THEOLOGY AND SANITY

FRANK J. SHEED

Theology and Sanity

IGNATIUS PRESS   SAN FRANCISCO

Cover design by Roxanne Mei Lum

Published in 1993 by Ignatius Press
ISBN 978-0-89870-470-9
Library of Congress Catalogue number 93-78529
Printed in the United States of America

CONTENTS

FOREWORD TO THE FIRST EDITION

I played with the thought of dedicating this book To All Who Know Less Theology Than I. It would have sounded flippant. But it would have been exact. There are thousands who know more theology than I, and for them I have no message: they must teach me. But there are thousands who know less, and less is not enough: I must try to teach them. This book contains theology, not the great mass of it that theologians need, but the indispensable minimum that every man needs in order that he may be living mentally in the real world—which is what the word "sanity" means in my title.

Sanity, remember, does not mean living in the same world as everyone else; it means living in the real world. But some of the most important elements in the real world can be known only by the revelation of God, which it is theology's business to study. Lacking this knowledge, the mind must live a half-blind life, trying to cope with a reality most of which it does not know is there. This is a wretched state for an immortal spirit, and pretty certain to lead to disaster. There is a good deal of disaster around at this moment.

F. J. S.

PREFACE TO THE REVISED EDITION

"Thirty-Three Years After"

When I wrote *Theology and Sanity,* I had been teaching the Faith under the open sky for a quarter of a century. The priests who had trained me and others for the work were Aquinas men; but it was from translating St. Augustine's *Confessions* that I went on to the writing of the book. So Augustine and Aquinas both went into it, in what proportion I could not tell. Now, a third of a century later, I am bringing out this revision. And I still cannot tell.

But Augustine and Aquinas—and Matthew and Mark and Luke and John and Paul—were not the only influences in its shaping. Every paragraph had been tried out on forty or fifty outdoor audiences before I got it down on paper. Listeners were free to walk away the moment they were bored—I tried to learn from their boredom. If they stayed, they could utter their reactions—anything from agreement to intelligent criticism to mockery to blasphemy—with a freedom which speakers who knew only the ivory tower of pulpit or lecture hall found unnerving. It was unbelievably educative. I doubt if there was any objection against the Faith in all the centuries that was not hurled at us. And, unlike the great theologians whose writings had helped to form our minds, we could not go off and think about the objection for a year or two, then write an article. We had to cope—somehow—there and then.

The crowd was truly co-author of the book; not a sentence that has not been reshaped by them. This really is *aggiornamento* —doctrines restated, not to be made more acceptable but more comprehensible, related to the questions people were actually asking, to the needs they were actually feeling, in the language they actually spoke. One early reviewer of *Theology and Sanity* liked the book well enough but observed that it did not contain the phrase "hypostatic union". I was reminded of an earlier incident. I had asked a learned theologian why the great third-century thinker Origen had not been canonized: "Good heavens," was the crushing answer, "he believed in the Apokatastasis." Theological language is a useful tool for specialists: I learnt to use it: then I learnt not to. I got more out of the specialists by forcing them into plain English.

The non-Catholic world has not made so full a contribution to the present revision, since in the last ten years I have done no outdoor speaking (it is not for septuagenarians). But Catholics, in groups and singly, have met me with as many difficulties and doubts and refusals as the old street-corner crowds.

Think of all that has happened within the Church since 1945. Pius XII had a dozen years still to reign, and the predisposition to accept what came from Rome was still fairly general. Pius never knew, and we never imagined, the angry refusal of such masses of Catholics which followed Pope Paul's encyclical on contraception. As it happened, that was only the culmination of a loss of confidence in the teaching Church, which had begun long before and came fully into the light when John XXIII opened the famous window.

But in 1945, none of this was apparent. Priests were not yet smiling their amusement over our accepting doctrines and practices which they themselves had been teaching us all our lives. We had not grown accustomed to hearing the Angel of the Annunciation bracketed with Santa Claus, or all the reality syphoned out of Resurrection and Ascension, leaving for our nourishment only the spiritual meaning of incidents all the truer for never having happened!

But in the same period, great things were happening. I list a handful, unique every one of them, which have made a difference to this revision.

In 1950, Pius XII issued the encyclical *Humani generis.* It had in it the words, to me totally stunning: "Without biblical theology, dogmatic theology becomes sterile." I have done no great reading in papal documents, but I wonder if that particular statement had ever been made before. If it had, why had I, in forty years of teaching the Faith, never come across it?

I had found more and more spiritual value in reading Scripture; I had happily used Scripture quotations in support of Catholic doctrine. Meditating on the word "sterile", I recognized at last that Doctrine and Scripture were two approaches from different angles to the same reality, under the guidance of the same Holy Spirit, each necessary to the fullness of the other. One result was that I made a new study of the actual words of Genesis, wrote *Genesis Regained,* and found the doctrines of Original Sin, Baptism, and Redemption desterilized for me.

At the very end of his life, Pius XII reminded a gathering of canonists and moral theologians that while they had always known that physical impotence was fatal to the union which was of the essence of marriage, there was a psychic impotence just as fatal, and he wanted them to give their minds to it. This statement has already worked a salutary revolution in the treatment of the anguish of failed marriages.

In his first Christmas Allocution, Pope John used a phrase as revolutionary in a different area. He referred to the other Christian churches as "bearing the name of Christ on their foreheads"—thus rolling back four centuries of mutual hatred and making possible at least a union of hearts among all who loved Christ our Lord.

With the whole Catholic sky exploding above them, the bishops of Vatican II kept their heads most marvelously. Somewhere else, I describe myself standing in front of St. Peter's as one session was concluding, watching the whole twenty-five hundred of them streaming out, and singing to myself the Gilbert and Sullivan lines—

> *Bishops in their shovel hats*
> *Were plentiful as tabby cats,*
> *In point of fact too many.*

But when I heard the same men singing the Nicene Creed together, I knew that something vast was in process. And the documents of the Council prove it.

I quote two:

(1) On the doctrinal differences between ourselves and the Eastern Orthodox Church: "It is hardly surprising if one tradition has come nearer than the other to the exact appreciation of certain aspects of a revealed mystery.... These varying theological formulations are often to be considered as complementary rather than competing." Surely this is a mildness unparalleled. And while the Protestant churches are not seen as in the same relation to us as the Orthodox, it would be hard to find any earlier statement even remotely like "Whatever is wrought by the grace of the Holy Spirit in the hearts of our separated brethren can contribute to our own spiritual up-building." That went one step beyond the point I myself had reached, after *Theology and Sanity* but before the Council, namely, that those other churches were doing an essential

work for Christ—since, for all sorts of reasons, there are countless millions of Christians who will not accept anything, even
Christ, from the Catholic Church, it is a great thing that He is
being brought to them by churches they *are* willing to listen
to.

(2) On the laity: "The Church's salvific work is to be done,
not by the hierarchy but by the whole Church." "The laity are
called in a special way to make the Church present *and operative*
in those places where *only through them* can she become the salt
of the earth."

The laity—90 per cent of the Church? 99 per cent?—are at
last called on to take their part in the saving of the world: that
is, in helping every member of the human race to receive what
Christ died and rose again to win for the race. The Sacrament
of Confirmation gave every Christian the right and the duty
to do precisely that. But right and duty do not of themselves
supply the equipment needed for the work. Precious little has
been done through the ages to equip the laity: precious little is
being done even now. Some of the training given to members
of individual Catholic groups seems to be merely pathetic, like
sending soldiers into battle with wooden swords and toy pistols.
The Council had summoned us all to the war in which there is
never a truce, the war between the mind of Christ and the
mind of the world. Bernard Shaw would not have seen himself
on Christ's side, but his summary of the situation has its own
aptness—"The class-war of the future will be a war of intellectual classes and the conquest will be the souls of the children."

For effective soldiering, we must give our own minds to the
study of both minds at war, Christ's primarily, but the world's
too. For the first, Paul had given us the formula: "We have the
mind of Christ", in Greek the *nous,* the element we do our
knowing with. We must be living mentally in the same world
as Christ. No one of us here on earth can live in it with Christ's

fullness, not even Paul. But we can study it, move into it, keep on growing in it.

To think we can do this by giving it as much of our free time as we can comfortably spare is foolishness. Paul would have delighted in Rudyard Kipling's phrase, "There's no discharge from the war." Unless we see it as of that urgency, we may as well stay on the sidelines while others fight for the souls of the children.

Theology and Sanity was first written as an elementary manual for laymen who accepted the call-up. It was minimum equipment, basic training. This revision takes into account the new conditions under which the struggle goes on.

Some of these have already been touched on. But there is one vast difference not yet mentioned; it is in the sheer number of human beings that both sides in the War of Minds hope to win over.

Back in 1945, the world at large was still not aware of any threat to humanity itself. Hitler was dead, and the world could now return to the progress which, they felt, the Nazi interlude had briefly interrupted. People in general seemed to have accepted the phrase that Pastor Bonhoffer had used before Hitler executed him—that mankind had come of age. That the notion of the human race as having come of age should have survived the war, that it should have survived the outbreak of peace, is surely wishful thinking's ultimate triumph.

For what a coming-of-age party mankind had—six million Jews cremated by Hitler, a hundred thousand or more Japanese killed by ourselves in a couple of atomic flashes, Stalin's endless slaughtering of Russians, on and on with barely a pause, to hundreds of thousands of Indonesians massacred, to Vietnam, to Uganda, to a million Americans slain in the womb by men paid by their mothers to slay them.

There would be those who would make a case for one or other of these bloodbaths. But they do not seem to add up to maturity. We are living in history's bloodiest century. The Vatican Council stated it better: the human race has reached a crisis-point on its way to maturity. And people are beginning — not exactly to call mankind's maturity into question, but to wonder if something hasn't gone wrong. The destroying things are too world-wide and too continuous.

Christ, we remember, had pity on the multitude, "harassed and helpless like sheep without a shepherd". To what country does that description not have more than a beginning of application? Everywhere we hear the two pathetic phrases — "It can't go on like this" (but what's to stop it?), and "Something has got to be done" (but by whom?). The mass of people find their nerve beginning to crack, as human life grows daily more complexly unmanageable.

The two-century hope that science will come up with something has lost its grip. Science can tell us more and more about life, but it can shed no light at all on what life is about — why we exist (why indeed anything exists), where we are supposed to be going, how we are to get there. On these questions, our rulers can tell us nothing either; most of them are not aware that those questions are fundamental to their work as rulers, or even that rulers have any bearing on it at all. But to handle human lives with no agreement as to what human beings are or what the purpose of life is — that is a formula for chaos.

Christ has the answers. And a discouraged world is more willing to listen than the world of yesterday, so sure of its own maturity. That is one difference between 1945 and now, and it should be all in our favor. But Christians, however aware of Christ's spiritual relevance for themselves, seem no more aware than everybody else of His relevance for the structure of mankind's life on earth.

That is not all. As we have seen, there is another difference between then and now—an uncertainty among Christians, Catholics included, as to what we can know of Christ or His teachings. There was a long moment in the sixties when we were left with the unhappy feeling that no passage of Scripture meant what it seemed to mean, so that Scripture was at once indispensable and impenetrable.

That nightmare moment has passed—or almost. The air is clearing. Much had been made, for instance, of the way words change their meanings with the centuries; however plain a phrase may seem, how can we know what it actually meant to the man—nineteen hundred years ago, three thousand years ago—who wrote it? The first shock over, one notices that there are a couple of countervailing elements.

One is that the changes are not as all-pervading as they had been made to seem. We can still know what Homer and Herodotus and Jeremiah and Amos are telling us—not everything, certainly, but enough for our enrichment: they are men like us, and so are the characters they wrote about—only too horribly like, often enough, too often for comfort. We can meet ourselves, not always with pleasure, all over both Testaments.

For the believer in Scripture's inspiration, the second element is even weightier. We do want to know what Jeremiah and Amos and Matthew and Paul and the rest are telling us. But what matters even more, the whole point of our reading, in fact, is what the Holy Spirit is telling us. And He has His own methods, today as always. His personal message for each individual reader is a continuing fact, but what He wants to tell mankind as a whole is a fact even more certain.

Quite apart from changing language and differences in civilizations, there is the simple fact that it is not possible to put together any selection of words in which some ingenious person may not find a meaning unmeant by the writer.

For God to have given His revelation and made no provision for its preservation would have been sheerly insane. Christ did not leave His teaching unguarded. He committed it to men He had trained: they were to teach it to all men till the end of time: He would be with them in their teaching. "No prophecy of Scripture is of private interpretation", said Paul, when the Church was new. The Dominican, Père Benoit, still with us, says the same: "Only a public authority divinely guided can spell out without error a public message divinely revealed."

The scholars have done a superb work on the actual text of Scripture: the Church needed them. As to the meaning, commentators without ceasing have produced their ideas; the libraries of the world are filled with them. But unless there is an authority to study them, sift them, compare them with the original revelation, channel them to the millions for whom Christ meant it—then they must add to the religious chaos and bring no light to the secular.

A small personal word.

In the period between the first publication and the revision, there have been major changes in the Church. But they are not mainly in the area of *theology* this book tries to cover. Such changes and additions as I have made are more the result of my own growth in understanding. One does not live thirty-three years stagnant.

As to *sanity*, nothing has happened to diminish either my devotion to it or my awareness of its difficulty. For me it is still a distant hope and a striving. It would be wonderful to die sane.

F. J. S.

PART I

PRELIMINARY

1. Religion and the Mind

My concern in this book is not with the Will but with the Intellect, not with sanctity but with sanity. The difference is too often overlooked in the practice of religion. The soul has two faculties, and they should be clearly distinguished. There is the will: its work is to love—and so to choose, to decide, to act. There is the intellect: its work is to know, to understand, to see: to see what? to see what's there.

(i) Seeing what the Church sees

I have said that my concern is with the intellect rather than with the will: this not because the intellect matters more in religion than the will, but because it does matter and tends to be neglected, and the neglect is bad. I realize that salvation depends directly upon the will. We are saved or damned according to what we love. If we love God, we shall ultimately get God: we shall be saved. If we love self in preference to God, then we shall get self apart from God: we shall be damned. But though in our relation to God the intellect does not matter as much as the will (and indeed depends for its health upon the will), it *does* matter, and as I have said, it is too much neglected—to the great misfortune of the will, for we can never attain a maximum love of God with only a minimum knowledge of God.

For the soul's full functioning, we need a Catholic intellect as well as a Catholic will. We have a Catholic will when we love God and obey God, love the Church and obey the Church. We have a Catholic intellect when we live consciously in the presence of the realities that God through His Church has revealed. A good working test of a Catholic will is that we should do what the Church says. But for a Catholic intellect, we must also see what the Church sees. This means that when we look out upon the Universe we see the same Universe that the Church sees; and the enormous advantage of this is that the Universe the Church sees is the real Universe, because she is the Church of God. Seeing what she sees means seeing what is there. And just as loving what is good is sanctity, or the health of the will, so seeing what is there is sanity, or the health of the intellect.

(ii) What does the Church see?

Now in that sense most of us have Catholic wills, but not many of us have Catholic intellects. When we look at the Universe, we see pretty well what other people see, plus certain extra features taught us by our religion. For the most part, the same influences that form other people's minds, form ours—the same habits of thought, inclinations, bodily senses, indolences, worked upon by the same newspapers, periodicals, best-sellers, films, radio programs. So that we have not so much Catholic minds as worldly minds with Catholic patches. Intellectually, we wear our Catholicism like a badge on the lapel of the same kind of suit that everyone else is wearing.

If that seems to you too sweeping, consider what the Church does see when she looks at the Universe. For one thing, she sees all things whatsoever held in existence from moment to moment by nothing but the continuing will of God that they should not cease to be. When she sees anything at all, in the same act she sees God holding it in existence. Do we? It is not merely a matter of knowing that this is so. Do we actually see it so? If we do not, then we are not living mentally in the same world as the Church. What is more, we are not seeing things as they are, for that *is* how they are.

Let us look a little longer at this first fact about anything. I can recall with great clarity the moment when for the first time I heard myself saying that God had made me and all things of nothing. I had known it, like any other Catholic, from childhood; but I had never properly taken it in. I had said it a thousand times but I had never heard what I was saying. In the sudden realization of this particular truth there is something quite peculiarly shattering. There are truths of religion immeasurably mightier in themselves, and the realization of any one of them might well make the heart miss a beat. But this one goes to the very essence of what we are, and goes there almost with the effect of annihilation. Indeed it is a kind of annihilation. God used no material in our making; we are made of nothing. At least self-sufficiency is annihilated, and all those customary ways that the illusion of self-sufficiency has made for us. The first effect of realizing that one is made of nothing is a kind of panic-stricken insecurity. One looks round for some more stable thing to clutch, and in this matter none of the beings of our experience are any more stable than we, for at the origin of them all is the same truth: all are made of nothing. But the panic and the insecurity are merely instinctive and transient. A mental habit has been annihilated, but the way toward a sounder mental habit is at least clear. For although we are made of nothing, we are made into something; and since what we are made *of* does not account for us, we are forced to a more intense concentration upon the God we are made *by*.

What follows is very simple but revolutionary. If a carpenter makes a chair, he can leave it and the chair will not cease to be. For the material he used in its making has a quality called rigidity, by virtue of which it will retain its nature as a chair. The maker of the chair has left it, but the chair can still rely for continuance in existence upon the material he used, the wood. Similarly if the Maker of the Universe left it, the Universe too would have to rely for continuance in existence upon the material He used—nothing. In short, the truth that God used no material in our making carries with it the not-sufficiently-realized truth that God continues to hold us in being, and that unless He did so we should simply cease to be.

This is the truth about the Universe as a whole and about every part of it. Material beings—the human body, for instance—are made up of atoms, and these again of electrons and protons, and these again of who knows what; but whatever may be the ultimate constituents of matter, God made them of nothing, so that they and the beings so imposingly built up of them exist only because He keeps them in existence. Spiritual beings—the human soul, for instance—have no constituent parts. Yet they do not escape this universal law. They are created by God of nothing and could not survive an instant without His conserving power. We are held above the surface of our native nothingness solely by God's continuing Will to hold us so. "In Him, we live and move and have our being" (Acts 17:28).

Therefore if we see anything at all—ourself or some other man, or the Universe as a whole or any part of it—without at the same time seeing God holding it there, then we are seeing it all wrong. If we saw a coat hanging on a wall and did not realize that it was held there by a hook, we should not be living in the real world at all, but in some fantastic world of our own in which coats defied the law of gravity and hung on walls by their own power. Similarly if we see things in existence and do not in the same act see that they are held in existence by God, then equally we are living in a fantastic world, not the real world. Seeing God everywhere and all things upheld by Him is not a matter of sanctity, but of plain sanity, because God *is* everywhere and all things *are* upheld by Him. What we do about it may be sanctity; but merely *seeing* it is sanity. To overlook God's presence is not simply to be irreligious; it is a kind of insanity, like overlooking anything else that is actually there.

It is part of the atmosphere in which we live—and which therefore we too must breathe—to take for granted that these considerations are edifying, and possibly even relevant if one happens to be of a religious temperament: but not otherwise. It may be a first step toward a fumigation of the atmosphere if we see the fallacy of this too easy view. If you were driving in a car, saw it heading straight for a tree, and called out to the driver to swerve or he would hit it; and if he answered "It is no good talking to me about trees: I'm a motorist, not a botanist", you would feel that he was carrying respect for the rights of the specialist too far. A tree is not only a fact of botany: it is a fact. God is not only a fact of religion: He is a fact. Not to see Him is to be wrong about everything, which includes being wrong about one's self. It does not require any extreme of religious fanaticism for a man to want to know what he is: and this he cannot know without some study of the Being who alone brought him into existence and holds him there.

I have discussed at some length this first thing that the Church sees when she looks at the Universe, what we may call the texture of the Universe, what it is made of. That, of course, is only a beginning of what she sees. Above all, she sees the *shape* of the Universe, all the things that exist and their relation one to another. Again it is worth our while to linger upon this and see what value it may have for the health of the mind. It is a plain fact that we do not know anything at all until we see it in its context, that is, in its place in the totality to which it belongs. Take the human eye as a convenient example. The human eye is very beautiful, as all lovers have seen. But the most ardent lover might find it hard to recapture his emotion if the lady, taking his praise of her eye too literally, decided to present it to him on a plate. The eye needs to be seen in the face; its beauty, its meaning, its usefulness all come from its position in the face; and one who had seen eyes only on plates would never really have known them at all, however minutely he might have examined the eye thus unhappily removed from its living context.

This is true of all things whatsoever. Nothing is rightly seen save in the totality to which it belongs; no part of the Universe is rightly seen save in relation to the whole. But the Universe cannot be seen as a whole unless one sees God as the Source of the existence of every part of it and the center by relation to which every part is related to every other. The man who does not see God may have vast knowledge of this or that section of being, but he is like a man who should know all about the eye, never having seen a face. His knowledge is of items in a list, not of features in a face. The shape of things, the proportion of things, the totality of things are unseen by him, indeed unsuspected by him. Because he does not know them he must omit them from his vision of things and his judgment of actions. He sees nothing quite right, because he sees nothing in its context. We live, indeed, in a vast context of things that are, events that have happened, a goal to which all is moving. That we should mentally see this context is part of mental

health. Just as knowing that all things are upheld by God is a
first step in knowing *what* we are, so a clear view of the shape
of reality is a first step toward knowing *where* we are. To know
where we are and what we are—that would seem to be the
very minimum required by our dignity as human beings.

Now the Church does thus *see* the Universe. Just as we
never think of an eye without at the same time being aware of
the face, she never sees anything at all without in the same act
seeing the face of reality: God, infinite and eternal, Trinity,
Unity; humanity, finite, created in time, fallen and redeemed
by Christ; the individual human person born into the life of
nature, reborn into the life of grace, united with Christ in the
Church which is His Mystical Body, aided by angels, hindered
by devils, destined for heaven, in peril of hell.

There in outline is the real Universe. Now it would be
plainly frivolous for most of us to pretend that we see things
like that. We know about the individual truths concerned, but
they do not combine in our minds to form the framework in
which, as a matter of course, we see everything. We know
about the Blessed Trinity, and the Incarnation, and Infinity
and Eternity, and our own creation from nothing. But we
know about them much as we might know that the sum of the
angles of a triangle is two right angles, or that Washington's
name was George. They are things we know, but we have not
got them into the mind's landscape. They are extras, immeasurably more important to us and more valued by us than
those mathematical or historical bits and pieces, but like them
in this, that we do not see them as a matter of course when we
see anything at all; we see them only when we advert to them.

The test of anyone's mind is what is in his mental landscape.
And it is not even enough that we should see the same things as
other people plus the things the Church teaches. Even the
things that we and they both see will not look the same or be

the same; because what the Church teaches affects even the things already in the landscape, the things of ordinary experience. It is like a physical landscape at sunrise: it is not that you see the same things that you saw before and now find yourself seeing the sun as well. You see everything sun-bathed. Similarly it is not a case of seeing the same universe as other people and then seeing God over and above. For God is at the center of the being of everything whatsoever. If we would see the Universe aright, we must see it God-bathed.

(iii) Intellect helps will

To many, the idea of bringing the intellect fully into action in religion seems almost repellent. The intellect seems so cold and measured and measuring, and the will so warm and glowing. Indeed the joy of the will is always figured in terms of warmth—such words as ardor, fervor, and the like come from Latin words for a fire burning: there is a fear that intellect can only damp down the fire. Many again who do not find the use of the intellect in religion actually repellent, regard it as at least unnecessary—at any rate for the layman—and possibly dangerous. One can, they say, love God without any very great study of doctrine. Indeed, they say, warming to their theme, some of the holiest people they know are quite ignorant. Plenty of theologians are not as holy as an old Irishman they have seen saying his Rosary. All this is so crammed with fallacy as to be hardly worth refuting. A man may be learned in dogma, and at the same time proud or greedy or cruel: knowledge does not supply for love if love is absent. Similarly, a virtuous man may be ignorant, but ignorance is not a virtue. It would be a strange God who could be loved better by being known less. Love of God is not the same thing as knowledge of

God; love of God is immeasurably more important than knowledge of God; but if a man loves God knowing a little about Him, he should love God more from knowing more about Him: for every new thing known about God is a new reason for loving Him. It is true that some get vast love from lesser knowledge; it is true even that some get vast light from lesser knowledge: for love helps sight. But sight helps love too.

After all, the man who uses his intellect in religion is using it to see what is there. But the alternative to seeing what is there is either not seeing what is there, and this is darkness; or seeing what is not there, and this is error, derangement, a kind of double darkness. And it is unthinkable that darkness whether single or double should be preferred to light.

Indeed light is the joy of the mind, as warmth is the joy of the will. But warmth and light are both effects of fire, warmth fire as felt, light fire as seen (and seen *by*). It seems strange to value the one effect and not the other of that fire by which the Holy Spirit is figured to us. It is an odd delusion that one is warmer in the dark, that one can love God better in the dark—or should we say in the half-dark, since a Christian can never be wholly in darkness.

We can be saved and even holy without a great deal of knowledge; for holiness is in the will, and we are saved by what we love, not by how much we know. But knowledge of the truth matters enormously all the same. It matters for the reason we have already stated, namely, that every new thing known about God is a new reason for loving Him. It matters also for a reason that may not at first sight appear: that, in the appallingly difficult struggle to be good, the will is helped immeasurably by the intellect's clear vision of the real Universe. Unless our minds have made that kind of study, then the position is that the Church is living in one world (which happens to be the real world) and we are living in another.

One practical consequence is that the laws of right living promulgated by the Church, moral laws generally, are the natural and obvious laws of that real world and would seem so to us if we were mentally living in it; whereas in the twilight world we are living in, they often seem odd and unreasonable, which does not make obedience any easier. Thus the whole burden of right living is cast upon the will—do it because the Church says it—with no aid from the intellect, or rather with active hindrance from the intellect, which naturally tends to judge by the half-reality it sees. And this is sheer cruelty.

The problem we shall consider in this book is how our minds are to "master" the Church's landscape, habituate themselves to it, move about easily in it, be at home in it. Somehow or other we must become fully conscious citizens of the real world, seeing reality as a whole and living wholly in it.

2. Examination of Intellect

We have, I hope, disentangled the special function of the intellect in religion; it is to explore Reality and make its home in it. The object of this book is to suggest the way for those whose intellects have not till now done any serious exploring— and note that serious exploring is not a quick job: the doctrines treated in this book cannot be rushed through, they must be worked through. The first thing necessary is to consider the intellect's equipment for an expedition so arduous. An intellect, of course, everybody *has:* intellect is not the property only of exceptionally gifted people; it is a piece of standard human equipment, like a nose. But the plain truth about most of us is that we have let our intellects sink into a condition in which they do not have the muscles or the energy or the right habits for the job, or any effective inclination toward it. We must see how they may be made fit.

(i) How imagination can hinder intellect

The first difficulty in the way of the intellect's functioning well is that it hates to function at all, at any rate beyond the point where functioning begins to require effort. The result is that when any matter arises which is properly the job of the intellect, then either nothing gets done at all, or else the imagination leaps in and does it instead. There is nothing to be done with the intellect until imagination has been put firmly in its place. And this is extraordinarily difficult. One of the results of the Fall of Man is that imagination has got completely out of hand; and even one who does not believe in that "considerable catastrophe", as Hilaire Belloc calls it, must at least admit that imagination plays a part in the mind's affairs totally out of proportion to its merits, so much out of proportion indeed as to suggest some long-standing derangement in man's nature.

Consider what imagination is. It is the power we have of making mental pictures of the material universe. What our senses have experienced — the sights the eye has seen, the sounds the ear has heard, what we have smelt, touched, tasted — can be reproduced by the imagination either as they originally came through our senses, or in any variety of new combinations. A moment's reflection upon what life would be like if we lacked this power will show how valuable a part the imagination has to play; but it is a subordinate part, and entirely limited to the world of matter. What the senses cannot experience, the imagination cannot make pictures of.

But in the state in which we now are, this picture-making power seems able to out-shout almost every other power we have. It is a commonplace that it can storm the will. The will may have decided firmly for sobriety or chastity: the imagination conjures up the picture of a glass of beer or a girl and the will finds its decision wavering and breaking. But our concern is not with the effect of imagination upon the will, but upon the intellect. There is practical value in dwelling a moment on this unpleasing business.

I pass over the damage imagination does to our thinking by way of distraction, because the experience is too poignantly familiar to need emphasis. Time and again we set out upon a train of abstract thought and come to ourselves at the end of an hour with the sickening realization that for the last fifty-nine minutes we have been watching imagination's pictures flash across the mind and the abstract thinking is still to do. Yet bad as that is, it is not the worst of the ways in which imagination hinders the functioning of intellect, because we are aware of our unhappy tendency and, when the urgency is great enough, can take steps to control it. But it has two other ways of interference, very dangerous because we do not suspect their danger or even their existence, and very important in our inquiry because they operate most powerfully in the field of religion.

The first of these is that the imagination acts as a censor upon what the intellect shall accept. Tell a man, for instance, that his soul has no shape or size or color or weight, and the chances are that he will retort that such a thing is inconceivable. If we reply that it is not inconceivable but only unimaginable, he will consider that we have conceded his case—and will proceed to use the word "unimaginable" with the same happy finality as the word "inconceivable". For indeed in the usage of our day, the two words have become interchangeable. That they are thus interchangeable is a measure of the decay of thinking, and to sort them out and see them as distinct is an essential first step in the mind's movement toward health.

To distinguish them we must distinguish spirit from matter, and this distinction is worth a little space here because it will be vital at every point of our inquiry. We shall return to it many times; this is only a beginning. Of spirit we have already spoken as lacking the properties of matter. But it would be a poor definition of anything to say of it simply that it is not something else. If all one can say of a thing is that it is not some other thing, then in the absence of that other thing one would not be able to say anything of it at all. But spirit would still be something even if matter did not exist, and we cannot feel that we have made much advance in our knowledge of spirit until we can speak of it thus in its own proper nature.

Spirit, we say, is the being that knows and loves; and this is a positive statement of its *activity*, what it does. But we can say something also of its *nature*, what it is. Briefly, *spirit is the being which has its own nature so firmly in its grasp that it can never become some other thing.* Any material thing is in the constant peril of becoming something else: wood is burnt and becomes ash, oxygen meets hydrogen and becomes water, hay is eaten and becomes cow. In short any material thing is what it is at any given moment, but precariously. A spiritual thing is what it is, but tenaciously. My body, being material, might be eaten by a cannibal, and some of my body would be absorbed to become his body. But my soul can never thus be made into something else. The reason is bound up with a truth we have already mentioned — that material things have constituent parts, and spiritual things have not. What has parts can be taken apart. Because material things have parts, molecules and such, these parts can be separated from one another and made to enter into new alliances with other parts similarly separated from the company they had, until that moment, been keeping. But a spirit has no parts: therefore it cannot be taken apart. It can exist only as a whole. God might annihilate it, but while it exists, it can only be what it is: it can never be anything else. Worms will one day eat my body: but not my mind. Even the worm that dieth not finds the mind too tough to consume.

What has parts, then, can cease to be what it is and become something else: that is one limitation from which spirit is free. But there is another. What has parts can occupy space—space indeed may be thought of as the arrangement matter makes to spread its parts in. It is from the occupation of space that those properties flow which affect the senses. That is why matter does. That is why spirit does not.

We may now return to the distinction between "unimaginable" and "inconceivable". To say that something is unimaginable is merely to say that the imagination cannot make a picture of it. But pictures are only of the material world; and to that, imagination is limited. Naturally it cannot form pictures of spiritual realities, angels, or human souls, or love or justice. Imagination cannot form mental pictures of these, because none of our senses could experience them. To complain that a spiritual thing is unimaginable would be like complaining that the air is invisible. The air is beyond the reach of one particular sense, namely sight, because it lacks color. Spirit is beyond the reach of all the senses (and so of imagination) because it lacks all material qualities. With the eyes of your body you cannot see justice. You can see a just man or an unjust man, but justice itself you cannot see with your eyes. Nor can you hear it or smell it or run it across your palate or bark your shins on it.

Thus the reality of any spiritual statement must be tested by the intellect, not by the imagination. The intellect's word of rejection is "inconceivable". This means that the statement proffered to the intellect contains a contradiction within itself, so that no concept can be formed embodying the statement. A four-sided triangle, for instance, is in this sense inconceivable. It is a contradiction in terms, because a triangle is a three-sided figure; and a four-sided three-sided figure cannot be conceived and cannot *be*. The less-instructed atheist will ask whether God can make a weight so heavy that He cannot lift it, in the happy belief that, whichever answer we give, we shall admit that there is something God cannot do. But the question is literally meaningless: a weight that an omnipotent Being cannot lift is as complete a contradiction in terms as a four-sided triangle. In either case the words are English, but do not mean anything because they cancel each other out. There is no point in piling together a lot of words, regardless of their meaning, and then asking triumphantly "Can God make that?" God can do *anything,* but a contradiction in terms is not a thing at all. It is nothing. God Himself could not make a four-sided triangle or a weight that Almighty power could not lift. They are inconceivable, they are nothing; and nothing—to give a slightly different emphasis to Scripture—is impossible to God.

Thus the first test of any statement concerning spiritual reality is not can imagination form a mental picture of it, but does it stand up to the examination of the intellect, do the terms of it contradict each other, is it conceivable or inconceivable? Imagination can say nothing about it either way. It cannot reject it. It cannot accept it either. It must leave it alone, and that is precisely one of the things that imagination hates to do.

Which leads us to the other of the two ways in which imagination hinders intellect without our perceiving it. In the ordinary way, if concepts are beyond its reach, imagination acts as censor and simply throws them out: while the intellect, grown flabby with disuse, tiredly concurs in a rejection so beneficent because it saves so much trouble. But this happy arrangement receives a check if one happens to be a Catholic. For the Faith binds us to accept many truths altogether beyond imagination's reach, and will not allow imagination to reject them. Here imagination does its subtlest piece of sabotage. It cannot forbid intellect to accept them: so it offers to *help* intellect to accept them. It comes along with all sorts of mental pictures, comparisons from the material world. Thus for the doctrine of the Blessed Trinity imagination offers the picture of a shamrock, or a triangle, or three drops of water poured together to form one drop of water.

Now there is in fact a definite role for such analogies as these in religion. God's dealings with mankind may often be seen more clearly by some comparison drawn from the material universe, because both human beings and the material universe are creatures of the same God, and there are all kinds of family resemblances between the various works of the one master. Our Lord's parables are a marvelous application of this principle. But useful as such comparisons may be as illustrations of God's dealings with us, they shed no light whatever upon the innermost being of God in Himself. The shamrock simile tells us absolutely nothing about the Blessed Trinity, nor does the triangle, nor the drops of water. The excuse for them is that they help us to *see* the doctrine. But they do not. They only help us to swallow the doctrine. They prevent the doctrine from being a difficulty; but they do it by substituting something else for the doctrine, something which is not a difficulty, certainly, but not the doctrine either. What is the gain of this, I do not know. Certainly it prevents the truth about God from being a danger to our faith; but in the same act, it prevents the truth about God from being a light to our

minds. The same objective might have been attained a great
deal more neatly by not mentioning the doctrine at all.

If we are to get anywhere in that grasp of reality which is
the purpose of this book, the intellect must learn to do its own
job. It will be rigorous and exacting work for the intellect, but
there is no advance in theology without it, nor indeed any real
mental maturity. (And mental maturity is worth having: what
more suitable companion could there be for that commoner
phenomenon, bodily maturity?) Thinking is very hard, and
imagining is very easy, and we are very lazy. We have fallen
into the habit of using imagination as a crutch, and our intellects have almost lost the habit of walking. They must learn to
walk, and this must mean great pain for muscles so long
unused. It is worth all the pain: not only for the intellect but
for the imagination too. Once the intellect is doing its own
work properly, it can use the imagination most fruitfully; and
the imagination will find new joy in the service of a vital
intellect.

(ii) Mystery and how the intellect may cope with it

So far we have been considering the limitation of the mind's
power that results from bad habits. But there is a vastly more
important limitation which arises from the nature of the mind
itself. Bad habits or good habits, our minds remain finite, and
so can never wholly contain the Infinite. This is the fact about
us which accounts for the existence of what we call Mysteries
in religion. At first thought this might seem a reason for
abandoning the whole venture: if Reality is so utterly beyond
us, why not leave it alone and make the best terms we can with
our ineluctable darkness? But a Mystery is not something that
we can know nothing about: it is only something that the

mind cannot *wholly* know. It is to be thought of not as a high wall that we can neither see over nor get around: it is to be thought of rather as a gallery into which we can progress deeper and deeper, though we can never reach the end—yet every step of our progress is immeasurably satisfying. A Mystery, in short, is an invitation to the mind. For it means that there is an inexhaustible well of Truth from which the mind may drink and drink again in the certainty that the well will never run dry, that there will always be water for the mind's thirst.

As we examine the Mysteries of religion, we discover that the practical result of this effort of the finite to know the Infinite—which is also a determination of the Infinite to be known by the finite—is that any given Mystery resolves itself (for our minds, of course, not in its own reality) into two truths which we cannot see how to reconcile. Sometimes by the revelation of God, sometimes by the hard effort of man's own mind, we see that each of two things must be so, yet we cannot see why one does not exclude the other. Thus in the Mystery of the Blessed Trinity, we cannot see how God can be Three if He is infinitely One; in the Doctrine of the Incarnation, we cannot see how Christ can be wholly God and at the same time wholly man; in the mystery of our own will, we do not see how its freedom can be reconciled with God's omniscience; and so with all the other mysteries of religion. Left to ourselves, we should almost certainly say that there is a conflict, and therefore that both cannot be true; and even if under pressure we reluctantly admit that we cannot absolutely prove that there is contradiction, or exclude the possibility that there might be reconciliation at some point beyond our gaze, yet the point of reconciliation *is* beyond our gaze; and what lies within our gaze seems for ever irreconcilable.

Normally the mind would reject any doctrine proposed for its belief with this unbridgeable gulf in it. But when such doctrines are revealed by God, the Christian will not reject them; yet he still has to decide what to do about them in his own mind. One possibility for him is to make a large act of faith, accept them, and think no more about them. Thus he is not troubled by any apparent contradiction, nor illumined by the doctrine's truth. It simply lies in the mind, and he is no worse for it and no better for it. He has a shadowy feeling that if he looked at the doctrine very closely, it might be something of a trial to his faith. But he does not look at it very closely. He does not really look at it at all. This degree of intellectual unconcern makes for a quiet life, but not for any growth in the knowledge of God.

If the mind does do something with the mysterious truths God has revealed, it usually deals with the two elements whose reconciliation it cannot see in one of three ways. The first way is to select one of the component truths, make that the vital one, and simply accept the other half but without adverting to it very much. Thus, for example, in the doctrine of the Trinity, one might devote the whole force of the mind to the Three Persons, and leave the question of how Three Persons can be one God in the back of the mind; or one might concentrate upon the oneness of God and leave the threefold personality largely as a form of words whose meaning we shall discover in the next life. The trouble about this very natural expedient is that the mind gets no light from the element in the doctrine not adverted to, and the light it gets from the element of its choice is not as bright as it might be for want of the other: for although as the mind tries to master a doctrine it distinguishes the doctrine into two elements, in the living reality they are not two elements but one.

Yet even at that, this first way is immeasurably better than the second—which consists in accepting both elements, but shading them down to look like each other, thus getting no light from either. As applied to the Incarnation, this tactic involves accepting both the divinity and the humanity of our Lord, but making the divinity too human and the humanity too divine.

The third way is to accept both elements, and accept them both at white heat without bothering too much about whether one can see the reconciliation. The mind loses no integrity thereby, since it is already certain on other grounds of the truth of each element separately. Therefore in accepting and devoting itself with all its power to each, it is acting rightly. And the result justifies the method. For although we still cannot actually see the reconciliation, yet some mysterious reconciliation is in fact effected within us. We begin, as I have said, with a steady concentration upon each of the two elements, and a moment comes when we recognize that we are living mentally in the presence not of two truths but of one. We still could not say how both can be true at once, yet we truly experience them so.

There is a profound reason for this. It is involved in the kind of beings that we are. It is part of a larger truth about our whole experience of life. All life is a tension of apparent opposites. Life abides and life advances by a sort of counter-pull—what I have called a tension—between forces that seem to be the negation of each other. Thus our life is conditioned by death: the animal dies and man eats it and lives; man dies to himself in order to live to God, and, living to God, find himself too. Again our freedom is made perfect by obedience; thus a man is free to live if he obeys the laws of nutrition, is free to build himself a home, to sail the oceans of the world, to fly in the air, if he obeys the laws that govern his universe. One might go on endlessly listing such things. And no one of them is accidental or incidental. Our life is truly seen as a tension of opposites because we ourselves are a tension of opposites. We ourselves, like all created things, exist because omnipotence made something of nothing. We are best expressed as nothingness worked upon by omnipotence, the two most ultimate of all opposites. Because that is what we are, that is how we act. *Operatio sequitur esse,* say the philosophers. As we are, so we act, so we experience, so we know. There is this vast and fruitful combination of opposites within our very being, at the very heart of what we are, and you can trace it in everything we do. It means that there is an essential mysteriousness about us. Our minds cannot wholly grasp omnipotence: it has too much meaning for us; they cannot firmly grasp nothingness: it has not enough meaning for the mind to take hold of. Yet in these two terms we are stated.

That is why we tend to see the truths about God in the way I have described, as the union of two apparent opposites. We cannot see the reconciliation because we cannot see the union of the two opposites within ourselves. But although we cannot see it, we do experience it. We experience it in the plain fact that we actually are, and are aware of ourselves as one being. But as I have said there runs an element of duality through all our action. As soon as we say anything, we have to balance it by something almost diametrically opposite. And somehow it works. Consider one example. There is a rule of life, attributed to St. Augustine and to almost all the reasonably articulate saints since his day, and in any event verified in the experience of everyone who has made even the most meager attempt to live the Christian life. In its traditional form it runs "Pray as if everything depended on God; work as if everything depended on you." Here, in action, is that wholehearted acceptance of two opposites which somehow fuses into one continuing act of successful living.

(iii) The splendor of Mystery

That there should be Mystery in our knowledge of God, and
that this should show itself to us as truths about God, each of
which we know to be true while yet we cannot see how to
reconcile them, is plain common sense. And indeed most people
would admit as much if they happen to believe in God at all.
But here we come upon a curious phenomenon. Many Christians who are theoretically aware of all this are yet completely
shattered in their faith the first time their attention is drawn to
one of these apparent contradictions. Someone asks them some
such question as "If God knew last Tuesday what you are
going to do next Tuesday, what becomes of your free will?"
We shall be glancing at this question later, but for the moment
my concern is only with the curious effect upon the assailed
Christian. He knows that there are truths about God that he
cannot reconcile; he knows that if he could totally comprehend God, then God would have to be no larger than his own
mind, and so not large at all. He knows that the very fact that
there is a God requires that there should be elements we cannot
reconcile; yet the moment he meets two such elements he is
driven to wonder whether there can be a God after all.

But, this logical monstrosity apart, there is something
marvelously inviting to the mind in an infinite being of whom
we can know something, but whom we cannot wholly know;
in the knowledge of whom we can grow, yet the truth of
whose being we can never exhaust; we shall never have to
throw God away like a solved crossword puzzle. And all this is
contained in the concept of Mystery.

Thus a Mystery is not to be thought of as simply darkness: it
is a tiny circle of light surrounded by darkness. It is for us so to
use our own powers and God's grace that the light will grow. It
means using the mind upon what reality may be made to tell us

about God, and upon what God, through His Church, has told us about Himself; it means praying for more knowledge, and using the knowledge one gains to enrich one's prayer. Thus the circle of light grows; but it is always ringed round with darkness: for however our capacity may increase, it remains finite, and God remains Infinite. Indeed the more the light grows, the more we see what His Infinity means, what His Immensity is. The theologian sees far more problems about the Blessed Trinity than the ordinary Catholic. But this is an ordinary accompaniment of knowledge. The man who knows nothing about a subject has no difficulties either, sees no problems, can ask no questions. Even to be able to ask questions is a kind of knowledge. The theologian can ask far profounder questions because he knows more about God; by that same knowledge he knows that there are depths that he will never know. But to see why one cannot know more is itself a real seeing; there is a way of seeing the darkness which is a kind of light.

The circle of light grows as the mind acts upon God and is acted upon by God. The mind sees certain problems, and advances in their solution. Quite literally, it questions God, asks how and why, not as heckling God, challenging Him to defend the truth of His own being, but as begging Him for more light. Nor must it be thought that growth in the knowledge of God is a continual wrestling with problems in an effort to push back the darkness. Pushing back the darkness does of course increase the extent of our light. But there is a question not only of the extent of light but of intensity. And that grows in us by our sheer enjoyment of the light we have. It would be a pity if we were so obsessed with the darkness as to be unable to enjoy the light, so troubled by what we do not know or cannot know that there is no joy to us in what we know. The way of life for the mind is to live in the light and revel in the light and grow in the light in all tranquillity.

(iv) Keeping the intellect cleansed

In all tranquillity, I say, but with immeasurable labor. That is
another of those opposites whose tension makes our life. There
is, as I have said earlier, real pain for the mind as it brings its
almost atrophied muscles into action without the comforting
crutch of imagination. This activity gets a little easier as the
habit grows. Slowly the mind grows out of its reliance upon
images that has stultified it. But this cleansing of the intellect
is not a thing that can ever be done once and for all in this
life. Imagination is forever creeping up on us, betraying us
without our knowing it. God gave the Israelites a command
ment against the use of graven images. Truly I believe the
mental images can be even worse for religion than graven.
Certainly the habit clings. Scripture regularly compares idolatry with fornication. The Israelites went whoring after images.
The mind can do that too, and most of our minds have been
doing it. Even after they have been converted to better ways,
they still long for their old sins, very much as St. Augustine
did. Certainly the battle gets easier as one goes on. The intellect begins to develop its muscles, and begins even to enjoy
using them. But imagination is always lurking in the background: the intellect is still, unknown to itself, affected in its
own proper processes by images it had rejected and even
forgotten. "The price of freedom is eternal vigilance." That
applies to all freedom, including the freedom of the intellect to
do its own laborious housework.

PART II

GOD

3. He Who Is

There is no better illustration of the way in which a mental image can still affect thinking even after it has been formally expelled from the mind than the picture of God as a venerable man with a beard, rather like the poet Tennyson, or perhaps Karl Marx. Nobody who can think at all any longer believes that this is what God is like. But even those who laugh most scornfully at its naïveté would, I think, if they were skilled at exploring their own thoughts, find that they were still dangerously affected by it. It is rather like what happens when we read a novel with illustrations. Without in the least being aware of it, we absorb a certain impression of the characters from the way the artist has drawn them, and this impression affects our whole reading of the book.

(i) Errors about God

As I have said, the thing is below the level of consciousness. We take it for granted that we have formed our ideas of the characters from what the author has written. We may very well have forgotten even that the book had any illustrations. But their influence abides to color every judgment. I believe that a sufficiently penetrating analyst could discover some influence of the venerable man with the beard in all that is written about God—even by the most profound and profoundly orthodox theologians, but most notably by the most unorthodox modern thinkers in theology. Among these, for instance, there is a dead set against the idea of a personal God, an idea which their intellects find quite revolting. My own conviction is that they are not revolting against the philosophical concept of personality as applied to God: they are revolting against the venerable man with the beard. The influence of that long-established image is so great that the moment they begin to think of God as a person, they begin to think of Him as *that* person, so curiously like Lord Tennyson. Naturally they stop at once.

To the influence of this same image we may trace two of the principal modern tendencies about God, the tendency to treat Him as an equal, and the tendency to treat Him as an extra. Neither tendency could abide for one instant the light of the true idea of God's nature and person. But they do abide, and indeed they grow.

First, the tendency to treat God as an equal, the failure to grasp the relation of the creature to the Creator, may be stated very rapidly. It is commoner in the semi-religious fringe than among practicing Christians, but it is liable to show up anywhere. The commonest form of it is in the feeling that God is not making a very good job of the universe and that one could give Him some fairly useful suggestions. Another deadly effect of it is in the diminishing, to the point almost of disappearance, of the sense of sin. In the past, Catholics have not been much affected by such ideas; but in recent years those ideas have taken root. At any rate nothing would be lost by some kind of examination of intellect in this matter of the dwindling difference between the Infinite and ourselves. To

if he persuaded large numbers of people that the sun did not exist, his private error would be in a fair way to becoming a public nuisance; and if he were the captain of a ship, passengers' lives would not be safe with him: he could not be trusted to get them across the ocean. You could not discuss astronomy with such a man because, however much a man may be entitled to his own opinion, the sun remains a fact, and a fact essential to astronomy and navigation. Similarly, you cannot discuss the purpose of life with a man who denies the existence of God. You cannot profoundly collaborate in human affairs, in sociology, say, or education, with a man who denies the existence of God. You cannot simply agree to omit God from the collaboration for the sake of argument, any more than you could agree to omit the sun from navigation. The sun is a fact and essential to navigation. God is a fact and essential to everything.

That it is so has already, I trust, been made clear in the first chapter of this book. Everything exists because God called it into being from nothing and continues to hold it is existence. The formula for all created beings, from the speck of dust to the highest angel, is nothingness made to be something by the omnipotence of God. Omit God from the consideration of anything or everything, and you omit the reason why anything exists and make everything forever unexplainable; and this is not a sound first step toward understanding. Omit God and you are left with that other element, nothingness: what could be less practical? Living in the presence of God, that is, being at all times aware that God is present, is no more a matter of sanctity than being aware that the sun is there. Both are a matter of sanity. An error about either means that we are not living in the real world; but an error about the sun damages the reality of our world immeasurably less than an error about God, for that, indeed, falsifies reality totally.

We must then study God, if we are to understand anything at all. We must come to a knowledge of God and then grow in that knowledge. How? In two ways: the way of reason or philosophy, what the exploring mind can discover for itself; and the way of revelation, what God tells us of Himself.[1] We shall consider first the way of reason.

(ii) God is Infinite Existence

We may begin with the extraordinary compliment that the first Vatican Council paid to human reason in the year 1870. It defined that the existence of God can be known by the human reason without the aid of revelation. This is the mightiest compliment ever paid the human reason, and it is of faith. As Catholics we are bound to believe that the human reason can establish the existence of God. What the Vatican Council put in its carefully measured words, the Holy Spirit had said much more abruptly three thousand years before—"The fool hath said in his heart, there is no God." Both, as you see, come to the same thing—that the existence of God can be known by reason; therefore if you do not know it, your reasoning is defective, suggests the Vatican Council; you are a fool, cries the Psalmist under the inspiration of God.

There are various proofs for God's existence. The most famous are a series of five proofs formulated by St. Thomas Aquinas, working upon and supplementing the efforts of the great Greeks Plato and Aristotle some sixteen hundred years

[1] Marvelously supplementary to these is the way of Mystical Experience, whereby the knowledge of God gained by reason or revelation is given a new intensity which is almost a new dimension. But this is something each person must learn for himself, under the guidance of teachers more learned in the spiritual life than I.

before him: one way or another they are a development of and
a commentary upon St. Paul's words: "from the foundation of
the world, men have caught sight of His invisible nature, His
eternal power and His divineness, as they are known through
His creatures" (Rom 1:20). For a Catholic there is vast intellectual joy in these five proofs. There can be a kind of intoxication in his first meeting with them. But for many of us, once
the intoxication clears away, there is a certain sense of anticlimax.
They do indeed establish the existence of God with certainty:
but we were already certain of the existence of God. It was
delightful to find these proofs, but we did not need them. We
were already quite sure about God. It was only on reflection
that we became aware that these proofs still had a vastly
important function for us, even if we did not need them as
proofs. If a man is already certain by faith that God exists, he
should still study the proofs most carefully, not because they
lead to certainty *that* God is, but because no one can study
them carefully without coming to a far profounder understanding of *what* God is.

It is in this aspect that I shall consider reason's approach to
the knowledge of God in this place. This book is being written
not to prove the truths of Christianity to those who do not
hold them, but to aid those who do hold them in their
exploration. I shall take one of St. Thomas's five proofs, not
using it as a proof, but as a most useful way of exploration in
the nature of God. And it may be useful even to unbelievers:
much of the argument as to whether there is a God results
primarily not from doubt of His existence but from inability
to make head or tail of His nature. Even a little light upon
what God is would settle many doubts as to whether He is. We
shall see what light can be got from the argument from
Contingency, partly because it is in itself the most fascinating,
partly because it links up most closely with the truth we have

already twice considered, the elementary truth about ourselves and all things, that God made us of nothing.

The argument runs somewhat like this. If we consider the universe, we find that everything in it bears this mark, that it does exist but might very well not have existed. We ourselves exist, but we would not have existed if a man and a woman had not met and mated. The same mark can be found upon everything. A particular valley exists because a stream of water took that way down, perhaps because the ice melted up there. If the melting ice had not been there, there would have been no valley. And so with all the things of our experience. They exist, but they would not have existed if some other thing had not been what it was or done what it did.

None of these things, therefore, is the explanation of its own existence or the source of its own existence. In other words, their existence is contingent upon something else. Each thing possesses existence, and can pass on existence; but it did not originate its existence. It is essentially a receiver of existence. Now it is impossible to conceive of a universe consisting exclusively of contingent beings, that is, of beings which are only receivers of existence and not originators. The reader who is taking his role as explorer seriously might very well stop reading at this point and let his mind make for itself the effort to conceive a condition in which nothing should exist save receivers of existence.

Anyone who has taken this suggestion seriously and pondered the matter for himself before reading on, will have seen that the thing is a contradiction in terms and therefore an impossibility. If nothing exists save beings that receive their existence, how does anything exist at all? Where do they receive their existence from? In such a system made up exclusively of receivers, one being may have got it from another, and that from still another, but how did existence get into the system at all? Even if you tell yourself that this system contains an infinite number of receivers of existence, you still have not accounted for existence. Even an infinite number of beings, if no one of these is the source of its own existence, will not account for existence.

Thus we are driven to see that the beings of our experience, the contingent beings, could not exist at all unless there is also a being which differs from them by possessing existence in its own right. It does not have to receive existence; it simply has existence. It is not contingent: it simply is. This is the Being that we call God.

All this may seem very simple and matter of course, but in reality we have arrived at a truth of inexhaustible profundity and of inexhaustible fertility in giving birth to other truths. Not all at once does the mind comprehend the immensity of what it has thus so easily come upon. But consider some of the consequences that may be seen almost at first look. We have arrived at a being, whom we call God, who is not, as all other beings are, a receiver of existence: and this satisfactorily accounts for their existence—they have received it from Him. But what accounts for *His* existence? At least we shall not be guilty of the crudity of those who ask: Who made God? For to make anything is to confer existence upon it; and as we have seen, God does not have to receive existence. He is not made, He simply is. He does not come into existence, He is in existence. But the question remains as insistent for Him as for any contingent thing: *why* does He exist, what accounts for His existence?

Here one must follow very closely. God exists not because of any other being, for He is the source of all being. Therefore the reason for His existence, since it is not in anything else, must be in Himself. This means that there is something about *what He is* which requires that He must be. Now *what a being is* we call its nature; thus we can restate our phrase and say that there is in His nature something that demands existence, better still something that commands existence. In other words His nature is such that He must exist. Consider how immeasurable a difference this makes between God and all contingent beings. They may exist or may not. God must exist. He cannot not-exist. Their nature is to be able to exist. God's nature is to exist. They can have existence. God *is* existence.

For there are not two elements, namely, God and His existence. And indeed if they were two, the question would arise, what accounts for their being found together? But they are not two, they are one. God is existence. Existence *is.* All the receivers of existence exist because there is one who does not have to receive existence. He does not have to receive existence because He is existence.

This, then, is the primary Truth about God. It was the crowning achievement of Greek philosophy in the fifth century before Christ to have reached the threshold of this most fundamental of all truths. Christian philosophers have continued their process, and for us it is a truth of philosophy and not only a truth of revelation. But all the same it *is* a truth of revelation, otherwise the philosophically gifted would hold it with less certainty, and the philosophically ungifted would not hold it at all. We have not only the word of human reason upon a matter so important. A good thousand years before the Greek intellect came so close to it, the Jewish people got the thing itself, and not by any effort of their intellect: God told them. You will find it in the third chapter of Exodus, when God appeared to Moses "in a flame of fire out of the midst of a bush". God had told Moses to bring his people out of Egypt. And Moses said to God: "Lo, I shall go to the children of Israel, and say to them: 'The God of your fathers hath sent me to you.' If they should say to me, 'What is His name?' what shall I say to them?"

And God said to Moses: "I am Who Am. Thus shalt thou say to the children of Israel: He Who Is hath sent me to you."

This, then, is God's name for Himself, He Who Is. When we have said He is, there is no more to be said. We have said everything. The only trouble is that we do not know all we have said. But we can begin to find out. All theology consists in finding out what is meant by the words "He Is". Let us begin.

What we see at once is that since God is existence, that existence must be utterly without limit, for there is no principle of limitation in a being thus self-existent. Limitation is a deficiency of existence, something lacking to fullness of existence. But what deficiency of existence could there be in one who *is* existence; or what could be lacking to the fullness of existence of one who *is* existence? God is infinite. What is not infinite is not God, not the source of all contingent beings.

Another consequence that we see at once is that God must contain in Himself all the perfections we find in things. "He that planted the ear, shall He not hear? or He that formed the eye, shall He not see?" (Ps 93:9). Since all things owe their existence totally to Him, all that they have is from Him and therefore all the perfections that they have must in some way be in Him. Obviously they will be in Him in a way immeasurably higher. For He made all things from nothing, and these perfections will be in things only insofar as nothingness can receive them, or, to put it crudely, with a certain mingling of nothingness: whereas they are in God in utter purity. Some notion of what that means we shall try to arrive at in the next chapter. But meanwhile the truth stands that whatever perfections are to be found in created existence must be in God, who is the source of all existence. Thus since knowledge and love are to be found in created things, knowledge and love must be in God. God must know and love. And this is the bare minimum that we mean when we speak of God as personal: a person is a being who can know and love.

(iii) God is Personal

Earlier in the chapter we referred to the modern tendency to revolt against the idea of a personal God. I suggested then that people are revolting not against the application of the philosophical concept of person to the true idea of God, but against the picture of God as a venerable man with a beard. They have a feeling that the only way to get rid of the beard is to drop the notion of person. Unknown to themselves, the idea of personality is still colored by the mental picture they think they have outgrown. That that is so appears in the very argument they use against attributing personality to God. It is, they say, a limitation imposed upon God's infinity; it is anthropomorphic, a scaling down of God to the measure of man. So they avoid the idea of God as Someone and make Him Something, not He but It. God is a stream of tendency, a transcendant other, a polarization.

But in the concept of person we have just outlined, there is nothing either limiting or anthropomorphic. To say that God can know and can love does not impose limitations upon God; it removes limitations—for to be unable to know and to love would be very limiting indeed. There is nothing limited about knowing and loving as such. There are limitations in my knowing and my loving, but these are limitations in me. Knowing and loving in themselves are expansive, not limiting. In an infinite being they will be as infinite as He.

By the same reasoning, we see that they are not anthropomorphic. They are not a scaling down of God to the measure of man. For we know that our knowing and loving are but the faintest shadows of His. We have them because we are made in His likeness, so far as creatures made of nothing are capable of receiving His likeness. Our concepts of knowing and loving are necessarily dimmed with our own finitude, stained with our nothingness. They are not adequate to God. But they are the best we have. To throw them away would be less adequate still. Knowledge and love in God are infinitely greater than in us, but they are not less. We can say them at least, and use the uttermost effort of our mind to purify them of the limitations that arise in them from our limitation. That is the way of advance for the mind. Human language is not adequate to utter God, but it is the highest we have, and we should use its highest words. The highest words in human speech are not high enough, but what do you gain by using lower words? or no words? It is for us to use the highest words we have, recognize that they are not high enough, try to strain upward from them, not to dredge human speech for something lower. God is Someone, not only Something; a Person, not only a Power. He, not It.

To this idea of God as at once Infinite Existence and Someone, the mind has to habituate itself if it is to grow in the knowledge of reality. It will be laborious work if one comes new to it, and, to begin with, totally unrewarding work. Cassian tells the story of the grief of Serapion, one of the Desert Fathers, when it was finally brought home to him that the God he had so loved and served was not in human form: how he "burst into bitter tears and a storm of sobbing and wailed aloud: 'Woe is me, they have taken my God from me, and I have no one to hold on to, I know not whom I may adore and pray to!'" (Coll. X., c3). We, of course, have always known better: yet Serapion's trouble is our trouble too, just a little. The mental picture of God as a venerable man had a kind of solidity about it, even though one knew that it was not the reality. In particular it was someone to say one's prayers to. By comparison, this new conception of God seems thin and remote and uncomforting. But this is the way with every advance. In the new field we lack the comfort of long custom. Bernard Shaw phrased the experience very admirably: "When we learn something, it feels at first as if we have lost something." It is so, for instance, with a new stroke at tennis. Our old stroke had been a pretty incompetent affair, of the sort to make a professional laugh. But it had been ours, we were used to it, all our muscles were in the habit of it. The new stroke is doubtless better, but we are not in the way of it, we cannot do anything with it, and all the joy goes out of tennis—but only until we have mastered the new way. Then, quite suddenly, we find that the whole game is a new experience.

So it is when we first begin to force the mind to do its own work in relation to God—particularly its praying, for it would be a shame to be thinking at a deeper level and praying at a shallower. A time will come when the mind will be happy and at home, functioning easily. But for the moment it hardly seems able to function at all. It can say the words, but it cannot handle the meaning. It is very much what happens when you first learn to play the piano. It is only when you start the exercises which are meant to make your fingers supple that you find out how utterly clumsy they are. They had always seemed to you reasonably competent fingers, and now all of a sudden they seem quite useless. It is because for the first time you are trying to use your fingers to make music. They were more comfortably employed making mud pies. But in the long run, music is better worth making.

4. The Mind Works on Infinity

We have arrived at the notion of God as Infinite Existence. But unless the mind fixes itself upon these words with the determination to find some meaning in them, they will remain no more than words, and of no more value for our knowledge of God than the mental picture we are trying to outgrow. As we shall see, we shall never get all the meaning out of them, but it is surprising how much we can get. Obviously there are a dozen ways of approach, but as convenient a way as any is by the consideration of a question often posed by unbelievers: "Where was God before the universe was created?" It is a convenient question for our purpose because it assails God's infinity in two ways. The word *where* raises the question of space and brings us to some first consideration of God's Immensity: the word *before* raises the question of time and brings us to some elementary consideration of God's Eternity. In finding the answer, we must use the intellect without imagination's aid; one of the neatest tricks imagination has played on us is the sense it has given us of the necessity of time and space: we feel that we simply cannot conceive anything without them. We must learn to. It goes with the maturity of the intellect to find itself more at home and at ease with the

61

timeless and spaceless, not deceived by the "imaginability" of time and space but finding them more problem than help. We shall not arrive at that maturity at once, or perhaps at all. But our present enquiry should bring us a little closer.

(i) God transcends space

The word *infinity* is built from the Latin words *finis,* a limit or boundary, and the prefix *in,* which negatives the main word. Thus it means "without limits or boundaries, limitless, boundless". But this word must not be taken as meaning only the absence of any external boundaries. To say that a being is infinite does not mean only that it spreads in all directions without any limit, that whether you are considering its being or its power you never reach a point where you must say "this far and no farther". It means the absence of all limitations, not only external but internal as well. At first sight, this may seem needlessly subtilizing and even meaningless. Actually it is quite vital to our knowledge of infinity. When we say that a being is infinite, we mean not only that there is no limit to what it can do, but no divisions within itself, no parts. An infinite being *must* be spirit.

Consider how the fact of having parts is a limitation. Our own bodies will serve to illustrate. My body has vast numbers of parts—arms, legs, kidneys, liver. No part is the whole of me. Thus my very being is divided up. No one element in me is me, and no one element in my body is my body. How limiting this is to my being should be obvious enough: among other things, it means that parts can be broken off me—fingers and such like; it means the possibility of that decisive break we call death; even while I live it means that I take a great deal of holding together. Its limiting effect upon my power is more obvious still. The things my body can do are distributed over the various parts of which my body consists. My foot can do one sort of thing, my liver another, my nose another. Thus my power to act is not concentrated but dispersed. As a consequence, I cannot perform any particular action without a preliminary bringing together of the various parts of me whose cooperation that particular action requires. Further, this dispersal of my power means that I cannot do all the things I am capable of doing at any one time. I cannot at once be playing the violin, writing a letter, and building a fire.

There is no need to labor the point. To have one's being in parts is an immense limitation, and under this limitation the whole material universe lies. It is because material things are thus made up of parts, that they are capable of occupying space. We glanced at this fact in Chapter 2: it is worth pausing here for a moment to consider it more at length. Division into parts means that one element in a being is not another element, and neither element is the whole being. This fact makes it possible for a material being to occupy space: for it is of the very essence of occupying space that there should be elements which are not each other: the thing may be microscopically small, or too small for any microscope, but if it occupies space, then one end is not the other end, the upper surface is not the lower surface, the outside is not the inside. Unless a being is composed of elements which are not each other, it cannot occupy space.

Thus we must not let imagination deceive us about the vastness of space. Let our universe be ever so vast, it occupies space only because it has the prior limitation of having its being broken up into parts. The occupation of space is a limitation, because it is grounded in a limitation. Scientists may argue whether there is any external boundary of the material universe, whether one can conceive a point in any direction beyond which the material universe does not extend. This is a pleasant argument, but it has no bearing on the question whether the material universe is infinite. It may extend in all directions without ever coming to an outer boundary; but it has the myriad boundaries within itself which arise from its being composed of parts. It is incurably finite.

God on the other hand *is* infinite. There are no parts in Him at all. He is wholly Himself in one inclusive act of being. Because He lacks the limitation of having parts, He is free from the consequent limitation of occupying space. Space cannot contain Him. He transcends space, and the things of space, and indeed all created things. He lives His life in utter and absolute independence of them. Here the mind must tread very delicately, or imagination will play a trick upon it. For imagination, the material universe is altogether enormous, spread out in its majesty throughout space; whereas God occupies no space at all, and therefore is for imagination unimaginably tiny. But in reality the universe is in space because it is limited; and God is outside space, not because His being is too small even for the tiniest pinpoint hold in space, but because His being is too mighty. "Heaven and the heaven of heavens cannot contain Him" (1 Kings 8:27).

God does not occupy space; yet we say, and say rightly, that God is everywhere. *Everywhere* is clearly a word of space: everywhere is the space occupied by everything. Therefore to say that God is everywhere means to say that God is in everything. We have seen that God transcends all things; but He is immanent, in some way abiding in all things too. Strictly, of course, since God is greater than the universe, it would be closer to the reality of things to say that everything is in God: the trouble is that if we say that, imagination tricks us with a mental picture of God as somehow the larger space of the two. Until imagination is under better control, let us stick to the phrase "God is in everything." But what does the word "in" mean when applied to a being totally spaceless? How can a being who occupies no space at all yet manage to be in everything that does occupy space? Clearly the word *in,* the word *where,* both need closer examination when we speak of God as being everywhere, in everything. A spiritual being cannot be in a material being as water is in a cup or a cup in water. God cannot be in everything by being spread out spatially to occupy everything. He is not in the material universe as water is in a sponge, or even as a sponge in the ocean. For all spaceless beings the word "where" has one meaning. A spaceless being is where it operates; it is in the things which receive the effects of its power.

God is at the central point of the being of everything whatsoever because He is infinite and all other things are finite, so that He can totally dominate them all by His power. And the first act of His domination is to hold them in existence, to keep them from being nothing. He is everywhere; that is, He is in all things, because the effect of His power is upon all things: "Do I not fill heaven and earth?" (Jer 23:24).

There is a still deeper and more mysterious level at which we must try to grasp God's presence in things. But what we have here will do for a first step. He is in all things, because His power operates upon them, holding them in existence; that is to say, He is in all things not because He needs them, but because they need Him. The universe therefore is to be thought of not as a necessity for God, providing Him with a place to be. He transcends things by the power of His own Nature; He is immanent in things only to meet their need. Thus the question we began with—where was God before the universe existed?—fades away into the inconsiderable question: what created thing was being held in existence by the power of God before there was any created thing?

(ii) God transcends time

We have seen that the first part of the question led us to consider space in relation to God, and thus to God's total transcendence of space, which we call His Immensity. Now let us look at the second part of the question: "Before the universe was created." For just as the word "where" raises the question of space, the word "before" raises the question of time, and we must be as clear about God's transcendence of time as about His transcendence of space. What, then, is time? Philosophers use the word in two closely related senses; most of us find that one of these senses is sufficient for us. Time, say the philosophers, is the duration of that which changes; time, say the philosophers again and we with them, is the measurement of the changes of the universe. What is common to both statements is the relation of time to change. Where nothing changes, there is nothing for time to measure. Where nothing changes, time has no possible meaning. Thus time and the universe started together. God is infinite and therefore changeless. He is "the Father of lights with whom there is no change or shadow of alteration" (James 1:17). He possesses the utter fullness of existence, so that nothing can go from Him, for that would be to reduce Him; and nothing can come to Him, for He already possesses all. The universe He created is a changing universe. And because change belongs to it and not to God, time belongs to it and not to God. To repeat, time and the universe started together: time is the ticking of the universe.

Thus the phrase "before the universe was created" has no meaning at all. *Before* is a word of time, and there could be no time before the universe because time began with the universe. To say "before the universe" means when there wasn't any "when"; which is to say that it doesn't mean anything at all.

Let us look a little more closely at what is implied by change. It means that the being which is subject to it is never at any moment the whole of itself: it possesses its being successively, as the philosophers say. You, for instance, are never at any moment the whole of yourself. What you were last year, what you will be next year, all belongs to the totality called you. But last year has gone, and next year has not arrived. It is obviously an overwhelming limitation that one never wholly possesses one's self, that one possesses one's being in successive moments and not simply in one act of being, that one is never wholly there. There is no such limitation in God. He possesses Himself wholly in one act of being. This is what we call His eternity. Thus eternity does not mean time open at both ends, time stretching away back into the past with no beginning, stretching away forward into the future with no ending. In fact we are back at our earlier principle: that infinity means not only the absence of external limits, but of internal divisions as well. Just as space has parts lying alongside one another, time has parts following one another. The Infinite has no parts, of either (or any other conceivable) sort. Eternity is not time, however much we may try to glorify the concept of time. The philosophic definition of *eternity* is in two Latin words, *tota simul,*[1] which may be roughly translated as "all at once". God's eternity means that He possesses the totality of what He is, not in successive acts as we do, but in one single act. Just as time is the duration of that which changes, eternity is the duration of that which simply is, the duration of the Being who, in one infinite act of being which does not change and does not cease, is all that He is, and does all that He does.

---

[1] These are the key words of Boethius' definition of eternity—"Vitae interminabilis tota simul et perfecta possessio"—the whole and perfect possession in one act of life without end.

We may help to clarify our notions of eternity and time by considering what the word *now* means as applied to each. Our now, the now of time, is the *nunc fluens,* the flowing now. It does not apply to the same instant of time as when I used it in the last sentence. At every use of the word "now", it applies to a different instant. It does not even remain the same while we are saying it. For it consists of two sounds, n- and -ow. While we are saying the n-, the -ow is still in the future; when we are saying the -ow, the n- is already past. In other words, time's present is a very fleeting present indeed: God's present abides. He lives in the eternal now.

Apply all this to the consideration of one further absurdity that tends to shadow the back of our minds, even when in the front of our minds we are by way of knowing better. It is the vague feeling we have that eternity had been going on for some time before God decided to create the universe. In the light of what we have said, this is seen to be sheerly meaningless, for it brings time into eternity. We must not think of God creating the universe after a certain amount of eternity had rolled by, because there are no parts in eternity, and it does not roll by. This mental monstrosity is perhaps related to the picture of God as an old man. But God is not only not an old man, He is not even an old God. He is not old at all. For "old" simply means that one has lived through a long time; and there is no time to God.

How then are we to conceive creation, if we are not allowed to think of time stretching back to its beginning and eternity stretching back before that? We must try to conceive it in some such terms as these: God, who possesses the whole of His being in one single act of infinite existence, wills that a universe should be which possesses its being in successive acts, bit by bit. Eternity belongs to the one, time to the other. God's creative act, like all His acts, is in eternity because God is in eternity. The result of His creative act is in time. We get something faintly comparable in human affairs: a man speaks into a microphone at a certain time in London, his voice is heard a measurable moment later all over the world: the man acts where and when he is, the effects of his action are where and when they are. It is only a shadowly comparison not shedding much light on creation in eternity and time. The discouraged intellect may feel itself utterly incompetent to make anything at all of such concepts. But there is no gain in trying to imagine eternity in terms of the bit by bit. It is easier, of course, but it is a denaturing of eternity and therefore of God.

(iii) Infinite activity and changelessness

We have seen God as infinite and utterly changeless; and these two ideas might tend to combine in our minds in a concept of infinite stagnation. But God is alive, and life is activity; and God is infinite, so that His activity is infinite too. Thus we are in the presence of two truths about God, that He is infinitely in action and utterly immutable. Both truths are certain, yet it is immeasurably difficult for minds like ours to see how they can be reconciled. In all our experience of activity, change seems to be of activity's very essence. Certainly it is of no use to call upon the aid of imagination. Imagination can furnish no picture at all in which these two elements are happily combined for our comfort. If we are to make anything of them at all, the mind must be prepared to strip away every vestige of the effect that its long immersion in time and space has had upon it. We shall never wholly succeed, of course; but we shall go far enough to be able to see what further road lies ahead, and why we cannot yet tread that further road—far enough to see how the difficulty of reconciling these two truths lies not in the truth but wholly in us.

Let us at least make a beginning, some first steps in the knowledge of God's activity. God is not simply something but Someone. He is personal; that is, He knows and loves. Therefore we can see that His activity will be personal activity, His life will be a life of knowing and loving, knowing infinitely, loving infinitely. In our thought of God's activity, we very naturally tend to think first of His actions in relation to the universe and so to us. Indeed we tend to think of these not only first but pretty much exclusively. It is something of a wrench to realize that we do not belong essentially to God's life and activity at all—it is of *our* essence that He acts upon us, but not of His. It is not mere crudity to say that running the universe is God's hobby, not His real life. We must of course study closely God's dealings with us; but we must not stop there. We must also study Who and What that God is who thus deals with us. Otherwise we shall fall short not only in our understanding of God, but also, as a consequence, in our understanding of His dealings with us. One result not infrequently observed of this concentration upon God's Providence and neglect of God is a tendency to figure God's activities as one's own action, to assume that He acts as one would act oneself, to read His purposes as one would read one's own, and indeed to be prepared to play Providence oneself on occasion. Religious people are in a certain danger of talking of their own will as if it must be God's will and, in that misapprehension, forcing it upon others. Nothing is so strong a safeguard against this silliness as a grasp of the nature of God in Himself.

Here, then, we shall concentrate upon God's own life, so far as we can come to any knowledge of it. It is a life of knowing infinitely and loving infinitely. The innermost secrets of the personal life of God remain to be considered in the light of the revelation given to us by Christ our Lord. Here we shall consider them only in relation to our present problem, which is to see how infinite activity can be one thing in God with His changelessness. At this first level we can see that the combination of these two truths means that God knows infinitely and loves infinitely, and that these two infinite activities imply no faintest shadow of change within Himself. In one way we can see it simply enough. Change would imply either that some new element, which had not been there before, entered into His knowing or His loving; or that some element, which had been there, ceased to be there. But His knowing and His loving are in their very being the perfect expression of His own infinite perfection. By the mere fact of being, they possess all the perfection that knowledge and love can have, so that nothing could be added to them; and they possess this perfection abidingly, so that nothing can be taken from them. They cannot grow, because God is perfect; they cannot diminish, because God is perfect. Infinite knowledge and infinite life are *infinite* activities, and change can find no point of entry. So far we have been considering how these two apparent irreconcilables, activity and immutability, are one in God's personal life within Himself. Later we shall consider how our minds may see a reconciliation for them in God's dealings with the universe. How the changeless Being lives His own changeless life is one thing: how the changeless Being handles the affairs of this changing universe is another.

Meanwhile let us return to the problem as it affects our understanding of God's own life. I have said that in one way we can see the reconciliation without any great difficulty. That is, we can demonstrate to ourselves unanswerably that it must be so. But there remains the practical problem of *seeing* it so.

(iv) An exercise upon infinity

Not till we have the face-to-face vision of God in the next life shall we be able to see the two as totally one, so that we shall see the immutability as identical with the infinite activity. Here below we have no direct mental experience of the infinite. We know that it is the complete negation of limits, but we cannot conceive the infinite as it *is*. Yet immense progress is possible toward it. We can at least develop an awareness of the elements of limitation in our own being and our own action, and try to conceive what the absence of these limitations must mean in God. I shall try to show by an example how we may make a first step toward this awareness. We have spoken of God's knowing. Now all we know about knowing, we derive from our own knowing. From it we get our positive concept of what knowing means in itself; from it we can, if we make the effort seriously enough, discover some of the limitations there are in our knowing, arising from our finitude; and by concentrating upon what knowing means in itself, and trying to strip away the limitations of knowing as it is in us, we can make some stumbling steps toward the realization of what God's knowing must be.

Let us consider our own knowing to find out both the positive meaning of knowing and its limitations in us. Positively, we discover that we know a thing when what it is, is present to our minds. Knowing will not be less than that in God: the mode of it may be beyond our conception: the majesty of it may be beyond our conception: but the essential of it we have hold of—all things are present to the mind of God as what they are.

Now for some of the limitations of our knowing. I do not pretend to list them all.

(1) In the first place, we know so little; there are such vast masses of things that we do not know. (2) A second limitation is that in our efforts to acquire knowledge, we have to proceed

one step at a time; we cannot know about anything by the mere act of looking at it. (3) Even of the things that we do know, we cannot hold more than two or three in our mind at once—attention to one set of things means that we cannot be attending to another set of things at the same time.

These three are limitations in our knowing that no one can possibly fail to hit upon at once. There is no great difficulty in seeing that God's knowledge will be free from them—there is nothing He does not know. He does not have to acquire knowledge. He knows all that He knows in one act of knowing; the same light bathes them all.

But there are certain other limitations in our knowing less obvious than these, which one who comes new to such thinking might not discover as limitations. Two of these will lead to very considerable advance in the knowledge of God. The first of these not-immediately-obvious limitations is that our knowledge is dependent upon the object known. Our knowledge of an orange, for instance, depends upon our having an orange to study. We know about anything by closely considering that thing. In its absence, we cannot know it. Our knowledge demands a real submission of our intellect to the evidence of the thing. We are so accustomed to knowing things this way, that it does not even strike us as limitation. But to be dependent is always a limitation. What our dependency means in its actuality in God, we cannot see. We have no experience of being infinite or of knowing infinitely. We cannot know God as He knows Himself; we cannot even know ourselves as He knows us.

The second of these not-immediately-obvious limitations is less obvious still and very much harder to see. But it leads us to a most profound truth about the nature of God. It is a fundamental limitation in our knowing that our act of knowing is distinct from our selves. My knowing is something that I do, but it is not I. This may at first glance seem either no limitation at all, or at best, mere hair-splitting. But in fact it is a very powerful limitation. If my knowledge were the same thing as I, I should not have to make the distinct effort of setting about knowing: I should be engaged in the act of knowing, and of knowing all that I know, all the time; nor should I ever forget anything if my knowing were myself. Because it is not, I am sometimes knowing and sometimes not knowing, always under the necessity of making a distinct effort in the matter, often totally incapable of making the effort. God's knowing is not subject to this limitation any more than to any other conceivable limitation. God's knowing is not distinct from Himself. God and His knowledge are one. God is His knowledge. God's knowledge is God. Once again, there may be vast difficulties for the mind in actually seeing it so, but there is no great difficulty in seeing that it must be so. For if God's knowledge were not identical with God Himself, then there would be some distinction between God and His knowledge, something that God has and that His knowledge lacks: but that would mean that His knowledge would not be infinite: which is impossible.

A moment's reflection will show us that the same line of thought, which leads us to see that God and His knowledge are one, applies to all the other attributes of God—His love, His justice, His mercy, any you please. God's mercy is not something God has; it is God. If His mercy or His justice were in any way distinct from Him, it would mean that there was something in Him that they lacked, and so His mercy or His justice would not be Infinite, and that again is impossible. Thus there is no distinction between God's attributes and God, and therefore no difference between one of God's attributes and another. God's justice is God Himself, and God's mercy is God Himself. Infinite justice and infinite mercy are not two opposing tendencies in God: they are one same God.

Let us make one further effort toward the understanding of this point. All perfections are in God, yet not distinct from one another because not distinct from God Himself. But our minds cannot handle all concepts in one concept. We must see them as distinct in order to see them at all. The mercy of God is an infinite reality. The justice of God is an infinite reality. In the being of God they are the same reality. But if we try to begin our thinking by seeing them as the same reality, we shall simply not see them at all. Because God's mercy is real, let us contemplate God's mercy; and because God's justice is real, let us contemplate God's justice. Here indeed is the perfect opportunity for what has already been suggested as the right approach to the polar elements in any mystery: accept them both at white heat, and in some utterly unsayable way they will tend to fuse into one. So with God's attributes. There is not one of them that will not immeasurably repay our study. And as we thus in the mind live with them, our sense of their distinction from one another will grow less, and there will form in our mind some faint suggestion of their oneness with God. For this oneness of God and His attributes is merely the living consequence of that oneness we have already seen between God and His existence. We have all sorts of attributes, and they are not we. But there is no real distinction between what God has and what God is. God is what He has.

(v) The going is hard

But whatever light may be about to grow in us as we grow in the knowledge of God, our first steps are pretty much in the dark. Our going is heavy going. We begin by stripping away limitations which are part of the very atmosphere we have always breathed, and we find breathing very difficult. The stripping away of limitations seems a very thinning process, since we have nothing so familiar to put in their place. There is at first an intolerable sense of thinness about the idea of God that results. We may know that we are not taking anything away from God, because to subtract limitations is to add reality. But at first it does not seem so. Reality as we are accustomed to it, with all its limitations, has a kind of thickness compared to the thinness of infinite Spirit. It is true that what I have called thickness results from the element of nothingness, and that all the realities we know as mingled with nothing-ness because they are created, are to be found in utter purity in the Creator. But it is hard to see that this purity increases their intensity.

The truth is that if we had only the God of philosophy, God as the exploring mind can discover Him by its own powers, most of us would probably always feel Him just too remote. Ideally, we should be able to make vast progress in knowledge of Him and some sort of intimacy with Him. But we are not ideal. Fortunately man's seeking for God is not the whole story. God has also sought man, a seeking with a long history that culminated when God became man and dwelt amongst us. Nothing could be less remote than Jesus Christ.

5. God Tells Man

Why God became man we shall consider in the second part of this book, together with certain precisions as to what is meant by the truth that Christ is God and some of the immeasurable things that flow from it.

(i) Christ teaches us by being God

Our present concern is simply with the new way opened to man for the knowledge of God by the sheer fact of the Incarnation, the fact that at a given moment of history, God the Son took a human nature and made it so utterly His own that, remaining God without diminution or dimming of His Divinity, He was still truly man, and remains forever man. To know that Christ is God sheds a great light upon Christ, as we shall see; for the moment our concern is with the light it sheds upon God.

A moment's reflection will show why this new way to the knowledge of God is so vast and vital. Apart from the Incarnation, man could know of God only in God's Nature. Man could, for example, know God as Infinite Power, creating the universe from nothing, and this is true knowledge and very valuable. But if it is true knowledge, it is undeniably rather remote knowledge. We have in ourselves no experience of creating anything at all from nothing, none of the insight that comes from shared experience. We have no notion of what is involved in creating something from nothing and only the most shadowy notion, born of reflection and not of experience, of what is meant by being infinite. For such things we have in ourselves no measuring-rod. But to see God not simply in His own nature, but being and doing and suffering in our nature, is a very different matter. And when we are reading the Gospels, that is precisely what we do see—God obeying His mother, God paying taxes, God receiving hospitality, God receiving insults, God tormented by hunger and thirst, God loving, God angry: and these things we can measure, for we have done them all ourselves.

In all this first part, we are in search of light upon God as He is in Himself. Christ our Lord gives us a great flood of light by what He has to tell us about God, as we shall see later; but with all reverence we may feel that He gives us more light upon God by being than by saying.

This, I think, explains something about Our Lord's way of revealing the primary fact about Himself which puzzles many readers of the Gospels. They feel that He made an unnecessary mystery about it: if He was God, it would surely have been simpler for Him to say so in the plainest words at the very outset of His mission. So people say—believers in His Divinity as an expression of puzzlement, unbelievers as a challenge to the truth of the doctrine. Notice, at any rate, that Our Lord's action in this matter was of set policy: He did, quite deliberately, make a certain mystery about who and what He was. His enemies felt it. We have the Jews demanding indignantly: "How long wilt thou go on keeping us in suspense? If thou art the Christ, tell us openly" (Jn 10:24). But it was not only from His enemies that the full knowledge was long held. Between the Birth in Bethlehem and the Death on Calvary, there is probably no single episode of Our Lord's life better known than the scene by the lake at Caesarea Philippi, when Peter answered and said: "Thou art Christ, the Son of the living God"; and Jesus answered him: "Blessed art thou, Simon son of Jonah; it is not flesh and blood, it is My father who is in Heaven that has revealed this to thee. And I tell thee this in my turn: that thou art Peter, and it is upon this rock that I will build my Church: and the gates of Hell shall not prevail against it."

In the splendor of this climax, we tend to see what went before it rather in shadow. However often we have read the passage, the mind leaps forward to this, and thus is in danger of missing a good deal of the light in what immediately leads up to it. We remember, of course, St. Peter's great answer. If we press our memory a little harder, we remember what question St. Peter was answering: but it may be doubted if many of us see how very startling a question it was. For Our Lord had asked the Apostles: "Who do you say that I am?" Recall that these were the men who had been His inseparable companions so long: and yet so late in their companionship He could ask them who they thought He was. Clearly He had not told them; just as clearly, He had had good reason for not telling them.

The reason, one may in all reverence surmise, why He did not begin by telling either His friends or His enemies that He was God is that they were Jews, and the Jews believed in God. It is only an age deficient in apprehending God's majesty that could be surprised that Christ Jesus should only gradually have led men to the realization of a truth which such men would find so shattering. I have already spoken of our modern tendency to treat God as an equal, or at any rate to overlook the immeasurable difference between His infinity and our finitude. In such an atmosphere, men think with a certain naïveté of God as an interesting person to meet, and of themselves happily engaging in an interchange of views with Him upon the running of His universe, they making their suggestions and God explaining His difficulties and everybody feeling the better for the interchange. In such an atmosphere nothing seems more natural than that God should simply introduce Himself, and with the minimum of ceremony.

I have called this way of thinking naïve, and naïve it is to the point of drivelling. No Jew of Our Lord's day, however sinful he might have been, would have felt like that for an instant. If Christ our Lord had begun with the announcement that He was God, and they had believed Him, they would simply have fallen flat on their faces and never got up. To men with their awareness of the majesty of God, the truth that Christ was God had to be broken very gradually or it would have broken them. If we read the Gospels with that in mind, we can see how marvelously Our Lord brought the Apostles to realization. His method was not to tell them, but to bring them to a point where they would tell Him. They saw Him doing things and heard Him saying things—things that only God had a right to do (like forgiving sins and supplementing the law God had given on Sinai), things that only God could truthfully say ("I and the Father are one"; "Before Abraham was made, I am"; "No one knows the Son but the Father, and no one knows the Father but the Son"); and they reflected upon what they had seen and heard; and a wild hypothesis began to form in their minds; and at times they felt surer of it as certain things seemed incapable of any lesser explanation, and again at times they felt unsure, as certain things could not be fitted at all into their present concept of God. But with endless advance and recoil, the sum of their movement was advance: and at last came St. Peter's confession: "Thou art Christ, Son of the Living God", rewarded so marvelously by Our Lord, as we have seen. Yet as far as the words of Peter go, they contain nothing that had not been said by another Apostle at the very first calling of the Apostles. For Nathanael had said (Jn 1:49): "Thou, Master, art the Son of God, thou art the King of Israel."

What difference did Christ our Lord see between the confession of Nathanael, and the confession of Peter? Partly, we may suppose, the difference lay in this: that St. Peter's confession was a true act of faith, made under the impulsion of the grace of God—"It is not flesh and blood, but My Father who is in Heaven that has revealed this to thee." Nathanael's confession was an act of human reason; Christ had just made a mysterious reference to a fig tree, obviously some incident Nathanael thought known only to himself, and the only way he could rationally account for Christ's knowing it was to assume that Christ must be more than man. Similarly we find all the Apostles reaching out toward a supernatural explanation when Our Lord calmed the storm with a word; and they said one to another: "Who is this, who is obeyed even by the winds and the sea?" (Mk 4:40). But bit by bit their human reason was bringing them to see that there could be only the one explanation; was bringing them, that is, to the point where their minds were ready to receive the impulsion of God's grace and make the act of Faith, after which they held the truth not by human reason, which of itself can go on wavering endlessly, but with the sure support of the grace of God. That point Peter reached first.

Nor was that the only difference between Peter's confession and Nathanael's. In Peter's words there was a far fuller content of meaning: they look toward that moment when Thomas, totally renouncing his too human doubt, cried out to Jesus: "My Lord, and my God."

Today it is almost a distinguishing mark of Catholics that they see a real function for the Apostles. In non-Catholic writing, no more important function can be found for them than to be foils to the brilliancy of their Master, which is to say, fools asking their foolish questions to bring out the wisdom of His answers, very much the function of Dr. Watson in the Sherlock Holmes stories. Yet they meant something very important to Our Lord—"You have not chosen me, I have chosen you." And even if we hold it not surprising that those Christians who have lost the sense of the divinely founded hierarchical structure of the Church should not see the function of the Apostles as the first members of that hierarchy, it is still surprising that any Christian should overlook this other function to which we have been leading up. For these were the men who knew Christ before they knew He was God. Had they known from the beginning, they might simply have feared Him, and fear would have made a bar to any progress in intimacy. But by the time they knew beyond the possibility of uncertainty that He was God, it was too late to have only fear. For by the time they knew He was God, they had come to know that He was love. If they had known that Christ was God first, then they would have applied their idea of God to Christ; as it was, they were able to apply their knowledge of Christ to God. The principal fruit for them and for us of their three years of companionship with Him was the unshakable certainty of His love for mankind; and it was St. John, the Apostle He loved best, who crystallized the whole experience for us in the phrase of his first Epistle, "God is Love" (4:8).

We may ask why the Jews did not know that already, for God had shown them His love often enough; and in the Old Testament His love is wonderfully stated. "The Lord is compassionate and merciful, long-suffering and plenteous in mercy" (Ps 102:8); that is strong enough, yet it is not the strongest thing of its sort. In Isaiah (49:15) there is a phrase which would seem to reach the very limit of divine tenderness: "Can a woman forget her infant, so as not to have pity on the son of her womb? And if she should forget, yet will I not forget thee." The truth is that love arises and abides most easily and naturally where there is community of nature; and until God took our nature and became man, that way did not exist. God-made-man could love us with human love—and this, though a lesser thing than divine love, can be very comforting to our weakness. Nowhere in the Old Testament did it occur to anyone to call God what they were to call God-made-man, "the friend of sinners". The Jews knew that God had spoken to and done great things for mankind, but He had not *been* man.

The moral for us is simple: in our approach to God we are helped enormously by seeing Him in our nature; and for the mind, this means a continual study of Him whereby the Apostles' experience of Christ becomes our own personal experience, their intimacy becomes our intimacy. We cannot always analyze intimacy; but there is no mistaking it: we know the person quite differently. You do not learn intimacy, or reap the fruit of someone else's. You grow into it. In the Gospels, one really can grow into this intimacy with Our Lord, precisely because the evangelists do not obtrude their own personalities. Anyhow, know Him we must. There is no other way to full knowledge of God; Christ has said so. In other words, we have to vivify all that hard thinking about the Infinite by the closest companionship with our Lord Jesus Christ. By both, the mind grows toward the knowledge of God which is its health. At first we may find one more instance of an experience we have had already, namely, the difficulty of getting two apparently dissimilar things into the one picture. We can think with ease and joy about Christ our Lord; we can exercise our minds with no ease at all and precious little joy upon the Infinite; but our problem is to conceive the two as one God. The solution is as before, to use our mind with all its might upon both, and bit by bit we shall begin to find that one sheds light upon the other, and we begin at least in glimpses to see that it is but the one light.

As a practical matter, then, it is to be recommended that the user of this book will accompany all the rest of his reading and thinking by a steady reading of the Gospels, steadily reminding himself at each incident and each phrase of Our Lord that He who said this and did this is God the Son, Infinite Existence. This is the way to make the philosophy come alive. Francis Thompson has said that no pagan ever saw the same tree as Wordsworth; it is certainly truer to say that no pagan ever saw the same Infinity and Eternity and Immensity as we who have seen God companioning with men.

(ii) Christ teaches us by speaking of God

One result of this reading of the Gospels will be to find what Our Lord showed us about God by being God. Another will be to find what Our Lord shows us about God by what He has to say of God. There is a lot to be said for making one's own list of the texts in which Christ our Lord tells us of God, grasping them in their context and returning to them again and again.[1] Most of them, naturally, treat of God in His dealings with and judgments of the human race. Save perhaps in the proportion of statements about God's love to statements about His justice, it would be hard to find among these anything that has not already been told us in the Old Testament. There is a new atmosphere, but if it is impossible not to feel the difference, it is almost impossible to lay a precise finger on it. If one happens to know the Old Testament at all well, everything makes us see how vast a communication about Himself God had already given His chosen people.

In a handful of statements, Our Lord covers the ground of the philosophers: God is a spirit (Jn 4:24); He is perfect (Mt 5:48); He dwells in secret (Mt 6:18); He is good and He only (Mt 19:17); to Him all things are possible (Mt 19:26); He has never ceased working, that is, maintaining creation in being (Jn 5:44); He is the one only God (Mk 12:33).

It is a vast reassurance to the mind to have God as it were ratifying the words with which human language has tried to utter Him. It is true that no word of human speech, no concept

---

[1] It will be useful later if all texts are noted which tell why Christ came among men.

of the human mind, is adequate; but word and concept are not therefore useless, for God has used them. We may have precious little notion of what they mean in an infinite nature, but the little *is* precious. They do not give all light, but light-giving they are. God uses them for that.

Our Lord uses them: God had already used them: for not here either do we find anything that is not in the Old Testament. But there is a third sort of statement, which does constitute a new element in God's revelation of Himself to men. As we read what Our Lord tells us of God, we are bound to become conscious of two elements constantly recurring, and recurring in combination—the element of oneness and the element of plurality.

I say that this was new. There are in the Old Testament stray hints and gleams of it, but they are no more than that. Thus in the first chapter of Genesis, God says (verse 26), "Let *us* make man to *our* image and likeness", and in the next verse we read, "And God made man to *his* image and likeness": the plural words "us" and "our" seem to suggest that there were several persons; the singular word "his" that they were somehow one. I do not mean that the human writer of Genesis knew how apt to the reality of God were the words he wrote: but God who inspired him knew it. Anyhow it did not strike the Jews, even by Christ's day, as requiring any special comment. To us again, there is something fascinating in the fact that the word for God, "Elohim", is plural: yet it takes a verb in the singular, and if an adjective goes with it, that is in the singular too. But again it did not strike the Jews, or the Canaanites (who had the same usage), that this grammar had any special significance. Of another sort, there are descriptions of Wisdom which seem to suggest a second person within the Godhead: for example, "And thy wisom with thee, which knoweth thy works, which then also was present when thou madest the world" (Wis 9:9).

If this is no more than a way of saying that God was not without the attribute of wisdom at the time He made the world, it seems a rather elaborate way of stating an obvious truth. To us who have heard Our Lord's explicit revelation, such things are full of suggestion. But they did not lead the Jews, nor were they of a sort inescapably to lead them, to the truth that God, remaining one, is yet in some mysterious way more than one. To a truth so astounding indeed, one must be led inescapably or one will not arrive there at all. It is not the sort of truth that one will leap to embrace on a mere hint.

Our Lord did not stop at a hint. As I have said, He insists on an element of plurality, returning to it again and again. There is, of course, no faintest mitigation of the utter monotheism of the Jews. Our Lord quotes God's own revelation to them: "Hear, O Israel: the Lord thy God is One God." But there is a new element of more-than-oneness, which does not contradict the oneness but somehow enriches it. Thus (Jn 10:30) He says, "I and the Father are One." Here there is clearly a statement of two who are yet one. In the last two verses of St. Matthew's gospel we find Our Lord saying: "Baptizing them in the name of the Father, and of the Son, and of the Holy Spirit". Here we have plurality again, this time three, yet the unity is stated in the use of the word "name", not "names".

This combination of oneness and plurality is most evident in Our Lord's discourse to the Apostles at the Last Supper. The whole of this discourse, from the thirteenth chapter of St. John to the seventeenth, should be read and read again: everything is in it. But for the moment our concern is with these two elements in what Our Lord has to tell us of the Godhead. In this discourse the special note is what can only be called a certain interchangeability. What I mean by this will appear from some examples. Thus in the fourteenth chapter we find Philip the Apostle saying to Our Lord, "Let us see the Father", and Our Lord answering him, "Whoever has seen me, has seen the Father."

We find this same notion, which I have been driven to call clumsily interchangeability, in what Our Lord has to say of answer to prayer, the sending of the Holy Spirit, God's abiding in our souls. Thus He says (Jn 16:23): "If you ask the Father anything in My name, He will give it to you." But He had already said (Jn 14:14): "If you shall ask Me anything in My name, that I will do."

Of the sending of the Holy Spirit, He had said (Jn 14:16): "I will ask the Father and He shall give you another Paraclete, that He may abide with you forever." Thus the Father is to send the Holy Spirit. But a little later (Jn 14:7) Our Lord says: "If I go, I will send the Paraclete to you."

We have just heard Our Lord saying that the Paraclete, the Holy Spirit, is to abide with us forever; but a few verses later, in answer to a question of St. Jude, Our Lord says: "If anyone love me He will keep my word and my Father will love him and we will come to him and will make our abode with him."

Heaven knows what His hearers made of all this as they heard the words come from His lips. What He was revealing was the doctrine of the Blessed Trinity. He revealed it because He wanted us to know it. We must try.

6. Three Persons in One Nature

The notion is unfortunately widespread that the mystery of the Blessed Trinity is a mystery of mathematics, that is to say, of how one can equal three. The plain Christian accepts the doctrine of the Trinity; the "advanced" Christian rejects it; but too often what is being accepted by the one and rejected by the other is that one equals three. The believer argues that God has said it, therefore it must be true; the rejecter argues it cannot be true, therefore God has not said it. A learned non-Catholic divine, being asked if he believed in the Trinity, answered, "I must confess that the arithmetical aspect of the Deity does not greatly interest me"; and if the learned can think that there is some question of arithmetic involved, the ordinary person can hardly be expected to know any better.

(i) Importance of the doctrine of the Trinity

Consider what happens when a believer in the doctrine is suddenly called upon to explain it—and note that unless he is forced to, he will not talk about it at all: there is no likelihood of his being so much in love with the principal doctrine of his Faith that he will *want* to tell people about it. Anyhow, here he is: he has been challenged, and must say something. The dialogue runs something like this:

Believer: "Well, you see, there are three persons in one nature."
Questioner: "Tell me more."
Believer: "Well, there is God the Father, God the Son, God the Holy Spirit."
Questioner: "Ah, I see, three gods."
Believer (shocked): "Oh, no! Only one God."
Questioner: "But you said three: you called the Father God, which is one; and you called the Son God, which makes two; and you called the Holy Spirit God, which makes three."

Here the dialogue form breaks down. From the believer's mouth there emerges what can only be called a soup of words, sentences that begin and do not end, words that change into something else halfway. This goes on for a longer or shorter time. But finally there comes something like: "Thus, you see, three is one and one is three." The questioner not unnaturally retorts that three is not one nor one three. Then comes the believer's great moment. With his eyes fairly gleaming he cries: "Ah, that is the mystery. You have to have faith."

Now it is true that the doctrine of the Blessed Trinity is a mystery, and that we can know it only by faith. But what we have just been hearing is not the mystery of the Trinity; it is not the mystery of anything, it is wretched nonsense. It may be heroic faith to believe it, like the man who

Wished there were four of 'em
That he might believe more of 'em

or it may be total intellectual unconcern—God has revealed certain things about Himself, we accept the fact that He has done so, but find in ourselves no particular inclination to follow it up. God has told us that He is three persons in one

Divine nature, and we say "Quite so", and proceed to think of other matters—last week's Retreat or next week's Confession or Lent or Lourdes or the Church's social teaching or foreign missions. All these are vital things, but compared with God Himself, they are as nothing: and the Trinity is God Himself. These other things must be thought about, but to think about them exclusively and about the Trinity not at all is plain folly. And not only folly, but a kind of insensitiveness, almost a callousness, to the love of God. For the doctrine of the Trinity is the inner, the innermost, life of God, His profoundest secret. He did not have to reveal it to us. We could have been saved without knowing that ultimate truth. In the strictest sense it is His business, not ours. He revealed it to us because He loves men and so wants not only to be served by them but truly known by them. It is the surest mark of love to want to be known. The revelation of the Trinity was in one sense an even more certain proof than Calvary that God loves mankind. To accept it politely and think no more of it is an insensitiveness beyond comprehension in those who quite certainly love God: as many certainly do who could give no better statement of the doctrine than the believer in the dialogue we have just been considering.

How did we reach this curious travesty of the supreme truth about God? The short statement of the doctrine is, as we have heard all our lives, that there are three persons in one nature. But if we attach no meaning to the word *person,* and no meaning to the word *nature,* then both the nouns have dropped out of our definition, and we are left only with the numbers three and one, and get along as best we can with these. Let us agree that there may be more in the mind of the believer than he manages to get said: but the things that do get said give a pretty strong impression that his notion of the Trinity is simply a travesty. It does him no positive harm provided he does not look at it too closely; but it sheds no light in his own soul: and his statement of it, when he is driven to make a statement, might very well extinguish such flickering as there may be in others. The Catholic whose faith is wavering might well have it blown out altogether by such an explanation of the Trinity as some fellow Catholic of stronger faith might feel moved to give: and no one coming fresh to the study of God would be much encouraged.

(ii) "Person" and "Nature"

Let us come now to a consideration of the doctrine of the Blessed Trinity to see what light there is in it for us, being utterly confident that had there been no light for us, God would not have revealed it to us. There would be a rather horrible note of mockery in telling us something of which we can make nothing. The doctrine may be set out in four statements:

In the one divine Nature, there are three Persons—the Father, the Son, and the Holy Spirit.

The Father is not the Son, the Son is not the Holy Spirit, the Holy Spirit is not the Father: no one of the Persons is either of the others.

The Father is God, the Son is God, the Holy Spirit is God.

There are not three Gods but one God.

We have seen that the imagination cannot help here. Comparisons drawn from the material universe are a hindrance and no help. Once one has taken hold of this doctrine, it is natural enough to want to utter it in simile and metaphor—like the lovely *lumen de lumine,* light from light, with which the Nicene Creed phrases the relation of the Son to the Father. But this is for afterward, poetical statement of a truth known, not the way to its knowledge. For that, the intellect must go on alone. And for the intellect, the way into the mystery lies, as we have already suggested, in the meaning of the words "person" and "nature". There is no question of arithmetic involved. We are not saying three persons in one person, or three natures in one nature; we are saying three persons in one nature. There is not even the appearance of an arithmetical problem. It is for us to see what person is and what nature is, and then to consider what meaning there can be in a nature totally possessed by three distinct persons.

The newcomer to this sort of thinking must be prepared to work hard here. It is a decisive stage of our advance into theology to get some grasp of the meaning of *nature* and the meaning of *person*. Fortunately the first stage of our search goes easily enough. We begin with ourselves. Such a phrase as "my nature" suggests that there is a person, I, who possesses a nature. The person could not exist without his nature, but there is some distinction all the same; for it is the person who possesses the nature and not the other way round.

One distinction we see instantly. Nature answers the question *what* we are; person answers the question *who* we are. Every being has a nature; of every being we may properly ask, What is it? But not every being is a person: only rational beings are persons. We could not properly ask of a stone or a potato or an oyster, Who is it?

By our nature, then, we are what we are. It follows that by our nature we do what we do: for every being acts according to what it is. Applying this to ourselves, we come upon another distinction between person and nature. We find that there are many things, countless things, we can do. We can laugh and cry and walk and talk and sleep and think and love. All these and other things we can do because as human beings we have a nature which makes them possible. A snake could do only one of them—sleep. A stone could do none of them. Nature, then, is to be seen not only as what we are but as the source of what we can do.

But although my nature is the source of all my actions, although my nature decides what kind of operations are possible for me, it is not my nature that does them: I do them, I the person. Thus both person and nature may be considered sources of action, but in a different sense. The person is that which does the actions, the nature is that by virtue of which the actions are done, or, better, that from which the actions are drawn. We can express the distinction in all sorts of ways. We can say that it is our *nature* to do certain things, but that *we* do them. We can say that *we* operate in or according to our *nature*. In this light we see why the philosophers speak of a person as the center of attribution in a rational nature: whatever is done in a rational nature or suffered in a rational nature or any way experienced in a rational nature is done or suffered or experienced by the person whose nature it is.

Thus there is a reality in us by which we are *what* we are: and there is a reality in us by which we are *who* we are. But as to whether these are two really distinct realities, or two levels of one reality, or related in some other way, we cannot see deep enough into ourselves to know with any sureness. There is an obvious difference between beings of whom you can say only *what* they are and the higher beings of whom you can say *who* they are as well. But in these latter—even in ourselves, of whom we have a great deal of experience—we see only darkly as to the distinction between the *what* and the *who*. Of our nature in its root reality we have only a shadowy notion, and of our self a notion more shadowy still. If someone—for want of something better to say—says: "Tell me about yourself", we can tell her the qualities we have or the things we have done; but of the *self* that has the qualities and has done the things, we cannot tell her anything. We cannot bring it under her gaze. Indeed we cannot easily or continuously bring it under our own. As we turn our mind inward to look at the thing we call "I", we know that there is something there, but we cannot get it into any focus: it does not submit to being looked at very closely. Both as to the nature that we ourselves have and the person that we ourselves are, we are more in darkness than in light. But at least we *have* certain things clear: *nature* says what we are, *person* says who we are. Nature is the source of our operations, person does them.

Now at first sight it might seem that this examination of the meaning of person and nature has not got us far toward an understanding of the Blessed Trinity. For although we have been led to see a distinction between person and nature in us, it seems clearer than ever that one nature can be possessed and operated in only by one person. By a tremendous stretch, we can just barely glimpse the possibility of one person having more than one nature, opening up to him more than one field of operation. But the intellect feels baffled at the reverse concept of one nature being totally "wielded", much less totally possessed, by more than one person. Now to admit ourselves baffled by the notion of three persons in the one nature of God is an entirely honorable admission of our own limitation; but to argue that because in man the relation of one nature to one person is invariable, therefore the same must be the relation in God, is a defect in our thinking. It is indeed an example of that anthropomorphism, the tendency to make God in the image of man, which we have already seen hurled in accusation at the Christian belief in God.

Let us look more closely at this idea. Man is made in the image and likeness of God. Therefore it is certain that man resembles God. Yet we can never argue with certainty from an image to the original of the image: we can never be sure that because the image is thus and so, therefore the original must be thus and so. A statue may be an extremely good statue of a man. But we could not argue that the man must be a very rigid man, because the statue is very rigid. The statue is rigid, not because the man is rigid, but because stone is rigid. So also with any quality you may observe in an image: the question arises whether that quality is there because the original was like that or because the material of which the image is made is like that. So with man and God. When we learn anything about man, the question always arises whether man is like that because God is like that, or because that is the best that can be done in reproducing the likeness of God in a being created of nothing. Put quite simply, we have always to allow for the necessary scaling down of the infinite in its finite likeness.

Apply this to the question of one person and one nature, which we find in man. Is this relation of one-to-one the result of something in the nature of being, or simply of something in the nature of finite being? With all the light we can get on the meaning of person and of nature even in ourselves, we have seen that there is still much that is dark to us: both concepts plunge away to a depth where the eye cannot follow them. Even of our own finite natures, it would be rash to affirm that the only possible relation is one person to one nature. But of an infinite nature, we have no experience at all. If God tells us that His own infinite nature is totally possessed by three persons, we can have no grounds for doubting the statement, although we may find it almost immeasurably difficult to make any meaning of it. There is no difficulty in accepting it as true, given our own inexperience of what it is to have an infinite nature and God's statement on the subject; there is no difficulty, I say, in accepting it as true; the difficulty lies in seeing what it means. Yet short of seeing some meaning in it, there is no point in having it revealed to us; indeed, a revelation that is only darkness is a kind of contradiction in terms.

(iii) Three Persons—One God

Let us then see what meaning,—that is to say, what light,—we can get from what has been said so far. The one infinite nature is totally possessed by three distinct persons. Here we must be quite accurate: the three persons are distinct, but not separate; and they do not share the divine nature, but each possesses it totally.

At this first beginning of our exploration of the supreme truth about God, it is worth pausing a moment to consider the virtue of accuracy. There is a feeling that it is a very suitable virtue for mathematicians and scientists, but cramping if applied to operations more specifically human. The young tend to despise it as a kind of tidiness, a virtue proper only to the poor-spirited. And everybody feels that it limits the free soul. It is in particular disrepute as applied to religion, where it is seen as a sort of anxious weighing and measuring that is fatal to the impetuous rush of the spirit. But in fact, accuracy is in every field the key to beauty: beauty has no greater enemy than rough approximation. Had Cleopatra's nose been shorter, says Pascal, the face of the Roman Empire and so of the world would have been changed: an eighth of an inch is not a lot: a lover, you would think, would not bother with such close calculation; but her nose was for her lovers the precise length for beauty: a slight inaccuracy would have spoiled everything. It is so in music, it is so in everything: beauty and accuracy run together, and where accuracy does not run, beauty limps.

Returning to the point at which this digression started: we must not say three separate persons, but three distinct persons, because although they are distinct—that is to say, no one of them is either of the others—yet they cannot be separated, for each is what he is by the total possession of the one same nature: apart from that one same nature, no one of the three persons could exist at all. And we must not use any phrase which suggests that the three persons *share* the Divine Nature. For we have seen that in the Infinite there is utter simplicity, there are no parts, therefore no possibility of sharing. The infinite Divine Nature can be possessed only in its totality. In the words of the Fourth Council of the Lateran, "There are three persons indeed, but one utterly simple substance, essence, or nature."

Summarizing thus far, we may state the doctrine in this way: the Father possesses the whole nature of God as His Own, the Son possesses the whole nature of God as His Own, the Holy Spirit possesses the whole nature of God as His Own. Thus, since the nature of any being decides what the being is, each person is God, wholly and therefore equally with the others. Further, the nature decides what the person can do: therefore, each of the three persons who thus totally possess the Divine Nature can do all the things that go with being God.

All this we find in the Preface for the Mass on the Feast of the Holy Trinity: "Father, all-powerful and ever-living God, . . . we joyfully proclaim our faith in the mystery of your God-head . . . : three Persons equal in majesty, undivided in splendor, yet one Lord, one God, ever to be adored in your everlasting glory."

To complete this first stage of our inquiry, let us return to the question which, in our model dialogue above, produced so much incoherence from the believer—if each of the three persons is wholly God, why not three Gods? The reason why we cannot say three Gods becomes clear if we consider what is meant by the parallel phrase, "three men". That would mean three distinct persons, each possessing a human nature. But note that, although their natures would be similar, each would have his own. The first man could not think with the second man's intellect, but only with his own; the second man could not love with the third's will, but only with his own. The phrase "three men" would mean three distinct persons, each with his own separate human nature, his own separate equipment as man; the phrase "three gods" would mean three distinct persons, each with his own separate Divine Nature, his own separate equipment as God. But in the Blessed Trinity, that is not so. The three Persons are God, not by the possession of equal and similar natures, but by the possession of one single nature; they do in fact, what our three men could not do, know with the same intellect and love with the same will. They are three Persons, but they are not three Gods; they are One God.

7. Father, Son, and Holy Spirit

Consider where we now are in our exploration. Concentrating, not upon God's dealings with His creatures, but upon His own proper being and His own proper life, we saw God first as Infinite Existence, possessing all that He is in one single act of being, living His life of infinite knowledge and infinite love, without change and without end. Then, by revelation from God Himself, we learnt that the one Divine Nature is possessed in Its totality by three distinct Persons. And this is a truth of God's own proper life: whatever it may mean to us, its primary meaning is within the life of God Himself. We must now see how these two truths about God are one truth.

God, we have said, knows and loves, for these are the proper operations of Spirit. Because He is infinite, His knowledge and love are infinite. Because He is infinite, His knowledge and love are simply Himself. It is in the further consideration of God living within His own nature a life of infinite knowledge and infinite love that we shall come to some further knowledge of the three Persons and of their relations one to another.

(i) The First Person generates the Second

We begin with the relation of the Second Person to the First. For this relation, Scripture provides us with two names: the Second Person is the Son, and He is the Word. It must be understood that these two words refer to one and the same vital process in the Godhead. As St. Augustine put it, the Second Person is called Word for the same reason as He is called Son. But in our human experience, each word provides an element that the other does not; we naturally think of a son as a distinct person, and we naturally think of a word (a mental word of course) as within the same nature; and both are needed for our understanding of the Second Person of the Blessed Trinity. Therefore there is gain for us in examining the two words separately.

Take the word son first. The relation of father and son is the most familiar of all relations to men. If we come to analyze our ideas about it, we find that the essence of being a son lies in these two elements: (1) that the son is like in nature to the father and (2) that he receives his nature from his father. These two elements are combined in the philosophical definition of sonship: "the origin of a living thing from another living thing, by communication of substance unto likeness of nature".

The phrase "likeness of nature" simply means that the son of a man is a man, and the son of a horse is a horse; and "communication of substance" means that the father does not make the son from some external matter, as one might make a chair, but in some way produces him from within himself. All this is of the very essence of sonship. So that God, in teaching us to call the Second Person the Son, is teaching us both that the Second Person is like in nature to the First and that He proceeds from the First; not as a being that the First has made from some external matter or created from nothing, but as produced[1] within the very nature of the First; further, since the Son is like in nature to the Father, the Son too is infinite in nature, is God—"the only begotten Son, born of the Father before all ages, God of God, light of light, true God of true God, begotten not made", says the Nicene Creed. Further again, to come at the same truth in another way, whereas a father and son who are alike in nature but finite may have every kind of inequality between them, a Father and Son who are alike in nature *and infinite* must be totally equal, since infinity is the total possession of the fullness of existence. Therefore the Son is infinite, omnipotent, eternal.

This last word, "eternal", might for a moment give us pause—because in human parenthood the father is of necessity older than the son, and our minds, easily deceived by the habitual, tend to think that what is invariably present to a given thing in our experience is of the essence of the thing. Here we may apply the principle already stated about arguing from the likeness to the original. Fatherhood in man is a certain

---

[1] Some theologians dislike the word "produced" as suggesting a coming into being, or a causal effect of the Father upon the Son. But all the verbs of our language are in themselves misleading in one way or another. We must make the necessary corrections in our own mind as we use them.

likeness of fatherhood in God. In man, the father has to exist first, and indeed for an appreciable interval, before his son. But we must ask ourselves whether that is because fatherhood is such, or because man's nature is such.

To ask the question is to answer it. We have seen the definition of sonship, the origin of a living thing from another living thing by communication of substance unto likeness of nature. Where you have that, you have the relation of father and son. In all this there is no question of a lapse of time between coming into existence and generating a son. That lapse of time arises not from the nature of sonship but from the finitude of man, specifically from the fact that he does not come into existence in full possession of all his powers, but has to grow slowly. A man needs a little time before he is able to generate a son. But there is no question of God's needing a little eternity before He is able to generate a Son; there is no such thing as a little eternity — eternity is one indivisible thing; God simply is, and in one act of being is all that He is, and simply by being Himself is Father of His Son. God never had any existence except as Father: Father and Son are co-eternal: and it is but one consequence for us of their equality that we can see that they are equally necessary. Not for one moment must we think of the Father as necessary and of the Son as in some way contingent. There could be no equality between the necessary and the contingent. It is true that the Son receives His Nature from the Father, but not as a result of a decision which the Father might just as well not have made. By the same infinite necessity the Father both is and is Father: that is to say, by the same infinite necessity, the Father is and the Son is.

Thus far we have come following up the clue contained in the word son. There is a Second Person, equal in all things to the First, God as He is God, infinite as He is infinite. Yet here we come up against an apparently enormous difficulty. In plain words, we seem to have established two Gods, two Infinities: and two Infinities is a contradiction in terms, since the moment we try to conceive two Infinities, we see that each would be limited by the fact that the other was beyond His power; and also that two limited Infinities would not be infinite at all. The trouble is that the concept of human sonship brings us to likeness of nature but not to oneness of nature; a father and son are like in nature: both are human, but each has his own separate equipment as a man, his own separate human nature.

To make the one further step from likeness in nature to oneness of nature, we must turn to the second word that Scripture provides for the relation of the Second Person to the First, the word *Word*. Already in Scripture (Eccl 24:5) we have a hint of a word—"I came out of the mouth of the Most High"—a Word which is also a son—"the firstborn before all creatures". But the explicit reference to the Son of God as the Word we get from St. John, and so, we may believe, from Our Lady, since Christ our Lord on the Cross entrusted her to St. John that he might be her son and she his mother. To open his Gospel, he writes: "In the beginning was the Word, and the Word was with God, and the Word was God, . . . and the Word was made flesh and dwelt among us. And we saw His glory, the glory as of the only-begotten of the Father." Thus He who became man and dwelt among us, that Jesus of whom St. John was to write his Gospel, was the only-begotten of the Father—with that phrase we are back at the concept of the Son; and He who lived among men as Jesus of Nazareth, who was the Son of God, was the Word of God: and the Word was God.

It is clear that if God has a word, it will not be a vocal word, a thing of air, shaped by lungs and throat and tongue and teeth. God is not like that. God is a pure spirit, and His word must be a word in the mind, *verbum mentale;* in other words, a thought or idea. We must follow very closely to see what is the meaning of

> the thought or idea in the mind of God,
> which was in the beginning with God,
> which was the only-begotten Son of God,
> which became flesh and dwelt among us.

God, so His Church teaches us, lives an infinite life of knowledge and of love. Concentrate upon the knowledge. God knows, knows infinitely, but knows what? If we conceive of God as knowing only the universe He created, then we stunt our own conception of God intolerably. For however immense the universe may appear to us, it remains finite, and the finite can never be an adequate object of infinite knowledge; it remains contingent; that is, it might never have existed at all if God had not willed to create it, and it is a plain absurdity to think of God making the universe in order to have something to exercise His power of knowing on. Obviously the only adequate object of infinite knowledge is the Infinite, God Himself. So far we could go by reason, but at that it is not very far. The concept of God's knowing Himself is true, but seems rather a barrier to thought than an invitation. It seems like a closed circle, which leaves us nowhere to go. Yet by itself, reason would not go beyond that. It is only God's revelation that tells us what reason never could, that God, knowing Himself with infinite knowledge, thinking of Himself with infinite power, conceives an idea of Himself. With that piece of information, the closed circle is suddenly opened, the barrier is down, and the whole vast inner life of God invites us.

The next paragraph must be read by beginners with the greatest care; studied minutely.

An idea is, so far as we can make it so, the mental double or image of the object we are contemplating; it expresses as much of that object as we can manage to get into it. Because of the limitation of our powers, the idea we form is never the perfect double or image, never totally expresses the object; in plain words, is never totally adequate. But if God does, as we know from Himself that He does, conceive an idea of Himself, this idea must be totally adequate, in no way less than the Being of which it is the Idea, lacking nothing that that Being has. The Idea must contain all the perfection of the Being of which it is the Idea. There can be nothing in the Thinker that is not in His Thought of Himself, otherwise the Thinker would be thinking of Himself inadequately, which is impossible for the Infinite. Thus the Idea, the Word that God conceives, is Infinite, Eternal, Living, a Person, equal in all things to Him Who conceives It— Someone as He is, conscious of Himself as He is, God as He is.

We can see how all this brings us to the same truths as the analysis of the word *son*. The Son is like in nature, equal in all things to the Father, God as He is God. The Idea is like in nature to what the Infinite Thinker is thinking of—namely, Himself—equal to Him in all things, God as He is God. So it is that St. Paul can speak of the Son as "the image of the invisible God". We sometimes speak of a son as the image of his father— even the living image. This Son is. It is of the essence of a son, any son, that he should be like his father; it is of the essence of an idea, any idea, that it should be like what the thinker is thinking of. The Infinite Father generates an Infinite Son, resembling Him infinitely; the Infinite Thinker, thinking of Himself, conceives an Infinite Idea, resembling Him infinitely.

So far, the word *Word* has brought us to the same truths about the relation of the Second Person to the First as the word *Son* did. And we can find one further parallel. A son is not his father, and if God's Son is a Person, He is a distinct person. A thought is not the thinker, and if God's thought is a person, He is a distinct person.

But with Word, we can now take a further step. For though the thought is not the thinker, the thought is in the nature of the thinker; it is not a separate nature, as the nature of a son in all our human experience is a separate nature from his father's. Thought is within the very nature of the thinker. Thus we have God within His Own Nature conceiving an Idea, which, because it *is* an idea, is wholly in that one same Nature; and because it is an adequate idea, it contains that nature wholly. The Son has nothing that He has not received from the Father; but the Father has nothing that He has not given to the Son. The one has the Divine Nature as unreceived; the other as received: but each has It in Its totality, and there is no shadow of inequality between them.

It is pleasant to observe that, to tell us of the production of the Second Person, we have these two figures—the Father generating a Son, the Thinker conceiving an Idea. Thus, the male and female roles in producing human beings are both used to convey the infinite fecundity of God.

(ii) The Third Person proceeds from First and Second

The Second Person, as we have just seen, proceeds from the First by way of knowledge. The other primary operation of spirit is love; and it is by way of love that the Third Person proceeds.[2] To a point, the two "processions" are parallel. The

---

[2] We have seen that God's attributes are one with God Himself and so with one another. God's knowledge and love are not in themselves two distinct principles. But their reality and power and productivity are not thereby lessened. God can produce a perfect act of knowledge and a perfect act of love.

First Person knows Himself; His act of knowing Himself produces an Idea, a Word; and this Idea, this Word, the perfect Image of Himself, is the Second Person. The First Person and the Second combine in an act of love—love of one another, love of the glory of the Godhead which is their own; and just as the act of knowing produces an Idea within the Divine Nature, the act of loving produces a state of Lovingness within the Divine Nature. Into this Lovingness, Father and Son pour all that they have and all that they are, with no diminution, nothing held back. Thus this Lovingness within the Godhead is utterly equal to the Father and the Son, for they have poured their all into it. There is nothing they have which their Lovingness does not have. Thus their Lovingness too is Infinite, Eternal, Living, Someone, a Person, God. Observe that here again we are still within the Divine Nature. For love is wholly within the nature of the lover. But this love wholly contains the Divine Nature, because God puts the whole of Himself into love.

The name of this Third Person of the Blessed Trinity is not in itself as revealing as the two names of the Second Person. He is *Spiritus sanctus* in Latin, *to Pneuma to hagion* in Greek, Holy Spirit in English. Observe that these words do not mean exactly what the word *spirit* means when we use it of God, or the angels, or the human soul. It goes back to a prior meaning. The words *Spiritus, Pneuma,* and *Spirit* (*Ghost* as it was in Old English) all convey the same idea of the movement of air, breath or breathing, or the wind blowing. And Our Lord stresses this suggestion: He speaks of the Spirit that bloweth where It listeth; He breathes upon the Apostles and says, "Receive you the Holy Spirit"; and when He sends the Holy Spirit upon them at Pentecost, there is at first the rushing of a mighty wind. The connection with love is not immediately evident, but as we dwell with the idea, we begin to see a kind of aptness which we would find it difficult to pin down in words, and certain ideas do stir vaguely in the mind: for instance, the sigh that lovers breathe.

Let us repeat in a little more detail two of the truths already stated concerning the procession of the Third Person. The first is that the Holy Spirit proceeds from the Father and the Son as from one principle of love. We have this in the hymn "Tantum Ergo", where we salute the Holy Spirit as "procedenti ab utroque"—to Him who proceeds from both; and this is a simple re-phrasing of the Nicene Creed's "qui ex Patre Filioque procedit"—He who proceeds from the Father and the Son. The word *filioque,* which means "and from the son", was not in the Creed as originally drawn up, but was added later in France, spread rapidly, and was accepted by the Church as giving fullness and precision to the doctrine. The Council of Florence (1438–45) defined that "the Holy Spirit is from the Father and the Son eternally, and has His essence and subsistence from Father and Son together, and proceeds eternally from both as from one principle and one single spiration."

Notice further that the word *generate* is reserved for the procession of the Second Person from the First. The Father and Son do not generate the Holy Spirit. For this second procession, the Church uses the word *spirate,* breathe. The father generates the Son; the Father and the Son *breathe* the Holy Spirit. The reason lies in this, that the likeness of the Second Person to the First results precisely from the fact that it is by way of knowledge. It is a property of knowing to produce in the mind a likeness of the thing known, as it is a property of generation to produce a likeness of the being who generates. But it is not the nature of loving to produce likeness. The Third Person is like the First and Second not because loving as such produces resemblance but because in this instance the lovers have put themselves wholly into their love. As with the Son, so with the Holy Spirit, the Divine Nature is possessed as a gift received, but as a gift truly received and in its totality; so that here again there is no shadow of inequality.

Thus the Three Persons, to use a philosophical term, *subsist:* that is to say, they have the whole perfection of personality; each is wholly Himself, not merely a modification of the Divine Nature; each is the whole of Himself, not a part of some greater entity. Using the technical word *hypostasis* for person, we can say that whereas our finite human nature is singly hypostatized, the infinite Divine Nature is triply hypostatized. It is wholly expressed, hypostatized, as Existence in the Person of the Father, as Knowledge in the Person of the Son, as Lovingness in the Person of the Holy Spirit.

(iii) Processions in eternity

There may still remain one error clinging to our knowledge of the processions of the Persons in the Blessed Trinity because of our own immersion in time. As far as the statement of it goes, we are not likely to make the error of thinking that the Son is in some way less eternal than the Father, or the Holy Spirit in some way younger than the Father and the Son. We know that there is no succession in Eternity, no change in God. God the Father did not first exist as a Person and then become a Father. God, by the very act of being God, generates His Son; God the Father and God the Son, by the very act of being God, spirate the Holy Spirit. As I say, there is not likely to be any error in our statement of this: the error will tend to cling to our idea in such a way that when we are looking directly at it, we do not see it, yet it is profoundly there: and, because time is so deeply woven into all our experience, our advance in the knowledge of God depends upon our deliberate effort to rid our mind of it. The trouble is that we have no language for what we are trying to say. We cannot make any statement at all without tenses, past or present or future; but God's actions have no tense. He has no past; he has no future. He has only an eternal present, but it is not our present, poised between past and future; it is not a tense at all. How then are we to utter God's actions with man's verbs? Our nearest tense to His timelessness is the present tense. Thus if we say God generated His Son in Eternity, we are making it a past operation, at least verbally, and words do affect our thinking even when we know better. It would be closer to the reality to say God is generating His Son in Eternity, for it is the very essence of the Father's abiding life as Father to be generating His Son: the trouble is that the phrase "*is* generating", although it does convey the notion of present operation, also conveys the notion of incompleteness—the operation is still going on because the operation is not yet complete; and this also is a shadow upon the truth. The truth is that each phrase—"God generated", "God is generating"—contains something that the other lacks. The one gives the notion of completeness, the other of present action. It may be well for the mind to use both phrases, moving from one to the other, until the mind finds itself in some way seeing both in one new verb for which it has no word.

As it is with the eternity of the Son, so it is with the eternity of the Holy Spirit. And it is in the eternal relations of Father, Son, and Holy Spirit within the one Divine Nature that the Divine Life is utterly lived. The mind can form only the most shadowy notion of what that life of Three-in-One means in itself—what it means that, within the Divine Simplicity, Three should possess one another totally, give themselves to one another totally, utter their life-secret to one another totally, in the changeless stillness of infinite Life. Our greatest words are only a lisping or tinkling. The earlier theologians coined the word "circumincession"—the flow of vital activity within one another; modern theologians alter one letter and make it "circuminsession"—the utter repose of Three dwelling within one another. Both words are magnificent; and both are all but nothing.

8. Some Further Precisions

The doctrine of the Blessed Trinity means that the Divine Nature is wholly expressed as Thinker, wholly expressed as the Thinker's Thought of Himself, wholly expressed as Love. Remaining the One identical nature—which, because it is infinite, cannot be repeated, or shared, or possessed in part but only totally—it is owned by Three Persons. It is an infinite, rational nature in which—to repeat our definition of *person*— there are three centers of attribution: an infinite principle of operation in which there are three operators. This, we have seen, is what the doctrine means. But does this definition mean anything?

(i) "Nature" and "Person" again

In a finite nature, which is the only kind of nature that we have any experience of possessing, we assume instantly that the same identical nature could not be possessed by even two distinct persons; that one single source of operations can be possessed, "wielded" by one single operator only. Yet even examining the concepts of person and nature in their finiteness in us, we have seen a certain glimmer of distinction, which should prepare us for at least the possibility of that plurality of persons which we find in an infinite nature: person and nature are not so indistinguishably one that we can dismiss as unthinkable the idea that, if the nature were infinite, there might be more than one person in it. You could not be a person unless you had a nature, yet it is not your nature that makes you a person, makes you *who* you are. The philosophers say that a person is essentially (1) a substance of a rational nature, (2) incommunicable—i.e., not a part, or not capable of being a part, of some other substance. We can put it for our present purposes a shade more simply. You are a distinct person not because you have a distinct nature but because you are you, you are wholly you, you are the whole of you, you are not someone else. Your nature is bound up in all this, but it is not the whole explanation of it. Now the concept of person thus stated applies in its fullness to each of the three Persons in the Divine Nature. Each is Himself, each is wholly Himself, each is the whole of Himself, no one of the Three is either of the others.

(ii) How are persons equal if distinct?

So far what we have said of the Blessed Trinity should have had the effect of widening the area of light. We know that the ring of darkness is still there, but the light has been growing and we in it. We know that we cannot see the Blessed Trinity as it is in itself, yet in a sense we have been seeing it. We have clarified the ideas represented by the words of our formula; we have done something to strip away from the concepts involved certain limitations that we have seen as belonging not to them, but to our finiteness. If the unfolding has meant anything to us at all, the whole thing has been a kind of joy. We feel that if we cannot see the concrete reality of the Three Persons in One God, at least we can see why we cannot see; we can see that the difficulty of seeing lies in us, not in God.

But the darkness that belongs to Mystery presents itself to us not simply as something we cannot see because our eyes are not strong enough for so much light; it presents itself also in a very much more irksome fashion as the appearance of contradiction in so much of it as we *can* see. So far we have not been much bothered by this more troubling kind of darkness; but it is there, and as we advance we shall become increasingly aware of it.

Consider our problem: if each of the three Divine Persons is not either of the others, what has each got that the other two have not got? And if each has something that the others have not, then obviously it is only another way of putting the same truth to say that each must lack something that the others have: and does that not contradict at once their equality and their infinity? Or at least the infinity of all but the first? It does not diminish the Father that He is not generated as the Son is, but does it not diminish the Son that He does not generate as the Father does? Likewise one may feel that it is surely some kind of diminution in the Holy Spirit that He does not produce a Person by spiration as Father and Son do.

To say that one sees the answers clearly would be to say that the mystery of the Blessed Trinity is no mystery at all. We know that the Three Persons are not each other: we know that each is Infinite and wholly God. If we knew no more than that, we can still know *that*. Even if we come to see further, by that very fact we come upon some new problem even more apparently insoluble — because we are limited and God is infinite.

It is of the very nature of partial seeing that we cannot see all the reconciliation of the parts we see, because it is only in the whole that they are one, and we do not see the whole. The words we form cannot wholly express God: only the Word He generates can do that. To be irked at this necessary darkness is as though we were irked at not being God.

But none of this is any reason for not asking the questions. We may not see the answer: but if we do not ask the questions, we certainly will not see even a glimmer of the answer. We have already seen that we must not ask the questions as though we were God, calling upon Him to defend His statements about Himself before the bar of our reason. We must ask the questions simply as requests for light. And upon these particular questions, we shall find that we can push back the surrounding darkness a little. The theologians, with their discussion of the Three Persons as Subsistent Relations, can get more light than we, but even at the level of our present knowledge we can get *some* light.

Thus far we can see that the Son and the Holy Spirit have the same infinite knowledge as the Father because they possess the same infinite nature of which infinite knowledge is one operation; the Father's possession of that knowledge generates an Idea, the Son's does not, nor does the Holy Spirit's: not because the Son and the Holy Spirit have any less knowledge, any less knowing power, than the Father, but because the Divine Knowledge has already produced the Idea, so that the Divine Nature is wholly expressed as knowledge. The same can be said of the Divine Love. The Holy Spirit has the same infinite love as the Father and Son. Their possession of that love produces a state of lovingness which is a Person; His does not: but again not because He has less love, less loving-power, than the Father and the Son, but because the Divine Nature is already utterly expressed as Love.

Thus no one of the Three has anything that the others have not; each possesses the whole Godhead, but each possesses it in His own way—contained in that, if we could see deep enough into it, lies the secret of the distinction of Persons.

(iii) Reason and revelation

What we must recognize is that success in finding answers to this and such-like questions has a bearing upon our *understanding* of the doctrine of the Blessed Trinity, but none at all upon our *acceptance* of it. If we were trying to arrive at the doctrine by the effort of our own minds working upon the concept of the Infinite, then a problem, en route to which we could not see the answer, would effectually bar our progress; till it was solved, we should never arrive at the Trinity. But we have received the doctrine from God Himself. Therefore we make this examination not to discover the doctrine (for God has revealed it); still less to verify it (for no effort of our mind could make it more certain than God's word); but to understand it better, to get more light on it and from it, to know more of God as a result of it.

The further examination can be very profitable—provided we do not underrate its difficulty. From the sure ground of revealed truth, we are adventuring outward into the Infinite. The trouble is that we cannot get the Infinite itself under our microscope. Even if we have formed as good a concept of the Infinite as finite mind can form, yet our Infinite (that is, the Infinite as we conceive it) is a synthetic affair compared with its own incredible reality. Therefore we move slowly: a glimmer of light pleases us, a mass of darkness does not surprise us. There is a type of foolish philosopher who reasons from his human concept of the Infinite as though it actually *were* the

Infinite, and gets into hot quarrels about his deductions with other philosophers as foolish as himself. Against that folly of confidence we must be on our guard. Logic misused can mislead us: not that logic is less valid here than elsewhere but that we have not sufficient knowledge to apply the methods of logic with certainty. To argue too confidently about the inner being of the Infinite is to overlook the myriad things that we do not know about it: our premises are a shadow and an approximation of the Infinite Reality: how can our conclusions be sure?

What is sure is what God has revealed. With that we can start our exploration. In our exploring, what is sure is that what the Church has defined is true, what the Church has condemned is false: Christ established a Church that could do us this essential service. For most of us, exploration will be only the effort to understand as much as is thus certain. And it is immensely rewarding. For the great theologians, exploration means the effort to enlarge the boundaries of the certain: in this effort, they use logic with superb power; but they too know that nothing can be known as infallibly certain till the Church has spoken: the mind of man is not sufficient.

But the light is the light, however darkness may hem it in. The difficulties in extending the area of our understanding do not in the least affect the certainty of what we do know of the Blessed Trinity. And what we know is a knowledge from which the mind can draw light and upon which the whole soul can feed.

9. Concluding This Part

What Our Lord's first hearers, ignorant of the doctrine of the Blessed Trinity, made of His allusions to it we cannot know: we may guess that they were utterly puzzled. But there is a great profit for ourselves, knowing the doctrine, in listening to those same words of Our Lord. I shall not attempt any full treatment here, but shall indicate how the reader may go about it for himself.

(i) Our Lord's teaching on the Trinity

Begin with Luke 10:22 and Matthew 11:27: "No one knows the Son but the Father, and no one knows the Father but the Son, and him to whom the Son shall reveal Him."

Here we have two capital points of the doctrine: first, that it can be known only by revelation, the power of the human mind cannot reach it without the aid of God: second, that the central point of the mystery of the relation of Father and Son, that in which its being as a mystery can be summarized, is the knowledge each has of the other—which seems at least to suggest the first procession by way of knowledge.

Self-existence and the timeless present of eternity are in

"Before Abraham was made, I am" (Jn 8:58); equality of nature in "All things whatsoever the Father hath are mine" (Jn 16:15); distinction of persons and identity of nature in "I and the Father are one" (Jn 10:30); circuminsession in "The Father is in me and I in the Father" (Jn 10:38).

Remembering that nature is the principle of operation—the person does what his nature allows—the identity of nature is asserted by Our Lord in an identity of operation: "My Father works until now and I work" (Jn 5:17); "Whatsoever things He [the Father] does, these the Son also does in like manner" (Jn 5:19).

Of the Third Person, Our Lord says less: but it is enough. The Spirit is a person: "When *He,* the Spirit of truth is come, He shall lead you unto all truth" (Jn 16:13); He is equal to the Son, and each is a Paraclete: "I will ask the Father and He will give you another Paraclete" (Jn 14:16); He is equal to Father and Son: "baptizing them in the name of the Father and of the Son and of the Holy Spirit" (Mt 28:19). To see just what that phrase means as to the Godhead of the Holy Spirit, try substituting any other name, however mighty. "In the name of the Father and of the Son and of the Archangel Michael." The thing would sound ridiculous. With all possible respect to the Archangel, one would feel that the company was too exalted for him.

But there is another truth Our Lord makes clear: that though He, the Son, possesses the Divine Nature in total equality with the Father, it is still as a nature received: He is not the origin: "The Son cannot do anything of His own impulse, He can only do what He sees His father doing" (Jn 5:19–23) because the Divine Nature in which He lives and moves and has His being is wholly received from His Father.

With this we may compare Our Lord's parallel phrase about the Holy Spirit: "He will not speak of His own impulse, He will utter the message that has been given to Him" (Jn 16:13).

For the Holy Spirit, too, has received that Divine Nature which is totally His—received it not from the Father only, but from the Son also, so that Our Lord can go on to say: "It is from me that He will derive what He makes plain to you."

This same truth about the procession of the Second Person from the First, and of the Third Person from the First and Second, is illuminated in another way as well. Our Lord speaks of Himself, the Second Person, as being "sent"—always by the Father. He speaks of the Third Person as to be sent—sometimes by the Father, sometimes by Himself. In this "sending" we must see no glimmer of subordination of the Son and the Holy Spirit. They come to us by the divine will, which is their own as totally as it is the Father's: but inasmuch as they received the nature in which that will is, they may be thought of as sent. That is why the Father, who possesses the Divine Nature as unreceived, is never spoken of as sent; that is why the Son, who receives the Divine Nature from the Father alone, is spoken of as sent by the Father but not by the Holy Spirit; that is why the Holy Spirit, who receives the Divine Nature from Father and Son, is spoken of as sent by the Father and by the Son. But it must be repeated, the sending is not to be thought of as a command imposed but as the free decision of a nature possessed in total equality by each.

(ii) The Trinity and creatures: "appropriation"

What we have just had is not in any sense an exhaustive analysis of Our Lord's teaching on the Blessed Trinity: it is no more than an indication of how one might go about making such an analysis. But the last paragraph has brought us to a new stage in our study of the Trinity. So far we have been treating of God solely as He is in Himself. With the "sendings", we see

God in His action upon the universe He has created. We pass from the inner life of God to His operations upon things other than Himself. With these the rest of the book will be concerned. But before we come to them, one clarification is necessary.

The operations of the Divine Nature upon the created universe and everything within it are the operations of the Three Divine Persons acting as one principle, not of any one or other of them. Creation from nothing, conservation in being, sanctification, answer to prayer—the work of God in these and all other matters is the work of the Blessed Trinity, the Three-in-One. There is *no* external operation of the Divine Nature which is the work of one Person as distinct from the others.

Yet both the New Testament and the Church's Liturgy are packed with phrases which do seem to attribute certain divine operations to Father or Son or Holy Spirit. The Nicene Creed leaps to mind with its reference to the Father as Creator, the Son as Redeemer, the Holy Spirit as Life-giver or Sanctifier. Now Redemption was (as we shall see in much detail later) not a work in the Divine Nature, but in the human nature which the Son of God made His own; therefore no question arises about the title of Redeemer given to the Son alone, for He alone assumed a human nature and *in that nature* suffered and died for us. But Creation and Sanctification are definitely operations in the Divine Nature: they are definitely, therefore, the work of the Blessed Trinity and not of the Father alone or the Holy Spirit alone (as Redemption *is* of the Son alone). Why then is Creation attributed to the Father and Sanctification to the Holy Spirit?

Observe that the thing is no accident; the attribution is not haphazard. The Church does it of set purpose, as we find St. Paul doing it of set purpose, upon a system learnt from Our Lord Himself. The theological name for it is "appropriation". We are encouraged to attribute this or that external operation of the Blessed Trinity to that Person to whom the corresponding operation within the Godhead belongs. Thus the works of origination and of omnipotence are appropriated to the Father; the works of knowledge or wisdom to the Son, who subsists by the way of knowledge; the works of love to the Holy Spirit, who subsists as Love.

That Our Lord Himself wishes us to do this is clear. Consider one fact only. Our sanctification is to be by the indwelling in our souls of Father, Son, and Holy Spirit. Once indeed, as we have seen, He says: "If anyone love me he will keep my word, and my Father will love him, and we will come to him and will make our abode with him"—thus showing that the indwelling is to be of Father and Son too. But for the most part, it is the Holy Spirit that will come and abide in our souls, it is of the Holy Spirit that we are to be temples. Once given appropriation, the reason is obvious: the gifts of God to the soul are an outpouring of Love, and the Holy Spirit is subsistent Love. But why have appropriation at all? Apparently in order to bring home to us the reality of the distinction between the Three, and what we may call the hypostatic character of each: so urgently does God want to be known by us. If we always thought of the operation of God upon us as the operation of all three Persons, we should be in danger of regarding the three Persons as only a form of words, with no distinction of one from another: and so God's purpose in revealing the central living fact of His own infinite life would be frustrated. Whereas appropriation to one Person or another continually reminds us of the distinction: and the specific appropriations that we make remind us that the Father is Origin and Power; the Son, Knowledge or Wisdom; the Holy Spirit, Love. Thus each Person is for us a distinct reality, and the reality that He really is. Provided we keep clear in our minds the complementary truth that the action appropriated to each Person is in fact the action of all Three, then there is only gain for us.

The principle of appropriation thus taught by Our Lord is adopted with thoroughness in the remaining books of the New Testament and especially by St. Paul. Thus we find that, while teaching with great clarity that all three Persons are God, he usually keeps the name God for the Father, the Second Person being Lord (*Kurios, Dominus*), and the Third, Spirit: as we have seen, not to question the identity of nature, but to bring into relief the distinction of the persons. Nor does he keep to these terms invariably. But usually he writes of the Three as God, Lord, Spirit. And so we find it in many early Christian writers. This practice accounts for a curiosity that has occasionally puzzled the faithful, in the Nicene Creed: which speaks of "*one* Lord, Jesus Christ" and then speaks of "the Holy Spirit, *Lord* and giver of life". The reason is that in the original form of the Creed, the Second Person was called "one Lord" in accord with our present formula; and the Third, "Spirit". Later the word *Lord* was added after "Spirit" to assert the equality of the Holy Spirit with the Son as against some who had questioned it.

But to return to St. Paul. There is one famous text (1 Cor 12:4) in which he uses his three titles, and appropriates certain things to each: "There are different kinds of gifts, though it is the same *Spirit* who gives them, just as there are different kinds of service, though it is the same *Lord* we serve, and different manifestations of power, though it is the same *God* who manifests His power everywhere in all of us." On the same principle, St. Paul has given us another formula (Rom 11:36): *from* the Father, *through* the Son (that is, through the Divine Wisdom or according to the Divine Idea), *unto* the Holy Spirit (that is, unto sanctification, which is love); and the liturgical form of prayer *to* the Father, *through* Jesus Christ, *in the unity of* the

Holy Spirit, keeps similarly close to the hypostatic character of the Three Persons.

We shall see more of all this in the remaining two parts of this book. But before embarking on the troubled story of creation, let us glance once more at the doctrine of the Blessed Trinity as it enables us to see into the blissful life of God Himself.

(iii) Rejoicing in the doctrine

God, the infinite fullness of Existence, is wholly Himself in one infinite act of being, utterly fulfilled in infinite knowledge and infinite love, utterly simple, utterly single: yet not solitary. Mankind has always feared the solitary God. In flight from that terrifying idea, the Pagans imagined a multitude of Gods: it was the wrong answer, but to the right question or, perhaps better, to the right quest. The Trinity was the right answer. God is one, but it is not the oneness of infinite solitude: it is the oneness of one infinite Godhead triply uttered: a communication of infinite truth and infinite love among three, infinite self-revelation, infinite self-donation, companionship at the level of divinity.

Contemplating it, we find that the concept of infinite love comes to life for us. God lives a life of infinite love. But whom does He love? What is an adequate object for a love that is infinite? Not men, nor angels. If God has only these to love, then His love never has an object worthy of it, for they cannot conceive infinite love and cannot return it. If that is all, God is forever loving His inferiors, as He is doomed to the companionship of His inferiors. The only adequate object of infinite love is an infinite being, God Himself. Certainly there is a real truth in the concept of God's loving Himself infinitely, but it is not a truth we can make much of: it does not issue in anything: we *know* that it is not an infinite egoism, but we cannot be rid of that feeling about it. But with the doctrine of the Blessed Trinity, that feeling vanishes: there is an otherness within the Godhead. Infinite love among three who are infinite with one same infinity means infinite love infinitely received, infinitely returned.

It may be that the glory of the doctrine does not shine for us at once. We see it, perhaps, as immense, but not as satisfying anything particular in ourselves, touching no nerve in us. We accept it, but in all honesty we cannot feel that it makes any great difference to our spiritual or mental life, to our love of God or to our comprehension of reality. But the prime question about a doctrine is not what does it do to us, but *is it so.* The doctrine of the Trinity is reality about God. If we thrill to it, so much the better. But thrill or no thrill, let us keep hold of it and mentally live with it, for it is reality, and whether we perceive its effects on us or not, reality nourishes. And nothing else does.

PART III

CREATION

10. God as Creator

God is infinite, the utterly sufficient All. There is no need of His nature not satisfied by what He is. There is not the smallest chink through which anything can be added to His fullness of existence, to the limitless perfection of His happiness. Besides Himself He needs no other. How could beings with nothing in them that He has not given, provide Him with anything He lacks? Yet other beings exist, and exist because He brought them into existence. Why? Not only did creation provide nothing that His nature needed, it provided, so to speak, no luxury either; it brought Him no profit, no increase, for there was nothing in it that was not already in Himself in greater, because uncreated, perfection. Why, then, is the created universe here at all?

(i) Why God created

The answer that leaps to our lips still leaves our precise question untouched. The created universe exists, we say, for God's honor and glory, each thing necessarily glorifying God simply by being what it is: neither creation as a whole nor any element of it could have any other reason for existence. Created beings achieve their own perfection in glorifying God: but it still remains that they do not add anything to His: so that our question likewise remains, Why did God create the universe at all?

God knows. But we need not leave it at that. From all we hear Him say of the world, it is clear that He created it out of love, especially love of man. The simple answer is that He created it because He knew that we should like it. It brings Him no gain, but it can bring us tremendous gain. And apparently it goes with the infinite goodness of God that our gain can be a motive for Him. It is of the nature of goodness that it wants to spread outward, to confer itself, and God is Supreme Goodness. In some ways one of the most staggering phrases in all Scripture is St. John's statement (Jn 3:16) that God loved the world, yet St. John had come to know God's love so well that he could make a statement so breathtaking almost casually and in his stride. God could love things less than Himself and could act to give them pleasure. So he brought them into existence. He knew that there were possible beings capable of enjoying Him, and He made them. "The Lord has made all things for Himself" (Prov 16:4): apart from Himself there existed nothing to make them for. He made them for His own sake, for His own pleasure. But it was His pleasure to bring into existence things which could take pleasure in existence. For our sakes, He made us for His sake. To us there is something mysterious in an altruism so total, but something exciting in the mystery. Among all the mysteries, many are greater, but it is hard to think of one more pleasing.

(ii) What it means to be created

We have thus caught some glimpse of why the created universe exists. That must always be the primary question. Until we know why a thing exists, we cannot properly know anything else about it. Whatever details we can discover by studying it, our interpretation of the details must always be governed by our understanding of why the thing exists at all. If we are wrong about that, the details we do know are as likely to mislead us as not. But if "why" is the primary question and its answer the key to all knowledge, there are other questions to be answered in due order. The question "why" is followed by the question "how". The universe exists because God loved the very idea of it. But how did the universe come into existence?

Note that this is not at all the same as the scientist's question about the origin of the universe. Science always starts with something in existence, and its efforts to explain the origin of that something simply mean looking for some earlier something of the same created order. This study is of immense value, but our present inquiry undercuts it. Quite simply, we are asking how is it that anything is here at all. When philosophers and theologians ask why *anything* exists, the alternative they have in mind is *nothing*. There might have been nothing; why is there something? This is a question which quite properly science does not put. If in his backward progress from cause to earlier cause the scientist suddenly found himself faced with nothing, he would be inexpressibly startled. Neither his instruments nor his scientific methods are made to cope with nothing. If he found nothing in his series, he would have to call upon philosophy and theology.

But a question is none the less a question and none the less urgent because science cannot cope with it. If one may venture a criticism of the scientists one meets, one does sometimes feel that they have a tendency to treat questions which science cannot handle as if they were by that very fact not questions at all. But the question how anything exists is second only in importance to the question why anything exists; and we must consider both in the light of philosophy and theology, which can answer them, not blaming science because it cannot, but not treating the questions as unimportant because it cannot.

We have seen why God exists: He exists because what He is demands existence, cannot not-exist. But this created universe does not thus demand existence. How then does it exist? It can exist only because God, who alone possesses existence as of right, confers existence upon it. God made it. And He made it of nothing. What else was there for Him to make it of? He could not make it of Himself, for He is utterly simple and changeless: there are no parts in Him which could be subtracted from Him and set going as a universe that was not He. In one sense, then, the act of creation can be stated quite simply. God willed that things which had not been should be. "He spoke and they were made; He commanded and they were created" (Ps 148:5). To create is to make a thing in its totality, that is, to make the whole of it. A carpenter does not make the whole of a chair—the wood is not of his making; a poet does not make the whole of a poem—the words already existed; but God does make the whole universe—there is nothing in it that is not of His making, nothing that already existed.

We must not misunderstand the statement that God made the universe of nothing. It does not mean that God used nothing as a kind of material which He proceeded to shape into a universe. It means that God used no material whatever in the making of the universe. That He could do this goes with His infinity. We have some faint glimpse of what this means when we see a human agent in action. It is the measure of human power to be able to make a little go a long way. It is the measurelessness of infinite power that it can make a universe with no material at all. If we honestly focus our minds upon the act of creation, really and honestly consider what is meant by "making something out of nothing", we find it almost totally baffling. The mind seems unable to see anything at all. It is not that the mind is blinded by sheer darkness, but dazed both by too much light and by its own lack of habituation to moving by its own strength. Upon the act of creation, our habit of relying upon the imagination lets us down most evilly.

We think we are *thinking* about the production of something from nothing by infinite power, whereas in fact we are trying desperately to form some mental picture of the process. Such an attempt is forever doomed to failure, because one of the terms in the process, nothingness, has no image. If we are to come to any understanding at all of creation, we must insist that our mind handle the concepts concerned, without the distraction of trying to picture them. And the concepts concerned are very simple. God is infinite. There is no limitation to His being, there is no limitation to His power. Because there is no limitation to His power, there is no limitation of His power of making. But it would be a great limitation to His power of making if it needed material to work upon. God does not need things at all; He is not dependent upon them in any way whatever. We have already seen (Chapter 4) that God does not depend upon things for His knowledge of things: as St. Augustine says (*De Genesi ad Litteram*): "He made the things He knew: He did not get to know the things He had made." His power of making is as independent of created things as His power of knowing. The most skillful carpenter is dependent upon the wood, and without it would be a very helpless carpenter, sitting with folded hands and all his skill within him. But that would be a very meagre figure for the omnipotent God. "He can send His call to that which has no being as if it already was" (Rom 4:17).

This fact, that God made us and all things of nothing by a sheer act of His will, is not simply a fact of history, something that happened an immeasurably long time ago. We may very well think of it as something that happened, because it did happen. But it implies as its corollary something that is happening here and now, happening from instant to instant and of the most vital importance to us. Because we are made by God of nothing, then we cannot continue in existence unless God continuously holds us in existence. There is an emptiness at the very center of the being of all created things, which only God can fill; not an emptiness merely in the sense that it cannot be happy without God; but in the sense that it cannot *be* at all without Him. God does not simply make us and leave us. To return for a moment to the carpenter: he can make a table and leave it, and the table will continue, none the worse for his absence. But that, we saw in chapter 1, is because of the material he used, namely, wood. Wood is so constituted that it will retain a shape given to it. Similarly, if God, having made the universe, left it, the universe would have to rely for its continuance in existence upon the material it was made of: namely, nothing.

Another comparison from human experience may help. If I stand in front of a mirror, my image is in the mirror, but only while I stand there. If I go, it goes. Only my continuing presence keeps the image in being. The reason is that the image is not made *of* the mirror but only *in* the mirror. The mirror contributes nothing but receptiveness: it is purely receptive, purely passive. So of the nothingness in which God mirrors himself: we may figure it as receptive or passive—carrying receptivity, passivity to the ultimate power. Thus the image is sustained by my continuing presence: the universe is sustained by God's continuing presence. Take me away and the image ceases. Take God away and the universe ceases.

Whatever illustration we find helpful, the point to be grasped is that if God abandoned anything He had made, it would simply cease to be. In the words of the Roman Catechism (part I, chapter II): "Unless His continuing Providence were present to the things He created, and preserved them by the same power by which they were established in the beginning, they would instantly lapse back [into their original nothingness]."

Therefore we must see the universe and everything in it (ourselves included) as held in existence from moment to moment by nothing save God's continuing will to hold it (including us) there. This is the plain truth about all created things: not to see it is to be in error, tragic or comic or sheerly farcical, about ourselves and everything else. The failure to see it is what causes man to play such fantastic tricks before high heaven as make the angels weep. So far this is no more than a summary of the truth already stated about the presence of God in all things. But we can now add something enormous. The God who is thus continuously present in us as in all things is the Blessed Trinity. At the very center of our being, Father, Son and Holy Spirit are living their infinite life of knowing and loving.

Thus the formula for everything from Adam to the Archangel is nothingness made into something and kept in being by the infinite power of the Blessed Trinity. Note especially the phrase "made into something". Things are not simply thoughts in the mind of God. He has given them real existence, real be-ing. He does not simply think them: He has made them. The universe is not a system of ideas thought by God; it is a system of things made by God. The universe really *is*.

But not as God is. Here we may pause to make the effort already made once or twice in this book and to be made once or twice again before the end, to distinguish between the absolute being of God and the relative being of created things — what philosophers call the analogy of being. God alone wholly *is* with all that *is* can mean. You can say of the universe that it is, but you cannot leave it there: you have to keep adding *words,* and every word you add subtracts. Thus you must say of the universe, "It is because . . . "; "It is, but it was not"; "It is, but it might not have been"; "It is, so long as . . . "; "It is this or that — e.g., man or cat, little or big." All of these and the thousand other additions one must make to the simple statement "It is" are limitations, subtracting something from the fullness of what "is" can mean. Each thing *is,* but dependently, but conditionally, but as this or that limited selection of limited excellences. It is, but relatively, partially. But when you have said of God, *He is,* in the first place you have said everything; and in the second, if you still want to add words — e.g., He is infinite, He is omnipotent, He is all-good, He is omniscient — the added words subtract nothing but merely draw out for consideration some special perfection already contained in the fullness of *is.* Nothing else is with all that *is* can mean: it is only some of what *is* can mean. Nothing else is good with all that goodness can mean. Only God is absolute Good, absolute *is.*

Because the universe is created of nothing, it does not add up to God. God plus the universe does not total up to something greater than God, in some such way as we might feel that a man plus his image in the mirror is not greater than the man. The created universe contains nothing that is not the result of His power, a power needed not only to bring it into existence but to maintain it in existence. Nothing else is in the finite save what God puts there and keeps there.

Observe how delicately the truth treads in this matter. The created universe really is — not with the fullness of being that is God's, but existing in the real order all the same, not simply thought or dream or illusion. It is really something, not simply nothingness masquerading as something. Yet in a matter so delicate we can understand the error of the pantheist who thinks the created universe is simply a mask of God and no more, or the not so very different error of those who think that the created universe is an illusion. Both have the wrong solution to the right difficulty: both have recognized the inferiority of created being in comparison with the majesty of infinite being. What they have failed to grasp is the majesty of created being in comparison with nothingness.

We must keep both truths steadily in mind, if we are to see reality right. Created being is small enough in comparison with the Uncreated: "All nations are before Him as if they had no being at all, and are counted to Him as nothing and emptiness": so says Isaiah. But all the same, God looked upon what He had made of nothing, and found it good (Gen 1:31); all the same, God loved the world. In the eleventh chapter of the Book of Wisdom, we find the two truths perfectly balanced: "The whole world before Thee is as the least grain of the balance, and as a drop of the morning dew that falls down upon the earth": but all the same, "Thou lovest all things that are, and hatest none of the things which Thou has made: for Thou didst not make anything hating it. And how could anything endure if Thou wouldst not? or be preserved if not called by Thee?"

(iii) Creation is by the Trinity

Our first answer to the question how God created the universe is that He brought it into being from nothingness by the sole act of His will. So much we might have reasoned out for ourselves, assuming that our reason was as good as reason theoretically can be. In any event, whether we could have *arrived at it* by sheer reasoning or not, we can now *establish it* by sheer reason without appeal to any direct statement by God on the matter. But there is a further answer to the question how, which we can give only because God has given it to us.

Creation is the work of the Blessed Trinity, Father, Son, and Holy Spirit. So we should know, once it has been revealed to us, that God is Three Persons in one nature: for the nature is the principle of operation, that *by which* God acts, and this principle is wholly and in utter equality possessed by all Three. The Fourth Council of the Lateran (1215) speaks of Father, Son, and Holy Spirit as "one principle of all things, creator of all things visible and invisible". The Council of Florence (1439) gives us a further clarification: it compares the fact that Father and Son are not two principles but one in the spiration of the Holy Spirit with the fact that Father, Son, and Holy Spirit are not three principles but one in the creation of the universe. It may be worth a moment's pause to consider the sequence (understanding that it is not a sequence in time but in order of being)—

The Father generates the Son;
Father and Son as one principle spirate the Holy Spirit;
Father, Son, and Holy Spirit as one principle create the universe.

But though creation is the work of the Three Persons, it comes under the Law of Appropriation in two ways. In the first place, the Father is always called Creator: we find this in all the Creeds and indeed universally. The fitness of this name is obvious. To Him who is Origin within the Godhead, the origination of all things external to the Godhead is naturally attributed.

But there is an appropriation of creation to the Second Person as well, and this is worth most careful examination— not only in itself but as showing us why it was to be the

Second Person who should become man to restore the created order from the profound catastrophe into which it was plunged by Adam's sin. Consider first the *fact* of this appropriation to the Son.

We have already looked at the opening words of St. John's Gospel: "In the beginning was the Word, and the Word was with God, and the Word was God. All things were made by Him, and without Him was made nothing." This had already been foreshadowed in the Old Testament, where Wisdom says, "I was with him, forming all things" (Prov 8:24). And indeed before St. John wrote his Gospel, the same thing was already clearly stated in other books of the New Testament. We find in Hebrews (1:2): "his Son, whom he hath appointed heir of all things, by whom also he made the world"; and again in Colossians (1:14–17): "In the Son of God, in his blood, we find the redemption that sets us free from our sins. He is the true likeness of the God we cannot see; his is that first birth which precedes every act of creation. Yes, in him all created things took their being, heavenly and earthly. . . . "

There is at first something puzzling here. The fitness of attributing creation especially to the Father is obvious: He is Origin and Omnipotence within the Godhead, and the origination of the finite universe is naturally appropriated to Him. But in that event, why the appropriation to the Son?

Clearly Scripture envisages two elements in creation, and appropriates one to the Father and one to the Son. The Father creates: He creates *by* or *through* the Son. We may see this as the Father's *will* to create, *executed by* the Son. Or again: the Father as creating, that is, bringing the first elements of being out of nothingness — the direct work of Omnipotence — and the Son as forming those first elements into the created order we know — the work of Wisdom as distinct from Power. This may be the explanation of the wording of the first chapter of

Genesis: "In the beginning God *created* the heavens and the earth." The verb "created" is not used again except for *man* (whose soul is in fact a fresh creation) and *whales* (if there is any significance in this, I do not know what it is). With these two exceptions, the verb used is "made". However this may be, we can see that creation involved both Omnipotence and Wisdom: Omnipotence was needed to make something from nothing; so that it might not be just anything, but an ordered, purposeful system of things, Wisdom was needed too. As a work of Omnipotence, it is attributed to the Father; as a work of Wisdom, to the Son.[1]

Under these and all other possible explanations lies a great truth, God made the universe. But what does "making" mean? Two things we can say: First that all making is in some way self-expression: the maker expresses himself in the thing he makes. Again we can say that the maker makes in accordance with an idea or image in his mind.

But, as to the first, the making of our universe was not the first fruits of God's infinite productivity, or God's self-expression. The Father had already uttered Himself, expressed Himself wholly as the Son, the Word, the Second Person of the Blessed Trinity. God is not only infinite activity but infinite productivity, too, the infinite productivity from which proceeds the Word and the Holy Spirit; and since it is the same God, His finite productivity mirrors His infinite productivity. He had expressed Himself once in the uncreated—that is, as the infinite nature could receive the expression of Him—and thereby produced the Word; He now expressed Himself in the created order— that is, as nothingness can receive the expression of Him—and

[1] The Holy Spirit is also called creator—e.g., in the hymn *Veni Creator Spiritus.* This refers directly to the creation of the "new man" in grace. But insofar as the creation of the universe was to express divine love, there may be an appropriation to the Holy Spirit also.

thereby produced the universe. We can catch some glimpse of the relation between God uttering Himself in the uncreated as the Second Person of the Blessed Trinity, and God uttering Himself, so far as He can be uttered in nothingness, as Creation.

And, as to the second, if making is according to an image in the mind of the maker, the image already in the mind of God was the Second Person of the Trinity: and it is now relevant to add one further truth to what has already been said of the Second Person as the image of the First. In the Word, the Father utters Himself totally: therefore in the Word He utters His Knowledge, all His Knowledge: and this means His Knowledge not only of Himself, but of all the beings He can create. Thus the Second Person expresses the idea of all creatable things as they are in the Divine Nature. That is why St. Thomas can say that in the Word, God utters both Himself and us.

11. The Created Universe

God's nature is one in utter simplicity; yet the created universe in which He has chosen to mirror His nature is multitudinous and complex. When God mirrored Himself in the infinite, He produced one Image with all the perfections of the Infinite; we might have expected that when He mirrored Himself in the finite, He would have produced one single being with the highest perfections that the finite can have. But, even if that had meant a more perfect mirroring of Himself, God did not need to see Himself thus mirrored; and though that was *how* He created, it was not *why* He created. He created because He conceived all sorts of creatures capable of enjoying Him, and out of love for them He willed that they should have the chance. Such a theoretically best mirroring in one single finite being would have left out all of us human and only moderately admirable beings, all angels less than the highest, to say nothing of cats and dogs and such-like: all of them getting their measure of enjoyment out of existence, and so, though they may not know it, out of God. Thus the multiplicity of the created universe seems to suit the abundance of His love, whether it mirrors Him so well or not.

(i) Spirit (likeness) and matter (imprint)

In fact it mirrors Him better. The simplicity of the Infinite is reflected most glowingly by the vast complexity and variousness of the finite. It is true that no multiplication of finite beings at any level of splendor is any more adequate to express the Infinite than the most microscopic piece of fluff: but to our finite minds the sheer multiplicity and variety of things can convey the sense of the Infinite—especially of infinite power and richness—most overwhelmingly.

Yet a merely chaotic complexity would not have conveyed God but betrayed Him. The universe is not just a heap of things or a whirl of things, each one showing the power of God in some measure. It is an *arrangement* of things, ordered in their relations to each other by the amount of God's power each expresses. In short, the universe has a shape; its various elements have a place and a function: underlying the multiplicity of things is the unifying design of God, making one universe alike, as our minds grow in the mastery of the order of things.

To begin with, we see one vast principle of differentiation producing the two major divisions of created being. All things are made by God: but some things He has made *in His likeness:* other things not so. The things made in His likeness are spirit. The rest, matter. And there is one being, man, in whom both sorts are combined.

It is impossible to exaggerate the importance of this distinction or exhaust its fruitfulness. Everything that any maker makes has a certain resemblance to him: *his* mind conceived it: *his* workmanship made it. From anything at all that is made you can learn something of its maker: it bears his imprint, we say: it is physiognomical of him. But for all that, there is a world of difference between the resemblance a thing cannot help having to its maker and the resemblance where the maker has definitely set out to produce his own likeness. A chair is something like the carpenter; but Rembrandt's self-portrait is much more like Rembrandt.

The universe God has made is of these two sorts. Material things God simply makes; but when He comes to the making of man, He says, "Let us make man to our own image and likeness"; and this He can say because man's soul is a spirit, as God Himself is. And this, or something like it, He might well have said already of the angels, for they also are spirit. But if this consideration leads us to see a special splendor in the world of spirit, it must not lead us to any contempt of matter, for it is His workmanship too. It bears the imprint that is only His. He has uttered it, and it can utter Him to us. The heavens show forth the glory of the Lord. So indeed does everything—from dust to archangel—by being what God made it to be, but the heavens more spectacularly than either, for only the most powerful mind sees dust as glorious, and you and I have never seen an archangel at all.

(ii) Grades of "is"

In order to see why created spirits are in the likeness of God, as merely material beings are not, we must return to the meaning of spirit as set out somewhat lengthily in Chapter 2. Of spirit we make two positive statements, one as to what it is, one as to what it does. Spirit is that being which has a permanent hold upon its own nature, which cannot be changed into anything else, which can be only itself. Again, spirit is the being that knows and loves. Both statements are verified to the utmost limit of their meaning only in God. But with limitations proper to the finite, they are true also of angels and the souls of men; and they are not true of matter. Material being cannot know or love; and it has no permanent, but only the most precarious, hold upon what it is at any given moment: it can always be changed into something else.

What we have here are real differences of being—what we may call grades or measures of being. Spirit has more being than matter. This will be to many an unfamiliar and therefore unluminous way of talking. We are accustomed to think more of what things do than of what they are; and even when we are concentrating on what they are, we usually stop at the ways in which they make themselves known to us, that is, the ways in which they act upon our senses or our minds; in plain words, what they do *to us*. So that even our considera-tion of what they *are* is still a consideration of what they *do.* It might help if we recognized that be-ing is a kind of doing, like thinking; but a profounder doing than that "doing to us" which fills so much of our horizon. We could probably man-age this better if only the verb *to be* were a regular verb. If we could say "Spirit be-s more than matter be-s", the truth there stated would hit the mind more powerfully for having first hit the ear. But we have to say "Spirit is more than matter is"; and it is the hardest thing in the world to take the word "is" seriously. It is the most rich and the most dynamic of all words; it is the key word in the name of God Himself, but it is surely the most miserable and meagre-sounding of all words. Anyhow, spirit *is* more than matter *is:* there is more *to* it, it *has* more being, it *does* more being.

The amount of anything's being is the amount of its response to the power of God: and this response depends upon what God conceives it as having and wills it to have. As what He is, God is present to all things equally, sustaining them in existence; but as what He does, He is present to them variously according to the amount of being He wills that they shall have. He wills that some things shall have more being than others: the measure of every creature's being is the power God gives it to reflect God. Spirit has more be-ing than matter. Within these two orders there are still further grades of being, and these we shall come to later. For the moment let us consider these two major divisions as a whole.

(iii) Eternity, aeviternity, time

We might at this stage consider our concept of being as at three levels—

> Infinite Spirit
> Created Spirit
> Matter

—but we must never let such an ordering of things trick us into the idea that we have here some kind of mathematical progression. Infinite Spirit, the Absolute, does not belong in the same series as finite spirit. Strictly speaking, we are not rising step by step from matter to angels to God. The gulf between infinite and finite being is so vast that differences between one finite being and another, be it between the highest and the lowest, are derisory by comparison.

We can see this by seeing how far even the beings made in God's likeness fall short of that God in whose likeness they are. Spirit, remember, has a firm hold upon its own nature. Angels and human souls are immortal. And by comparison with matter's transience, this is a great glory. But their hold upon existence depends upon their having been brought into existence and being continuously maintained in existence, for they too were made of nothing; and in them as in all created things there is a certain element of nothingness. God, on the other hand, possesses His nature by no gift but by its own necessity; and there is no negative element to dim His utter positivity.

But, this said, we can return to consider the glory of spirit in the created order. Its permanence is conditional, but the condition will not fail. Its permanence is as certain as matter's transience.

This transience of matter is worth a closer look. We have already seen that any material thing can become some other material thing because it does not possess its being in one single simple reality but dispersed in parts, in such a way that one part is not another. This dispersion in parts has two consequences: matter occupies space: and again its parts can be broken up, subtracted, added to so that it is no longer the kind of material being it was but some other kind; and this other kind is just as much subject to change, and so on endlessly. From the moment matter begins to be, it begins to change.

Indeed we have here another way of grading things. We have already seen them graded according to the amount of being in them. Equally they can be graded according to their subjection to change. The two gradings will give the same order because they are two aspects of the one fact. Change is always the result of something lacking: the more defective a thing is in being, the more it is subject to change; the more perfect the being, the less it is subject to change.

Thus the *Infinite Being* having all perfections is utterly changeless. Nothing else is changeless. Every created being, however glorious, contains a certain negative element, lacks something, from the fact that it is made of nothing. So St. Augustine writes (*De Natura Boni*): "All the things that God has made are mutable because made of nothing." And the Council of Florence tells us that creatures are "good, of course, because they are made by the Supreme Good, but mutable because they are made of nothing". But all are not subject to change to the same extent.

Created spirit, having no parts, cannot suffer *substantial* change; that is to say, it can never become something else. Yet it is not therefore totally exempt from change. It can, for instance, have a change of operation, as when an angel is sent to announce the birth of Christ, or when a human soul passes from one intellectual activity to another; it can change its relation to other beings, God above all, but finite beings too; it can receive new knowledge, it can love more, or less. All these are what we call accidental changes, changes in a creature's qualities or operations or relations which leave it still itself.

With *matter,* we have of course ceaseless accidental change and the ever-present threat, only too often realized, of substantial change, of being so changed that it ceases to be what it was and becomes something else. So much is this so, that change is almost matter's definition.

Thus we have three relations to change—the utter changelessness of God; the substantial permanence combined with occasional accidental change that belongs to spirit; and the liability to substantial change and the continuous accidental change that goes with matter. To each of these three corresponds its own kind of duration. For the changelessness of God, there is Eternity; for the continuous changefulness of matter, there is Time. Time is the duration of that which changes, as eternity is the duration of that which changes not. But what of spirit? Because it knows change at all, even if only accidental change, it is not in eternity; but because the changes it knows are not continuous, it is not exactly in time either. The spirit does indeed know a before and after. If God gives an angel a particular revelation, for instance, then something in the angelic mind is aware of his state when he did not have the revelation and his state when he has it. But there is nothing in the nature of spirit which requires these changes; they happen when they happen—they do not bring change into his nature itself; and in between, the spirit rests in the changeless possession of what he has. His "now" is more closely akin to the abiding now of eternity than to the flowing now of time. For his duration too, there is a word—the word *aevum* or *aeviternity*, the duration of that which in its essence or substance knows no change: though by its accidents it can know change, and to that extent is in time too, but a sort of discontinuous time, not the ever-flowing time of matter.

Aeviternity is the proper sphere of every created spirit, and therefore of the human soul. But the soul's special relation to the matter of the human body gives it a necessary and proper relation to continuous time (which is the body's duration), which other spirits are not troubled by. At death, this distracting relation to matter's time ceases to affect the soul, so that it can experience its proper aeviternity. But during this life, time presses upon the soul, if only by way of the heartbeats that never cease. The soul can become too much immersed in matter, in the limitations of time and space and change. Love of change is a disease that the soul contracts from the body— one sure symptom of it is the inability to contemplate. During contemplation, time really does stand still for the soul, which is one reason why we should practice it: for it means practicing the soul in its own proper element.

(iv) Creation in time

We have discussed *why* God created the universe and *how,* and we have had a first glance at *what* He created. Before going on to a fuller examination of *what,* we might glance at the question *when* — that is to say, at what time did God create the universe? We have already seen enough of what time is to save us from certain cruder misconceptions as to what the present inquiry is about. Time is the duration of that which changes; again, time is a measure of change. Either way, unless there is in existence a being that changes, there is no time either.

The reader new to this kind of discussion should pause here to make sure that he has grasped the point. There is in existence a kind of being, namely, matter, which is in ceaseless change. Time is the measurement of change. Apart from a being whose changes time measures, time is nothing at all. Creation means that God, who is infinite and possesses the whole of His being in one single act of being, brought into existence a universe which does not possess its being thus in one single act, but part by part and moment by moment. The fact about the material universe which we express in the phrase "part by part" accounts for its being spread out in space; the fact about it which we express in the phrase "from moment to moment" accounts for its being spread out in time. Space and time express its finitude. There is the one limitation by which its being is dispersed over parts which are not each other so that it is nowhere wholly itself; there is the other limitation by which it works out its reality gradually and is at no one time all it can be.

As has already been noted, we may, if we like, think of both space and time as ways of expressing the division of our universe into parts: space is the division into parts which coexist; time is the division into parts which follow one another. But either way, space and time are not realities which can exist apart from the universe. Space is simply the arrangement that matter makes for the convenience of its parts: space is that which surrounds and lies between material objects: if there were no material objects, there would be no space either. Similarly, time measures the changes of beings that are subject to change, and if there were no such beings, there would be no time.

As we have seen, time may be, somewhat crudely perhaps, thought of as the ticking of the universe as it works out its existence from moment to moment. Thus we see the fallacy of conceiving a running stream of time into which God suddenly dropped the universe. Time and the universe began together. From the moment the universe existed, it began to tick. Naturally there was no ticking before there was anything to tick.

Thus we may say quite literally that there never was a time when the universe did not exist, which does not at all mean that the universe did not have a beginning, but only that when the universe did not exist, time did not exist either, and time and the universe began together. In St. Augustine's phrase, "Obviously the world was made not *in* time but *with* time." So that the question, when was the universe created? can only mean how long ago was it created? How far back do we have to go before coming to that first moment before which there was no moment, that first moment in which something existed where nothing had been, something which *in* that first moment had no past, though in the next moment it had one, one that has never ceased to lengthen.

Was there indeed such a *first* moment? Did the material universe have in a sense a beginning? As we look *forward,* we know that for the human soul at least there is no limit in the future; might our gaze backward through time similarly find no limit in the past? There are Catholic philosophers, though they are in the minority, who hold that reason alone cannot settle the question. Personally I feel that even if the mind had to make its decision without aid from God, it would opt for a beginning. A succession that did not begin bothers the mind, as it is not bothered by a succession that will not end. But whatever the unaided mind might make of such a question,[1] it is not left unaided.

God Himself has told us. We shall discuss later the question of the divine inspiration of Scripture. Here we need only remind ourselves that the human writers wrote what God willed them to write, so that He is Himself the guarantor of the truths they set down. And the first book of Scripture in its first sentence tells us: "In the beginning God made the heavens and the earth." The Church has amplified this. The Fourth Council of the Lateran defined that God "by His almighty

---

[1] The question whether the universe had a beginning in time, a first moment, does not touch the question whether the universe has a creator. It is not because the universe once was not and now is that we argue that God must have brought it into being. It is because whether the universe had a beginning or not, it does not contain within itself the reason for its own existence, so that its existence can be accounted for only by a being who *is* in Himself the sufficient reason for His own existence. God must have made it, and made it as to its totality. There are theists who hold that it is impossible to prove from reason that the universe does not go back endlessly into the past. But just as this does not destroy the need of a self-existent being to give the universe existence and maintain it in existence, so it does not mean that in this hypothesis the universe would be eternal. We have already sufficiently seen that endlessness in time does not constitute eternity.

power created together in the beginning of time both creatures, the Spiritual and the Corporeal, namely, the Angelic and the earthly, and afterwards the human, as it were a common creature, composed of spirit and body".

How long ago? Genesis does not say: nor does the Church. The truth is that Genesis is concerned with the things that matter vitally in God's own nature and in His dealings with the human soul, and the "date" of creation is not one of them. That God is personal and distinct from his creation (as against pantheism), that there is one God (as against polytheism), that Evil is not a separate creative principle but arises from a misused will (as against dualism), that God created sun and stars and sky and earth (as against nature worship); that man is created by God, in His image and likeness, that woman like man is made in God's image, what God planned for man, how man reacted to God's plan, the effect upon the whole human race of man's reaction—these things are of towering importance. But how long ago did it all happen? It would be interesting to know, of course, but it would be almost frivolous to think that it matters very much in comparison with the things that Genesis does tell us.

A word on Genesis, or rather on its first three chapters. Scholars seem to be agreed that chapters 2 and 3, which tell of the creation and fall of Adam and Eve, were compiled from earlier material around 900 B.C., perhaps in the time of Solomon. Around 500 B.C., there was a kind of official "edition" made of the first five books of the Old Testament. It seems that our chapter 1 of Genesis, the "hymn of creation", was added then as an introduction. That chapter reads like a meditation on the name "I Am", which God had told Moses was His own.

The next two chapters read as if they were born of their writer's meditation on the contrast between the world as it is and any world God could possibly have invented. Why should the living God create a world in which even the highest creatures must die? Why should the all-pure God create a world in which these same creatures find purity impossible to preserve, sin impossible to avoid? He saw the two problems as related. For him, death would not have come to man if sin had not come first. He saw sin as a kind of death, diminishing life.

It was his special insight that the essence of sin was the desire to be like God—in fact, to be one's own god. And this desire must have been at the heart of the breakdown in man's relation with God. Did God reveal that insight to the Genesis author? Or was it his own thinking, aided by what we should now call actual graces, light and strength given by God?

He did not know the details of the story, only the essence. So he cast the central truths into figurative language, telling them as the story of a man and a woman in a garden. He could have told it equally well of a larger human group if the thought had occurred to him. He was not writing a mere parable, a story of which the whole point is the meaning, so it would be naïve to ask if it really happened. Unless the things he tells in figures did happen, sin and death are not accounted for, nor is the breach between man and God.

He saw the man and the woman as real people committing the sin that is at the root of history—"history" for him meaning the story of man's continuing and varying relation with God. If we think of the man and woman as humanity, male and female, we get all he had to tell us of humanity's brokenness.

12. Angels, Matter, Men

As we have seen, all things are God's workmanship and bear His imprint, but some things He made in His likeness, too. These are spirit. Those that bear only His imprint are matter.

(i) Angels

Highest in the created order come the angels, pure spirits, as we call them—spirits with no material element in them. That such beings exist we might guess; indeed, as we shall see later, a consideration of so much of the created universe as we can discover for ourselves would lead us to feel that creation would be incomplete without them. Yet it remains that there is nothing in our experience that forces our reason to postulate the angels as its cause: we know of their existence as a fact only by revelation, taught us by God through His Scriptures and through His Church.

The Church has told us, as we saw in the last chapter, that angels exist, and that they are created by God. There is not a great deal actually defined by the Church about them, but the writings of the Fathers, Doctors, and theologians are rich in development of what Scripture has to tell us of them; and

Scripture, both the Old Testament and the New, is so filled with their activities that it is difficult to see why in the religious awareness of so many Christian bodies they occupy so small a part—so small that many appear to have forgotten them altogether.

Probably this has something to do with a feeling that belief in angels is unscientific—it may have been all right for our ancestors, but modern science has made it just too difficult for us. This feeling is all but universal and all but meaningless. Science can no more disprove the existence of angels than it can prove it. If by some odd freak science offered to prove that angels exist, we should have to refuse so well-meant an offer; if science denies their existence, its denial is as irrelevant. If angels exist, they will be beyond the range or reach of the sciences which man has developed for the investigation of matter. To refuse to explore our universe by any but one set of methods is much as if our ancestors had refused to discover any more of the world than they could reach on horseback. Philosophy can discuss the possibility of pure spirits; theology can discuss whether the fact of their existence has been revealed to us. But what can science say? That it has never seen one? Naturally: they are immaterial and so beyond the reach of sight as of all other senses.

After all, men exist who know and will: there is nothing unscientific in believing that beings higher than men exist who know and will. What science does it offend? Or why should science in general be offended that the tests it has developed for things in space should not be applied to beings outside space?

Among men, there are good and bad: there is nothing unscientific in believing that among pure spirits there are good and bad.

Again, men intervene in the affairs of beings less than themselves, often enough without those lesser beings having the faintest notion of it—the cats and dogs of Hiroshima could hardly have known that their catastrophe was man-made: since men do thus intervene all the time, there is nothing unscientific in believing that angels do.

Perhaps the feeling that angels and science do not fit is merely a sense that angels would be too marvelous or mysterious an element in the sober prosaic world that science has analyzed for us. But that will not do. Science has shown us a world at once fantastic and mysterious. Angels are no more incredible than atoms, and a great deal more comprehensible. Ah, you say, but atoms are not persons, and angels are. Why this terror of persons? We are persons ourselves. As we have seen, there is no iron law that only one sort of person can exist in the universe. It is simply a question of fact: do angels exist or not? Science is not equipped to answer the question, but that does not keep it from being a question. The answer is not less important because science cannot provide it. The answer is not less certain because God has provided it. God has told us that angels exist.

Scripture, I say, is full of them. Actually their first two appearances in Scripture seem to constitute a rather bleak beginning of their relations with us, for the first appearance is of a bad angel tricking man out of paradise, and the second appearance is of good angels keeping him out. This Scriptural division of angels into good and bad we shall examine later. For the moment we may make some rough analysis of what Scripture has to tell us of the function of angels in God's plan.

The word *angel* itself is from a Greek word meaning messenger: that we should make this the name by which we habitually know them is perhaps evidence of man's tendency to think of himself as central: there are countless instances in which God has used these pure spirits as messengers to men, and theologians teach that God uses them to convey illumination from Him to one another; yet that is not the reason for their existence or their chief function. Their chief function, their proper life-work, is to glorify God. "Adore Him, all you His angels" (Ps 96:7) puts it with perfect succinctness; and in the great vision of Daniel (7:9-10) we have the same truth in resplendent detail: "I beheld till thrones were placed and the Ancient of days sat: His garment was white as snow, and the hair of his head like clean wool: his throne like flames of fire: the wheels of it like a burning fire. A swift stream of fire issued forth from before him: thousands of thousands ministered to him, and ten thousand times a hundred thousand stood before him."

Besides the adoration and service of God, they have certain other functions, which can be understood only in the light of a certain vital truth about God's dealings with His creatures. All that any creature is, all that any creature has, is from God. There is no other possible source than Existence Itself from which even the tiniest scintilla of existence should come to any creature. But God has shown us with overwhelming evidence that He wills to give His gifts to creatures through other creatures so that we may learn by the receiving of God's gifts from one another and the transmission of God's gifts to one another, our family relationship within the great household of God. Our human life comes from God, yet God chooses to give it to us through a father and mother; the bread that sustains our bodily life comes from God, but by way of the farmer and the miller and the baker; the truth that nourishes the soul comes to us from God, but through men—the men who wrote the Bible, the bishops of His Church.

I have picked a few more spectacular instances of a rule which is the norm of God's dealings with His creatures. In the light of this rule, we can understand the second great function of angels: God uses them to implement His will, in relation to one another, in relation to the physical universe: in relation to the whole functioning of the laws of nature and of grace. This is magnificently put by the Psalmist: "Bless the Lord, all ye His angels: You that are mighty in strength and execute His word, harkening to the voice of His orders" (Ps 102:20). Thus angels are in charge, under God, of the universe as a whole, and of the various parts of it. They are responsible for the operation of the general laws by which God rules the universe, and for such special interventions as God chooses to make in the affairs of men: as when He sends an angel before the camp of Israel during the flight out of Egypt (Exo 14:19), or when He sends an angel to strike Jerusalem with a pestilence as a punishment for the disobedience of David, the king (1 Chron 21). At the Last Judgment, "the angels shall go out, and shall separate the wicked from among the just, and shall cast them into the furnace of fire" (Mt 13:49). They are responsible for individual countries: Daniel tells us of the angel of Persia, and the angel of Greece; they have a mission of guardianship to individual persons. The angel Raphael tells Tobias, "I offered thy prayer to the Lord" (Tob 12:12). And the Epistle to the Hebrews says (1:14): "What are they all of them, but spirits apt for service, whom he sends out when the destined heirs of eternal salvation have need of them." It is not absolutely of faith that each one of us has a guardian angel, but it would be rash to dismiss it in face of the continuous teaching of the Church. Never think of angels without dwelling on the words of Our Lord: "See to it that you do not treat one of these little ones with contempt; I tell you, they have angels of their own in heaven, that behold the face of my heavenly Father continually" (Mt 18:10).

One further thing we learn about angels from Scripture, definitely as to the main fact though cloudily as to the detail. We learn that there is not one undifferentiated level of pure spirits, but that they are of different levels of excellence, according to the degree of His power that God has willed to make manifest in them. Scripture gives us nine names, and it is the

general view of Catholic writers that these are the names of
nine choirs, in one or other of which all the countless myriads
of angels come. Five of these names we owe to St. Paul.
Writing to the Colossians (1:16) with the purpose of correcting
certain faulty and exaggerated notions about angels which had
taken hold of them, he writes in the first chapter: "In him [the
Second Person of the Blessed Trinity] were all things created in
heaven and on earth, visible and invisible, whether *Thrones* or
Dominations or *Principalities* or *Powers.*" Three of these names
recur together with a fifth in the Epistle to the Ephesians,
where he tells us that Christ is raised "above all Principality,
and Power, and *Virtue,* and Dominion, and every name that is
named, not only in this world, but also in that which is to
come" (Eph 1:21).

To these five names we may add the word *angel,* which
occurs throughout the Scriptures, and *archangel,* which occurs
twice in the New Testament, together with the Cherubim
with flaming sword who guarded Paradise against fallen Adam,
and were in Ezekiel's vision (1:14) like flashes of lightning, and
the Seraphim (the name is from a Hebrew word meaning to
burn or flame), who touched the mouth of Isaiah with a live
coal (Is 6:6).

St. Thomas adopts a division of the nine choirs into three
groups, according to their intellectual perfection and consequent nearness in being to God—Seraphim, Cherubim, Thrones;
Dominations, Virtues, Powers; Principalities, Archangels, Angels.
Other writers suggest different arrangements; and there is a
mass of magnificent theological speculation as to the difference
of function between one choir and another. But the Church
has defined nothing upon this matter.

(ii) Matter, living and non-living

Glorious as created spirit is, it has limitations, deficiencies in being, that God has not. As we have seen, it cannot account for its existence by itself, but needs to be brought into being and maintained in being by the absolute power of God. Mighty as are the angel's powers of knowing and loving, they are not infinite, and it can receive increase of both.

If created spirit lacks the perfection of being that God has, matter lacks the perfection of being that created spirit has. By comparison with God, we see the angel as diminished; by comparison with the angel, we see matter as diminished. Actually the gulf between God and the highest angel is immeasurably greater than the gulf between the highest angel and the lowest of material things; but owing to our familiarity with things and our lack of familiarity with God, the lesser gulf impresses us more. And if we must correct our perspective in this matter for the sake of intellectual health, we must correct it by becoming more aware of the difference between finite and infinite, not by becoming less aware of the difference between created spirit and matter. For this lesser difference is still enormous.

Whereas spirit has—conditionally upon the will of God but no less certainly for that—unending permanence in being, matter has not even what we might call temporary permanence: any material object can at any moment be changed into some other; seems in fact almost avid for change, *any* change; seems so little in love with what it is at any moment that it would almost rather be something else.

Again, whereas spirit has all its being at any given moment concentrated in one single reality, so that there is no element in a spirit that is not the whole of it, matter has its being dispersed in parts that occupy space; and partly as a consequence of this condition, partly as a consequence of a deeper deficiency still, a material being is limited in its power to individual material things with which it can make contact, whereas spirit can range over the whole universe by knowledge and love.

Yet matter has this resemblance to spirit, that it is not one undifferentiated level: it, too, has different levels of excellence, according to the degree of His power that God has willed to make manifest in each.

The dominating division in the material order is between living and non-living. Animals are living and vegetables are living: stones are not living. So much we all see. But as to what life is, which is in animals and vegetables (to say nothing of angels and God) and not in stones, most of us feel rather as St. Augustine felt about the meaning of time: that we know what it means provided no one asks us. And to this point at least we are justified, that although there may be borderline cases where it is difficult to tell whether the thing belongs to the living or non-living order, there are vast fields in which we know, and without hesitation. We might find it hard to make a list of just what qualities in a thing mark it as living: the chances are that the reality of the distinction strikes us most violently when we see what happens when life goes out of a living body. It rots; and though again we might be hard put to it to analyze the difference between the rotting of what has once been living and the mere breaking up of what never has, the difficulty arises merely from our lack of skill in analyzing a fact, not from any uncertainty about the fact. A rock may wear away from wind and weather, but we should never confuse this with the decay of vegetation once growing on it, to say nothing of the decay of the animals that once lived on it.

This is not the place for any very close analysis of the fact called life. It is a fascinating inquiry, and even one who is neither scientist nor philosopher can gain immense profit from watching scientists and philosophers at work on it. Here we may take the simplest and most fruitful definition: living being is one which has *within itself* some principle by which it operates: and operates not just anyhow but in fulfillment of its nature, in the development of what it is and the achievement of its proper functions. Living things act from some power or necessity within them, and do really (in subordination to God) initiate action; non-living things are only acted upon (though they are, of course, not purely passive in face of such action upon them: they have their own sort of energy and in consequence their own sort of reaction).

What we have said of living being applies to all living beings—fully and supremely to God; in the created order, to angels, human souls, and all the material beings that have life. But naturally the operations which thus find their source within the nature of each being differ according to that nature. Here our concern is with the operations of material living things—powers of movement (anchored to a root in vegetables, unanchored in animals), nutrition and growth (growth which does not simply mean being added to but developing toward a total shape), and reproduction of their kind.

The life principle in a material being is called its soul. It is the soul of the vegetable, the soul of the dog, that accounts for the activities of vegetable and dog while they are alive, and for the decay of vegetable and dog when they are dead.

Thus there are three divisions of the created universe:

Spirit
Living Matter
Non-living Matter.

Life reaches down from the beings made in God's likeness to some of the beings that only bear His imprint. At any level, life is a great glory: but living matter is still very much matter. This is obvious if we consider what the proper operations of spirit

are—*knowing,* which means having things present to the mind
in their concept or meaning and not simply in their look, or taste,
or smell; and *loving,* which means being attracted to things thus
known. The plant may be said to have some sort of rudimentary knowledge and love: it may seem, for instance, to know
where the sun is and to move toward it: but all this is so rudimentary that we feel we are using a figure of speech. When we
speak of animals as knowing and loving, we feel that we are
straining language less—at least when we are talking of the
higher animals: we do not feel so sure about oysters, say, as we
do about dogs—especially our own dog. But even at the highest
we see that the knowledge of an animal (and therefore the love
of an animal, since there is always a proportion between love and
knowledge) is only a good imitation: it has not the ranging
power of spiritual knowledge. Indeed, animal knowledge is
limited in comparison with spirit knowledge, very much as the
animal's being is limited by comparison with the spirit's being.
The spirit can know the universal and the abstract: the animal
seems to know only the individual and concrete, and this is so
much less that it can only by courtesy be called knowing at all.

A very crude example must suffice here instead of the
longer discussion the matter will find in a book of philosophy.
A man, having a spiritual soul, can be aware not only of this or
that dog but of the general notion of dog which is expressed in
all the dogs that have been or will be or could be. When he
remarks that the dog is a useful animal, he is employing—and
employing with the ease of an entirely natural operation—a
universal concept. He is not thinking of any individual dog of
a particular shape and size and color; he is abstracting that
essence of dog which is common to all the numberless combinations of size and shape and color in which dogs are found.
He can do this precisely because his soul is a spirit. His body,
which is material, cannot make any sort of contact, enter into

any sort of relation, with that universal dog. His eyes can see only individual dogs, each dog with its own shape and size and color. That is what we mean by saying that matter is limited in its contacts to the individual and concrete.

If we examine all that we can of the animal's awareness of things, there is nothing to suggest that this awareness ever goes beyond the individual and concrete to make any sort of generalization or abstraction, that it ever goes beyond the sight and the taste and the smell to what the thing *is*. As someone has observed, if one ever met a pig capable of knowing that it was a pig, it might be safer to baptize it, on the ground that it must have a spiritual soul to be able to arrive at the general idea "pig" and apply it to itself as one realization of that general idea. As I say, none of the animal activities that we call knowing seem to go beyond awareness of the individual and concrete; that is, none of them seem to go beyond the material order, for that *is* the material order. Nothing that the animal's psyche does takes us so obviously out of the range of matter that we are forced to postulate a spiritual principle. The animal's soul does nothing that leads us to feel that some higher-than-material principle must be in operation. Therefore there is no reason to believe that it is not a material soul, "immersed" in the matter of the animal's body.

Neither by permanence in being, nor by rational knowledge and love, do even the highest material beings, those that have life, transcend the sphere of matter. The gulf between matter and spirit remains. But if it is a real gulf, it is a bridged gulf, too, bridged at one point—man.

(iii) Man as the union of spirit and matter

That man has at once a material and a spiritual element, and therefore belongs to both worlds, we *might* know merely by looking at him and thinking about what we see. But on the whole, though man is much given to looking at himself, he is not at all good at thinking about what he sees. Nothing in the world is more fantastic than the variety of answers man has proposed to the simple question, What is man? Fortunately we are not left to our own incompetent devices: God has told us, through the men whom He inspired to write His Scriptures.

The account of creation in the first two chapters of Genesis gives us two principal statements about man: "Let us make man to our image and likeness" (Gen 1:26). "And the Lord God formed Man of the slime of the earth: and breathed into his face the breath of life and man became a living soul" (Gen 2:7). There you have the two-fold element in man, the slime of the earth and the likeness of God. And both elements belong. The matter of our body is not simply an extra, something we should be better without, something to be grown out of as the butterfly grows out of the grub, something in some happier future to be discarded as the butterfly discards the cocoon. Matter is part of the very nature of man; he would not be man without it. And he would not perform his function in the universe without it. For it is precisely his function to join the two worlds of matter and spirit into one universe, and he does it by belonging essentially to both of them. We are to think of creation not as two closed circles which nowhere meet but as a kind of figure-eight with man on both sides of the joint.

Thus if man is not, as he sometimes thinks, the center of the universe (in the sense of that upon which all revolves), he is in this other sense *at* the center of the universe, bestriding the lower world of matter and the upper world of spirit. In both worlds he has the closest and most vital contacts: it is a pity that he is so much more keenly aware of the lower one, and so sketchily and intermittently aware of the upper, for both are realities, and realities that affect him profoundly. Angels can guard him; cows can nourish him, and so can sunsets. Angels, again, can tempt him, insects can bite him. The trouble is that we are more concerned about insects than about devils, more concerned that cows should nourish us than that angels should bless. We must recover a total view of our universe if only in order to know where we are — and that in the interest of sanity. As to answers for the question, How did angels get to tempting, how did man become temptable and biteable — so very biteable that he bites himself more fatally than any insect can bite him — these things too we must get to know. They will begin to appear a little later in the story, when we come to see what man made of himself. Here we are concerned with man as God made him.

He is, we have seen, a union of spirit and matter. But what does that mean? The meaning at the first level may be set out simply enough. Man has a living body; therefore, there is some principle in him which makes his body to be alive. And whether a body be vegetable or lower animal or man, that principle in it which makes it living is what we call its soul. Man, then, has a soul; so has a dog, so has a cabbage: and man's soul does for his body what their souls do for theirs, makes it a living body. But whereas their souls are material, limited to matter, not producing any operation that goes beyond matter, man's soul is spirit. It does not only the things that souls do, but the things that spirits do. By intellect and will it knows and loves as spirits know and love: in its thinking it handles the abstract and the universal. Man, having a body and soul, is an animal; but he is a rational animal, for alone of the animals he has a soul which is a spirit.

But how are we to conceive a union of two beings, one of them in space, the other not. And note that it is not just any kind of union, but a union so close that the two constitute one being. The soul, which is spirit, is in every part of the body; no smallest part of the body is outside the union. Now it is obvious that in all this the effort to give the soul some sort of shape in order to make the union seem easier to grasp is waste of time. There is no gain in trying to think of the body as thinly buttered all over with soul, or as a sponge interpenetrated with soul, or of the soul as shaped like the body so that it can have a point by point contact with each part of the body, only made of some spirit stuff more refined than matter.

A moment's reflection will show us why imagination is driven to such odd acrobatics. In its efforts to make the problem easier for itself, it is introducing a difficulty that is not there. It sees it as the problem of how a body so large that it occupies quite a lot of space can be totally occupied by a soul so small that it occupies no space whatever. But the soul is outside space not because it is too small to occupy even the smallest section of space, but because it lacks the limitations which would make space necessary for it. If we are to think of a difference of largeness between soul and body, then we must think of the soul as larger: for it has more being in it, has fewer limitations to diminish it, is every way greater in being. Thus for the intellect the question of how spirit can totally occupy matter is simply the question of how the greater can totally occupy the less; and the answer is simple—by superiority of being and of energy. A spirit is not in space, but it can act upon a being that is in space. And this is the only kind of spatial presence that a spirit can have. It is where it acts. The soul acts upon every part of the body, and its action is to vivify, to make alive (indeed, according to St. Thomas, the soul not only makes the body alive, it makes it a body). In some ways the presence of the soul in every part of the body is comparable to the presence of God in every part of the universe.

There is in the purely material order a comparison which the mind may find helpful provided that it gets what is to be got from it and then resolutely throws it away. When a pot of water is boiling over a flame, there is a sense in which the flame is in every part of the water, although the flame itself occupies none of the space that the water occupies. The energies that come from the flame are what set every part of the water bubbling and hissing. The casual onlooker might easily be deceived into thinking that the water is the energetic thing and might overlook altogether the flame with its utter stillness. If the flame happened to be invisible, there would be people to assert that all this talk of flame was superstitious nonsense. But all the movement of the water is due to the superior energy of the flame. And the water, if it could think about the matter at all, might easily think that the flame had no other business than to heat it. But the flame has a life of its own and can continue as a flame whether the water is there or not.

All this can be applied easily enough to the relation of soul and body. The body is so very alive and clamorous that the soul can be overlooked altogether. But all the vitality of the body is derived from the energizing upon it of the soul. One need not be told what happens to any part of the body, the finger, say, if it gets separated from the body and thus removed from the field of the soul's energies. Which reminds us that the union of soul and body has this double flower of intimacy, that the soul acts upon every part of the body, but only upon that particular body: with no other material thing can it make direct contact at all. My soul is meant for the vivifying of my body. It is the perfect specialist.

The illustration, I have said, must be used for what it has to give and then discarded. For it is valid only up to a point. The flame and the water are two separate realities brought into relation for a specific purpose, but each quite capable of existing fully as itself apart from the other. But soul and body are not thus casually brought together; they are united to form one complete individual reality; they would not come into existence without each other; if they are separated, they suffer loss—the body ceases to be a body, and the spirit, although it survives, survives with a large part of its powers idle within it for lack of a body to use them on. You must never think of your soul simply as a more powerful thing which dominates your body: soul and body are partners in the business of being you.

So much, for the moment, for the nature of man. Let us return to the account of his creation. "The Lord God formed man of the slime of the earth", and "breathed into his face the breath of life; and man became a living being." It would be difficult to conceive anything more compressed. The word "formed", for instance, tells us of the fact but not of the process: there was an assembling of elements of the material universe, but was it instantaneous, or spread over a considerable space of time? Was it complete in one act, or by stages? Were those elements, for instance, formed into an animal body which as one generation followed another gradually evolved—not, of course, by the ordinary laws of matter but under the special guidance of God—to a point where it was capable of union with a spiritual soul, which God then created and infused into it? The statement in Genesis does not seem actually to exclude this, but it certainly does not say it. Nor has the Church formally said that it is not so. What the Church would say if she ever felt called upon to make a statement on the matter, I do not know. So far she has made no explicit statement. On the surface, no specifically religious question seems to be involved. Whether God formed the body of man in one act or by an unfolding process, it was God who formed it. But man does not come into being until God creates a human soul: if anyone should teach that *that* evolves from some lower form, he would not have to wait long for the Church's comment.

What may have been happening to the elements of the human body before it was a human body is not of the first importance, and Genesis does not tell us. What *is* of the first importance, it does tell us: that man was made of the slime of the earth in the image and likeness of God; and it tells us one other thing that has never ceased to matter. In the first chapter of Genesis we read: "And God created man to his own image: to the image of God he created him: male and female he created them. And God blessed them, saying: Increase and multiply." In the second chapter, the origin of woman is given in more detail: "And the Lord God said: It is not good for man to be alone: let us make him a help like unto himself. . . . Then the Lord God cast a deep sleep upon Adam: and when he was fast asleep, he took one of his ribs, and filled up flesh for it. And the Lord God built the rib which he took from Adam into a woman: and brought her to Adam. And Adam said: This now is bone of my bones, and flesh of my flesh; she shall be called woman, because she was taken out of man." Then come the words that Christ spoke of as God's: "Wherefore a man shall leave father and mother and shall cleave to his wife: and they shall be two in one flesh."

It would take a long time to unwrap all that is contained here. At a first glance we see certain obvious elements in it. We see, for example, that the first woman came from the first man. The mind shudders at the thought of all the jokes that have been made about this, largely perhaps because man has always found something comic in his ribs. Genesis seems to make it clear, anyhow, that woman was made from some element of the body of man: there is nothing particularly comic about this, nor indeed anything improbable, considering that every human being is made of elements taken from the body of other human beings. And there is an enormous importance in it, for it preserves the unity of the race: we are all from one.

The second truth that leaps to the eye is that God, in giving a wife to Adam, revealed His plan for the cooperation of the sexes in the continuance of the race. The moment husband and wife exist, Adam sees them as father and mother, and this by the revelation of God: it was from no experience of his own that he talked of a man leaving father and mother. Thus God made the production of all other human beings to depend upon the cooperation of man and woman. He did not so act with the angels. Angels have no progeny; they were not told to increase and multiply and fill the heavens. There is no race of angels. They are related to one another as children of one God, and so are we; but they are not, as we are, related to one another as children of one father of their own kind. The fatherhood of God is shadowed forth to us, as it is not to them, by a fatherhood of our own. And indeed our part in God's creative act—what we call procreation—is our greatest glory in the natural order; it is the act in which we come closest to the creative power of God. And it is a glory peculiar to man. For the angels do not procreate at all, and the animals reproduce their kind without rational choice or any awareness of the majesty of that in which they take part.

We must not exaggerate this procreative power into some fancied superiority of ourselves over the angels. Man's body comes from his parents, but not his soul. That is still the direct creation of God. God still takes slime of the earth and breathes a soul into it, only now He takes it not *from* the earth but from the children of Adam. The reason why we do not generate our children's souls is the reason why angels do not generate at all: namely, that the spirit, mightier in being than the body, has no parts, no constituent elements, one of which may be separated from it and set up in being on its own account. Thus our power to reproduce is bound up with the lesser perfection of our material bodies, and the angels do not envy us. It comes from our lowliness, but in our lowly way we can glory in it.

Meanwhile they remain our superiors and there is profit for us in their contact. It is a pity that any man should be so very conscious of the material beings below him, and altogether ignore these spiritual beings above him. It means that he is spending too much of his life in the company of his inferiors — not, one imagines, through mere preference for low company, but through mental inertia. It is not for nothing that the Church lists sloth among the capital sins. There may, of course, even among those who accept the existence of angels, be a feeling that there is not much we can do about them — they *are* above our heads, and there they must stay. But we are not so helpless. We can habituate the mind to the fact of them, exercise the mind in the comprehension of them, and pray to them for aid. The Church is rich in suggestions for prayer. In the Mass for the feast of the archangels Michael, Gabriel, and Raphael, we pray: "God our Father, . . . may those who serve you constantly in heaven keep our lives safe from all harm on earth."

(iv) Law and providence

Here, then, is the created universe in its broadest division from non-living matter through living matter, through man, who is a union of matter and spirit, to the angels, who are pure spirits. God brings it into being from nothing, God sustains it in being, and unsustained by Him it would be nothing as before. His will which is love is the sole reason for its existence; therefore His will must be the rule of its operation, its law. But even as law, His will is still love. The laws which govern this universe and all things in it are the result of God's knowledge of what the universe is, and this knowledge is perfect knowledge, because there is nothing in the universe which is not His.

But a very brief consideration of the laws by which our universe is run shows us two rather different sets of laws, what we may call physical law and moral law. The practical distinction for us is that physical law is God's ordinance as to how all things *must* act, moral law is His ordinance as to how spiritual beings *ought* to act. There is an element of choice in the operation of the moral law which does not exist in the operation of the physical law. But the element of choice, although it is there, may not be precisely what we think. That fire burns is a physical law, at times extraordinarily useful for man, at times catastrophic. But, useful or catastrophic, fire still burns. At first sight the moral law seems different. It tells us that we ought to do this and ought not to do that, and in those very terms implies that we are free to choose whether we will do this or that, whereas there is no freedom of choice about being burned if we put our hand in the fire. But in actual fact the moral law merely casts into the form of a command something that is already as much a law of nature as that fire burns. God's command to us not to bear false witness implies that we are free to bear false witness if we choose; but to bear false witness— even if we do not know of God's command and no question of sin arises—will damage us spiritually just as certainly as to put our hands into the fire will damage us bodily. We can if we choose bear false witness: we can if we choose put our hand into the fire: in either event we shall be damaged. In other words, physical laws and moral laws *are* laws because we are what we are. If we were asbestos instead of flesh, fire would not burn us; if we were stags, adultery would not damage us either. Physical or moral law, to know what it is, is to know the reality of things: to act in accordance with it, is to act by the reality of things. And that is sanity.

God's laws are there to enable the universe as a whole and each being in it to achieve what God meant it to achieve. For the universe as a whole and for each being, God has a purpose; and He has made provision that each being should fulfill His purpose. This overruling provision which God has made, that His plan be not stultified or any way frustrated, is His Providence. The universe is not crashing toward a chaos, for it would not have been consonant with God's all-wisdom and all-knowledge to bring something into existence which would escape His control and by its own aimlessness mock Him rather than mirror Him. The universe is not crashing toward a chaos but growing toward a harmony. All that anything is, all that anything does, has its part in the harmony. Nothing must be left out. Into the harmony are woven the actions of beings who have no choice but to act according to the nature God has given them, and the inweaving of these presents no difficulty to our mind. What does seem difficult is that into the harmony are woven also the acts of beings who can choose, and can choose to act inharmoniously. But God, who rules all things, knows what they will do to wreck the harmony and knows what He will do to turn their discord into concord, so that the harmony is not wrecked. God, says the Portuguese proverb, writes straight with crooked lines.

Nor are we in this to figure God anxiously watching us to see what note we will play wrong and feverishly rushing to play the notes that will harmonize our discord into concord. God does not match the successiveness of our acts by a successiveness in His, so that every wrong act of ours is counteracted by a right act of His. Just as the spirit can dominate every part of the body by not being in space, so God can dominate every part of time by being outside of time. In the objection mentioned on page 16, the opening phrase — "If God knew last Tuesday" — shows unawareness of this. God did *not* know last Tuesday! Tuesday is a period of time and part of the duration in which I act. But God acts in eternity, which has no Tuesdays. God acts where He is: we receive the effects of His acts where we are. He acts in the spacelessness of His immensity and the timelessness of His eternity: we receive the effects of His acts in space and time. He acts in the singleness of His simplicity, and we receive the effect of His action in the multiplicity of our dispersion. We find this hard to comprehend, because we have no direct knowledge of eternity. Like our concept of infinity, our concept of eternity is far stronger and clearer on the side of what it is not than of what it is. Even the smallest extra glimpse of what it is would make a world of difference. After all, we should never have guessed that infinity was Triune; there will be similar fruitful surprises about eternity. Meanwhile the truth stands; God knows all things and provides for all things: we choose, and He lets us choose, but He has His own way of acting upon our choice: and all in a single, timeless operation of wisdom and love.

13. The Testing of Angels and Men

We cannot handle anything intelligently until we know the purpose for which it was made. Without that knowledge we act only blindly upon things. When we are in doubt, there is only one certain way of finding out what things are made *for*, namely, to ask their maker; for the purpose of anything is not in itself but in the mind of the maker. With what purpose did God make material beings, spiritual beings, and beings who are both?

(i) God's purpose for His creatures

Each thing He made to serve Him, and to serve Him by being totally itself. But within this total ordering of everything toward God, there is a division: for, under God, spiritual beings are an end in themselves, matter is not. The earth is made for man, whereas man is not similarly made for the angels, but men and angels alike for God only: they can serve one another, but it is not the service of a means to an end but reciprocal service of the children of one father: the immortal beings have no end but God Himself.

The subordination of the earth to man is stated by God at man's creation: "Increase and multiply, and fill the earth, and subdue it, and rule over the fishes of the sea, and the fowls of the air, and all living creatures that move upon the earth." Thus man's domination of the animals is not simply a tyranny, based upon man's misuse of the superior power that his intellect gives him. It is a fulfillment of God's plan for animals and men. It is a natural consequence of this domination that Adam was given by God the charge of naming the animals: "And the Lord God having formed out of the ground all the beasts of the earth, and all the fowls of the air, brought them to Adam to see what he would call them: for whatsoever Adam called any living creature the same is its name." To our modern taste there seems something grotesque about all this: but we have imported the grotesqueness into it ourselves. Clearly it would be a comical sight to see a modern man on Clapham Common, say, summoning the animals and naming them at his whim with this or that meaningless collection of sounds. Substitute a court of Solomon's temple for Clapham Common, and the Genesis writer might have found it equally comic. But that, I think, is not the point here. This naming matter he saw as important. He chose to tell it in terms of the garden-metaphor, into which he had cast the whole of his insight on sin at the beginning of the human race.

For us, a name has come to be little more than a label attached for convenience of reference; a number would do as well. But in Scripture, "name" is of enormous importance; it is the being's whole reality as uttered. One of the names for God Himself is simply "the Name". Given all this—the picture of the man naming the animals was a way of saying what the "hymn of creation" was to say: "Man was given dominion over every living thing." The whole point of the naming episode was the inferiority of the animals to man. For a companion, man needed an equal; and we hear God say, "I will make him a companion of his own kind."

(ii) Spirits meant for the Beatific Vision

For angels and men the only purpose could be the most perfect possible relation with God. Had we no revelation from God Himself as to the purpose for which He made them, we might at least hazard a guess; that as the highest powers of their nature are knowledge and love, it must be their destiny to come to know God and love God to the very limit of their power, using no element of energy upon anything that would distract them from this knowing and loving. Again considering their nature, we might hazard the further guess that this knowing of God would be by way of a richer and richer concept of Him, and that their love of God would bear a proportion to their growing knowledge. Such a natural destiny would be a thing of unbelievable splendor; yet that is not their destiny, but something more splendid still. No examination of the nature of angels and men would tell us what this more splendid destiny is; we can know it only from the word of God. God has told us that the destiny alike of men and angels is to see Himself, the Uncreated Splendor, face to face, not by means of any concept however rich, but directly—God Himself taking the place in the intellect of the idea of Himself, so that between the spirit of angel or of man and God, nothing whatever shall intervene, not the purest concept, not anything at all. This is the Beatific Vision, the seeing that is our bliss. This is the end for which God has destined spiritual beings: it is an end for which their natural powers are totally inadequate— which is why we could not discover it for ourselves by examining those natural powers. Angels and men alike need to have ingrafted into them by God powers enabling them to achieve this end which their natural powers could not achieve.

Life, we have seen, is a principle of operation. Natural life is the principle by which we carry out the kind of operations that go with the kind of beings we are.

The principle which is to enable us to operate above our nature is called *supernatural life.* The object of this super-natural life is the Beatific Vision, the direct gaze upon God. Without it we cannot have the Beatific Vision. We lack the power.

(iii) Testing of the angels

But in God's design, neither angels nor men were to have the Beatific Vision without a previous testing. Consider the angels first. God created them in the perfection of their nature as pure spirits. Further, He endowed them with the supernatural life of which we have just spoken. But they were not as yet admitted to the Beatific Vision. They must first be tested. What the testing was, we do not know; but we know that some of them failed in the test, and we know too that they failed through some form of self-assertion, assertion of self against God. In the Book of Job we read: "In His angels He found wickedness" (Job 4:18). Further, we know that one of these rebellious angels was the leader of the rest. We find such phrases as the "Devil and his angels" (e.g., Mt 25:41) and "the Dragon and his angels" (Rev 12:7). This chief of rebellious angels is most commonly called Satan, a Hebrew word meaning adversary or accuser, which is roughly the meaning also of the Greek word *Diabolos,* from which our word "Devil" comes. He is worth closer study.

Strictly speaking there is one Devil: the rest are demons: he is *princeps daemoniorum* (Mt 9:34). It is usually held that the rebellion was his affair primarily: he seduced the rest. The words Satan, Diabolos, Devil express his nature: he is the enemy. What is his name? We say that he was Lucifer, the light-bearer, before his fall, though he is not called by that name in Scripture. Scripture has a handful of names for a devil of great power, and it is commonly thought that they are all his — the rest remain a nameless multitude of wickedness. He is Asmodeus, the murderous fiend of the Book of Tobias (3:8); he is Beelzebub, Lord of Flies, in the Gospels; he is Belial, the one without use or profit (2 Cor 6:15); he is Apollyon, that is, the exterminator (Rev 9:11).

Our Lord describes him (Jn 8:44): "He, from the first, was a murderer; and as for truth, he has never taken his stand upon that; there is no truth in him. When he utters falsehood, he is only uttering what is natural to him; he is all false and it is he who gave falsehood its birth" — or in the Douay Version, "He is a liar and the father of lies." If Christians can be found to ignore the other angels, it seems an excess of rashness to ignore this one.

But to return to their great rebellion. We have seen that their sin was some form of self-assertion. It may be worth pausing at this first and most catastrophic of all sins to consider the nature of sin. In angels or men, sin is always an effort to gain something against the will of God. Thus for angels and men sin is essentially ludicrous. All alike are made by God of nothing; all alike are held in existence by nothing save the continuing will of God to hold them so. To think that we can gain anything by hacking or biting or furtively nibbling at the Will which alone holds us in existence at all is a kind of incredible folly. It is precisely because apart from God we should be nothing that Pride is the worst of all sins, for it is the direct assertion of self as against God. It is sin in its nakedness: all other sins are sin dressed up a little. Other sins are an effort to *gain* something against the will of God; pride is the claim to *be* something apart from the will of God.

I have said that sin is incredible folly. But it is made to look credible by the ease and frequency with which we do it. Sin is madness, but it is possible. Why? There is a profound mystery here: a mystery at its very darkest when we ask how pure spirits could have been guilty of a folly so monstrous, but still a mystery even when any one of us considers his own most recent effort to gain something against God's will. The rebellious angels must have known that it was madness, yet they did it: but after all, any instructed Catholic knows that it is madness, yet he does it. Sin, in fact, is not simply a matter of knowledge, mysterious as knowledge is; it is a matter of that far more mysterious thing, will, at the very ultimate point of its mysteriousness, its freedom of choice. The will, if it wants intensely enough, can ignore the intellect's information and go for what it wants. Even if the intellect knows that the thing will bring disaster, the will can choose it; even if it knows that the thing cannot be had at all, the will can still fix itself upon it. Not even by the intellect is the will coerced. Created beings are the resultant of infinite power working upon nothingness, and they are free to fix their choice anywhere between those two extremes. To choose anything at all as apart from God is quite literally to choose nothingness, for apart from God everything *is* nothing. To choose God is to choose the infinite. Either way, whether we choose nothing or the infinite, we cannot *be* either, but we can possess either. We are free to choose.

The word *freedom* may easily mislead for it has two meanings, or perhaps three. In its first and most rudimentary sense it is the absence of coercion: when we say that the will is free, we mean that we make our choices uncoerced: we choose what we like. This does not mean, of course, that the will has no proper object of its action: as the object of sight is color, so the object of the will is the good. Unless a thing is seen by us as good in *some* sense, we cannot choose it at all. But even a thing that we see as good, we *need* not choose. And of two alternatives seen as good, we can choose which we will. It is not simply a matter of a passive will tugged by conflicting attractions and yielding of inescapable necessity to the stronger tug. It is the will which gives the victory to one tug or the other: the will is not coerced by the objects of its desire.

So much our own experience of choosing tells us. But the question instantly arises: how can our freedom to choose be reconciled with the omnipotence of God? If we are really free, then there is something that escapes the power of God. That created things cannot coerce our will is one thing: but that God cannot is quite another. The problem is deeply mysterious because there are too many elements in it that do not lie under our gaze. One feels toward a reconciliation, or, perhaps better, one fumbles in the direction where the reconciliation may prove to be: but that is all. We are free: but clearly there is a proportion between the "free" and the "we": our freedom must have as much reality as we, but not more. Our being is real but contingent, created of nothing: it is therefore no limitation to the infinity of God's *Being* that we lie outside it. It may be, perhaps, that just as our being does not limit God's infinite Being, so our freedom does not limit God's infinite Power. In any event, the *fact* of our freedom is certain: God has said it. He has told us of the alternatives of right and wrong, urged us to do right, warned us against doing wrong, promised reward for the one, threatened punishment for the other: told us in a hundred ways that we are responsible for our choices. He who made us makes clear that He made us free to choose.

But freedom to choose does not mean freedom to choose the consequences of our choice, for we are living in a universe, not a chaos: we can choose to do this or that, but the consequences of that choice will be governed by the laws of the universe in which we are. It is only if we use our freedom of choice—that is, our freedom to choose without coercion—to make choices in harmony with the reality of things—in harmony with what God is, with what we are, and with what all other things are—that we achieve freedom in its second sense, namely, fullness of being, the act of being all that by nature we are, and doing all that by nature we are meant to do. And at this second level of freedom, we shall find that choice without coercion which was part of our initial equipment, but now at a level of development which makes the rudimentary thing almost infinitesimal by comparison.

Summarizing all this: we can choose what we want, and within our own limits, what we shall do; but we cannot choose the consequences of what we do, nor can we prevent any action of ours—even our rebellion—from being used by God to His glory; we can only prevent its being used for our glory too. "Them that glorify me I shall glorify: but they that despise me shall be ignoble" (1 Sam 2:30).

All this, as we have seen, applies to angels and to humans.

Let us return to the sin of the angels. They had chosen self as distinct from God: so far they were free, that is, their choice was not coerced. But they had collided with reality. And the result could only be tragedy to them. St. Peter tells us starkly: "God spared not the angels who sinned" (2 Pet 2:4). There are references in Scripture to a battle in heaven, not between the rebellious angels and God but between the rebellious angels and the loyal. Thus we find in the last book of the New Testament, the Book of Apocalypse or Revelation (12:7): "Fierce war broke out in heaven, where Michael and his angels fought against the dragon. The dragon and his angels fought on their part, but could not win the day, or stand their ground in heaven any longer." It would seem that St. John here has in mind the continuing struggle between good and evil, but it is hard to think that he has not in his mind the first battle in that long campaign. What we know with certainty is that Satan and his angels were cast out of heaven into hell. Our Lord warns human sinners that their ultimate place may be "that eternal fire which has been prepared for the devil and his angels" (Mt 25:41).

What was their state in hell? They had lost grace "by pride", says St. Ambrose; their nature was badly damaged, particularly in the will: "the Devil and the other demons were created good in nature by God, but by their own act they became evil" (Decree *Firmiter,* Fourth Council of Lateran). Of their own choice they had demanded independence of God, a life without God. Faced with a choice between God and self, they had opted for self: love of self grown monstrous turned them to hatred of God, and in this hatred of God their wills were now set so that they would not change. Totally without God they could not be, if they were to continue in existence at all; but by their own choice they were to have, from now on forever, nothing of God but His presence sustaining them in being. They would not accept anything else He might do for them.

Both ways, the result could only be anguish. Angels, like human beings, are made by God and made for God: their very being is interwoven of needs which only God can satisfy. The fallen angels refused the satisfaction, because that would have meant turning to God, whom they hated; so that they were left to the torment of needs which could not be satisfied. Grasp that in their new state, not merely the major need of created things, but even the need for God, could not be satisfied. No need could be satisfied. They could not make any sort of solace for one another—in their new destitution they had nothing to give one another, nor perhaps any will to give. Torn away from God, they were torn away from one another; torn away from the love of God, the very source of love was dried up in themselves. Whatever positive values were still in them were there by the continuing action of God: hating God, they could only hate one another. It may be fanciful to see a hint of this in the plea the demons made (Luke 8:31), when Our Lord cast them back to hell, but let them instead go into a herd of swine—as though any sort of occupation upon earth was better than the company of their mightier fellows at home. But there is nothing fanciful in the total domination of their will by hatred, and the domination of all lesser hatreds by hatred of God. In their continuing hatred of God, they were to continue their warfare against good; having lost their battle with the other angels, they were to continue to fight against the souls of men, and in that warfare they were to have victories, but such victories could only be minute satisfactions in an abyss of unsatisfaction.

But for the angels who triumphed in the test, there was the Beatific Vision: they "behold the face of my heavenly Father continually" (Mt 18:10). Now, gazing forever upon the unveiled face of God, their wills were united to His in love so utterly, that sin was impossible to them: uncoerced, in the intensity of their love, they could will only what God willed. And in that life they were fully themselves, every power in fullest operation, utterly fulfilled. That is freedom.

(iv) Natural and supernatural equipment of Adam

Man, too, was intended by God for the Beatific Vision, and he, too, was to have his probation. But whereas the proving of the angels was a test for each separate angel, for the proving of man the test was by a representative man, the first man from whom all others come. There is an obvious fittingness in this. Angels, as we have seen, do not procreate. Being pure spirits, each has to be created separately as to his totality; there is no element in them that is not the direct creation of God, so that there is no organic connection between one angel and another. They are not related to each other in anything comparable to the family relationships of human beings. In that sense there is a human race but no angelic race. In that sense again there could be a representative man but not a representative angel.

We shall consider the story of man's testing, as the main line of Christian theology has developed it. The first man had, what no animal has, a spiritual soul. Whatever prehistory his body may have had, his soul was a new reality, a direct creation of God, perfect in its own finite kind, and capable with God's aid of living in harmony with Him. The body was ruled by the soul and accepted the soul's rule without rebellion. Within the soul, reason ruled, and the first law of reason, which is acceptance of the will of God. As well as this total integrity, Adam had certain other perfections which, like it, we can only call preternatural. He did not have to find out everything for himself, by experience and meditation upon experience and the comparison of his own experience with other people's. He began with an initial equipment of knowledge, simply given to him by God. Contained in this knowledge was all that he needed in order to live intelligently according to the plan God had for him, and all that he needed in order to fulfill his function as ruler of the material universe. There is no suggestion in all this that, starting out in this universe with no men before him, he had from God all the knowledge that he needed.

He had another gift, or rather two other gifts, which we may think of as utterly preternatural in relation to what man has become, yet almost natural according to man's first sinlessness. The first is what theologians call impassibility: the universe, made for the service of men, literally *could* not harm him. God would not allow it. Man was lord of the world, until he threw away his dominion.

The other gift was immortality. Death was not in God's original design. "God made not death, neither hath he pleasure in the destruction of the living" (Wis 1:13). In the perfection He had planned for man, man was not to suffer the separation of soul and body, which comes to us when the body is damaged to such a point by accident or the mere wear and tear of living that it can no longer respond to the animating power of the soul, and so disintegrates and is no more a human body. In one sense, death is natural because the body has parts and therefore can fall apart; but in another sense, we feel it as an unnatural interruption of man's existence. His immortal destiny is to be forever soul and body, so why the temporary separation? God would allow no accident to fall upon unfallen man; and the sinless soul in its first perfection was quite strong enough to supply for any wear and tear of the body in a world which could not harm man. But unfallen man was given powers of another, greater sort. Genesis shows him in close intimacy with

God. After Christ, we see more clearly what that intimacy could have meant.

This paragraph and the three that follow must be read with the closest attention. The doctrine they contain is essential to the understanding of the purpose of our existence, and therefore to the intelligent living of our lives. As we have seen, God intended that man should come to the Beatific Vision, the direct gaze upon Himself. We have seen likewise that this was beyond the powers of man's nature. Man's intellect is made to know things by dint of ideas, and by its natural powers it has no other way of knowing. When I say that I know someone, I mean that in my mind there is an idea of him and a mental picture of him. As I get to know him better, the mental picture gets a little clearer and the idea gets enormously fuller and richer. But the person himself is never in my mind, save by way of the idea. That is the kind of knowing proper to man's intellect—to know things not directly but by means of an idea. But our destiny is to know God directly, with no idea, however perfect, aiding or intervening. The intellect will be in direct and conscious contact with God Himself. Since by nature direct knowledge is impossible to us, we must receive in our soul new powers to enable us thus to act above our nature, and for this God gives us, as He gave the angels, supernatural life.

Grasp with all possible clearness that this supernatural life is not a development of our natural powers; it is something over and above, something that our nature could never grow to, something that it can receive only as a direct gift from God. The gulf between non-living and living is not so great as the gulf between natural life and supernatural. The purpose of this supernatural life, as we have seen, is that in heaven we may see God directly. But we do not wait until then to receive the supernatural life. It is given to man in this life, and what man does with it is the primary story of his life. Everything else is incidental, on the fringe, of no permanent importance. When we come to die we are judged by the answer to one question—whether we have the supernatural life in our soul. If we have, then to heaven we shall surely go, for the supernatural life is the power to live the life of heaven. If we have not, then we cannot possibly go to heaven, for we could not live there when we got there. Grasp clearly that the supernatural life, which we call also sanctifying grace, is not simply a passport to heaven: it is the power to live in heaven.

But if we are given the supernatural life here upon earth, it does not here upon earth have its full effect of enabling us to see God directly. If it did, our probation would be over. But it has vast effects in the soul all the same, enabling the soul to do things that by nature it could not do. For a full discussion of the operation of sanctifying grace in the soul, we must wait until the third section of this book. Here we can state it in summary. By the gift of faith, the intellect is given a new way of attaining and holding truth, upon the word of God: by the gifts of charity and hope, the will is given a new mode of loving God and effectively desiring to be with Him. These three are called the theological virtues, because their direct object is God—we believe in God, we hope in God, we love God. In addition, our souls are given what are called the moral virtues—prudence, justice, temperance, and fortitude—by which man is helped to handle the things of this created universe for the salvation of his soul. Further still, there are the gifts of the Holy Spirit. Thus supernaturally endowed, we can act so as to merit the supernatural reward.

And by this supernatural endowment we are raised from being merely creatures of God to being children of God. For the power to see God as He is is a power which by nature belongs to God alone. Thus by the supernatural life we are being given a share, a created share certainly, in God's own life. Merely as created spirits we are in the likeness of God; but this natural likeness is as nothing to the supernatural likeness whereby, enabled to do what belongs to the nature of God, we are raised to such a likeness of His nature as joins children to their father.

God created Adam with this gift too. There was no first moment, however short, in which Adam existed simply as the perfect natural man. From the first moment of his creation until his fall, Adam had two lives in him, the natural life and the supernatural life. He dominated the world: he was subject only to God. And in him the whole human race was tested. The first member of the human race to come from him was Eve—the word is connected with "life" or "living"—and she too had the same gifts.

There is much in their life in this first stage upon which we can only speculate, as did the Genesis writer. It is too far removed from anything we have experienced. But on the side of their relations with God, we get some light. Their first duty, and also in that happy unfallen state their supreme pleasure, was prayer, both in the wider sense of the direction of the whole of life to God, and in the special sense of conversing with God, talking to Him and listening to Him. That anyone, knowing that God both is and is everywhere, should not talk to Him is a kind of ridiculousness. There is no one else in whose company we so intimately and continuously are; and never to address Him is plainly funny—reminiscent of W. S. Gilbert's poem about the two Englishmen cast up on a desert island who would not speak to each other because they had not been introduced.

But if it is natural for us, as for Adam, to talk to God, what kind of thing would one say? Obviously there is the acknowledgment of God's glory by adoration and love; and the acknowledgment of our obligations to God by thanksgiving; and, because God wishes it so, there is the asking for what we want. All this was in Adam's prayer as it should be in ours. But at first his prayer lacked what should be the most poignant element in ours, sorrow for sin.

Again, his prayer (like ours) would be an offering of the whole of himself to God, not of his soul only but of soul and body, too. It would be a stunting of prayer to find nothing for the body to do. But we have not seen the whole of man's approach to God, in seeing it as the offering of the whole of himself, soul and body. There is the offering of other things, too, by way of sacrifice, which is the setting apart and consecrating to God of some part of all that He has given us by way of acknowledgment that He has given us all; and there is the offering *along with others,* by way of prayer and sacrifice in common. God gave Eve to Adam because it is not good for man to be alone. It is not indeed in the nature of man to be an isolated unit all by himself. By his needs and by his powers he is bound up with others. This element too in his nature must be offered to God. The excuse a modern man gives for staying away from Church—that he finds that he prays better alone— misses the point. What he is doing is refusing to join with his fellow men in the worship of God. That is to say, he is leaving the social element in his nature unoffered to God. Adam and Eve would have had their private prayers to God, but they would have talked to Him together too.

It is tempting to speculate upon other elements in this paradisal life and upon what it would have meant for the generations to follow if they had remained faithful and triumphed in their testing. But it would be no more than speculation. What matters is that they began with all that was needed to reach their goal, and they threw it away.

(v) The testing of man

For remember that this first period of human life, like the first period of angelic life, was one of probation, of testing. What the test was for the angels, we do not know; but we know that it was a personal individual testing, one which each angel had to meet for himself; and that some of them failed in the test. Of the testing of man, we know something more, though there is obscurity about it; but as we have seen, there was this difference between the testing of men and of angels, that the testing of the human race was not in each of us individually, but in the representative man from whom we are all sprung.

As I say, we know something about the testing of Adam, or rather of the human race in Adam. God made Adam lord of the world, but there was a condition attached. In the phrase of Genesis, which may be interpreted literally or may have a figurative meaning but in either event states something that did really happen—"The Lord God brought forth of the ground all manner of trees fair to behold and pleasant to eat of; the Tree of Life also in the midst of Paradise: and the Tree of Knowledge of Good and Evil . . . and he commanded him, saying: Of every tree of Paradise thou shalt eat: but of the Tree of Knowledge of Good and Evil, thou shalt not eat for in what day soever thou shalt eat of it, thou shalt die the death."

Now all that this means, we cannot clearly know. If the Tree of Knowledge of Good and Evil literally means a tree, at least it is a tree unknown to our botanists: the trees we know do not bear fruit of such profound intellectual and spiritual consequences. Certainly we have no reason to figure it as an appletree, nor its fruits as apples. The phrase is profoundly mysterious: therefore the condition God set for Adam's continuation in happiness must also be mysterious.

How long Adam and Eve remained in union with God, the

Genesis writer did not know and did not pretend to know. Was it so much as one day? He does not say. All he says is that the Serpent tempted Eve to eat of the fruit, promising that the result would not be death but that their eyes should be opened and they should be as gods, knowing good and evil. Eve ate of the fruit and gave to her husband, who ate too. They had failed in the test. They had sinned against God; and their sin was some form of assertion of self as against God: "they should be as gods", the Serpent had said, perhaps in wry mockery of his own futile dream. Like the rebellious angels, they had been free to choose and had chosen, but had not been free to choose the consequences of their choice. The consequences were calamitous for themselves and for the human race, at that moment and until the end of time: the consequences will not cease in the next life. We shall not understand what has happened to mankind since, what is happening now, even within our own selves, unless we grasp very clearly just what resulted from the Fall of man in Adam.

14. The Fall of Man

The immediate effect of Adam's sin, as stated in Genesis, is surprising enough. Whereas before the Fall "they were both naked, to wit, Adam and his wife: and were not ashamed", now, instantly upon their eating they were aware of each other's nakedness and proceeded to fashion themselves some sort of clothing. And as they could no longer look upon each other untroubled, so they could no longer face God without fear. "Adam and his wife hid themselves from the face of the Lord God, amidst the trees of Paradise." Nor was their fear without reason.

To Eve, God said: "I will multiply thy sorrows, and thy conceptions. In sorrow shalt thou bring forth children, and thou shalt be under thy husband's power, and he shall have dominion over thee."

To Adam, He said: "Cursed is the earth in thy work: with labor and toil shalt thou eat thereof all the days of thy life. Thorns and thistles shall it bring forth to thee, and thou shalt eat the herbs of the earth. In the sweat of thy face shalt thou eat bread till thou return to the earth, out of which thou wast taken: for dust thou art and into dust thou shalt return."

The rest of the story is in a couple of sentences: "And the Lord God sent him out of the Paradise of pleasure, to till the earth from which he was taken. And he cast out Adam; and placed before the Paradise of pleasure cherubim, and a flaming sword, turning every way, to keep the way of the tree of life."

(i) Loss of grace, damage to nature

Upon the story of the Fall of man set out with such appalling brevity in Genesis, mankind has had a long time to meditate; Christ himself came to give us a clearer knowledge of what was involved in it, and for two thousand years His Church has been thinking upon it in the light of His revelation. In the remainder of this chapter an attempt will be made to summarize the Church's teaching.

In giving Adam the order not to eat of the fruit of this one tree, God had told Adam that to eat of it would mean death. But Adam, as we remember, had two lives in him—the natural

life of body and soul by which he was a man, and the supernatural life of sanctifying grace by which he was a son of God
and might one day look upon the living reality of God in
Heaven. To each of these lives corresponded a death, and by
his sin Adam fell under both.

Consider first the death which was the loss of the supernatural life. His soul had possessed sanctifying grace, and with it
faith, hope, and charity, the moral virtues of justice, prudence,
temperance, and fortitude, and an extraordinary wealth of
God's gifts besides. But the key to supernatural life, as to all
life, is love. The vivifying element in sanctifying grace is
charity, which is the love of God. Adam, setting his own will
against God's, in that very fact annihilated love, thus lost the
living principle in sanctifying grace, was supernaturally dead.
From his soul had gone the power whose full effect was to have
been the direct vision of God.

Thus he was left with natural life only, whereas before he
had had both supernatural and natural life. But the natural life
he was left with was not as it had been before. In losing the
right relation of his own person to God by rebellion, he had
lost his original integrity, the right relation of body and soul,
and the harmonious working of the powers of the soul with
one another; he was punished too by the withdrawal of freedom from suffering and death, gifts which in any event would
have sat oddly upon a nature as disordered as his now was.
Death had come upon man, and it had come as a penalty for
sin; for though by the material element in his nature man is
liable to death, yet if man had not sinned God would have
stood between him and that liability.

Let us look more closely at the damage within his nature.
The soul had ruled the body while the soul preserved its right
relation of loving obedience to the Infinite Source of all life.
But the soul in rebellion against its God had quite literally lost

its rights and found the body rebellious against it. The soul's various powers had maintained harmony because all alike were directed toward God as their supreme end; but having turned aside from God, they no longer had any one end to unify them and hold them in harmony, and each must pursue its own devices, one seeking its satisfaction in one direction, one in another. So that the soul was faced at once with the rebellion of the body, and with warfare within its own powers. The splendor was most miserably and thoroughly wrecked. Adam had to struggle, as we all since have to struggle, against the insubordination of the body and a wavering in the soul's direction. In two ways Adam first and we after him are most obviously afflicted in consequence. We find it nearly impossible to control our passions. Upon these matters even one who does not believe mankind fell in Adam must still see that something has gone appallingly wrong with human nature: if man was created by God, then he could not have been created like this! If we did not know that man had fallen in Adam, we should surely know from observation that he had suffered some sort of fall.

Of the imagination and the undue place it takes in affairs which should be exclusively of the intellect or the will, we have already spoken at some length in the first part of this book. Imagination by itself is simply a picture-making power, of real utility to the intellect. As a result of the derangement of man's nature produced by the Fall, imagination has passed far beyond the condition of a useful servant. For about nine-tenths of our living activities, imagination practically runs the whole show. It might be well at this point to reread Chapter 2, where this particular disorder is treated at length.

Of the passions and the emotional life generally, we can do no more than indicate the main trouble caused by the Fall, leaving every person to document the outline from his or her own experience. That man should have passions is natural: what is tragic is that they should escape the domination of his mind. Before the Fall they did not. Of this we have already had one clear instance. Before the Fall, Adam and his wife were naked, and not perturbed by the fact. They had already been given God's blessing that they were to increase and multiply and fill the earth; they had had the Revelation of God that the relation of husband and wife was to be even closer than that of parents and children. They had sexual passion, but it was not their master. They could summon it up at will, use it and enjoy it and return to tranquility. Sexual union was not a matter of frenzied and inescapable urgency. But with the Fall, the passions passed out of control of will and intellect: from now on they were to harry man perpetually. We have seen that Adam and Eve's first recorded action after their sin was to perceive their nakedness. Their first recorded action after being cast out of Paradise was sexual intercourse: "Adam knew Eve his wife: who conceived and brought forth Cain"—the first murderer was the first fruit of sexual passion uncontrolled. In their paradisal state they would have had the sexual intercourse when they wanted it: now they must have it when it insists.

Adam, of course, was not bound to remain as low as he had fallen. He was still a man; he was still free to make choice of worse or better, still free, in fact, to place his love anywhere between nothingness and God Himself. He had lost his innocence but not his memory. What he knew of God before the Fall he still knew after it. Knowing God's goodness, he still had motive for repentance: and any natural movement in that direction would not have been hindered by his enormous awareness that his sin had not paid. Because he was a man and so had free will, he was not bound to repent, but he was able to repent; and theologians have never doubted that by God's grace he did repent and received the supernatural life again into his soul, though not in its former plenitude — his troubled nature was not capable of that. If he had not thus received the supernatural life and died with it, he could not have entered heaven: for, as we have seen and cannot too often remind ourselves, the supernatural life is the power to live in heaven.

But the restoration of the supernatural life did not of itself heal the damage in his nature. We may here use a somewhat crude comparison. If a jug filled with cream falls from a high shelf, there will be two results: the jug will be cracked, the cream will be spilled. Provided the jug has not been smashed to pieces, the cream can be poured back into it: but this will not heal the crack. The comparison is admittedly a crude one, and will need to be refined and corrected later, because the supernatural life, here figured by the cream, can have very profound effects on our nature. But in a general way it remains true that the damage done to our nature has to be healed by an immense striving within our nature itself. So that Adam, though he regained some measure of sanctifying grace, still had the warfare of body against soul, the warfare of the soul's powers among themselves, the swollen power of imagination, the clouding of the intellect and the distorting of the will by passion, the ever-present possibility of falling again into sin.

(ii) Broken relation between man and God

The third effect of the Fall he could do nothing about at all, namely, the broken relation between mankind and God. Man had been at one with God. He was no longer at one with God. There was a breach between God and the human race, and this was the most serious result of sin at its origin. Oddly enough, it is almost invariably overlooked, because we have lost the habit of thinking of the human race. We concentrate upon

individuals, specially upon ourselves; then upon others according to their closeness to us, our family or our nation; we may
even say that our affections embrace all living men, though
our sense of oneness with them can hardly be very strong. But
we have no natural and spontaneous response to the concept of
the human race itself—not only all men now living but all men
who have ever lived or ever will live. It is a defect in us that we
find the human race as a whole too large to love effectively or
even realize. It is because of this defect that so many find the
notion of the whole race being tested in one man improbable
and almost grotesque. But it would be strange if God, who is
equally the creator of all men, to whom no man is more
immediately present than any other, to whom no idea is too
big, did not see the race as a whole and treat it so; and it is at
once an enlargement of our limitedness and a strengthening of
our own relation with all human beings to see Him do it. In
the story of the first dealing of God with man, that is what we
see.

Let us look at it more closely. As a beginning we should be
clear about what was involved in the original relation of
oneness between God and our race. He had conferred upon us
supernatural life, which, as we have seen, lifts us from mere
creatures into sons of God. The gift was to Adam, but to
Adam as head of the race, and so far the whole race seen by
God as incorporated in him. The race of man stood in the
relation of a son to God; had that relation remained unbroken,
we should all have received from God the same supernatural
life merely by being members of a race that had it, we should
have been sons of God individually because our race stood in
the relation of sonship. But by Adam's act the relation was
broken. The human race was put to the test in Adam; Adam
failed to pass the test. He sinned. And in that act the human
race became a fallen race, a race no longer at one with God;

a race to which heaven was closed. The race had been at one with God, as a son with his father: now it stood facing God as a servant his lord. There was a breach between.

It is held that Adam, and Eve too, died in a state of sanctifying grace, personally united with God by charity, but members of a race which was no longer at one with Him. And so died many after them. They could not be damned because they had sanctifying grace in their souls; but they could not enter heaven because the race they belonged to was no longer at one with God. The problem for the human race was precisely the restoration of this oneness: it was the problem of at-one-ment which we disguise with the pronunciation "atonement". God knew how He would solve the problem: how the human race might be reunited with Him, how sonship might be restored to it. But until God chose to act, there was nothing that man could do to remake the oneness. It is one of man's unhappier powers that he can destroy what he cannot rebuild: for instance, he can kill another man but cannot restore him to life. So here. Supernatural oneness between man and God is something that only God can make: man could destroy it, but could no more re-make it once destroyed than he could have made it in the first place. Only God could re-make it.

But the re-making was complicated by an element that had not been in the first making—the element of the sin that man had committed. Mankind now was not simply a zero, but a minus; or, to put it another way, mankind was not simply penniless but in debt. Whether or not God chose to exact it, in strict justice something was certainly due from man—in expiation of the sin, in payment of the debt. And by justice I mean not merely avenging justice, punishing an offense, but a just vision of things requiring that a damage to the right order of reality be repaired. "The man who commits sin violates order: sin of its nature is disorder" (1 Jn 3:4). The glory of God had been denied by an act of human nature: the glory of God is the key to reality; its denial makes everything unreal, so that by its own act human nature is set in the way of unreality; some act of human nature at least as definitive in the opposite direction would seem to be required to restore the right order of things.

Thus there was not only the problem of restoring man's broken relationship to God—how to heal the breach—at-one-ment in its original sense; but the problem of expiation—what to do about the sin which had caused the breach—atonement in the word's commoner present sense. It was for God to decide whether expiation must be made. But if it must, how? Nothing that man—Adam, or any other man or humanity as a whole—was now in a position to offer to God in expiation of this first great crime of human nature would suffice, for man himself was too badly damaged to offer any perfect act of reparation: damaged man had nothing but damaged acts to offer. No man could offer even the whole of himself, for man was no longer in total possession of himself; too much of him was beyond his own control. God's love desired the restoration of oneness, of the relation of sonship: but if expiation must first be made, how was expiation possible?

Thus one may muse over the problems that man had set by his sin. But it is only musing, valid enough while we are seeing what man could not do, but only hints and glimpses of probabilities when we try to see what required to be done. There is profit for the mind in speculating as to what God might have done; but it is as nothing to the profit in studying what He did do. In the event, both problems were to find one solution in which love and justice were miraculously fused.

But not yet. And until God Himself remade the oneness, holy men and women could receive the supernatural life, but as a gift personal to themselves, a reward for their love, *not* through the human race; they could die with the supernatural life in their souls, and that meant that they had the power to live the life of heaven; but they must wait until heaven should be once more open to the race to which they belonged.

(iii) Natural effects upon Adam's descendants

Let us consider more closely the personal effect upon Adam's descendants of his Fall. For, as we have seen, we were all involved in it. St. Paul writes (Rom 5:12): "It was through one man that guilt came into the world; and since death came owing to guilt, death was handed on to all mankind by one man." There were two lives in Adam with a death corresponding to each: and we fell under both. Because he sinned, we are all born into this life without the supernatural life, with natural life only: and that natural life is a damaged life, doomed inescapably to break up in death.

Consider these two effects separately. For our natural life, we are dependent by inheritance upon Adam. Our natural life is the life of soul and body, and though our souls are a direct creation of God, yet their relation with our bodies is so close that the variously damaged bodies with which each soul is united at the beginning of each person's life are quite sufficient to ensure for each a damaged nature. We have the same sort of disorder in the elements of our nature that Adam had: a body rebellious against the soul, warfare of the soul's powers against one another, imagination far too powerful, passions and emotions swinging us toward sin. We too must die. Further, we must live in a world that has lost the necessity of obeying us. From Adam onward, man has been fighting for his life and his rights in a universe that no longer acknowledges him as its lord. The greatest conqueror can be brought down to his death by a snake, or more humiliatingly by a microbe. Nor does man treat the animals any better than they treat him. The harmony is wrecked. To man in his perfection, God gave "dominion" over the animals: but when He comes to bless Noah after the Flood, there is a new note: "Let the fear and dread of you be upon all the beasts of the earth, and upon all the fowls of the air, and all that move upon the earth: all the fishes of the sea are delivered into your hand. And everything that moveth and liveth shall be meat for you: even as the green herbs have I delivered them all to you" (Gen 9:1–3).

There remains in the natural order one most mysterious result of Adam's sin. The order of the material universe was damaged by it. God said to Adam: "The earth is cursed in thy work." At the creation, God had looked upon all that He had made and seen that it was very good. But now there was a curse upon it. It was still good, but there was a disorder in it, all the same, which was not part of God's design or the result of material causes only but resulted from Adam's sin. The material universe is so closely interlinked, inter-balanced, that the catastrophe in its highest part spread damage downward through all its parts. We have fallen into the naïve habit of thinking of matter as wholly self-contained, affected only by material causes. But it is created by Spirit, preserved in being by Spirit, wholly under the control of Spirit; and there is no reason to think that what happens to spirit at any level leaves it unaffected. And quite apart from such possible direct effects, the action of man in the perverseness of his will and the darkness of his mind can produce the most appalling destructions of the equilibrium of the material order. We do not know what damage the earth took from Adam's sin, but there is *some* new element of perversity in it as a result. This too Christ will make good (Rom 8:22).

(iv) Original sin and man's helplessness

So much, though it is sketchy enough, for the natural effects upon us of Adam's sin. The supernatural effect is immeasurably more serious. We are born without the supernatural life—not because Adam, having lost it, could not transmit to us what he did not have himself (as we have seen, Adam almost certainly regained it for himself). The supernatural life is not transmitted by inheritance as our bodies are. It is a free gift of God. But God had decreed that it should be hereditary in this other sense, that it should accompany the nature that human beings were to inherit from Adam, if Adam had not sinned. We are born without it, not because Adam did not have it to give to us, but because the condition on which God would have given it to us at the first moment of our existence was that Adam should not fail; and he failed.

Here we come to one of the more mysterious of the doctrines that treat directly of man, the doctrine of Original Sin, which is bound up with the truth that Adam's sin involved the whole race. In some profoundly dark way Adam's sin is in his descendants as real sin: they are not only affected by the results of his sin, they are somehow involved in the guilt of it: "a multitude, through one man's disobedience, became guilty" (Rom 5:19).

It is in us not as an actual sin, a personal sin, as it was in Adam, who actually committed it, but as a habitual sin, a state of unrighteousness, which most theologians equate with the absence of the supernatural life, which, had Adam not sinned, would have been there. Thus the Council of Trent says that "unrighteousness follows natural birth precisely as righteousness follows regeneration"—in other words, we are born into unrighteousness (absence of sanctifying grace) just as we should have been born into sanctifying grace but for Adam's sin, just as (to anticipate things to come) we are reborn into sanctifying grace by baptism.

But wherein lies our guilt? That this privation of grace should be in us as an effect of sin, we can see. But how is it sin? It is, as we have seen, not a personal sin. But if it is not personal, how is it ours? Because of that other element in us, our nature. It was a state of sinfulness in Adam's nature, and Adam's nature was the source of our nature. Theologians teach that it is transmitted by the natural way of sexual generation: it comes to us because we are "ex semine Adae", of Adam's seed. If we could see more clearly into the relation of person and nature within ourselves, and into the relation of each man's nature with the nature of those through whom and ultimately from whom it comes to him, there would be no mystery. Lacking that clear vision, we find it darkly mysterious. To me it seems that the twelfth-century writer Odo of Cambrai came very close to the limit of lucidity, in his work *De Peccato Originali* (Migne, P.L. 160:1085):

"The sin wherewith we sinned in Adam is natural in me, personal in Adam. In Adam it is graver, in me less grave; for in him I sinned not as who I am but as what I am. It was not I that sinned in him, but what I am; I sinned in him as man, not as Odo; as substance, not as person. Because the substance does not exist save in the person, the sin of the substance is the sin of the person, yet not personal. That sin is personal which I commit as who I am, not as what I am; by which I sin as Odo, not as man; by which I sin as person, not as nature."

Our first reaction is quite likely to be a sense that we are being treated unfairly in thus being started off in life with a damaged nature and with no supernatural life at all, because of something done by someone else unmeasured ages ago. The unbeliever finds it matter for mockery—Eve, he says, ate the apple; we get the stomach-ache—and even the believer can be troubled by a seeming want of fairness in God. But if such a reaction is spontaneous, it should not survive a little reflection. The accusation of unfairness is particularly fragile. We have no *right* to supernatural life at all, because as human beings our nature is fully constituted without it; if God chooses to give it to us, it is an entirely free gift on His part, a gift, therefore, that He can give or withhold or give conditionally entirely as He pleases, with no question of right upon our part arising. As to our nature, we and all our ancestors owe it to Adam, and we cannot complain if he had only a damaged nature to transmit to us: it is still better than no nature at all. We had done nothing to earn a nature. Before we existed we were not entitled even to human nature; once we exist we are not entitled to a supernature. We cannot say that we have earned and been cheated out of a better nature than we were conceived with: we had not earned any nature at all, and there was nothing to cheat us out of.

As I have said, the accusation of unfairness will not stand a moment's consideration. But even the complaint at our being thus bound up with Adam's disaster shows a failure to grasp the organic solidarity of the human race. We are not isolated units, but even in the natural order members of one thing: it would be no advantage to us to be separated out, cut off, from the consequences of other men's ill deeds, but cut off, too, from a sharing in the fruits of other men's virtues: "One man", so St. Paul writes to the Romans (5:18), "commits a fault, and it brings condemnation upon all; one man makes amends, and it brings to all justification, that is, life. A multitude will become acceptable to God through one man's obedience, just as a multitude, through one man's disobedience, became guilty." The same solidarity of the race by which we receive the effects of Adam's defeat enables us to receive the fruits of Christ's victory. But of that, more, much more, later.

(v) The Devil's part

There remains to consider one of the personages taking part in the tragedy of the Fall — the Devil. The account in Genesis tells us that Eve was tempted by the serpent. It tells us no more about the tempter than that. It does not say that it was the Devil. That it was no ordinary serpent as known to zoology we understand as clearly as that the tree of the Knowledge of Good and Evil was no ordinary tree as known to botany. So much we shall scarcely need to be told. If we did not guess for ourselves that it was the Devil, we should find it in later passages of Scripture. In the Book of Wisdom we read, "God created man incorruptible, and to the image of his own likeness he made him. But, by the envy of the devil, death came into the world" (2:23–24); and in the Apocalypse we read of "that old serpent, who is called the devil and Satan, who seduceth the whole world" (12:9).

From now onward the Devil is to play a continuing part in the affairs of men. What he gained by this first and most resounding defeat of man it is hard to say with absolute precision, or any precision. But the general result is only too clear. Man had been established by God as lord of the world, and some sort of lordship passed to his conqueror. Again and again (e.g., Jn 14:30) the Devil is referred to as the Prince of this world. It is obvious enough that he became lord of the world in fact, in the sense that alcohol can become lord of a man; for as an angel he was superior in power to man, and he had found a weakness in man and could play on it with murderous effect. The world had him for its lord much as Scripture speaks of the man whose god is his belly. But did he gain some sort of rights over the world? It is hard to see how he could, for his own action in tempting Adam was sinful, and no rights can be acquired by sin. He could say to Our Lord (Lk 4:6): "The

Kingdoms of this world have been made over to me" and could offer them to Our Lord on a condition; nor does Our Lord say that it is not so. But what exactly does "made over to me" signify? Anyhow the Devil's *power* over fallen humanity was a horrifying fact. Individuals might resist, but the race looked as if it had sold out to the Devil.

Whatever his lordship involved, it is clear that following upon the success of this first effort to tempt man, he continues as tempter and adversary. We find Satan moving King David to make a census of Israel against the command of God; and there are scores of other instances. St. Paul tells us, "Our wrestling is not against flesh and blood; but against Principalities and Powers, against the rulers of the world of this darkness, against the spirits of wickedness in the high places" (Eph 6:12). There is an extraordinarily full working out of this special relation of Satan to the human race in the Book of Job. Satan brings every kind of evil upon Job to try his faith in God: but we are especially told that he could do so only by God's permission. To say that Satan gained the right to tempt mankind by his victory over Adam would be too strong. Satan's action was sinful, and, as has been said, one can gain no rights by sin. But it would seem that God saw a certain fittingness in allowing Satan to tempt man: the human race, in Adam, had chosen to listen to Satan; very well, let them go on listening to Satan. God was there to help them, as He was there to help Adam. All the sins of all men since Adam have followed the pattern of Adam's sin, and make a sort of solidarity in sin between us and him that is a horrid parody of the solidarity in nature. We all have some sort of replica of Adam's experience in this matter. And on the whole our record is not very glorious. Nor is this surprising. If Satan could win a victory so resounding over unfallen man, his task would not necessarily be harder over fallen man. But strife against so powerful an enemy is very maturing to the soul if we stand firm; and this also God may have had in mind in allowing Satan to tempt us.

As we have already indicated, there was to be Atonement. God knew what He would do so that the race of man might return to His friendship: otherwise there would have been no point in giving sanctifying grace to individual men. For the ultimate object of sanctifying grace is to enable men to live the life of heaven; and this they could do only if Heaven were once more to be opened to the race to which they belong. In other words, there was to be for mankind a second chance. The nature of this second chance we shall discuss more thoroughly later; note here that it did not remove the need of testing but involved that each man should be tested individually. That, now, is what man's life upon earth is. And just as Adam's representative testing involved temptation by the Devil, so likewise for our individual testing.

Fundamentally this testing is of the will. The will is free to choose God or to choose self as against God: and this latter choice is seldom a direct choice of self, but develops by way of seeking for happiness according to one's own desires—which may be directed to anything whatever that is—against the will of God. Given that the created order is so full of things capable of attracting us, and our nature so damaged, one might wonder why anything more should be needed to make the test severe. In other words, we can so easily choose some lesser thing by our own momentum, so to speak, that one wonders why the Devil should bother with us. Certain elements in the answer must wait till we come to a more detailed treatment of our own nature, as we have received it damaged and have damaged it further; but there is one element which must be stated here. With every man simply following his own tendency to damage and diminish himself by making this or that choice against the will of God, evil might very well have a carnival, but it would be a somewhat chaotic carnival. It is hard to look upon this world without coming to a sense that evil is not simply chaotic, that there is a drive and a direction in it which suggests a living intelligence coordinating what would otherwise be only scattered and unrelated plunges of the human will—though the uncoercible will of man sets the Devil problems too.

The modern mood, out of touch with the very notion of religion as a statement of the reality of things, will have none of this notion of a personal Devil. It does not deny that evil is abroad: but it prefers to talk of forces and tendencies. In one sense this refusal to see the Devil as a person is a natural piece of wishful thinking: for if there is such a person, he is rather a terrifying person: it is more comfortable to believe that there is no such person: if one has to be terrified in the dark, it is better to be terrified of a tendency than of Someone. But in a profounder sense, the refusal of personality to the Devil is part of the general modern attack upon personality. We have already seen it in operation denying personality to God. Later we shall see it in operation denying personality to man. Why should the Devil be treated any better?

At any rate you must tear out a vast amount of Christianity if you will reduce the Devil to a tendency. From end to end of the story of man the Devil appears as Someone, as a being of intelligence and will. We have said that God knew what He would do to undo the catastrophe of man's Fall. It is not for nothing that the first statement God made of what He would do, He made not to Adam and Eve but to the Devil, and He made it in terms of victory over the Devil: his head was to be crushed.

15. Between the Fall and the Redemption

God knew what He would do, but He would not do it yet. "In the dispensation of the fullness of times," St. Paul tells the Ephesians (1:10), "God was to re-establish all things in Christ." What does "the fullness of times" mean? At least it means that the Redemption was to take place not at a moment arbitrarily chosen, as though God suddenly decided that the mess had gone on long enough and He had better do something about it. There was a fullness of time, a due moment. Looking at it from our own angle, we feel it fitting that God did not heal the disease at once: a disease should run its course. There is a rhythm of sin, as of revolution. Mankind had started on the road of self-assertion: it must be allowed to work out all the bleak logic of self-assertion to discover for itself all the unwholesome places into which self-assertion could take it. To be redeemed instantly might have left a faint "perhaps" to trouble mankind's peace: the Devil had said that we should be as gods—perhaps, if we had been allowed to try it out thoroughly, we *might* have become as gods. Well, we were allowed to try it out thoroughly: and we did not become gods.

When mankind knew at last and beyond a doubt that the game was up, might not that have been "the fullness of time"? Certainly there is an element of that in it. St. Paul perhaps is only putting the same idea more positively when he speaks of mankind as growing up, coming to maturity. By sin, mankind threw away the maturity God had planned for it and had started it toward. Instead it had gone after a childish dream and must now go through all the pains of growing toward maturity. It would be an element in that growth to know that the dream was childish, to be prepared to put away the things of a child.

Mankind did, in some way clear to the eye of God and half-clear to the eye of man, grow up. The fullness of time came. And in it, to quote St. Paul again (Gal 4:4), "God sent his Son, made of a woman, that we might receive the adoption of sons." Observe that it took man a vast time to grow thus far. How long? We have no notion. We have a close and detailed account of God's continuous dealings with one race, His chosen race the Jews, from about the year 2000 B.C., when he called Abraham. Recorded history as a whole does not go so very much farther back, even for the handful of favored races whose earlier history is to be read at all. Scripture, as we have seen, is not concerned to tell us how long ago man was created. Archaeology and geology give us glimpses of civilizations behind civilizations, and some certainty that the race was already incredibly old when our history begins to take hold on its doings. What had happened to the human race between Adam's expulsion from Eden and the beginning of a continuous historical record? Above all, what had happened to man's relations with God?

(i) What happened to religion

The one astonishing fact is that at the time history takes hold, we find religion everywhere. And although there is an enormous variety of creed and rite and spiritual and moral atmosphere, there is a solid core of common principle. There is a universal belief in a creator of heaven and earth and, in especial, of man, in the existence of a moral law, in some sort of survival after death; there is also the practice of prayer and sacrifice; and an almost universal belief in an earlier state of earthly happiness which mankind had and lost. All these things are not found everywhere with equal clearness: any one of them will be in one place strongly held and dominating the whole religious outlook, in another hardly realized, living or half-living in the background of the mind. But it is all there; and at any stage of clarity or shadowiness, its universality is remarkable. We cannot know all the twists and turns of the road religion took from Adam onward; but there is sufficient resemblance between what it was in him and what we find it to be in these remote descendants of his, to enable us to get some notion of the main forces at work.

What did the human race bring out of Paradise for the start of the vast adventure of regaining in the hardest possible way the maturity it had rejected? Two things principally: The first was religious knowledge: what God had revealed to Adam and Eve. They would teach it to their children, and they to theirs: it would become a tradition, a memory, a half-memory. The second was their human nature—made of nothing by God and held in existence by His continuing presence in them; a mind and a will wounded, but functioning; a body clamorous and hard to control, and no continuing will to control it. Had the human race been left to its own devices, the interplay of these two factors—the memory of truth revealed and the nature of man—would have governed the state of religion at any given time and place. But the human race was not left to its own devices, and two other factors must be regarded as in continuous action: Satan did not lose his interest in man after his first spectacular victory; and God never ceased in His care for the world He loved.

One can imagine what would happen to the tradition, the handing on from generation to generation of the religious truths that Adam knew. As the generations lengthened and the families of man spread to cover the earth, there was an inevitable dilution and distortion of the original message. We have seen what happened to the deposit of faith given by Christ to the Apostles, how it has been split into fragments and most of it lost, save where the infallible Church preserves it. The deposit of faith given by God to Adam, with no infallible Church to guard it, would not have fared better. The memory *as* a memory could only fade: the weakness of the human mind and human will would be too heavily against it. But human nature, if on this side it would make against the preservation of religious truth by memory, would on another side make for its rebuilding. The mind of man was deranged by sin but not destroyed. Quite apart from what might survive of the tradition, or if nothing at all survived, the mind of man could establish the foundations of a religious interpretation of the universe; and the will of man, with all its tendency toward self as apart from God, could not rid itself of an impulse to move toward God too. How could it, since God is more intimately present to it than it is to itself? Only a final rejection of God could annihilate finally the impulse to move toward him; and in this life, men and women do not finally reject Him.

Just what elements in the universe and in himself led man to construct the religious interpretation of things which came to the aid of the religious memory that was fading, or supplied for it if it was faded altogether, we cannot know with any certainty. With the scraps of evidence that archaeology and anthropology provide, with inferences from the mental processes of savage peoples still existent, with a coloring from the personality of the theorist, admirable theories are constructed. Any of them may be true; possibly all of them represent an element in a complex process.

The human mind can, as we have seen, by its own powers and without the aid of revelation, establish the existence of God. There are the five proofs set down by St. Thomas, for instance. But *did* every man set about it like that? We do not know. We know that he did pretty universally believe in a God (or gods) responsible for creating heaven and earth, in a moral law that expressed the divine will, in prayer and sacrifice as a way to approach the divinity. We do not know how he arrived at this belief; there are any number of ways leading to it. But after all, how could he have failed to arrive at it, since all ways lead to it?

He saw the universe being and happening, so to speak. Things are done: he would assume (quite rightly as it happens) that someone does them. There is an order, of day and night and seasons and such: he would assume, rightly again, that someone arranged it so. If anyone had suggested to him that no one arranged it, that it merely happened, he would perhaps not have known the philosophical answer to that untruth; but it *is* an untruth, it would not have occurred to him spontaneously, and no one seems to have suggested it to him: or if anyone did, he gave the perfectly good answer, "Don't be silly." Atheism arrived later, and was not widely popular then.

Toward the Someone who made things and did things, he naturally felt dependence (for he knew his own helplessness in the grip of the universe), and he naturally felt awe in the presence of one so immeasurably more powerful. Prayer would be natural (and it may in exceptional souls have reached a high point of union with God); so, at a further remove, would sacrifice—prayer and sacrifice being, at the lowest, likely to win the divine favor, and at the highest, capable of expressing the profoundest reality about man himself. The reality of man must always be kept in mind. Man would not thus early have arrived at the freakish notion of leaving his body out of account in religion; therefore, there would always be some sort of ritual; and the natural tendency to find outward expression for the soul's deepest states would lead to the idea of sacrament and symbol—such as the notion of the ritual use of water for spiritual cleansing.

All this is at once right and pretty well inevitable. What other attitudes man would adopt, or what embroidery he would put upon these, would depend on what further attributes—beyond personality and omnipotence—he considered that the Divinity would have. Upon this matter there is no limit. According to the elements in the universe which have most impressed their mind or their imagination or their fear or their fancy, men and women have in one time and place or another credited their gods with the strangest attributes and acted toward them accordingly. But the root of all this has been the assumption that God can be known from what He has made, an assumption in itself reasonable, but likely to mislead those who argued back from the thing made to the maker without allowing for the difference between Infinite and finite. It would be impossible to pursue all the ways in which man has argued back from creation to Creator and the strange religious beliefs and practices that have resulted; but two seem to be especially widespread and of special importance—two elements in man himself upon which he has built a notion of God.

The one is the human experience of sex—universal, life-giving, the closest union of two human beings, at once nonrational and ecstatic, lifting men and women for the moment out of themselves. It was inevitable that they should attribute some sort of sex-experience to the Divinity, and natural enough that they should (as so many did) introduce sexual union into their religious rituals as a symbolic means of union with the creative power.

The other is the human experience of conscience—worked out for us magnificently by Newman. The root of it is the awareness of something within us that says "You shall" or "You shall not": the sense of a law written in our nature, asserting an obligation not imposed on us by ourselves to do right and avoid wrong. It might or might not have led men to believe in a Supreme Being: but once they *did* believe in such a Being, it was inevitable that they should connect that inner voice with Him, should see the law it utters as His, should see Him as a source of morality, and so even of holiness: as One whom they would worship, with whom they would seek some sort of mystical oneness.

All this, man following his own nature could do: and all this, whether by some such process as we have sketched or by some quite other, man did so. Yet precisely as by the reality in it, human nature tends to build religion, so by the wounds in it, it tends to deform what it has built.

Thus the human intellect would tend to see that there must be some sort of Supreme Being. But only a human intellect at full strength would by its own unsupported powers hold on to *one* God, and that God spiritual, just as a human will at less than full strength would find one God too overwhelming, and a purely spiritual God too remote. Polytheism and idolatry came crowding in everywhere; pantheism was an escape in a different direction. Moral corruption naturally corrupted religion too. Sexual rites could only grow monstrous: man's fallen nature gets too much excitement out of sex to be trusted with sexual ritual. Nor did man's fallen nature always keep blood rituals in control: animal sacrifice suggested human sacrifice, and human sacrifice could grow to hecatombs. And if this means aberration by excess, there was the possibility of aberration by defect, religion falling to a mere ritual relation without love or holiness or sense of moral obligation, but only gods to be placated and a routine of placation.

Scripture makes it clear that the Devil played a large part in it. The prophet Baruch (4:7) tells the Jews that their captivity in Babylon is a punishment from God for having worshiped false gods. "For you have provoked Him who made you, the eternal God, offering sacrifice to devils and not to God." So St. Paul, advising Christians not to eat meat that is known to have been offered in sacrifice to idols, makes clear that this prohibition is not because what is offered in sacrifice to idols is anything, or that the idol itself is anything, but that "the things which the heathens sacrifice, they sacrifice to devils and not to God. And I would not that you should be made partakers with devils." In the very worst of religions, you can see what good thing they are travestying: somewhere below the travesty, there is a basis of reality. The Devil indeed prefers to work with reality gone astray: there is more *to* it than to total fictions. The religions of heathendom gave him wonderful scope. Just how much he made of it, we see in a grim passage of Wisdom (14:21–27): "Men, serving either their affection or their kings, gave the incommunicable name to stones and wood. And it was not enough for them to err about the knowledge of God; but whereas they lived in a great war of ignorance, they call so many and so great evils peace. For either they sacrifice their own children, or use hidden sacrifices, or keep watches full of madness. So that now they neither keep life nor marriage undefiled: but one killeth another by envy or grieveth him by adultery. And all things are mingled together,

blood, murder, theft and dissimulation, corruption and un-
faithfulness, tumults and perjury, disquieting of the good;
forgetfulness of God, defiling of souls, changing of nature,
disorder in marriage, and the irregularity of adultery and
uncleanness. For the worship of abominable idols is the cause,
and the beginning and end, of all evils."

It was a carnival for the Devil. Yet religion did not perish.
Nor is the history of religion a history of corruptions growing
ever worse. There is degeneration, but there is revival too.
Between Adam and Our Lord, we see now one section, now
another, of the pagan world, but we see no one section steadily,
and a vast part of the world we scarcely see at all. So that it is
impossible to figure a rhythm of degeneration and revival: but
on the whole the movement of paganism strikes us as not
downward, certainly, upward if anything. So history seems to
show: so we should expect. For the pagans were made by
God in His own image, and God loved them all. They had all
fallen in Adam, but the Redemption was for them all. His
providence did not ignore them in the immeasurable ages
between. Wherever we look in time or place, we see a calling
upon God; it would be strange if God did not answer.

Just how God's providence worked, we do not know.
St. John tells us in the first chapter of his Gospel that the Word
who is God "enlightens *every* soul born into the world", so
that besides the supernatural illumination of the soul in grace,
which, as we have seen, is appropriated to the Third Person of
the Blessed Trinity, there is an illumination of every human
soul appropriated to the Second. St. Irenaeus, who knew
paganism—he lived in the midst of it in Asia and in Italy and in
Gaul—writes in the second century: "One and the same Divine
Father and His eternal Word are from the beginning and in
every age close to the human race and approach man by many
ordinances and many operations of assisting grace."

The formula for this period, as for all periods, is man's desire for God (not, alas, man's sole desire, nor always his strongest, and in some men no longer there at all) and God's love for man. Given that, we might expect to find what in fact we do find. With all the fantastic perversions wrought by man's weakness of mind and will, there are true values, that is to say, resemblances to the Christian revelation, to be found in every part of paganism. Some elements in the true approach of God to man and of man to God are to be found in all religions; there is hardly one that is not to be found in some.

(ii) God's special choice of the Jews

But in God's plan for the re-establishment of the whole race, a special part was to be acted by one race, the Jews, and therefore God brought them into a special relation with Himself. The story is told in the forty-six books of the Old Testament, from which I have already quoted so much. They are the sacred books of the Jews, and form a body of religious writing without parallel in the world. They cover the whole period from the creation of Adam to just before the coming of Christ; but they treat mainly of God's choosing of the Jews and what followed from it. The Church that Christ founded teaches that they were written by men under the inspiration of God—inspiration consisting in this, that God so illumined the minds and energized the wills of the writers, that what they wrote was what God wanted written. Thus these books truly have God for their principal author. That is why the arguments as to when and by whom the various books were written do not affect our acceptance of the doctrine they contain: our acceptance is based not on the human author, but on God, who inspired him.

The special relation of one people with God begins at a time and a place—the time roughly 2000 B.C., the place Haran in the land of Canaan. There had come Abram, with his father and his brothers, from the Chaldaean town of Ur. And God said to Abram (Gen 12), "I will make of thee a great nation, and I will bless thee, and magnify thy name: and thou shalt be blessed. I will bless them that bless thee, and curse them that curse thee; and in thee shall all the kindred of the earth be blessed." In the years that followed, God renewed the promises many times: but it was twenty-five years later that the great covenant was made which constituted the Jews God's people (Gen 17): "God said to him: *I am God Almighty.* ... And my covenant is with thee; and thou shalt be a father of many nations. ... And I will establish my covenant between me and thee, and between thy seed after thee in their generations, by a perpetual covenant: to be a God to thee, and to thy seed after thee." God changed Abram's name to Abraham, which means "father of nations", and gave the command of circumcision "as a sign of the covenant".

God then had singled out a particular family, which was to grow into a nation: not for their own sake but for the sake of all mankind: they were chosen not simply for a favor but for a function, something God was to do through them for the whole race. This God makes clear again (Gen 22): "In thy seed shall all the nations of the earth be blessed."

The promises were repeated to Abraham's second son, Isaac (he had already had a son Ishmael by a bondwoman), and to Isaac's second son, Jacob (for the elder, Esau, had forsworn his birthright). In all this we see the hint of Redemption—all mankind is to be blessed through the seed of Abraham. And soon comes the hint of a Redeemer, and even of the mode of the Redemption—Jacob, dying, prophesies one who is to come from his fourth son, Judah: "The sceptre shall not be taken away from Judah, nor a ruler from his thigh, till he come that is to be sent: and he shall be the expectation of nations. Tying his foal to the vineyard, and his ass, O my son, to the vine. He shall wash his robe in wine, and his garment in the blood of the grape" (Gen 49:10–11).

By now the children of Jacob, to whom God had given the new name of "Israel", were in Egypt, and there they were to be for four hundred years. The last part of that time they were fiercely oppressed, until God brought them out of Egypt under the leader Moses, as Exodus 12 describes it. The last act of their time in Egypt was spectacular. The angel of God visited the houses of the Egyptians, slaying the first-born: but he passed over the houses of the children of Israel, who had marked their door-posts with the blood of a lamb sacrificed by God's ordinance. And God ordered that this passing over (*pasch* is the Hebrew word) should be celebrated each year by the sacrifice of a lamb.

So the Israelites went from Egypt, crossed the Red Sea, and came into the Arabian Desert: and there, upon Mt. Sinai, the Covenant was renewed and the Law was given. God gave the Jews through Moses the ten commandments and a great mass of moral, ritual, and legal precepts covering every detail of their lives. Sacrifices were offered; and Moses, "taking the book of the covenant", read it in the hearing of all the people: and they said: "All things that the Lord hath spoken, we will do. We will be obedient. And he took the blood and sprinkled it upon the people, and he said: *This is the blood of the covenant which the Lord has made with you concerning all these words*" (Ex 24).

Let us repeat that the Jews were chosen because of something God meant to accomplish through them for the whole world. The essence of their function lay in this—that from them was to come the Redeemer, who should redeem all mankind. Meanwhile, they were to bear witness to truths which were in danger of perishing, which indeed seemed to have perished utterly: the truth that there is but one God, the truth that God will send a Redeemer of mankind.

Observe that the Jews showed no great natural aptitude for, or any very tenacious hold upon, either truth. Monotheism, for instance, made no more appeal to them than to all that ocean of polytheistic people which surrounded them. All their instincts ran to strange gods and to idols: the thing seems to have been a craving as strong as a person might feel for alcohol. They were forever going after the gods of the heathen, and God was forever restoring them to right ways. God's pedagogy was of two sorts: He allowed their enemies to work their will upon them as a reminder that they were in the hand of the one God and could achieve nothing without Him; He sent them the Prophets to bear glowing and glorious witness to the same truth. If they found monotheism difficult, they found not much easier the true doctrine as to the nature of the Messiah, the Anointed One, who was to come, and of the Kingdom He was to found. Here again the Prophets were their instructors; and as the centuries pass, the picture of the Messiah and His Kingdom grows in detail and in clarity.

Yet we should be mistaken if we exaggerated the clarity. There is a mass of prophecy, and a magnificence over all of it. But much of it is obscure even to us who have seen its fulfillment; certain elements which now seem most wonderfully fulfilled appear buried in their context, not emphasized as prophetical or especially likely to catch the ear or the eye. The Prophets did not provide a blackboard diagram and then proceed to lecture on it. Indeed our modern use of the word *prophet* may give us a wrong notion of their office. *To prophesy* does not mean to foretell but to speak out. They were not there primarily to foretell the future but to utter the eternal and judge the present by it. The Jews not unnaturally found morality harder even than monotheism: the Law had imposed upon them a morality stricter than any other known among men, and they fell from it. The Prophets thundered against this faithlessness as against strange gods. For here too they must judge the present by the eternal.

But precisely because that was their function, they did speak much of Him who was to come. Consider how the picture builds up. We have already seen that One who was to be the expectation of nations should come from Judah. From the Psalms (e.g., Ps 131:11) we gather the further detail that He was to be a descendant of David the King, and that is confirmed by the statement of Isaiah (11:1) that He is to be "a rod out of the root of Jesse", for Jesse was David's father: "In that day, the root of Jesse, who standeth for an ensign of the people, him the Gentiles shall beseech: and his sepulchre shall be glorious." There is no explicit statement that this is the Messiah: but St. Paul takes it for granted (Rom 15:12), and in any event no Jew imagined a Messiah not sprung from David.

In the seventh chapter of Isaiah we read, "Behold a virgin shall conceive and bear a son: and his name shall be called Emmanuel." From St. Matthew (1:23) we know that this is a prophecy of the virgin birth of Christ; yet in the context, one might well think that the prophecy referred to an event immediately expected and actually described in the next chapter of Isaiah, the eighth, as having happened. In the light of our new knowledge, we can re-read the eighth chapter and see that though there is some sort of fulfillment there and then, yet some mightier thing is involved: the language used is of a grandeur too great for the actual episode.

The fifth chapter of Micah tells us that the Messiah is

to be born in Bethlehem: "And thou, Bethlehem Ephrata, art a little one among the thousands of Judah: out of thee shall he come forth unto me that is to be the ruler in Israel: and his going forth is from the beginning, from the days of eternity. . . . And this man shall be our peace."

There are other details we see fulfilled, but they could hardly have meant so much to their first hearers: thus Zechariah (9:9) writes: "Rejoice greatly, O daughter of Sion, shout for joy, O daughter of Jerusalem: Behold thy King will come to thee, the just and saviour. He is poor and riding upon an ass, upon a colt, the foal of an ass."

Such details as we have been considering—that the Messiah was to be of the tribe of Judah, of the family of David, born of a virgin and in Bethlehem—are not the primary things about Him. Two things that matter far more are Himself and what He was to do. Upon both, the prophecies are fuller and clearer.

As to what He was: there is a central stream of teaching which shows him a man triumphant, and two parallel streams, one showing Him as more than a man, the other showing Him as less than triumphant. It would seem that the Jews concentrated on the central stream, and made little of either of the others. Yet these others are of such vast importance that, missing them, one hardly sees Him at all.

That He was to be more than man, not simply the greatest of men, is indicated again and again. We have already seen the phrase of Micah—"his going forth from the beginning, from the days of eternity". The same truth is to be found in Psalm 109—"Before the day star, I begot thee." But it is not only by pre-existence that the Messiah seems to be more than man. The hints are everywhere—as in the suggestion that He is to be son to God in a special way. (It is hard to see how they could be more than hints: the truth about the divinity of the Messiah could not well be conveyed to a nation that did not know the doctrine of the Trinity.)

The reverse of the medal is the even clearer stream of prophecy that the Messiah is to be poor and suffering. There is Psalm 22(21), from which Christ quoted on the cross, as well as Isaiah 53, to which He drew attention at the Last Supper (Lk 22:31). Here note a few verses from Isaiah, summing all up: "Despised and the most abject of men, a man of sorrows and acquainted with infirmity. . . .

"He shall be led as a sheep to the slaughter and shall be dumb as a lamb before his shearer. . . .

"And the Lord was pleased to bruise him in infirmity. If he shall lay down his life for sin, he shall see a long-lived seed. . . ."

To say that the Jews ignored a great deal of all this is not to accuse them of any startling malignity. The assertion of the Messiah's preexistence, for example, was difficult to reconcile with the certainty that he was to be a descendant of David: one gets the impression that the Jews, faced with two elements difficult to reconcile, simply took the intellectual line of least resistance, concentrated upon the clearer one and left the other in its mysteriousness. Similarly it is hard to see how anything short of what did in fact happen to Christ our Lord could have shown the fulfillment both of the splendor and the suffering: lacking that clue, they concentrated on the more obvious.

But if their intellect followed the line of least resistance in the picture they formed of the Messiah in Himself, their will seems to have followed the line of greatest complacency in the picture they formed of the Kingdom He was to found. They saw it as a Kingdom of Israel in which the Gentiles, if they came into it at all, should be very much in a subordinate place; and they saw it as an earthly and not as a spiritual Kingdom. The Prophets, properly read, supply correctives for both.

Thus they assert that the Messiah is coming for a light to the Gentiles and that the Gentiles are to share in the joy of His Kingdom. When Psalm 71 says, "In him shall all the tribes of the earth be blessed: all nations shall magnify him", it simply reasserts what God said to Abram in the first of the promises. Isaiah is filled with the same teaching: and he indicates the possibility that there may be Jews excluded from the Kingdom and Gentiles admitted. So St. Paul (Rom 10:20) explains the contrast (Is 65) between what God says of the Gentiles, "Those who never looked for me have found me: I have made myself known to those who never asked for word of me", and what He says of the Jews, "I stretch out my hand all day to a people that refuses obedience and cries out against me."

But if we find from the Prophets that the Gentiles were to have a place, and a place of joy, in the Kingdom, it was left for St. Paul to utter in plain words the intimate secret of the total equality of Jew and Gentile in the Kingdom, the mystery of Christ "which was never made known to any human being in past ages . . . that through the gospel preaching the Gentiles are to win the same inheritance, to be made part of the same body, to share the same divine promise in Christ Jesus" (Eph 3:5–6).

Thus all who belong to Christ are of the seed of Abraham, and the promises of the Kingdom are to us. But what sort of Kingdom? The Jews, as we have seen, seemed to expect an earthly Kingdom. The Prophets do not precisely and explicitly contradict them, but they give a mass of teaching which should have made the notion of a merely earthly Kingdom untenable and not even desirable. Thus Ezekiel (36:24–26): "And I will pour upon you clean water and you shall be cleansed from all your filthiness: and I will cleanse you from all your idols. And I will give you a new heart and put a new spirit within you: and I will take away the stony heart out of your flesh and will give you a heart of flesh. And I will put my spirit in the midst of you." And Zechariah (9): "And he shall speak peace to the Gentiles: and his power shall be from sea to sea, and from the rivers even to the end of the earth. . . . And the Lord their God will save them in that day, as the flock of his people: for holy stones shall be lifted up over his land. For what is the good thing of him and what is his beautiful thing, but the corn of the elect and wine springing forth virgins?"

Indeed it is plain enough, for us who read the Prophets now, that there was to be a spiritualization at every point: even at the point of priesthood and sacrifice, where Israel had most scrupulously observed the Law. For the Jewish priests and the Jewish sacrifices were but figures of, and preparations for, something that was mysteriously to transcend them. The Messiah was to be (Ps 109) "a priest forever according to the order of Melchisedek"—a strange phrase, for Melchisedek, who had offered a sacrifice of bread and wine (Gen 14), was not a Jew. As for the priesthood, so for the sacrifices: "From the rising of the sun even to the going down, my name is great among the Gentiles: and in every place there is sacrifice and there is offered to my name a clean oblation. For my name is great among the Gentiles, saith the Lord of hosts" (Mal 1:11).

Everything in Israel was preparatory, looked forward to something which should complete it. The Law given by God to Moses was not a consummation. It was a preparation: a hard and heavy preparation: not maturity, but a superb training for maturity.

(iii) The fullness of time

The hour came. Look again at what St. Paul told the Galatians (4:3–5): "So we also, when we were children, were serving under the elements of the world. But when the fullness of the time was come, God sent his Son, made of a woman, made under the law: That he might redeem them who were under the law: that we might receive the adoption of sons." I have said that the fitness of the moment was clear to the eye of God, half-clear to our eye. We seem to see, though it would be absurd to pretend in such a matter that we could be certain, that the Law had done for the Jews all that it had in it to do. Trained by the Law and hammered by their enemies, they had come to a splendid point of development—poor enough in the light of the possibilities Christ was to reveal, but magnificent in comparison with what was to be found elsewhere. Their centuries-old temptation to polytheism and idolatry, they had conquered: from their return out of captivity in Babylon, five hundred years before, it seems not to have troubled them. Under the Romans who had ruled them now for sixty years, they had stood gloriously against the introduction of idols. They held unbreakably to belief in the one true God, and observed most scrupulously His ritual law; and if the moral law was harder to observe, they maintained its rights *as* law, and repented for their sins against it. It is easy enough to see defects here—as in the disproportionate observance of the outward act and failure to grasp that the inward state of the will was decisive. But the Jewish religion at the time of Christ's birth was a thing of grandeur: and showed by the holiness it produced in the best of the Jews how fit it was for the completion that Christ was to bring it and the use He made of it. The Law, says St. Paul (Gal 3:24), was a pedagogue—the word here does not mean a teacher, but the slave who took the children to school: and the school that the Law brought them to was Christ. To Christ the Law did in all reality bring the Jews.

But the preparation was not only of the Jews, nor the fullness of time only a matter of their coming to maturity. For the Gentiles too, the time was at the full. The history of the human race is one story from end to end, not a collection of unrelated short stories. The history of the race, says St. Augustine, is the story of one man. It was the race that fell in Adam, it was the race that was to be redeemed: in between, the race had to be made ready. One cannot pretend to see the Gentile world as God saw it. Yet even in what we can see, there is at least a suggestion of a pedagogic action of God upon the Gentiles, parallel (though at a lower level) to His pedagogic action upon the Jews. If the Jews were made ready in one way, the Gentiles were made ready in another. God had not given them the Mosaic Law, but His natural law was written in their hearts. And His providence was over them. He had not sent them Prophets like those He had sent Israel, but they had had powerful religious teachers and great religious revivals, countless movements upward to balance—and as it would seem more than balance—the countless movements downward: and God was not for nothing in all this. Indeed it is hard to see how, otherwise, religion, under the combined influence of man's weakness and the Devil's destructive skill, should have survived at all—whereas in fact the general religious standard of the heathen world was almost certainly higher at the coming of Christ than it had been two thousand years earlier when God made His covenant with Abraham.

But that continuing providence of God over the Gentiles, which a study of the Gentile world certainly suggests, we know as a fact from Scripture. St. John, we have seen, in the first chapter of his Gospel speaks of the Second Person of the Blessed Trinity as the True Light "Who enlightens every soul born into the world". St. Paul states unequivocally (Rom 1:19–20) that "the knowledge of God is clear to their minds; God himself has made it clear to them; from the foundation of the world men have caught sight of his invisible nature, his eternal power and his divineness, as they are known through

His creatures." Nor is it merely a matter of the intellect's power to draw inferences from the external universe: "As for the Gentiles, though they have no law to guide them, there are times when they carry out the precepts of the law unbidden, finding in their own natures a rule to guide them, in default of any other rule; and this shows that the obligations of the law are written in their hearts; their conscience utters its own testimony, and when they dispute with one another they find themselves condemning this, approving that" (Rom 2:14–15).

So that the Gentiles had a law uttering the will of God to them, but not supplemented as it was for the Jews by the Law given to Moses. Similarly the Gentiles had religious teachers, not Prophets inspired by God, but men working toward truth all the same and by and large serving truth—at least to the point of bettering the proportion of truth to error. Around five hundred years before Christ, the Jews as we have seen returned from the Babylonian captivity cleansed once for all of attachment to strange gods. About the same time there was a religious movement—or series of movements—throughout the pagan world. Zoroaster in Persia got closer to monotheism perhaps than any religious founder ever got outside the main stream of God's revelation to man; in different ways, Gautama Buddha in India and Confucius and Lai Tse in China founded systems based upon great truths from which, though they were mingled with error or hindered by insufficiency, men's souls surely gained far more than they lost. A couple of hundred years later, the Greek philosophers—Socrates, Plato, Aristotle—did a marvelous intellectual work upon the nature of things, which moved St. Justin Martyr to give them the title which St. Paul a century earlier had given the Law—"Pedagogues to bring men to Christ". Of the later religious movements—Stoicism, Neo-Pythagoreanism, and such—we may say what we have said of the great sixth-century movements: that, allowance made for their errors, they meant some sort of upward movement. Compared with Christianity, they are laden with imperfections: but compared with what actually lay around them, one can see how they had their part in the preparation. There were many other elements at work. The Roman Law spread a greater measure of better discipline over a wider area of the world than any secular law before it. The Jews were widely dispersed inside and outside the Roman Empire, and some of the truth of Judaism had seeped into the surrounding paganisms.

All these things are true, yet a glance at the state of the pagan world might lead us to feel that they bear too tiny a proportion to a whole ocean of iniquity. Look at St. Paul's powerful description in the first chapter of his Epistle to the Romans (a description blacker, if anything, than the passage already quoted from the centuries-earlier book of Wisdom):

"They, who claimed to be so wise, turned fools, and exchanged the glory of the imperishable God for representations of perishable man, of bird and beast and reptile. That is why God abandoned their lustful hearts to filthy practices of dishonouring their own bodies among themselves. They had exchanged God's truth for a lie, reverencing and worshipping the creature in preference to the Creator . . . and, in return, God abandoned them to passions which brought dishonour to themselves. Their women exchanged natural for unnatural intercourse; and the men, on their side, giving up natural intercourse with women, were burnt up with desire for each other; men practicing vileness with their fellow-men. Thus they have received a fitting retribution for their false belief.

"And as they scorned to keep God in view, so God has abandoned them to a frame of mind worthy of all scorn, that prompts them to disgraceful acts. They are versed in every kind of injustice, knavery, impurity, avarice, and ill-will; spiteful, murderous, contentious, deceitful, depraved, backbiters, slanderers, God's enemies; insolent, haughty, vainglorious; inventive in wickedness, disobedient to their parents; without prudence, without honour, without love, without loyalty, without pity."

In what sense can we speak of a fullness of time for such people? How can we feel that they too have in any way been made ready? Clearly we cannot *know*: yet certain possibilities leap to the eye. In the best of the Gentiles clearly, and in the average less clearly, there had grown up a contempt for the puerilities of the myths and a dissatisfaction with the mysteries; philosophy, which had promised so fair four centuries earlier, had come to a sort of barrenness and clearly could do no more for them; the pleasures of the flesh were horribly exacting but yielded less and less of joy. Despair lay over everything; and despair is a kind of maturity too, or at least a last stage on one road to maturity. It is not altogether fanciful to think that Jew and Gentile, having different roles to play in the design of the Messiah who was to come, were made ready by God in different ways. Israel was to receive the message from the Christ and bear it to the pagan world; the pagan world was to receive it from Israel. Israel was made ready to receive the new impulse because the Law had done so much for it; the Law had brought Israel as far as it could, but it had brought it there trained in mind and will and filled with hope—ready for what was to come. If Israel's preparation was by way of vitality and hope, paganism's was by way of devitalization and despair. The Jew had learned the glory of God, the pagan the worthlessness of all else. The spiritual energy of Israel needed this new relation with God: they had to do something with their energy. The spiritual destitution of paganism needed this new inpouring of life: they had to get energy from somewhere. For Jew and for

Gentile, it was the fullness of time. Christ came, that all things might be re-established in Him.

16. The Mission of Christ

Observe that the fullness of time, with all the mysterious spiritual resonances that the phrase has, actually *is* in time. It belongs to history. It has indeed been dated for us with some precision. Time came to its fullness during the reign of Augustus, who, having defeated Mark Antony and his ally, Cleopatra, ruled from 27 B.C. to A.D. 14 and out of the ancient Roman Republic and its conquests fashioned the Roman Empire, whose destiny was to be so closely linked with that of Christ's Kingdom on earth.

(i) The Incarnation

St. Luke tells us that Augustus decreed a census of the whole Empire: as a consequence, Joseph, a carpenter, "a man of David's clan and family", went from Nazareth in Galilee to register in David's city of Bethlehem in Judaea. With him was his wife, Mary, also of David's line, still a virgin and ever to be a virgin. And in Bethlehem she gave birth to Jesus, who was the Christ, the Anointed One, the expectation of the nations.

For this, the highest function to which any human person had ever been called, God had prepared Mary most exquisitely. Her own conception in the womb of Anne, her mother, had been in the ordinary way of nature. But in the doctrine of the Immaculate Conception, the Church teaches that from the moment that she was conceived, sanctifying grace was by the power of the Blessed Trinity in her soul: thus she was never stained by the sin at man's origin. All her life she was, by the power of the same most Holy Trinity, preserved from all personal sin. In due course she was betrothed, to Joseph the carpenter — whose glory in the eyes of God's Church has grown steadily, for all that we have not one word of his recorded.

During the time of betrothal, God (as St. Luke tells in his first chapter) sent the angel Gabriel to Nazareth where Mary was. And Gabriel greeted her: "Hail, full of grace; the Lord is with thee; blessed art thou among women."

Then came his message: "Mary, do not be afraid; thou hast found favour in the sight of God. And behold thou shalt conceive in thy womb, and shalt bear a son, and shalt call him Jesus. He shall be great, and men will know him for the Son of the Most High; the Lord God will give him the throne of his father David, and he shall reign over the Kingdom of Jacob eternally; his Kingdom shall never have an end."

Mary said to the Angel: "How can that be, since I have no knowledge of man?"

The Angel answered: "The Holy Spirit will come upon thee, and the power of the most High will overshadow thee. Thus that holy thing which is to be born of thee shall be known for the Son of God."

Thus she conceived. And to Joseph, profoundly troubled, an angel appeared in a dream and said: "Joseph, son of David, do not be afraid to take thy wife Mary to thyself, for it is by the power of the Holy Ghost that she has conceived this child; and she will bear a son, whom thou shalt call Jesus, for he is to save his people from their sins."

And now in Bethlehem Jesus is born: and forty days later Simeon, under the inspiration of God, hails Him as "the light which shall give revelation to the Gentiles, the glory of God's people Israel". Of the first thirty years of His life, we know almost nothing. Warned that Herod sought the life of the newborn Messiah, Joseph fled with his wife and the Child to Egypt: Herod died (A.D. 4), and the family settled in Nazareth. When Jesus was twelve, there was a curious episode (to which we shall return) when they lost the Child and found Him again in the Temple. Apart from that, nothing until He was around thirty.

Here again St. Luke dates the moment for us. In the fifteenth year of the reign of Augustus' successor, Tiberius (who reigned from A.D. 14 to 37), John the Baptist went all over the country round Jordan, baptizing and preaching that the Christ was at hand. To him came Jesus; and John cried, "This is the Lamb of God; this is He who takes away the sin of the world." From then we may date the three years of Our Lord's public life, ending in His death by crucifixion. On the third day after His death, He rose again to life; and forty days after that He ascended into heaven. The story in its main outlines is familiar to all Christians. What we want now is to get at its meaning.

(ii) What Christ came to do

We have to consider what Our Lord actually came into the world for. If you have taken the advice given in the first section of this book, you will have been taking special note of anything in the Gospels upon what Christ had come to do. The angel Gabriel, who announced His coming to the Blessed Virgin Mary, His mother, told her that He was to be called Jesus, which means "savior", and that He was to be ruler of a kingdom that would never end (Lk 1:31–34). The angel who appeared to St. Joseph added a precision to the word *savior* — He was to save His people *from their sins.* John the Baptist, sent by God to prepare the people for the coming of Christ, said: "This is the Lamb of God. This is He who takes away the sin of the world" (Jn 2:29).

The second phrase repeats what we already know, that He is to save and to save from sin, and adds perhaps, with the word "Lamb", the hint that He will be offered in sacrifice.

Our Lord Himself says many things upon what He had come for. Some of them represent not the purpose itself but rather what He knows to be the certain result of what He has come to do: "Do not imagine that I have come to bring peace to the earth; I have come to bring a sword, not peace" (Mt 10:34); or "I have come into this world so that a sentence may fall upon it, that those who are blind should see, and those who see should become blind" (Jn 9:39); or the intensely suggestive "It is fire that I have come to spread over the earth, and what better wish can I have than that it should be kindled" (Lk 12:49).

But what we must concentrate upon are His direct statements as to the purpose of His coming.

To Zacchaeus, the chief publican, He said (Lk 19:10): "That is what the Son of Man has come for, to search out and *to save what was lost."*

Compare this with what He had said earlier to Nicodemus (Jn 3:15): "This Son of Man must be lifted up, as the serpent was lifted up by Moses in the wilderness; so that *those who believe in him may not perish, but have eternal life."* Following this, we have either as part of Our Lord's speech to Nicodemus or written in commentary by the Evangelist: "God so loved the world, that he gave up his only-begotten Son, so *that those who believe in him may not perish, but have eternal life.* When God sent his Son into the world, it was not to reject the world, but *so that the world might find salvation* through him."

To the Roman Governor Pilate He said (Jn 18:37): "What I was born for, what I came into the world for, is *to bear witness of the truth.*"

To the Pharisees and Scribes, He said (Lk 5:32): "I have come *to call sinners to repentance.*"

He sent out His Apostles (Lk 9:2) *"to proclaim the Kingdom of God"* and to work miracles in support of their message.

To the Apostles, angry with James and John for seeking the first place in His Kingdom, He said (Mt. 20:28): "The Son of Man did not come to have service done him; he came to serve others, and *to give his life as a ransom for the lives of many.*"

Again to the Pharisees, He said (Jn 10:10): "I have come *so that they may have life and have it more abundantly.*"

These texts cover what He had to say directly as to why He had come. Observe that what He says of Himself is simply a development of what had already been said about Him—He is to save, to save from sin, to found a Kingdom; the hint in St. John's word "Lamb" is now made explicit—He is to give His life as a ransom for many; then there is the assertion of truth, the reality of things; and there is a further precision as to what salvation was from—He was to save a world that was lost, a race in danger of perishing—and a profounder statement as to what salvation was to be—life, more abundant life, eternal life: and, as we shall see from other things He said, life in union with God, as sons of God. But indeed upon every element in this summary of His purpose in coming, we shall get much light from the rest of His teaching.

So St. Paul was to find. He analyzed more fully and closely than any others what Our Lord came to do. It would be possible to make an immense list of the things he has to say on the subject; much of it will be quoted later. He uses a large number of different words to express the work Our Lord did, because what He did was as many-sided as the damage we received from Adam and the spiritual needs of man: and one word or another is more appropriate according to which particular effect of Our Lord's work St. Paul has in mind. Here we may note three words he uses again and again: the word "redeem", which means literally to buy back, to pay a price for something lost, so that it is roughly equivalent to "ransom"; the word "reconcile", which means restoring good relations, bringing harmony where there is discord, and so represents the heart of atonement; and the word "justification", which means giving us that natural and supernatural rightness which God designed for us and is therefore a way of expressing the result of reconciliation with God.

As an example of "redeem", we have "In the Son of God, in His blood, we find the redemption that sets us free from our sins" (Col 1:14).

"Reconcile" we find in: "Enemies of God, we were reconciled to him through his Son's death" (Rom 5:10); "It is God who, through Christ, has reconciled us to himself, and allowed us to minister this reconciliation of his to others. Yes, God was in Christ, reconciling the world to himself, establishing in our hearts his message of reconciliation, instead of holding men to account for their sins" (2 Cor 5:18–20).

For "justification", we find: "We have found justification through his blood" (Rom 5:9); "So, justified by his grace, we were to become heirs, with the hope of eternal life set before us" (Titus 3:7).

In the Epistle to the Romans (3:24) St. Paul gives us all three effects: "*Justification* comes to us as a free gift from his grace, through our *redemption* in Christ Jesus. God has offered him to us as a means of *reconciliation,* in virtue of faith, *ransoming* us with his blood."

The new relation to which reconciliation brings us, the living element in justification, is to be children of God by adoption, sharing the inheritance of Christ: "The spirit you have now received is not, as of old, a spirit of slavery, to govern you by fear; it is the spirit of adoption, which makes us cry out, Abba, Father" (Rom 8:14–15).

If we were to go no further than this into the meaning and mission of Christ our Lord, we should still have enough to see Him as our only hope. If we had never heard of Adam's sin (or having heard of it, did not believe it), we should still know our own sinfulness and need of cleansing; if we knew nothing of all the past, one look at the world would tell us of its urgent need for healing. Knowing these things, we need no very profound theology to tell us that in Christ our Lord is salvation for us and for all people. So millions have found Him, and millions will still find Him. Yet it remains that there are depths below depths of understanding possible, and theology can open them to us. There is immense gain of every sort in seeing the detail of the relation between men's need and Christ's work. For our special purpose in this study—to get some understanding of what life is about—it is indispensable.

(iii) How the God-Man could effect satisfaction and restoration

St. Paul's words, "redeem" and "reconcile" and "justify" are the fundamental ways of saying what Christ came to do; for they state the ways in which His one single action solved the twofold problem set by the sin of Adam.

As we have seen, the race had lost its oneness with God, and Our Lord did the work of at-one-ment or reconciliation, restoration of man to sonship. In this restored sonship lies man's right relation to God, which St. Paul calls "justification".

But also the race had, by its sin, put itself in debt to God's justice, and Christ paid the debt: for He offered to God an act that expiated, balanced, compensated for the act by which the race had chosen itself as apart from God. This the root idea of the word *redeem,* which literally means to buy something back, pay a price for the recovery of a captive. The metaphor must not be pressed too far: God was not a jailer holding men and women captive until Christ paid a ransom to free them from His hands: on the contrary, what held man captive was not God but sin, and the object of redemption was not to take men and women from God but to bind them to Him in a life-giving union. Yet there is a real sense of a price paid: something was due from man as a preliminary to restoration, and Christ rendered it for us by His death. St. Paul can say (1 Cor 6:20), "You are bought with a great price," and St. Peter (in his first Epistle 1:18–19), "You were not redeemed with corruptible things as gold or silver, . . . but with the precious blood of Christ, as of a lamb unspotted and undefiled."

Thus we have two elements in what Our Lord did. He made satisfaction for man's sins, and He merited for us the new life of sons reconciled to their Father. The word Redemption, though in its literal meaning it seems to apply especially to the element of satisfaction for sin, is ordinarily used also to cover the whole restoring work of Christ, and so to include the reconciliation and the justification: and that is natural. To "redeem" is to "buy back", and if the "buy" suggests the satisfaction, the "back" suggests the restoration. The important thing, when we use the word *redemption* for Christ's whole work of re-establishing humanity, is that we should grasp that there *are* two elements. The Council of Trent (VI.7) says that Our Lord, through the great charity wherewith He loved us, by His most Holy Passion on the wood of the cross, merited *justification* for us and made *satisfaction* to God on our behalf.

Notice again that it was not a question primarily of redeeming individuals, but of redeeming the human race to which these individuals belonged. As we have seen, St. John the Baptist speaks of Our Lord as taking away the "sin" of the world: not sins, sin. There was a sin of the world, which was the background against which all individual sins were written. The sin of the world was the breach between the human race and God, and it stood between men and the sonship of God. Christ healed it. It is in this widest sense that He is the Savior of mankind. The individual does not need to sin in order to have Christ as his Savior: the child who dies while still an infant never having committed any personal sin at all still has Christ for his Savior, because he shares in the benefits of the act by which Christ reconciled to God the race to which he belongs: Our Blessed Lady, Christ's Mother, who had God's grace in her soul from the first moment of her existence, could still call God her Savior, not only because He saved her from committing sin, but because He has saved the race of Adam, whose sinless descendant she was.

This thing that Our Lord came to do, the restoration of the broken relationship, is the primary thing if we are to understand His mission at all—what He came to do, and who He was that came to do it. We have already seen from the Gospels that Christ is God. St. Paul tells us so as clearly (Col 2.9): "In Christ the whole plenitude of the Godhead is embodied" (or in the Douay version: "In Christ dwells the fullness of the Godhead bodily"). We have seen also that Christ, not ceasing to be God, is man too. The opening of St. John's Gospel tells us how the Word, who was God, was made flesh, was incarnate; again St. Paul has his own way of saying it: "His nature is, from the first, divine, and he thought it no usurpation to claim the rank of Godhead; he dispossessed himself, and took the nature of a slave, fashioned in the likeness of men, and presenting himself to us in human form; and then he lowered his own dignity, accepted an obedience which brought him to death, death on a cross" (Phil 2:6–9).

The Incarnation was God's answer to the double problem that faced fallen mankind. The Second Person of the Blessed Trinity, God the Son, became man, took to Himself and made His own a human nature; and in that nature offered to God the sacrifice which outbalanced the sin of mankind, and merited the supernatural restoration of man: Adam's offense was expiated; the breach it had caused between God and man was healed, so that God and man might be at one again, and man brought back from servitude to sonship.

To see how totally the Incarnation answers the problem, we must consider more closely the relation of the humanity of Christ to his Godhead. It might be well for the reader to re-read Chapter 6, where the distinction between person and nature is discussed in some detail. Here I need only summarize. Given a rational being, the nature answers the question *what,* the person answers the question *who;* again, the person does what is done in the nature, but the nature conditions what the person does. The person does what his nature enables him to do. The nature is a source of possible actions: if any of those actions get done, it is the person who does them, not the nature. Where it is a question of a finite rational nature, there is a question not only of doing things but of having things done to one, suffering, in a general way experiencing. Here again the nature is decisive as to what may be done or suffered or experienced; but the person does and suffers and experiences.

We may now apply these distinctions to God-made-man, as earlier in the book we applied them to the three Persons of the Blessed Trinity. God the Son was a Person, a Someone, possessing the nature of God in its fullness, and this in the eternity of the divine Being. At a certain point in time, He took to Himself and made His own a human nature. Thus we have the unique instance of one single person with two natures, divine and human. To the question "Who are you?" Christ would have but one answer. He is the Second Person of the Blessed Trinity, God the Son, the Word. But to the question "What are you?" Christ our Lord would have two answers, for He has two natures; He is God and He is man. Note the consequences for Our Lord's actions. Nature decides what the person can do. This one Person had two natures, two sources of action from which He could draw. He had the divine nature, and so could do all that goes with being God. He had a human nature, and so could do all that goes with being man. But whether He was doing the things of God in His divine nature or doing the things of man in His human nature, in either event it was the Person who was doing them: and there was but the one Person and He was God.

Thus Christ, having a human nature, was able to perform a human act; but He who performed it was a divine Person. Being able to perform a human act, He could offer it in expiation of the human act of Adam. But because He was a divine Person, His human act had a value that no act of a merely human person could have had.

And this same union in Him of human and divine, which was the ground of His work of expiation, was the ground of His work of reconciliation too. If the human race were to be brought back from servitude to sonship, here was the man who in Himself was Son and not servant; if the human race were once more to be at one with God, here in Christ Jesus humanity was already united with the Godhead in a union of inconceivable closeness. Christ our Lord was the atonement before He made the atonement. He alone could perform an act at once human and divine. Thus He could offer to God an act of obedience in love which, as human, could rightly be set against humanity's sin of rebellion in self-love, and which, as divine, must have all the value needed, or immeasurably more than all the value needed, to satisfy for it.

17. The Redeemer

This doctrine of the one person and two natures of Christ our Lord, which is simply the answer to the questions *who* and *what* He is, is so vital to the understanding of what He did, and indeed to the understanding of all that we ourselves are and do, that we must examine it in more detail. There is not the tiniest scintilla of truth in it which will not cast a whole flood of light. The tendency to dismiss the mass of Christ's revelation upon it and the Church's meditation upon His revelation as mere theology can come only from a total unawareness of its meaning.

Notice that it was the Second Person of the Blessed Trinity who became man, not the First, not the Third, not all Three.

(i) A divine Person with a human nature

For the redemption of the world, why was the *Second* Person chosen? Some hint at the answer will be found in what we have already seen about the special relation of the Second Person to God's original plan of creation. God designed this creation according to the design of His intellect: and it is by way of intellect that the Son of God proceeds within the Blessed Trinity. God made this universe as a mirroring in the finite of His own perfection: but the Second Person of the Blessed Trinity is that same mirroring in the infinite. As St. John tells us in the prologue to his Gospel, all things whatsoever that were made were made by the Word of God, who was with God and who was God. Given this special linking of one Person within the Blessed Trinity to God's original plan for this universe, it seems fitting that when, owing to the sin of man, the damage had to be repaired, the repairing should fall to the same Person, and that He who had established all things should, in St. Paul's phrase, re-establish them. Thus it was the Word who became Flesh and dwelt among us so that we, believing in His name, might be made the sons of God: as He was.

God the Son took to Himself a human nature, not merely wearing it as a disguise or taking it up as an instrument He might use, but making it His own as my nature is my own, making it His own so utterly that we can express the new relation only by saying that He, God the Son, became man. He did not take a human nature simply to be able to do the things that a man does, to act the part of a man, to pass for a man. Let us say it again, He became man. To the question *what are you?* He could answer with no mitigation or reservation, "I am a man." That would not have been the whole answer, for it would not have reached His divine nature. But it would have been wholly true. The relation between His nature as man and His person was as direct, as intimate, as the relation between my nature and my person. He could say, "I am a man", as completely as I can say, "I am a man." Indeed He could say it with better title, for He was more of a man than I. His human nature was not diminished by sin, as mine is.

Notice again that it was a *real* human nature and a *complete* human nature. Take the reality first. The human nature of Christ was not simply a human body animated by a human soul, thus possessing all that the definition of a man requires, suddenly appearing among us. He actually belongs to us. His soul was a direct and individual creation of the Blessed Trinity, just like your soul and my soul; but by His body He was conceived of a human mother, just as you and I were.

Of a human mother, notice, but not of a human father. In the sense in which other human beings have a mother and father, He had a mother only. The bodies of other human beings result from the action of an element supplied by their father upon an element supplied by their mother. In the case of Our Lord, the effect upon the female element normally produced by the male element was produced simply by a creative act of the will of God. Thus He is a member of Adam's race on His mother's side; He is a Jew on His mother's side; but not upon His father's side, for in the order of human generation He had no father. He was descended from Adam as we all are, but not as much as we all are. None of us derived our souls from Adam, but we all derived our bodies from Adam; whereas He derived His body from Adam only as to part. It follows that we are all related to Him — through her, and only through her: we are all His maternal relations, His mother's people.

His was a real human nature: and it was a complete human nature, lacking nothing whatever that human nature requires for completeness. We read in Hebrews (4:15): "He was like us in all things but without sin" — sin not being required to complete human nature, but always operating to diminish it. To grasp the completeness of Our Lord's manhood, we have only to consider the elements of which manhood is composed, body and soul. His body was a real body, though conceived by miracle: He was born as an infant and grew through boyhood to manhood: in His body He knew hunger and thirst; when His body was scourged, it bled; when it had a weight to bear too heavy for it, it fell; when it was damaged beyond a certain point, it underwent that separation from the soul which is death.

Just as He had a human body, He had a human soul to animate it, a soul which like other human souls was a created spirit. He could cry in the Garden of Gethsemane, "My soul is sorrowful even unto death." Again, His soul had the faculties of intellect and will, human intellect and human will. He who by His divine intellect had all wisdom could in His human intellect grow in wisdom" (Lk 2:52). In the Garden He could say to God, "Not My will but Thine be done", thereby indicating that though His human will was totally united to the Divine Will, there was question of two wills and not one.

The co-existence in Christ of a human intellect with the divine intellect may at first seem more difficult to conceive than the coexistence of two wills. A human intellect proceeds toward knowledge "discursively", as the philosophers say, step by step as ordinary men say. The external world makes its impact upon the bodily senses; and from the evidence of the external world which thus gets through, the soul forms its concepts, and compares its concepts to form judgments; and as its experience increases, its knowledge grows. But all this in a necessarily limited way. It does seem difficult to conceive that the one identical person who by His divine nature knew all things could also proceed to acquire by the operation of His human intellect scattered sparkles of the infinite light of knowledge in which He already lived. It is, I say, hard to conceive, yet not inconceivable. The human nature and the divine nature belong to one person, but they are not one nature. The one person could operate, really and truly, in both natures. If Our Lord wanted to lift a load, He could have lifted it either by the effortless fiat of the divine will or by the hard effort of the human muscles. Our Lord's human nature was a reality; His human senses and His human intellect were reality. His human senses could not do other than receive the impact of the external world; His human intellect could not do other than act upon their evidence to form concepts and judgments. The Godhead did not swallow up the manhood.

While we are on this question of Our Lord's human intellect, there are two other things to be said about it. It has been the steady teaching of theologians that Our Lord's human intellect had both infused knowledge and the Beatific Vision. What it must have been like for the one human mind to move along so many roads at once we cannot well picture. But there is no contradiction in the idea of the mind moving by one road to a goal it has already reached by another. The point to be grasped is that neither infused knowledge nor beatific knowledge is beyond the power of human nature to receive from God. Many men have had infused knowledge—though not continuously; and all the saved will have beatific knowledge.

(ii) The need of the supernatural

Our Lord, then, as man, had a real body with a real soul, with a real intellect and a real will. His emotions were real too. He loved St. John. He wept over Jerusalem and over dead Lazarus. He stormed at the Pharisees.

But if Our Lord has a real human nature with a real natural life, then He needed the supernatural life too, to accomplish those things beyond the power of nature. By merely human natural power, He could not see God directly, any more than we could; but His human nature was capable of receiving sanctifying grace, just as ours is. The work of grace in the soul is, as we have seen, appropriated to the Third Person of the Blessed Trinity. The Second Person, as God, possessed all things; but as man, He needed the indwelling of the Holy

Spirit both for that elevation and sanctification which every human nature needs, and for the special guidance and illumination His human nature needed for the unique work which as Son of God He was to do in it and through it. Our Lord then had sanctifying grace in His soul. He did not have faith or hope because, possessing the beatific vision, He did not need them; but He had charity in the fullest measure possible to a creature: for, at the risk of wearying, we must constantly remind ourselves that His human nature was a creature: like ours.

His charity, like all charity, was love of God and love of neighbor. There is a modern fashion for concentrating on Christ's love for men and either totally ignoring His love for God or regarding it as an amiable weakness. It is easy enough to maintain this attitude if one has either not read the Gospels, or read them sketchily as a child and forgotten them. For Christ Himself, His Father's will was paramount and His one joy was in doing it: indeed it is the one joy that He can see for anyone—"Yea, rather blessed are they who have the word of My Father and keep it." Readers of this book who may be making a serious study of the Gospels for the first time will almost certainly be startled by the place that prayer to the Father takes in Christ's life. His first recorded words are that strange answer to His mother when after three days' loss she found Him in the temple: "Could you not tell that I must needs be in the place which belongs to my Father?" (Lk 2:49). His last words as He was dying on the Cross were "Father, into thy hands I commend my spirit" (Lk 23:46).

Here again, as with the co-existence of human and divine knowledge in the one Person, the mind sees a real problem. If Christ was God, in what sense was He praying to God? It is idle to try to avoid the difficulty by answering that the Second Person of the Blessed Trinity was speaking to the other two

Persons. Assuredly He was, but this converse within the divine nature is not the prayer we have in mind here, nor indeed is it prayer at all. Christ also prayed as we pray, as the creature prays to the Creator. And here precisely is the difficulty. What is done in the nature is done by the Person. To say that Christ prayed as the creature prayed to the Creator is to say that God the Son prayed the prayer of a creature. It is difficult, but it is precise. When God the Son took to Himself a human nature and was the Person in that nature, He took upon Himself all the obligations that a person has to his nature, and one such obligation is to express its creatureliness to its Creator. His prayer was the expression of a human nature in all the manifold relations that the human nature has to God; and because it was God who uttered that human prayer, it was the perfect human prayer. Nothing could be more repaying for our selves than to study it closely.

(iii) We must come to know Him

Thus, God and man, the Second Person of the Blessed Trinity in our nature, Our Lord moves through the Gospels: thirty years of all but complete silence, then three years of healing, teaching, in crowds or with the Twelve or alone in the prayer of God, moving steadily toward the thing He had come to do. But He must not remain for us simply a luminous figure, upon whom we dare not gaze too closely, upon whom we need not gaze too closely. In Christ, God is showing Himself to us. Not to look at that which is shown would leave the showing vain. Growth in the knowledge of Christ is growth in the knowledge of God, which He was; and of man, which He was. Quite literally we cannot grow to our capacity in the knowledge either of God or of man if we do not grow in the knowledge of

Christ. He is our best approach to the knowledge of God because, as we have seen, here God is to be studied not simply in His own nature, infinitely glorious but remote from our experience, but in our nature finitely glorious and thronging with experiences that we have shared. He is our best approach to the knowledge of man, because man, like everything else, is best studied in its most perfect specimen—only defective knowledge can result from exclusive concentration on damaged specimens.

This growth in the knowledge of Our Lord is not simply a matter of learning texts and seeing the detail of this or that episode of His life. We must get to know Him, as we know a person. But this effort involves something else, which I find it rather difficult to convey. I have already made one attempt. I shall try again. A knowledge of a person has to be personal. There is no such thing as an abstract knowledge of a person, which all who know him possess: there is your knowledge of a person and my knowledge of a person, and we may both know him intimately, but your knowledge will not be the same as mine. Knowledge of a person is a relation between that person and us: it is not only what is to be known about the person, but our reaction—the reaction of our whole self, intellect, will, emotions—to the person. As I have said, any number of people may know someone else intimately, and not only intimately but truly; yet if they could compare their knowledge, there would be vast surprises. It is so with any man: there are elements in him which one friend will respond to and another not, and to which those who respond will respond at different levels of intensity. It is so, above all, with Christ because of the very perfection of His human nature, its depth and universality. No one of us can see and respond to all that is there; no two of us will see and respond to the same things in Him. What is vital for each one of us is that we develop our own closest possible personal knowledge of Him and personal relation with Him.

That is why I shall not here attempt a description of the man Christ Jesus. I could at most give *my* picture of Him, which is not more valid or valuable than someone else's merely because it is mine. Nor is there any reason why I should try to impose my picture of Him upon others of His friends. It is for each one to develop his own personal intimacy by meeting Him. And the first place to meet Him is in the Gospels.

But if it would be at once impertinent and pointless to present the reader with a portrait of Christ by me, instead of letting him meet Christ for himself, it may be well to draw attention to certain elements in what I may call roughly the modern view of Christ our Lord, which may already be in the reader's mind, and which therefore he may bring with him to the reading of the Gospels and think he is finding in the Gospels. The mind needs to be cleansed of this particular error in order that it may be prepared to see the Christ who is actually there.

The error I have in mind is the picture of Christ as all love—"love" in this context meaning a sentimental weakness about human beings. This error is carved into thousands of statues—one feels that the artists are not close or recent readers of the Gospels. It is enshrined in the line "Gentle Jesus, meek and mild", an admirable line when it was written but now, by the wearing down of language, an appalling travesty. Meekness is a great and intensely dynamic virtue; so is mildness. But that is not what the words mean in the English of today. "Meek and mild" has become a term of contempt for the type of character which, if it does not deserve contempt, at least merits no particular admiration. It implies a passivity, a willingness to be pushed about, an amiable desire for niceness all around. It is doubtful if the money changers whom He cast out of the Temple would have called Him mild, or if the Syro-Phoenician would have called Him meek when He said, "It is not right to take the children's bread and throw it to the dogs" (Mk 7:27). It might be well, before proceeding to a new reading of the Gospels in the intent of meeting Christ, to begin with the twenty-third chapter of St. Matthew's Gospel, where you will find His terrifying attack upon the scribes and Pharisees: nothing could more violently purge the mind of the picture of ineffective niceness. Just consider a handful of phrases from it: "Woe upon you, scribes and Pharisees, you hypocrites that swallow up the property of widows, under cover of your long prayers. . . .

"Woe upon you, scribes and Pharisees, you hypocrites that encompass sea and land to gain a single proselyte, and then make the proselyte twice as worthy of damnation as yourselves. . . .

"Woe upon you, scribes and Pharisees, you hypocrites that scour the outward part of cup and dish, while all within is running with avarice and incontinence. . . .

"Woe upon you, scribes and Pharisees, you hypocrites that are like whitened sepulchres, fair in outward show, when they are full of dead men's bones and all manner of corruption within. . . .

"Serpents that you are, brood of vipers, how should you escape from the award of hell?"

This is not the whole Christ, but it is an element too often overlooked. It is an element not only in His character; what we must at every cost grasp is that it is an element in His love. Note that at the very end of this vast invective, Our Lord utters one of the most perfect expressions of tenderness: "Jerusalem, Jerusalem, still murdering the prophets, and stoning the messengers that are sent to thee, how often have I been ready to gather thy children together, as a hen gathers her chickens under her wings; and thou didst refuse it!"

Love is a more complex thing, in itself and Christ, than our shallowness always knows, more complex and more extreme. It is a curious phenomenon, which will lead a psychologist of the future, perhaps, to a deeper understanding of the mind of our age, that it has effortlessly and one would say automatically sorted out the tenderer elements in Christ to the total ignoring of the fiercer. In the Sermon on the Mount, for instance (Mt 5–7), everyone has heard of the eight opening phrases: Blessed are the poor in spirit, the patient, those who mourn, those who hunger and thirst for holiness, the merciful, the clean of heart, the peacemakers, those who suffer persecution in the cause of right. But almost nobody remembers that in the long sermon that follows these opening phrases, Our Lord threatens His hearers with hell no fewer than six times.

The plain truth is that we must bring to our meeting with Christ no preconceived ideas of what He ought to be, but a determination to learn what He is. He is not to be measured by our standard, for He is the God who made us. He is the standard.

(iv) His dual utterance

I shall say no more of what in our modern phrase we call the human personality of Christ (be careful of this phrase: Christ our Lord was not a human person, though He had a human nature: but the word *personality* as used today has got separated from the philosophical word *person* and only means the general effect of a person's character and temperament). What we must now consider is a certain difficulty already discussed, arising from the two natures of Christ.

The person very rightly "utters" his nature; this one person who had two natures rightly utters each nature. But the result is two quite different sets of utterances. He can say, "I and the Father are one", and "The Father is greater than I." In the one case it is the "I" who totally owns the divine nature and expresses a fact about His divine nature; in the second case it is the same "I" who owns a human nature and expresses a fact about His human nature. We must habituate ourselves to this dual utterance, holding firmly in the mind that in either utterance the person speaking is God the Son, the Second Person of the Blessed Trinity. Here again we must aim not at a mere verbal awareness but at a comprehension of the Man who was God. For the most part, I think, we tend to concentrate upon what it means to say that God took to Himself a human nature and became man. But we must also consider what it must have meant to this man, really man as we are man, to know that He was God. We see what it meant to His Apostles as they came gradually to be aware that the man was God: it stunned their human minds, then revitalized their human minds with its glory. We must try to see also what it meant to Christ Himself to be aware that He was God; for it was with a human mind that He was aware of it, a mind as human as theirs.

What the blaze of the glory and the wonder of the knowledge must have been we can barely begin to conceive: but that bare beginning of conceiving we must attempt. Here again, each must do it for himself. As the Apostles themselves grew to the knowledge of the fact, they could only be (as we should be, without the clue) utterly bewildered. They saw Him acting and speaking as man; they also saw Him acting and speaking as man has no right to act and speak, as only God rightly could. But they had no concept born of experience of one person with two natures, for there never had been such a person, any more than there ever would be such another.

Their bewilderment was not simply the difficulty of reconciling two sets of statements from the same person, one set entirely true of Him as God, one set entirely true of Him as man. The difficulty goes deeper. Until they recognized that He was God, they must have been uncertain even of His virtue as man. This is a truth which a great deal of modern talk quite incredibly overlooks. The expression "Christ was not God but He was the perfect man" can surely only be the product of a long and heroic abstention from Gospel reading. If He was not God, He was not a perfect man: He was a totally intolerable man. Consider one phrase only: "He that loveth father and mother more than Me is not worthy of Me." If the speaker was not God, then he was a man of an egoism so monstrous that no word short of insanity would fit it. And in one way or another, this note runs through all Our Lord's sayings. If He was God, then He was perfect man; if He was not God, then He was a very arrogant man. But we know what the Apostles came to know: He was God, and all falls into place.

He was man, but He was different. And the difference was not only in that He had a divine nature in which also He acted and spoke. Though the divine nature and the human did not mingle, though there was, so to speak, no spilling over of the divine into the human, yet even in the activity of the human nature many things had of necessity to be different because the person whose nature it was, was God. He loved the companionship of the Apostles, and they loved His companionship. But He knew the difference, and they felt His difference. He never asked their advice; never argued with them or indeed with anyone. He was the Master and He taught, and men must either accept His teaching or reject it: there was no place for argument about it. Nor did He ever pray with His Apostles: He taught them how to pray, but His own prayer was alone with the Father. Still they loved Him as no other man has ever been loved, though still not in the measure of His love for them. They were desolate without Him. And the one of them whom He loved most, summarized the doctrine of Christ's Godhead and his own experience of Christ in the key phrase of all religion, "God is Love."

18. The Redeeming Sacrifice

In the three words *Way, Truth,* and *Life,* Our Lord sums up what He is. In the same three words we may summarize what He did. He opened to men the way of salvation, gave them the truth by which they might know the way, and the life by which they might travel it.

The truth He gave by way of doctrine and law—doctrine as to the great realities of existence, and law to tell us how we should act, given that these realities are what they are. He teaches of God and of man, the breach between God and man and how it must be healed, the purpose of life, heaven and hell, the kingdom He is to establish and the laws of the kingdom— what things we must do, what things we must avoid, what food we must eat.

He not only taught us about the food we must eat. He saw to it that food should be provided. The way He had come to open could not be walked by the merely natural strength of man; it called for energies of action and resistance which the natural life cannot supply. Men and women needed a higher principle of action, a new life. Without this higher life, the Supernatural Life, they could neither live in heaven hereafter, nor so live here as to attain heaven. At the very beginning of His ministry He told Nicodemus that man must be born again, that is, born into this new life, by baptism: and He established baptism, and set His Apostles to baptizing. After the feeding of the five thousand, He told the multitude that they should not have life in them unless they ate the flesh of the Son of Man and drank His blood: and He established the Blessed Eucharist and so gave His Apostles the power to feed men with His Body and Blood.

But neither the truth, which gave knowledge of the way and of how to conduct oneself on the way, nor the life, which gave power for the way, would have had a great deal of point if the way itself were not open. The map of the road and the rules of the road and the food for the road would have been merely tantalizing to a race of men to whom the road itself was closed. The reopening of the road was, could only be, the act that would give meaning to all the rest of His immeasurable activity. The way was closed because the human race was not at one with God; Heaven was for the sons of God, and the way was closed to a race that had fallen from sonship into servitude. Christ opened the way. Let us see how He did it.

(i) Christ foretells His passion and death

He offered himself as a sacrifice to God for the sin of the race. That was the thing He had come to do, and it gave meaning to every other thing that He did. The prophets of Israel had said that it would be so, but—incredibly, as it now seems to us—their message had made no apparent impact on the mind of their people. Our Lord said it again and again, even more clearly, with almost as little impact. Right at the beginning, in that conversation with Nicodemus just quoted, Christ had foreshadowed the cross: the Son of Man must be lifted up as Moses lifted up the serpent in the desert for the healing of the stricken Israelites (Jn 3:14). Near the end of His ministry, just after the glory of Palm Sunday, and on the very threshold of the Passion, he uses the same comparison: "If only I am lifted up from the earth, I will attract all men to myself" (Jn 12:33). "In saying this," St. John comments, "He prophesied the death He was to die."

In between the first conversation with Nicodemus and Palm Sunday, He had more than once spoken of the same thing to scribes and Pharisees, but in language so veiled that they can hardly be held blind for not grasping His meaning. They had asked Him for "a sign", and He had answered, "The generation that asks for a sign is a wicked and unfaithful generation; the only sign that will be given it is the sign of the prophet Jonah. Jonah was three days and three nights in the belly of the seabeast, and the Son of Man will be three days and three nights in the heart of the earth" (Mt 12:39–40). Earlier still than the Jews' challenging Him for a sign, He had used language still more cryptic: "Destroy this temple, and in three days I will raise it up." His hearers then thought that He was referring to the great temple in Jerusalem, and in this sense His words were quoted against Him at His trial and hurled at Him in derision as He hung on the Cross. "But", as St. John comments, "He spoke of the temple of His body."

If His language to outsiders was veiled, what He said to His Apostles was quite clear and literal; yet, save by flashes, they seemed to have understood Him no better than the others, and the event found them as utterly unprepared as if He had never spoken a word. On three occasions Our Lord told them in great detail just what must happen. After the great scene at Caesarea Philippi when Our Lord had named Peter as the rock upon which He would build His Church, He told the Apostles "that He must go up to Jerusalem, and there, with much ill-usage from the chief priests and elders and scribes, must be put to death, and rise again on the third day" (Mt 16:21).

In Galilee a little later He told them the same thing with the added detail that He was to be betrayed (Mt 17:21). Just before Palm Sunday, which was the first day of the very week in which all these things were to be accomplished, He gave them the most detailed statement of all: "Now, we are going up to Jerusalem; and there the Son of Man will be given up into the hands of the chief priests and scribes, who will condemn him to death; and these will give him up into the hands of the Gentiles, who will mock him, and spit upon him, and scourge him, and kill him; but on the third day he will rise again" (Mk 10:33–34)—upon which St. Luke wryly comments, "They understood none of these things."

Some of these things they should certainly have understood: all that was to flow from Christ's death as a willed sacrifice might well have been mysterious; but that the leaders of the Jews would plan to kill Him was all but certain. From the great mass of prophecy, they had singled out certain elements to construct what we may call the orthodox hope of Israel. And His teaching, embracing and transcending the whole of prophecy, was a challenge and a denial of their hope: the Kingdom He talked of was not the Kingdom they dreamed of. His own personal claims were plain blasphemy if He was not God. Not believing Him God, they naturally took Him for a blasphemer. And then there was His scorn for them. The line of teaching and conduct upon which He had embarked meant that they would desire His death. His action was the logical consequence of His whole grasp, as their reaction was the logical consequence of their partial grasp, of reality. Once they made up their minds to kill Him, in the natural order they must succeed. The only question was whether God would prevent their doing the thing they planned. God willed not to prevent them. Since they would, as He knew they would, kill Christ, He would use their act as the occasion of the salvation of the race of man.

(ii) The Last Supper

On Palm Sunday, Our Lord entered Jerusalem humbly, riding upon an ass, and the crowds acclaimed Him wildly: for the last time.

With Palm Sunday past, things moved rapidly to the crisis. On the Wednesday of that week, He said to His Apostles, "You know that after two days the paschal feast is coming; it is then that the Son of Man must be given up to be crucified" (Mt 26:2). On the Thursday, "Knowing that his hour was come, that he should pass out of this world to the Father", He ate the paschal supper prescribed by Jewish law with His Apostles and then went on to make them the priests of the Eucharistic meal whereby until the end of the world, men should receive His own Body and Blood.

Matthew and Mark and Luke each gave their account of this; so does St. Paul (1 Cor 11). All four accounts should be read closely. Here is St. Luke's (22:19):

"Then he took bread, and blessed and broke it, and gave it to them, saying, This is my body, which is to be given for you; do this for a commemoration of me.

"And so with the cup, when supper was ended. This cup, he said, is the new testament, in my blood which is to be shed for you."

St. Matthew (26:28) phrases Our Lord's words upon the chalice slightly differently (leaving the meaning, of course, unaffected) and adds one further thing that He said: "Drink, all of you, of this; for this is my blood, of the new testament, which is to be shed for many, to the remission of sins."

The institution of the Blessed Eucharist tends to fill the mind's horizon when we think of the Last Supper. But though it was the towering fact of that night, it does not stand alone. At and after the Last Supper, we have the greatest mass of teaching that Our Lord ever gave at one time. All four Evangelists give their own account, and the reader of this book is urged to study them all; but it is St. John who gives us the fullest statement, and his chapters 13 to 17 should be read and read. Here we glance at two or three points of this great mass of teaching.

Our Lord has much to say to the Apostles by way of preparation for the role that must be theirs when He is gone from them and they must carry on His work. He tells them with no apparent anger that they are all about to desert Him and that Peter will deny Him thrice that night. But as though none of this had any great relevance, He goes on to the greater things to which they are called. "I dispose to you, as my Father hath disposed to me, a kingdom; That you may eat and drink at my table, in my kingdom; and may sit upon thrones, judging the twelve tribes of Israel" (Lk 22:29–30). "It was I that chose you. The task I have appointed you is to go out and bear fruit, fruit which will endure" (Jn 15:16). "You too are to be my witnesses" (Jn 15:27). But all this they shall not do in their own power, but in the power of the Holy Spirit. It is indeed necessary that Our Lord go to the Father in order that the Holy Spirit may come to them. There is a great deal about the Holy Spirit; and it is natural therefore that Our Lord should give His most extended teaching on the Blessed Trinity.

We have already taken some stock of what He said at the Last Supper on the Trinity; we shall return a little later to what He said on the role of the Apostles. What concerns us most at this point in the story, when He is within hours of His death, is that He states so clearly both elements in His mission. We have just heard Him state it as expiation: "This is my blood of the new testament which is to be shed for many, to the remission of sins." What He says of the restoration of oneness between man and God is as clear: He prays for all who through the teaching of the Apostles shall come to believe in Him, "That they all may be one, as thou, Father, in me, and I in thee; that they also may be one in us; that the world may believe that thou hast sent me. . . . Father, I will that where I am, they also whom thou has given me may be with me . . . that the love wherewith thou hast loved me may be in them and I in them" (Jn 17:20–22).

This then is the life-formula of the Atonement: men are to be united with Him as He is united with God. "I am in my Father: and you in me, and I in you" (Jn 14:20).

(iii) Gethsemane and Calvary

From the supper room Our Lord went with the Apostles to the Garden of Gethsemane, and the whole atmosphere changes most terrifyingly. Mankind, we know, was redeemed by the passion and death of Christ; but we tend to overleap the passion and concentrate upon the death. The loss is vast for our understanding of mankind's redemption, and for our understanding of the Man Christ Jesus. What happened in the Garden will cast a flood of light upon both. In a sense what happened there *is* the passion, at any rate its fiercest point. There is an immeasurable contrast between the serene mastery of Our Lord at the Supper and the fear and agony here; and the same contrast in reverse when Our Lord goes out from the Garden and suffers mockery and scourging and nailing to a cross with a mastery as serene.

Matthew, Mark, and Luke give similar descriptions. Here is Matthew's (26:37–39) of what follows the arrival at Gethsemane: "He took Peter and the sons of Zebedee with him. And now he grew sorrowful and dismayed; My soul, he said, is ready to die with sorrow; do you abide here, and watch with me. When he had gone a little further, he fell upon his face in prayer, and said, My Father, if it is possible, let this chalice pass me by; only as they will is, not as mine is."

St. Luke continues the account (22:43–44): "And there appeared to him an angel from heaven, encouraging him. And now he was in an agony, and prayed still more earnestly; his sweat fell to the ground like thick drops of blood."

A second and a third time He prayed, as St. Matthew tells: "My Father, if this chalice may not pass away, but I must drink it, thy will be done."

Quoting Isaiah 53, He had shown at the supper what the suffering was from which He shrank with so much anguish, of which, as St. Mark tells us, He was in fear. It was not simply, nor even primarily, the bodily torments that He was to endure, though He foresaw them in every detail and already felt their horror in His flesh. Other men had been through those torments. The ground of His anguish lay deeper. The prophet Isaiah had foretold it: "Sure he hath borne our infirmities and carried our sorrows. He was wounded for our iniquities, he was bruised for our sin. The Lord hath laid upon him the iniquity of us all." St. Peter, who slept while his Master was in agony, was to say the same thing: "Who his own self bore our sins in his body upon the tree" (1 Pet 2:24). Our Lord, offering Himself for the sins of the world, not only took upon His single self the punishment those sins have deserved: in some sense He took the sins themselves, everything of them save the guilt. Sin repented can still leave a crushing weight upon the soul, even one sin. Christ's soul bore the burden of all the sin of mankind.

That was His agony, that was the chalice He prayed might pass from Him. This is a key to the mysterious phrase of St. Paul: "Him, who knew no sin, God has made into sin for us" (2 Cor 5:21).

Yet Christ our Lord did not suffer unwillingly, did not make His sacrifice under compulsion. We have already seen that when, as Second Person of the Blessed Trinity, He speaks of Himself as sent by the Father, there is no implication that the Father has imposed His will upon the Son, for within the Blessed Trinity there is but the one divine will, which is the Son's will as totally as the Father's. Nor does Christ as Man, though He has a true human will, undergo His suffering and death unwillingly. He had already made it clear to His Apostles that He was subject to no compulsion of men: "I am the good shepherd. The good shepherd lays down his life for his sheep. . . . This my Father loves in me, that I am laying down my life, to take it up again afterwards. Nobody can rob me of it; I lay it down of my own accord" (Jn 10:11–18). Here in the Garden, in the very central point of His agony, He makes it clear that if He is obeying the will of God, He is obeying it willingly. The only compulsion upon Him was the moral compulsion to carry out an obligation He had already freely accepted. This was the thing He had come for. Earlier in that same week there had been some faint foreshadowing of the shrinking and the anguish of Gethsemane. It was a day or so after the triumphant entry into Jerusalem on Palm Sunday. Our Lord, having said that the hour was come and having shown that He must die in order to bring forth fruit, continues: "Now my soul is distressed. What am I to say? I will say, Father, save me from undergoing this hour of trial; and yet, I have only reached this hour for the sake of undergoing it" (Jn 12:27). And just before Palm Sunday He had said (Mt 20:28): "The Son of Man did not come to have service done him; he came to serve others, and to give his life as a ransom for the lives of many."

The weakness in the Garden was the shrinking in human nature from a burden greater than any that a man ever had had to bear or ever again should have to bear. But it did not carry the human will with it. Christ our Lord cried to God for help, and help was given Him. From that moment there was no return of weakness. It is the Christ of the Last Supper who returns to the sleeping Apostles and tells them (Mt 26:45–46): "The time draws near when the Son of Man is to be betrayed into the hands of sinners. Rise up, let us go our way; already, he that is to betray me is close at hand."

Then Judas came, with a band of soldiers and servants sent by the chief priests and Pharisees, and betrayed his Master to them with a kiss. As they made to arrest Our Lord, Peter drew his sword and attacked one of them, cutting off his ear. Our Lord rebuked him for his failure to understand the thing that was now in process: "Put thy sword back into its sheath. Am I not to drink the cup which my Father himself has appointed for me?" (Jn 18:11).

There is no need here to follow in detail Our Lord's various appearances before this and that court—two appearances before the Jewish Sanhedrin, and two before Pilate, separated by an appearance before Herod. Note that the accusation the Jews made against Him in their own court was not at all the same as the accusation they made against Him before Pilate. In their own court the accusation was that He called Himself the Son of God; and His admission settled the matter for them: He deserved to die. Before Pilate they accused Him of sedition— "Forbidding to give tribute to Caesar and saying that he is Christ the King" (Lk 23:2). As the night proceeded and merged into the day, He was mocked and spat upon, thorns were twisted into a rough wreath and pressed upon His head, and He was scourged. Finally He was made to carry His own cross to a hill outside the city, the hill of Calvary, which means "skull". There He was nailed to His cross and so hung for three hours between two thieves chosen for crucifixion with Him.

As with the Last Supper, so with the Crucifixion, each of the Evangelists gives his own account, and all four should be read most closely. We should especially concentrate upon the things Our Lord said during the three hours that he hung upon the cross. Among the four accounts we find seven such sayings. The last recorded by St. John is "It is consummated." The last recorded by St. Luke is "Father, into thy hands I commend my spirit. And saying this, he gave up the ghost." Matthew and Mark both tell us that at the moment of death, He cried out with a loud voice.

Christ our Lord died on the Friday. He rose again from the dead on the third day. What had passed in between? His body, separated by death from the animating power of His soul, lay in the tomb. But what of His soul? He had said to one of the thieves on the cross: "This day thou shalt be with me in paradise." From this we might imagine that Our Lord's soul— and the thief's—had gone to heaven that day. But after His Resurrection, Our Lord expressly told Mary Magdalen that He had not yet ascended to His Father. Where then was His soul, and what does "paradise" mean?

The English form of the Apostles' Creed says bluntly, "He descended into hell", and one might figure to oneself the consternation He would have produced if at this moment of His triumph over Satan He had appeared in Satan's realm. But He did not do that either: the Latin word translated by "hell" is *inferos,* which means not necessarily the hell of the damned but the lower regions. St. Peter tells us (1 Pet 3:19): "It was in his spirit that he went and preached to the spirits who lay in prison." It would seem that Our Lord's soul visited that place where those who had died in the grace of God before Christ's coming were awaiting the redemptive act which should open heaven to them. It is not difficult to see the fitness of all three names—*paradise,* by comparison with the hell of the damned, *lower regions,* because lower than heaven, *prison,* because there they must wait although they would rather be elsewhere.

(iv) Resurrection and Ascension

On the Sunday morning He rose from the dead. Observe that it was the Resurrection of the whole man, body and soul united and no more separable. For this was the conquest of death. By this victory over death, Our Lord's body had put off corruption and mortality and was now as immortal and incorruptible as His soul. The destiny which St. Paul sees for us in our resurrection, that "our mortal nature must be swallowed up in life" (2 Cor 5:4), comes to us only because in His Resurrection it had already come to Him. Already His body was glorified, in the state of a body in heaven, worthy of union with a soul that is looking directly upon the unveiled face of God.

For forty days more He was upon earth, in repeated though not continuous contact with His followers. He comes and goes with an independence of the restricting power of space, which is not now miracle but part of the consequence of the glorification of His body. He comes to the Apostles through a closed door, He vanishes from their sight. In all His contact with them He is continuing and completing their preparation for the work they must do once He has left the earth. Thus He gives them power to forgive sins or withhold forgiveness (Jn 20:22–23); He opens their understanding that they may understand the Scriptures (Lk 24:45); He gives them the commission to carry His doctrine and His sacraments to all nations till the end of time (Mt 28:19–20). But none of this activity is to begin until the Holy Spirit has come upon them; and the Holy Spirit will not come until Christ our Lord has gone to His Father— "for if I go not", He had told them at the Last Supper, "the Paraclete will not come to you: but if I go I will send him to you." At the end of forty days, He left this earth.

He gave them one more reminder that they should receive the power of the Holy Spirit coming upon them. "And when he had said these things, while they looked on, He was raised up: and a cloud received him out of their sight"—so St. Luke tells us in the first chapter of the Acts. St. Mark's account is as brief: "And the Lord Jesus, after he had spoken to them, was taken up into heaven, and sitteth at the right hand of God."

Notice that the Resurrection was not simply a convenient way for Our Lord to return to His Apostles and give them final instructions, nor His Ascension simply a convenient way of letting them know definitely and beyond question or perad-venture that He had left this world. Resurrection and Ascension belong organically to the Sacrifice He offered for us. The Sacrifice, insofar as it is the offering to God of a victim slain, was complete upon Calvary. But in the total conception of sacrifice, it is not sufficient—as Cain found long before—that a victim be offered to God; it is essential that the offering be accepted by God: and given that the nature of man requires that sacrifice be an action externally visible, it belongs to the perfection of sacrifice that God's acceptance should be as externally visible as humanity's offering. It is in this sense that Resurrection and Ascension belong organically to the Sacrifice. By the miracle of the Resurrection, God at once shows His acceptance of the Priest as a true priest of a true sacrifice *and* perfects the Victim offered to Him, so that whereas it was offered mortal and corruptible, it has gained immortality and incorruptibility. By the Ascension, God accepts the offered Victim by actually taking it to Himself. Humanity, offered to God in Christ the Victim, is now forever at the right hand of the Father.

19. Redemption

The very heart of the doctrine of the Redemption is that the human acts of Christ were the acts of a Person who was divine.

Everything that Christ did and suffered and experienced was done and suffered and experienced by one who was God. God's Son, wholly God, grew to manhood, was a carpenter, rejoiced, sorrowed, suffered, died. These last two words force us really to face the mystery and test our realization of it. Yet if God did not suffer and die, then no one did, for there was but the one person in Christ; that is, there was no suffering, no dying: no sacrifice, no redemption. The phrase "God died" gives us at first the greater shock, but afterward is less profoundly mysterious than the phrase "God suffered." The whole created universe, with everything in it from archangel down to electron, or any lower thing there may be, is held in existence from instant to instant solely by the continuing will of God to hold it so. And the words "God died" seem to carry annihilation to all things that thus depend upon God. But it is by the operation of His divine nature that God sustains all things in being, and it is not in His divine nature that God the

Son died, but only in His human nature, the most glorious of created things, but a created thing for all that. Death is a separation of soul and body. The phrase "God died" means that for that three days' space, God the Son's human soul was separated from His body: it was a real death, but it left the divine nature totally unaffected.

But what are we to make of the phrase "God suffered"? Again, the suffering was not in the divine nature, but in the human. Christ's suffering, the fear and agony in the Garden for instance, was real suffering; that is to say, someone really suffered it. And that someone was God the Son. How this can be, what indeed it means, we cannot fully know, indeed we can hardly feel that we know at all. The mind seems able to make no statement here. Yet it is literally true that, even if we cannot *say* it, there are momentary flashes of light, glimpses and glances, in which we half *see* it; and there is no measuring the fruitfulness of even this momentary half-seeing for sanctity; and not for sanctity only, but for plain human consolation.

(i) Necessarily effective

Summarizing this relation of nature and person in Christ's atoning act, we see that because He was man with a true human nature, He could offer a true human act in expiation of human sin, an act of total love to balance humanity's self-love; and because He was God, the human act He offered was of infinite value and so could satisfy and more than satisfy for the sins of men. But stating it thus, we see another question. Any act of Christ must be of infinite value, since the person who does the act is God. Why then does Christ offer His death, when some lesser act would have been of infinite value and therefore totally sufficient? Might He not have offered His thirst when He sat weary from His journey by Jacob's Well in Samaria? Or His patience under insult? Or any one of a thousand other things? Why had it to be His death?

In one sense the answer is clear. He had come into the world to teach the truth—about Himself as God, for instance, about Himself as Messiah, about the Kingdom which was to be *in* the world but not *of* it, about the Gentiles who would come into it, about the failure of the leaders of Israel to grasp the essentials of their own religion. His execution was the natural consequence. Only a miraculous intervention of the divine power could have prevented it. Given that He was to die, it is hard to think of His offering some lesser thing than His death as the sacrifice that should save mankind.

But all things are in the power of God. God could have intervened to prevent His death. Or He might have chosen a way of life that meant no such direct challenge to the rulers. Why, we may ask in all reverence, did the divine plan include the death of the Redeemer?

The two answers that instantly spring to mind are that nothing could show the love of God so overpoweringly as His willingness to die for us, and nothing could show the horror of sin so clearly as that it needed His death to expiate it. Now it is true that Calvary is a proof both of the awfulness of sin and of the love of God, but it would not be so unless there was something in the nature of sin that required Calvary. If the sin could as well have been expiated by some act of Christ less than His death, then Calvary would not show the horror of sin but would in fact exaggerate it. The same line of argument would not so obviously apply to Calvary as a proof of God's love, yet there would be something profoundly unsatisfying in the notion of God's showing His love for us by a needless death. There must certainly have been something *in what Our Lord had to do* which made His dying the best way to do it.

One element, at least, we can learn from Hebrews 5:8–9. Read these verses, memorize them, live with them:

> Although he was Son,
> he learned obedience through what he suffered;
> and being made perfect he became the source
> of salvation to all who obey him.

There are two statements here about Christ that might well make us rub our eyes, if we have not met these verses earlier. The first is that from His sufferings He learned obedience. What could there be for Jesus to learn about obedience? His Father was all-in-all to Him; He could say, "My food is to do the will of Him who sent me." Even when He shrank in agony in Gethsemane, He still uttered His submission to His Father's will: "*if it be your will,* let this cup pass from me." It was not that there was any disobedience in Him to be rectified. But there is something to be learned about obedience by dying for it, something which there is no way of putting into words, a new and ultimate dimension of obedience.

Possibly even more startling is to be told that by His sufferings He was "made perfect", and so could be our Savior. In plain words, without the sufferings He could not have been the source of our salvation. That surely is what St. John meant by saying that the Spirit *could not* be given because Jesus was not yet glorified (John 7:39). Jesus' first action *after* the Resurrection was to breathe on the Apostles and say, "Receive the Holy Spirit" (John 20). It is what St. Paul also meant by saying that Christ rose again "constituted Son of God *in power*".

Consequently, therefore, Jesus Himself, in His manhood, was the first beneficiary of His own redeeming sacrifice. Being made perfect, He could now be Head of a new humanity redeemed by Him, as Adam had been head of the old race fallen in him. Re-born with Christ, we are united with

His divinity, indwelt by Father and Holy Spirit. That is Redemption.

To discuss what the Redeemer might have done gives us certain lights upon the problem of our redemption. But they are as nothing to the light that floods out from what He certainly did. He gave all that He had upon Calvary: martyrs since have died in the strength of His death, knowing that even humanly speaking He gave more than they. He died: if He had not, we should not have had the Resurrection. As we shall see, by baptism we are buried with Him in His death, and rise with Him in His Resurrection. Only God knows what splendors might have been associated with some other way of Redemption; but we have seen the splendor of this way.

(ii) What was effected—overthrow of Satan, healing of breach between the human race and God

The sacrifice of Christ was totally effective. It could not be otherwise, given that He who offered it was God. But it is important to grasp *what* it effected. Whatever it was meant to effect, it did effect. But what was it? A little precision here will be extraordinarily clarifying later.

At the moment of His death on Calvary, Christ our Lord said, "It is consummated." Something was completed. But something was beginning, too, and the something that was beginning was not simply the paradisal enjoyment by men—either by all men or by an elect or even by Christ Himself—of what He had achieved by His sacrifice, but something with vast labor and anguish and the possibility of failure in it for men, and with work still for Christ to do. Something was completed. But, at the right hand of the Father, Christ Himself continues His work of intercession for us (Heb 7:25); and we have seen His last days upon earth filled with the preparation of His Apostles to continue His work among men until the end of time.

The thing that was completed was the Redemption of the race. The race had sinned in its beginning and as a result was no longer at one with God: so that heaven was closed to it. Bound up with the severed relationship of the race with God, there was a mysterious subjection to the Devil: by his victory over Adam, the Devil had secured some kind of princedom over Adam's race, so that he is called the Prince of this World. His princedom carried no legal rights but vast power: in the decree *Firmiter*, Pope Eugenius IV said: "No one has ever been liberated from the domination of the Devil save by the merit of the Mediator." The primary effect of Our Lord's sacrifice was the undoing of Adam's sin. The princedom of the Devil was destroyed. And the breach between the race and God was healed, so that heaven was opened to the members of the race. This fundamentally *is* the redemption.

Let us consider these two results in turn. "If the Son of God was revealed to us", says St. John, "It was so that he might undo what the devil had done" (1 John 3:8). It is, as we have noted, foreign to our habits of thought to attach any real importance to the Devil, that strange intervening third in the relations between man and God. But this is a defect in our mental habits. It can never be intelligent to take lightly anything that God takes seriously. And God takes the Devil very seriously indeed. It will be remembered that when, after the fall of man, God had foretold redemption, He had not only foretold it *to* the Devil, but had expressed it in terms of a victory *over* the Devil: the seed of the woman was to crush his head (Gen 3:15).

When the hour of the redemption came, Our Lord was intensely preoccupied with this aspect of it—as the struggle between Himself and the Devil issuing in victory for Himself over the Devil. Early in Passion Week, He cried out: "Now is the judgment of the world: now shall the prince of this world be cast out" (Jn 12:31). At the Last Supper He returns to the theme twice: "The prince of this world cometh; and in me he hath not anything" (Jn 14:30); and again "The prince of this world is already judged" (Jn 16:11). Why was Our Lord so pre-occupied with Satan? It may be because He was restoring the order of reality against which Satan is the great protest, so that Satan's power was ranged against Him at the peak of intensity. What is interesting is that the Devil so little understood the nature of Our Lord's mission, that he rushed upon his own defeat. For as St. Luke and St. John both tell us, it was Satan who entered into Judas to cause him to betray Christ into the hands of His enemies, thus precipitating Christ's redemptive sacrifice. It is some consolation to us to know that an enemy of intellect so powerful is not always well informed.

But the overthrow of Satan's princedom is only incidental to the healing of the breach between the race and God, by which heaven is opened to the race of men. Let us repeat that this was something done *for the race.* John the Baptist had hailed Our Lord: "Behold the Lamb of God. Behold him who taketh away *the sin of the world*" (Jn 1:29). There was a sin of the world, and Christ died to destroy it. "Now once, at the end of ages, he hath appeared for the destruction of sin by the sacrifice of himself" (Heb 9:26). As a result, heaven was once more opened to man. A man was enthroned there where no man had yet been, a man who had gone there to prepare a place for us.

Thus the sin of the race in the representative man, Adam, was taken away by the new representative man, Christ. "A man had brought us death, and a man should bring us resurrection from the dead; just as all have died with Adam, so with Christ all will be brought to life" (1 Cor 15:21). It is magnificent, and the soul rejoices. Yet the intellect, trying to comprehend, may be faintly troubled. At first glance there seems something arbitrary and almost capricious in it. Adam falls, and we are informed that Adam represented us and we have all fallen in him. Christ atones, and we are informed that Christ represents us and we are all redeemed in Him. Where, we might wonder, do we really come in? Who and what are these representatives? Above all, why?

But there is nothing arbitrary. Each is our representative because of a real relation of us to him. We have already seen that this is so of Adam. There is a solidarity of the human race, linking us physically to one another, and to the first man from whom we all come: and because of it our fate was involved in his. Christ is entitled to act for us by a double title: first on the side of His divinity, He is the God by whom and in whose image man was created; second on the side of His humanity, He is the perfect man, so that where Adam was the first man in time, Christ is the first man in value. Christ is the *moral* head of the race, as Adam was the *physical* head. Adam represents humanity in that all of us come from him, Christ in that there is no element of mind and will in any of us (Adam included) that is not better and richer and completer in Him. So that His act in compensation of Adam's is available for all men (Adam again included). The barrier erected by man's sin between the race and God is down. There is no longer a sin of the race to stand between us and sonship of God, between us and entry into heaven.

But our different relationships to Adam and to Christ involve a difference in the way of our sharing in the result of their acts. We fell in Adam inasmuch as we are united with him; we are restored in Christ inasmuch as we are united with Him. Adam's act becomes ours because we are (as we cannot help being) one with him. Christ's act becomes ours only when we become (as we may unhappily fail to become) one with Him. We are incorporated with Adam by the mere fact of being born; for incorporation with Christ, we must be re-born. "The man who came first came from earth, fashioned of dust; the man who came afterwards came from heaven, and his fashion is heavenly. The nature of that earthborn man is shared by his earthly sons, the nature of the heaven-born man, by his heavenly sons; and it remains for us, who once bore the stamp of earth, to bear the stamp of heaven" (1 Cor 15:47). We fell as members of humanity stemming from Adam; we are restored as members of a new humanity stemming from Christ.

We may now look again at what was completed by Our Lord's sacrifice on Calvary. Satisfaction was made, complete satisfaction, for the sin of the human race: the breach between God and the race was healed. That work was done, done completely, done once for all, because Christ had offered complete satisfaction for the sin of the race. He had not only satisfied but more than satisfied: He had merited for all mankind an elevation to sonship of God, to the supernatural life in which that sonship consists, the life by which we can look upon the face of God in heaven. Heaven was once more open to men.

(iii) Christ died for all; not all will be saved

But the opening of heaven does not mean that every person will get there. Some may fail: the defeat of Satan in his effort to hold the race does not mean that he will have no more victories over individuals. In other words, the salvation of the individual does not follow automatically upon the redemption of the race. It is a further problem, involving a further warfare. In plain words, though no one enters heaven save because Christ offered the atoning sacrifice, no one enters heaven simply because Christ offered the atoning sacrifice. His sacrifice availed both for the redemption of the race—satisfying for sin and meriting restoration—and for the salvation of the individual, but in different ways. It *effected* the redemption of the race; it made possible the salvation of the individual.

It is worth our while to pause for a moment on the distinction here made between *redemption* and *salvation*. Obviously, of course, there can be no hard and fast allocation of the word *redemption* to what Our Lord did for the race and *salvation* to what He does to the individual. He was the savior of the race as well as of the individual; by redeeming the race, He redeemed the individual. Yet I think there is a tendency in Scripture to use the words more often in the way here suggested.

However that may be, let us repeat that the sacrifice on Calvary was a propitiation not only for the representative sin of the race but for the personal sins of all members of the race: "He is the propitiation for our sins; and not for ours only, but also for those of the whole world" (1 Jn 2:2). "He hath washed us from our sins in his own blood" (Rev 1:5). But whereas the redemption of the race was entirely His work and therefore wholly achieved, the salvation of the individual depends upon our cooperation with His work, and some of us may fail. This is the reason for a variation of phrasing in Scripture—Christ being said at one time to have died for all and at another time to have died for some—which at first seems puzzling. The first phrase means that He excluded none from the reach of the sacrifice, the second that some have excluded themselves and so are not reached by it. "Being consummated, he became, *to all that obey him,* the cause of eternal salvation" (Heb 5:9). But nothing must dim our realization of the truth that He died for all without exception: "Such prayer is our duty, it is what God, our Saviour, expects of us, since it is His will that all men should be saved, and be led to recognize the truth; there is only one God, and only one Mediator between God and men, Jesus Christ, who is a man, like them, and gave himself as a ransom for them all" (1 Tim 2:5).

Christ died for all. "But though He died for all, yet not all receive the benefit of His death, but those only unto whom the merit of His passion is communicated" (Council of Trent VI:2). Salvation depends upon our receiving the supernatural life by which we become sons of God and having this life in our souls when we die. Christ merited it for all. But, as we have already seen, we do not receive it automatically merely by being born (for by birth we are one with Adam, in whom we fell), but by being re-born in Christ, made one with Him in such a way that in Him we are restored. If we do not receive His life, or if we receive it but lose it and die without it, then we shall not be saved.

Notice particularly how St. Paul emphasized the distinction between Christ's death on Calvary and our salvation by it. God "means us to win salvation through Our Lord Jesus Christ, Who has died for our sakes, that we, waking or sleeping, may find life with Him" (1 Th 5:10). In the Epistle to the Romans, he makes equally clear not only that there is some-thing to be done *by us* for our salvation, but that Christ's own part in our salvation is not confined to His death on Calvary: "For if, when we were enemies, we were reconciled to God *by the death* of His Son: much more, being reconciled, shall we be saved *by His life*" (5:10). Christ dying made our salvation possible; Christ living still operates to make it actual.

How? Christ works for us in heaven in His own Person, upon earth through His Church. Here let us consider for a moment Christ in heaven. We have seen that He is at the right hand of the Father in the whole of His reality, body and soul and divinity. We have also seen that He continues to make intercession for us: "Jesus continues for ever, and His priestly office is unchanging; that is why He can give eternal salvation to those who through Him make their way to God, He lives on still to make intercession on our behalf" (Heb 7:25). As St. Thomas says (S.T. III, q. 54): "interceding for us, He ever shows the Father what kind of death He bore for man." In other words, Christ our Lord is ever in the presence of His Father in that sacred humanity which He offered once for all upon Calvary: and by that continuing presence before God of that which was offered for us, our own continuance in the way of salvation is made possible. "He sits now at the right hand of God, annihilating death, to make us heirs of eternal life" (1 Pet 3:22).

We shall have occasion to return to this continuing priesthood of Christ in heaven. For the moment we must turn to a study of the Church, which is the continuation of His work upon earth, which is in fact Himself continuing to work upon earth. As we proceed in this study of the Church, we shall come to a fuller understanding than we have even yet indicated of what is meant by oneness with Christ, and with that, to the deepest meaning of Christ's redemptive work.

20. The Kingdom

We have observed the modern tendency to ignore the Devil; there is a tendency almost as great to ignore the Apostles. And if the first ignoring leaves unexplained a most important element in the work Our Lord came to do, the second badly falsifies Our Lord's plan for the continuation of His work upon earth. At any rate it is clear that Our Lord attached an enormous importance to what He would do to the Devil and to what He would do through the Apostles. Our concern now is with the Apostles.

(i) The function of the Apostles

Consider what He said to them at the Last Supper, these men who were just about to desert Him almost in a body: "I do not speak of you any more as my servants; a servant is one who does not understand what his master is about, whereas I have made known to you all that my Father has told me; and so I have called you my friends. It was not you that chose me, it was I that chose you. The task I have appointed you is to go out and bear fruit, fruit which will endure" (Jn 15:15–16). Clearly He was preparing them for some great thing, and clearly we shall not understand His plan for mankind unless we see their place in it.

In that plan for mankind there are many elements; but as His teaching proceeds, two emerge as dominant. One is the coming of the Kingdom, the other the spiritual shaping of men's souls by the gifts of truth and life that He brings. Take the teaching on the Kingdom first. The angel who announced to Mary that she was to be His mother said of Him: "His kingdom shall never have an end"; and it was on His claim to found a kingdom that the Jews framed the charge upon which Pilate sentenced Him to death. But Our Lord made it clear that His kingdom was not the kind of kingdom the Jews wanted, nor the kind of kingdom that Pilate would have thought worthy of drastic preventive action. The interchange between Our Lord and Pilate, indeed, is worth noting. Our

Lord had said, "My kingdom is not of this world." Pilate asks, "Thou art a king then?" Our Lord answers: "It is thy own lips that have called me a king. What I was born for, what I came into the world for, is to bear witness of the truth." Here as elsewhere we see that Our Lord's kingdom is bound up with the spiritual gifts He had come to bring. He was founding a kingdom in which those who believed in Him should receive truth and life.

Just as the kingdom and the gifts were two sides of the one reality, so we find the thing for which He was preparing the Apostles stated sometimes in terms of the Kingdom and sometimes of the gifts. Thus, at the Last Supper, Our Lord told them, "I dispose to you as My Father has disposed to Me a kingdom." The key words here are "as My Father has disposed to Me". We are all meant to enter the kingdom, but as citizens of the kingdom. Our Lord was set over the kingdom as ruler by His Father; and now we know that the Apostles are to be rulers in the kingdom, and not simply citizens. In that kingdom the ruler must be not only one who commands but one who serves. Christ serves supremely; but in their measure the Apostles likewise must serve. His service we have already seen as opening the Way to heaven by the sacrifice He offered, and giving the Truth and the Life that men need to tread the Way. He equips the Apostles to continue to serve in all those same ways. They may, in the religious sphere, require obedience to their commands, for without that there would be no unity, and very soon no society. But this is simply the background to service. They are to dispense the gifts of Truth and Life, for these cannot be given once for all; but each new generation born into the world, each new person born into the world, must receive them. This continuance of the gifts of Truth and Life strikes us as obvious once we grasp what the gifts are. But there is another continuance, too—the sacrifice is in some way to continue upon earth. At the Last Supper, Our Lord makes His Apostles not only teachers and ministers of the sacraments, but priests, too, offerers of sacrifice. For there was to be sacrifice in the kingdom. St. John says in the Apocalypse, "Thou wast slain in sacrifice—Thou hast ransomed us with Thy blood and given us to God. Thou hast made us a royal race of priests to serve God" (5:9).

Before coming to a detailed examination of the kingdom Our Lord founded, let us summarize rapidly the preparation He had given the Apostles. First, as dispensers of His Truth: there was the three-year period in which they heard Him teaching others, and received special teaching for themselves: "It is granted to you to understand the secret of God's kingdom; the rest must learn of it by parables" (Lk 8:10). At the Last Supper, Our Lord promised them further aid from the Holy Spirit: "Well, when the truth-giving Spirit, who proceeds from the Father, has come to befriend you, he whom I will send to you from the Father's side, he will bear witness of what I was" (Jn 15:26). After His Resurrection, "He enlightened their minds, to make them understand the Scriptures" (Lk 24:45).

As dispensers of Life, their preparation was as thorough. He sent them out to administer baptism, whereby men are born again into the life above nature; He gave them the power to change bread and wine into His Body and Blood and administer it to men, for unless we shall eat the Flesh of the Son of Man and drink His Blood we shall not have life in us (Jn 6:54); He gave them the power to forgive sins, that is, to restore to the souls of men the life they have lost by rejecting God's will in favor of their own. All this adds up to too vast a preparation for a dozen men who were, even the oldest of them, to survive Our Lord by so short a space and were then to leave the world, as He had left it. What He was doing was to establish the framework of His kingdom, the kingdom of which there should be no end. In that kingdom He would work upon men through men until the end of time. The Apostles were to be the first of a line. They would multiply successors, and the successors would die and their successors after them, but the line would never fail; and the come and go of men would not matter, since it is the one Christ operating through all of them.

But notice that although these men are simply to be human instruments in the hand of Christ and what they do is only of value because He does it, yet for the coming alive and continuance in life of His kingdom, the Holy Spirit must come upon it and abide with it. "I am sending down upon you the gift that was promised by My Father; you must wait in the city, until you are clothed with power from on high." So St. Luke tells us in his account of Our Lord's last words before the Ascension (24:49). In the first chapter of the Acts of the Apostles, St. Luke adds to this. The Apostles had been asking Our Lord about the restoration of the kingdom. He answered: "The Holy Spirit will come upon you, and you will receive strength from Him; you are to be my witness in Jerusalem and throughout Judaea, in Samaria, yes, and to the ends of the earth" (Acts 1:8). So saying, He ascended into Heaven, and ten days later the Holy Spirit came upon them: "When the day of Pentecost came round, while they were all gathered together in unity of purpose, all at once a sound came from Heaven like that of a strong wind blowing, and filled the whole house where they were sitting. Then appeared to them what seemed to be tongues of fire, which parted and came to rest on each of them; and they were all filled with the Holy Spirit, and began to speak in strange languages, as the Spirit gave utterance to each" (Acts 2:1–4).

(ii) The Church one and Catholic

Our Lord sees His kingdom and speaks of His kingdom with great precision of detail. Just before His Ascension, He said to His Apostles, "Go ye, teach all nations: baptising them in the name of the Father and of the Son and of the Holy Ghost, teaching them to observe all things whatsoever I have commanded you; and lo, I am with you all days, even to the consummation of the world" (Mt 28:19–20).

Notice first the threefold "all"—all nations, all things, all days. There has been plenty of disputation over the word "Catholic". But this one phrase of Our Lord's should have prevented most of it. Catholic, we say, means universal; but that is merely to exchange a Greek word for a Latin one. Examining the word *universal,* we see that it contains two ideas, the idea of all, the idea of one: universal is some sort of unity embracing all, some way of having all in one. But all what? All nations, all teachings, all times. So Our Lord says. It is not an exaggerated description of the Catholic Church. Not by the wildest exaggeration could it be advanced as a description of any other.

You will observe that the mission Our Lord gave the Apostles was to last till the end of the world, so that He was speaking to them not as themselves only, but as officials in His kingdom who should have successors until the end of time. Now look more closely at what He gave them to do. They were to teach, that is, they were to communicate truth; and they were to baptize, that is, they were to communicate life. He who is the Way and the Truth and the Life sends these men out to bring to the world His gifts of truth and life: and to bring men to the way, too, for in finding them we find Him. Where they are, He is—"I am with you all days, even to the consummation of the world." This continuous presence of

Christ with His Apostles gives us a double guarantee; first the certainty that the truth and the life we receive from them we are actually receiving from Him, so that they are true truth and living life, *His* gifts to us, not their gifts to us; second, and even more vital, the certainty that in contact with them we are in contact with Him. He had already given us some hint of this in His lifetime. Sending out the seventy-two disciples, He said to them (Lk 10:16): "He that hears you, hears Me": in the same sense we may note how St. John says in one place that Our Lord baptized people, and in another that He Himself did not baptize, but His disciples (Jn 3:22; 4:2): those who are baptized by them are baptized by Him.

But if Our Lord was to be with them in their teaching and baptizing and their work for the kingdom generally, why did they need the Holy Spirit? A little precision here will be rewarded with a great deal of light. Our Lord was the Second Person of the Blessed Trinity working among men in and through the human nature He had made His own. We have already seen that, because it *was* a human nature, it needed the supernatural life, the operation of the blessed Trinity in the soul by grace, which is appropriated especially to the Holy Spirit. As God, Our Lord was infinite; but as man, He needed the indwelling of the Holy Spirit, not to elevate and sanctify His human nature, but to give the special light and strength it needed for the special things which the Son of God was to do in it. We have seen how Our Lord is constantly spoken of as being acted upon by the Holy Spirit. "God anointed him with the Holy Spirit and with power, so that he went about doing good, and curing all those who were under the devil's tyranny" (Acts 10:38). For His temptation, He was led by the Holy spirit into a desert place. It was by the Holy Spirit that He offered Himself to God upon Calvary (Heb 9:14). It was by the Holy Spirit that He gave these commandments to the Apostles (Acts

1:2). Now just as the human nature through which He worked upon earth received light and strength from the Holy Spirit, so the human society through which He was to continue to work would need light and strength from the Holy Spirit in order that it might be maintained at the level of what He would use it to do.

We have seen that the word "Catholic" means all in one; and we have seen what the all is. Given that the Church was to teach all men all truths and that Christ was to be with it in the teaching, it seems hardly necessary to add that it was to be one Church. But there is another place in which Our Lord treats of the visible unity of His Church still more explicitly. At the Last Supper, having prayed for the Apostles, Our Lord went on to pray for all those who through their word should come to believe in Him. This was His prayer—"that they all may be one; that they too may be one in us, as thou, Father, art in me, and I in thee; so that the world may come to believe that it is thou who hast sent me" (Jn 17:21): a unity among men as intense, in the human order, as the unity of Persons within the Blessed Trinity; a unity externally visible so that the world could see it and be driven to conclude from it that only the power of God could account for it.

(iii) The function of Peter

Our Lord established His kingdom with officials through whom He would dispense His gifts of truth by way of doctrine, and of life by way of sacrament. The kingdom was to be in the souls of men since apart from that it could have borne no fruit; but it was not to be only in the souls of men. We must complete such phrases of Our Lord as "The Kingdom of Heaven is within you" and such phrases as "The Kingdom of Heaven is like a city set upon a hill." But for the protection of the truth and the preservation of the integrity of the channels of life, Our Lord made still further provision by choosing one of the Apostles and giving him special functions. When He first called the Apostles, He said to Simon, the brother of Andrew, "Thou shalt be called Peter"—a word which means "rock". When the end of His time upon earth was drawing near, He made clear the reason for the change of names: "Blessed art thou, Simon son of Jonah; it is not flesh and blood, it is my Father in heaven that has revealed this to thee. And I tell thee this in my turn, that thou art Peter, and it is upon this rock that I will build my church; and the gates of hell shall not prevail against it; and I will give to thee the keys of the kingdom of heaven; and whatever thou shalt bind on earth shall be bound in heaven, and whatever thou shalt loose on earth shall be loosed in heaven" (Mt 16:18–19).

At the Last Supper, when the dispute arose among the Apostles as to which should have first place in His kingdom, Our Lord settled it with the words: "Simon, Simon, Satan has claimed power over you all, so that He can sift you like wheat: but I have prayed for thee, that thy faith may not fail; when, after a while, thou hast come back to me, it is for thee to be the support of thy brethren" (Lk 22:31–32).

After His Resurrection, Our Lord appears among the Apostles and three times asks Peter if he loves Him. As Peter answers each question with an affirmation of his love, Our Lord utters the three phrases: "Feed My lambs", "Feed My lambs", "Feed My sheep" (Jn 21:16–17). Taking any one of these episodes, we must see that the function entrusted to Peter was very great; taking them all together, we see it is enormous. In the first he is to be the rock upon whom the Church (which Our Lord here calls also the kingdom of heaven) is to be founded. He is to have supremacy in the kingdom, for Our Lord promised him the "keys", which are the symbol of supremacy; and he is to have a final power of regulation and discipline, for his permissions and prohibitions are to be ratified in heaven. At the Last Supper, something is made explicit which before was certainly present, but implicitly. He is to safeguard the unity of the brethren, whom otherwise Satan would scatter like chaff, because by the prayer of God his own faith would not fail, would be unfailable—which brings us to the very word *infallibility.* The third is the richest of all. Peter is to shepherd the whole flock, the little ones and the great. He is to feed them. With what food? The spirit of man needs three kinds of food, and Our Lord came to provide them. "Man does not live by bread alone, but by every word that proceeds from the mouth of God." So truth is food. "My meat is to do the Will of Him that sent Me." So the law is food. "The food I shall give is My flesh for the life of the world." So sacrament is food. Peter must feed the flock with truth and law and sacrament.

Notice most particularly how in all this Our Lord, about to leave the earth, is conferring upon Peter His own special titles. Christ is the foundation (1 Cor 3:11), and He makes Peter the foundation. Christ is the key-bearer—He "bears the key of David, so that none may shut when He opens, none open when He shuts" (Rev 3:7)—and He makes Peter the key-bearer. It is to Christ that the power belongs to hold these whom God has given Him, but He gives to Peter the charge of being a support to the brethren. Our Lord had said, "I am the good shepherd"—and He makes Peter to be the shepherd. All this is in line with what we have already seen about the Church as a whole. Our Lord was truthgiver and lifegiver, and the Church is to be truthgiver and lifegiver: that is to say, He will continue to give truth and life through the Church. Our Lord is rock and key-bearer and shepherd: He will continue all that each title implies through Peter. Church or Peter, it is all the same.

Neither matters save as an instrument through which Christ has chosen to work.

This then was the provision Our Lord made for the souls of men that they might come to Him, be united with Him, and receive His gifts till the end of time. His kingdom would grow as it moved outward and onward toward its two limiting points—all the nations of the earth and the end of time—and there would be some increase of complexity in its structure to meet new needs created by its growth. But all would be within the living framework He established upon earth—one kingdom, with a smaller body of officials serving the great body of plain citizens, and among the officials one who is head over the rest and the servant of all. So the kingdom was, when the Holy Spirit descended upon it at Pentecost. So it still is. So till the end of the world it will be.

21. Dispensing the Gifts

Observe the aptness of all this to the nature of man. Religion is a relation of man to God, and a true religion must be true to both. God will treat man as man is, and man will react to God's act as man is.

(i) A social religion

Almost the first thing we see when we look at man is that he is not an isolated unit independent of others, but a social being bound to others both by needs that cannot be satisfied and by powers that must remain unused save in relation to other men. It would be strange if God, having made man social, should ignore the fact in His own personal dealings with man. To treat man as an isolated independent unit would be as monstrous in religion as it would be in any other department of human life. It would be to treat man as what he is not. But the one being who would not be likely to do that is God, who made man what he is, and made him so because that is what He wanted him to be. A religion which should consist in an individual relation of each person directly to God would be no religion for man. A social being requires a social religion. Within that social religion, the individual will have his own religious needs and experiences, but they will be within and not external to, or a substitute for, his approach to God and God's approach to him in union with other men.

Individualist religious theories there have always been, even among Christians. They have never been able to carry out the full logic of their individualist theory because their nature as human beings stood too solidly in their way. Something in religion they have had to get from other men. So the Bible-Christian despising priesthood and minimizing Church has yet had to fall back upon the Bible; and the Bible, although it is given to us by God, is given through men, the men who under His inspiration wrote it. A religion wherein the soul finds and maintains a relation with God with no dependence upon men is impossible, and what makes it impossible is the nature God gave man. The only question, then, is whether religion shall do its very uttermost to elude the social element in man's nature, accepting only so much as it can by no possibility avoid; or whether it shall wholly accept and glory in the social element as something given by God, something therefore to be used to the uttermost in religion as in the rest of man's life. In giving man the religion of the Kingdom, God showed what His own answer is.

Christ did not leave His followers free at their discretion to form their own groups if it seemed good to them, or to remain isolated if it seemed good to them. He banded them into a flock, a society, a Church. "He gave Himself for us, to ransom us from all our guilt, *a people set apart for Himself.*" What the Jews had been, the Church now is. We remember Moses' words: "This is the blood of the covenant." But now we have Christ's words: "This is my blood of the new covenant." There is a new covenant and a new people: not just millions of redeemed individuals: a people. The brotherhood of every Christian with Christ involved the brotherhood of all Christians with one another. His normal way of giving them His gifts of truth and life was to be through the society: in other words, the whole Christian life was not to be a solitary relation of each soul to Christ, but of each to all in Christ: this is what the Apostles' Creed means by the "Communion of Saints". In solidarity with other men, we fell in Adam and rose again with Christ; in the same solidarity, we live the new life.

God can and does give this or that man what he individually needs. But the great needs of the soul are not peculiar to the individual, but are the same for all. There is the need for the Life that Christ came to give, that we might have it more abundantly; and the need for knowledge—knowledge of what God is and what man is, and of the goal of life and how we are to attain it. It is through the society that God offers to all men the spiritual gifts by which these needs common to all are supplied. The relation of Christians with one another is essential in their relation with Christ. They are related to Him not one by one but in virtue of their membership in His Kingdom.

(ii) Truth taught infallibly

The close correspondence of religion with the nature of man is continued in every detail of the provision God made for the communication of His gifts of truth and life. We shall consider truth first.

The mind of man is capable of knowing reality and needs to know reality. It is of the nature of man to will his action in accordance with what he knows. His eternal destiny depends upon the choices he thus makes. Light therefore is essential for his proper operation as man. Further, man not only needs knowledge, he craves it and is capable of astonishing energy and even astonishing sacrifice in the pursuit of it. Within the Kingdom, all this side of man's nature is superbly provided for. There is no limit to the possibility of man's growth in knowledge, in the light. Further, his growth is not to be by way of spoon-feeding, but by way of an intellectual effort, which will call into play every muscle his mind has. It is to be noted that if Christ came to save men, He certainly did not come to save them trouble. It is not part of His purpose to do for men what they can very well do themselves, but only what they cannot. Just as in the act of *atonement* the humanity of Christ gave all that humanity had to give and the divinity of the person supplied only what human nature *could not give;* so in the matter of truth, and indeed in the matter of life too, God supplies what man cannot, but expects man to do the utter-most that he can.

There are certain things that the mind of man at its most powerful cannot compass. Merely by thinking, we cannot know what is in the mind of another or what some place is like that we have not visited. On these matters we must either be told by someone who knows, or else remain ignorant. That is why God has given us His revelation upon what He had in mind when He created man, upon what awaits us after death, and upon what kind of action here upon earth will bring us to our true destiny. There is a multiplicity of such truths which we could not find for ourselves, and God has supplied them. The Kingdom came into being endowed with an overflowing treasury of them, all the truths contained in the revelation of God written down in Scripture (completed now as men were inspired to write the books of the New Testament), or held securely in the mind of the Apostles—securely, for Our Lord had promised that the Holy Spirit would bring to their memory all things whatsoever He had taught them. Given this rich treasure of truths, the minds of Christians could work upon them in all the ways in which a mind can work—by close study of them in their direct statement, by meditation upon the implications wrapped up in any given piece of truth, and again upon its relation to other truths; by that intimacy which comes almost unawares from living by the truths; from prayer and contemplation.

All this the mind of man could do. It is its proper field. And thereby the mind of man could make vast progress, not adding to the truth but seeing more profoundly, more richly and vitally, finding new ways of stating the truths so as to get more light from them, and bring more of life within the circle of their light. What the mind of man could not do was to know with absolute certainty whether all its gains were really gains, or whether some admixture of error might not have crept in. Some men did make statements which other men thought to be false; and there was much controversy and at one time one man would seem to succeed, at another time another. But the mind of man has no faculty for settling such questions with certainty or finality. All human minds, even the most brilliant, are capable of error. One mind is better than another, but none is perfect; and if any one mind were perfect, the minds of others would not be perfect enough to know it. If God had given men a deposit of truth and left it to their mercy, there would soon have been no certainty of truth left in the world. But there are truths about which it is vital that certainty should be possible; since this certainty cannot be provided by man, God saw to it.

That is the whole point of the doctrine of infallibility. It is important to be clear on this. God made His Church infallible. In one sense it is surprising to see how little this means, yet how totally effective this little is. When we say the Church is infallible, we mean the bishops, for they are in the fullest sense successors of the Apostles; and their infallibility means simply this: that whatever is taught as to the revelation of Christ by the bishops of the Church cannot be wrong: God will not allow it. This does not mean that each individual bishop is prevented by God from teaching error, or that particular groups of bishops in this or that place might not teach error; but that when any teaching is so widely given by the bishops of the Church that we can say it is the teaching of the episcopate, then we can know that that teaching is true. If they teach that something is so, it is so. If they teach that something is false, it is false. And this not by their power, but by God's power.

Yet a situation might arise in which it would be difficult to tell with certainty what the common teaching of the episcopate throughout the world actually is. It might be a matter of some problem in theology newly posed and too urgent to be left to the sieve of theological discussion. One way or another the occasion might arise where a definite statement of truth, a statement which is certainly true, is needed, and there is dispute or doubt as to what the episcopate throughout the world teaches upon the matter. This is the normal ground of action for the infallibility of the pope. Just as the Apostles had their successors, the bishops, so Peter has his successor, the bishop of

Rome: for Rome was Peter's own See. And the pope is endowed with that same infallibility with which God has endowed the Church. Notice it is one and the same infallibility whereby God safeguards the bishops as a body and the bishop of Rome as head of the body from teaching error to His Church. There is no question of inspiration. God does not promise the pope some special message or illumination. The pope must learn his doctrine like anyone else. No hidden source of doctrine is available to him that is not available to any other citizen of the Kingdom. But God sees to it that when the pope gives the whole Church a definition of faith or morals bearing upon the revelation of Christ, there will be no error in it. If the pope defines that a thing is so, it is so. If he defines that it is false, it is false.

As we have seen, this is a tiny, almost penurious gift. In a sense, it gives nothing at all. By his infallibility, the pope acquires no truth. The truth that he infallibly teaches he had to acquire in the ordinary way of learning with ordinary or extraordinary effort. Infallibility does not account for any of the truth that is in his definition; it accounts only for the absence of all the error that might have been in his definition. In the struggle of the human mind for more light, infallibility, whether of Church or pope, saves the mind no trouble, does for the mind nothing that the mind could do for itself. What it does do is to guarantee the mind's true findings and to reject its false findings. The result is that the thinker can have all the luxury of thinking, yet the truth is safe: the flock of Christ is fed, and there is no poison in the food.

Infallibility is God's device to make it possible for the human mind to exercise its activity upon His revelation without destroying the revelation in the process. Grasp that the preservation of what God has revealed is the primary thing, incomparably more important than any conceivable mental activity—because the revelation provides truth which man must have in order to live intelligently, yet cannot find for himself. One way of preserving the truth would have been to give it to man as a set body of formulas, not to be discussed or subjected to the mind's action but simply to be learned and repeated. The result would have been some sort of stagnation and sterilization. The mind is so constituted that it cannot get much use out of what it cannot think about. Such a system would have preserved revealed truth from the adulteration of error, but would have reduced its fruitfulness for living almost to nothing.

Man being what he is, he could not be given truths to live by but not think about. Mental activity upon the revelation of God there has to be. But as we have seen, logically and historically, mental activity without the safeguard of an infallible teacher could have led only to chaos. The Bible, written by men under the inspiration of God, is a marvelous repository of God's revelation, but it cannot defend itself. If men differ as to what any one of its teachings may mean, it cannot intervene to settle the difference. The process terminates in chaos, and chaos is no terminus. One might be disposed to think that this is too gloomy a view. Free inquiry and free discussion with no safeguarding infallibility have not produced chaos in the physical sciences: why should they be more destructive in religion? But if they have not produced actual chaos, they have at least produced multitudinous error long reigning and only slowly corrected: and as often as not the correction turns out to be only an error in a different direction. This is tolerable in the physical sciences, but not in religion: for the truths of religion are the indispensable minimum that man needs to live by. And there is a further consideration. The errors of science tend to correct themselves because experience provides certain tests by which false theories are shown to be false. But with religion the decisive testing takes place after death, where we upon earth cannot see it.

Revelation and mental activity can be reconciled only by infallibility. It could of course, had God so willed it, have been a personal infallibility whereby God acted upon the soul of each Christian to prevent his arriving at error as a fruit of his thinking upon revelation. It could have been. But quite evidently it has not been, since outside the Church there is hardly agreement upon any single point of Christ's revelation; and in any event Christ made a different arrangement—an arrangement which, on the principle of leaving men to do as much as possible for themselves, with God supplying only what men cannot supply, is at once an indispensable minimum yet totally effective.

One fact at least is clear, and for a Christian should be decisive. Given that there is immense difference of opinion upon the meaning of every teaching Christ gave, there is no way of settling the difference; that is, there is no way of knowing with certainty what Christ means, unless there is here upon earth a living teacher who can settle it without the possibility of error. No other way is even suggested for attaining certainty as to what Christ meant. And what He meant is what matters.

Each truth thus attained and promulgated gives rise, of course, to further thinking, minds variously functioning on it, the air filled with speculations. On this particular question, there is a period—often a long period—of confusion. Only a solemn definition can clarify it: not that there is any magic in a definition. The point is that the Church is prepared to commit herself upon what Christ's revelation means.

(iii) *Life by sacraments*

Truth is the one great gift Christ gives us through His Church. Life is the other. There is the same close correspondence with human nature, both in the way life works in us when we have it and the channels through which it comes to us. What this supernatural life of sanctifying grace is we have already seen in some detail and will later see in even more detail. We need only summarize here. In order to live the life of heaven, for which man is destined, he needs new powers of knowing and loving in his soul over and above the natural powers of his intellect and will. Therefore a new life-principle, a new principle of operation, must be given to his soul. Though this new life is meant primarily to enable him to live in heaven, it is given to him while he is still upon earth, and its acquisition and preservation are man's principal business on earth. And if it does not yet have its full flowering in the direct vision of God, its effect upon the soul is still very great. It elevates the intellect to the level of faith and the will to the levels of hope and charity. It is not a gift given once for all. It may be lost and restored. What is more vital, it may be increased. While we live, there is no limit to the possibility of the growth of this life in us. It is indeed a result of the energizing of God's life in our souls; and precisely because God's life is infinite, there is no limit to the increase of its energizing in us, save the limit of our willingness to lay ourselves open to it.

Of how sanctifying grace operates in the soul and of the part played by actual grace and of the difference between the two we shall speak in Part Three of this book. Here we are concerned with the way in which Christ uses the Church to give sanctifying grace to us.

We have already seen that Christ meant the life to come to us in baptism—we are to be born again of water and the Holy

Spirit. We have seen that we cannot have life in us unless we eat the flesh of the Son of Man and drink His blood: and we have seen how this could be, for at the Last Supper He changed bread into His body and wine into His blood and gave them to the Apostles, at the same time giving the Apostles the command, and therefore the power, to do likewise for us. We have seen how He gave the Apostles the power to forgive sins, that is, to restore life to the soul which by sin has lost it: and since the power to forgive was accompanied by the power to withhold forgiveness, the minister of the power must be told what the sin was—so that the restoration of life was made consequent upon the material action by which one man told another his sins. Baptism and Eucharist and Forgiveness we see in the Gospels. When we come to the earliest days of the Church in action, we find another way by which life is given: "Is one of you sick? Let him send for the presbyters of the church, and let them pray over him, anointing him with oil in the Lord's name. Prayer offered in faith will restore the sick man, and the Lord will give him relief; if he is guilty of sins, they will be pardoned" (James 5:14).

Two other ways we also find used by the Apostles, which clearly they had been taught to do by Christ. There is the appointment of successors, for as we have seen they were to have successors until the end of time with the same powers as they to convey Christ's gifts to the souls of men. The New Testament story of the early Church is filled with the accounts of this communication of priestly power, and always in the same way, by the imposition of hands. We may notice one example: St. Paul writes to Timothy: "A special grace has been entrusted to thee; prophecy awarded it, and the imposition of the presbyters' hands went with it" (1 Tim 4:14). And there is another imposing of hands short of the communication of the priesthood by which men receive the Holy Spirit. It is the sacrament we have come to call Confirmation. There is an example in St. Paul's action in Ephesus (Acts 19:1–6).

These six, then—Baptism, Penance, Eucharist, Confirmation, Holy Orders, and Anointing—are evident from Scripture; and there is enough in Scripture to prepare our minds for the Church's statement that there was a seventh sacrament, established like these by Christ, the sacrament of Matrimony. What is to be noted in all seven is the combination of the spiritual gift with some material thing used as the vehicle by which the gift is brought to us. We have bread and water and wine and oil and the imposition of hands and the utterance of our sin and the union of a man and woman. Here again we must notice that God is treating man according to what man is. We have already seen that because man is a social being, God has made a social religion for him. We see now that because man is a union of spirit and matter, God treats him as both. The sacraments are a union of spirit and matter. Naturally: because they are God's approach to man, and that is what man is. A religion which took no proper account of man's body and left it inactive and unsanctified would be as monstrous as a religion which left out of account his essential relation with his fellows. Religion is the act of man—the whole man, soul and body. It is not the act of the soul only, for man is not only soul: it is his very raison d'être to be not only soul. The body is not as important as the soul, in life generally or in religion; but it is as truly part of man as the soul is, and has a real part to play both in life generally and in religion.

The supernatural does not ignore the natural or substitute something else for it. It is built upon or built into the natural. Sanctifying grace does not provide us with a new soul; it enters into the soul we already have. Nor does it give the soul new faculties but elevates the faculties that are already there, giving intellect and will new powers of operation. God-as-

Sanctifier does not destroy or bypass the work of God-as-Creator. What God has created, God sanctifies. All this means that the more fully man is man, the better his nature serves for the super-natural that is to be built upon it. Whatever damages man as man, damages him in his religious relation to God. His integrity as man requires a proper balance between spirit and matter; and he finds this proper balance at once appallingly difficult to keep and calamitous to lose. If the body becomes dominant, he is in danger of becoming a beast. But for spiritual men there is another danger—a spiritual pride leading to contempt for the body, which can bring them pretty close to the Devil.

The sacramental principle, continually reminding man of his body, will keep his feet firmly upon the ground and destroy pride in its strongest root; sanctifying his body will make it the fit partner of a soul indwelt by God.

The giving of supernatural life by way of sacrament, then, corresponds with the structure of man. Observe too how precisely this particular system of sacraments corresponds with the shape of man's natural life. Ordinarily we can count upon four determining points in human life: a man is born and a man dies: in between he grows up and he marries—or if he be a Catholic he may choose the direct ministry of God. For these four points, with their five possibilities, there are five sacraments. A man is reborn by Baptism, by which he gets a place in the Kingdom; for his growing out of childhood there is Confirmation, by which he gets a function in the Kingdom; for marriage there is Matrimony; for ministry there is Holy Orders, this latter bringing a fuller function in the Kingdom: and for death there is the Anointing. As life flows normally from one point to the next, there are two other needs, for daily bread and for healing in sickness. In the supernatural life there is a sacrament for each of these two, completing the seven. The

Blessed Eucharist provides our daily bread, the sacrament of Penance our healing in the soul's sickness.

Let us glance for a long moment at one of the sacraments. The Blessed Eucharist obviously differs from the others in this—that whereas by the others we receive the life of Christ, by the Blessed Eucharist we receive Christ Himself. The others all lead to increase of life, but the Blessed Eucharist is the basis of them all, for it is the very food of the soul, and without food there can be no continuance in life. The other sacraments, so to speak, take the Blessed Eucharist for granted. Baptism is a preparation for it, and so in another way is Penance. The others develop its possibilities.

Observe how the life of the early Church, as we see it in the Acts of the Apostles, is filled with it. At the Last Supper, Our Lord "took bread, and gave thanks, and broke it, and said, Take, eat; this is My Body, which is to be given up for you. Do this for a commemoration of me. And so with the cup, when supper was ended, This cup, He said, is the new testament, in my blood. Do this, whenever you drink it, for a commemoration of me" (1 Cor 11:24–25). He had changed bread into His body so that it was no longer bread, though it had all the appearances and properties of bread, but was really His body; and so with the wine. And He had told the Apostles: "Do this for a commemoration of Me." The *this* which they were to do in commemoration to Him was the thing that He had done: that is, they too were to change bread so that it was no longer bread but the body of Our Lord, and wine so that it was no longer wine but the blood of Our Lord: and Christians were to receive Our Lord's body and blood from their hands as they from Christ's hands. "Is not this cup we bless a participation in Christ's blood? Is not the bread we break a participation in Christ's body?" (1 Cor 10:16). St. Paul insists most urgently upon the reality of what we receive: "Whosoever shall eat this

bread, or drink the chalice of the Lord unworthily, shall be
guilty of profaning the body and the blood of the Lord" (1
Cor 11:27)—and he tells what "unworthily" means: each one
bringing his own food to the meal preceding the Eucharist, so
that "one is hungry and another is drunk".

It is, of course, the living Christ whom we thus receive. The
bread ceases to be bread and becomes His body. But because
death has no more dominion over Him, where His body is,
there He wholly is, body and blood and soul and divinity. The
wine ceases to be wine and becomes His blood: but where His
blood is, there He wholly is, body and blood and soul and
divinity. Therefore if we receive either, we are receiving the
whole Christ. And receive Him we must, for He is the food of
our life.

(iv) Continuance of sacrifice

That the Kingdom should have teachers and ministers of the
sacraments is obviously necessary; for till the end of time, men
will need Christ's gifts of truth and life, and He has chosen to
dispense them through men. That the Kingdom should have
priests is not at first so obvious. For Christ, our High Priest,
has offered the totally effective sacrifice, and it cannot be
added to. Yet priests there are, and a continuance of sacrifice.
Clearly if there are priests and a sacrifice, they will be men
through whom Christ is offering sacrifice, just as it is He who
is teaching through the teachers and giving life through the
ministers of the sacraments. The teachers of the Church are not
adding to His teaching; the ministers are dispensing no life but
His; the priests are offering no new sacrifice.

Observe how St. John insists both upon the unique priesthood of Christ, and upon the continuance of sacrifice in

Christ's Kingdom: "Thou wast slain in sacrifice; out of every tribe, every language, every people, every nation thou hast ransomed us with thy blood and given us to God. Thou hast made us a royal race of priests, to serve God; we shall reign as kings over the earth" (Rev 5:9–10).

That it should be so, the prophets had already told. Isaiah (66:21), telling how the Kingdom that was to be should contain the Gentiles in great numbers, adds: "I will take of them to be priests and Levites, saith the Lord"; and of the Sacrifice that is to be, we read in the Prophet Malachi. The Lord, having rebuked the priests of Israel for the way in which they are offering sacrifice, goes on: "I have no pleasure in you, and I will not receive a gift of your hand. For from the rising of the sun even to the going down, My name is great among the Gentiles: and in every place there is sacrifice and there is offered to My name a clean oblation" (Mal 1:10–11). We shall come a little later to discuss the Sacrifice of the Mass, wherein those who change the bread and wine into Christ's Body and Blood offer Him, thus wholly present, to His Father in Heaven. This is the clean oblation offered from the rising of the sun even to the going down in a vaster world than Malachi's readers knew of.

(v) A society divine and human

To know the Church of Christ, it is not sufficient to analyze the phrases in which Christ stated His design for it. We must study it in its actuality, as history shows it. That study can be a startling and even a shattering experience. The heavenly Jerusalem so often seems a very earthly Jerusalem. At one time or another the citizens of the Kingdom have practiced every sort of abomination; and not the citizens only, but the successors of the Apostles and even the successors of Peter himself. The study, I say, can be shattering. Yet not to make the study dooms one to an incomprehension of what was in the mind of Christ. To make it brings us to a very deep level of understanding of the nature of the human society here upon earth through which Christ has chosen to live and operate in His followers.

Note that it is a true human society. From this fact flow two consequences, the first easy to grasp, the other not so easy. First, a society of men, in order to be a society and not a rabble, has to have officials, and they have to have authority. Christ has given His society officials with authority. It is through them that He gives the gifts of life and truth and preserves the unity of the society. As ultimate custodian of the sacraments which convey the life, and the teachings which convey the truth, and ultimate authority for the preservation of unity, Christ uses the pope. Observe that all these gifts come *through* the society, not *from* it. They are from Christ, and their value is from Him, not from the society through which He has chosen to give them—through which He has *guaranteed* to give them. For these specified purposes, the officials (the pope included) represent Christ. And so far as they represent Christ, there is no defect in them.

No error is given to us as truth, the sacraments retain their integrity. Outside their representative capacity, the officials (the pope included) are simply themselves and must answer to God for their conduct like anyone else. The gifts we get from God through them in their representative capacity are so enormous in value, that it would be a kind of frivolity in us to object that we do not always approve of them personally: and, in any event, once we are sure that God has chosen to use them, it would be sheer impertinence to suggest to God that He should give us gifts so vast in some other way.

This is logically inescapable, but it leaves us with a troubling doubt. Would God be likely to use as His representatives, even for limited purposes, some of the men whom we find as priests or bishops or popes in His Church? The answer lies in what I have called the second, and less easily graspable, consequence of the Church's nature as a true human society, a society of human beings. Men do not become saints just by entering it: on the contrary their whole life in it is meant to be a striving toward sanctity. Further, men do not cease to be men by entering it. They retain their free will and the capacity to fix their will upon any object that seems to them desirable. Thus at any moment the human society, the Church upon earth, consists of millions of souls at various stages on the road that leads to sanctity. Some have attained it but must still struggle to remain in it; some are close to it, some not so close, some seem to have given up the struggle, some even seem to be headed viciously away from it. That is the reality of the human society at any given time. It is made up, in a proportion that changes from moment to moment, of men headed for heaven, men headed for hell, and men apparently not headed anywhere. And it is through *this* society that Christ is operating.

He guarantees that the truth and the life and the unity shall not fail. But He fulfills His guarantee without doing violence either to the nature of man or to the nature of human society. Having chosen to act upon men through a society of men, Christ is faithful to the logic of His choice. The men remain men; the society remains a society of men. They do glorious things, they do horrible things.

It is the especial meaning of the Church that in it Our Lord unites men to Himself *through humanity* — not through some ideal humanity, but through the humanity, good, bad, and indifferent, that actually exists. As Matthew Arnold notes, where other religions suggest a special type of man, Catholics suggest "all the pell mell of the men and women of Shakespeare's plays". There is a certain kind of spiritual man who finds all this intolerable. His every instinct is revolted at the thought of Christ's working in and through, and of himself being sanctified in and through, this mixed crowd of human beings. The hot smell of humanity is too strong for him. He would have his own direct relation with God, excluding the turbulence of humanity; or he would make his own choice of the men he feels God would choose. But this is preciousness and folly. It is as though the man Christ healed by the touch of His spittle had asked to be healed some other way—he was a refined man, perhaps, brought up to regard spittle as vulgar, or even unhygienic. One cannot be thus delicate about the gifts of God. Personally I like the company I find in the Church enormously. If another person dislikes it, that is his privilege. We do not join the Church for the company, but for the gifts.

There is a thoroughgoing democracy about salvation. Most people get into the Kingdom by being born of citizens, and what could be less exclusive than that: there is no way of testing babies for their fitness to be Catholics. Those who join later in life have to pass no intelligence test, or character test either. Provided they know what the Church is and still wish to join her, they are admitted, whatever their defects of intelligence or virtue. The plain truth is that Christ has chosen to unite to Himself and work through not an elite but an utterly unexclusive free-for-all cross-section of humanity. He solicits it, aids it, showers gifts upon it, but He does not force it. It responds to Him as the individuals in it will, sometimes better, sometimes worse. It acts according to what, by the measure of its cooperation with His gifts, it is. He does not "interfere" with it beyond what is necessary to carry out His guarantee that the truth and the life and the unity shall abide in it. Thus He does not appoint the officials after the first. He does not even appoint the pope. He has left the Church of Rome (meaning by that the Church in the Diocese of Rome) to choose its own rulers. The mode of election has varied from time to time, sometimes quite appallingly for the worse—as in the tenth century, when one scandalous family was able to force its choice on the Roman people. Now and for a long time, the cardinals choose the pope. They pray to the Holy Spirit for guidance in this, as Christians pray for guidance in every action; and according to the sincerity and integrity of the prayer it is answered: no less, no more.

This being so, anyone who knows what Europe has been like in the nineteen centuries of the Church's existence would be prepared for anything in the characters of the popes. And that is just about what one will find. Anything. Everything. The electors choose their man. He is consecrated bishop of Rome. God makes him infallible—which is to say that God will not let him teach the Church anything that is erroneous—and so safeguards his office. But the man himself remains a man. He has his own soul to save and his own struggle to save it, like any other Catholic. Being pope does not of itself help him in the struggle. There is no guarantee that he will save his soul even: for the pope is a man, and men do not get that guarantee. The only guarantee is that he will not teach the Church error, that the gifts of life and truth, of which it is his office to be custodian upon earth, shall not fail. The office of pope is not for the advantage of the pope; it is for the advantage of the Society.

This twofold nature of the Church—a society of human beings, Christ operating in it and through it—presents the same kind of puzzle and indeed scandal to the onlooker as the twofold nature of Christ himself—a true human nature assumed and made His own by a Person of divine nature. The puzzle is a sort of double effect. Looking at Christ, bleeding, thirsting, and dying, the onlooker would feel certain that here was a mere man with the limitations of a man. Seeing Him raising others from the dead and Himself raised, he would feel that this must be God. How could He be both? There is a similar double effect with the Church. Insofar as it is Christ Himself living in men—for the teaching of truth, for the promulgation of the moral law, for the lifegiving work of the sacraments—it is perfect. Apart from the field of operations thus safeguarded by the Founder, the Church's actions and policies will be affected by the limitations and imperfections of its human members. That first field is all that God has promised; and it is tremendous. If He gives more, that is over and above the bargain. We are not entitled to expect it. That He does give more, there can be no doubt: it would be hard to follow the Church's history without the recurrent feeling that we are in the presence of something more than human, something that human powers and purposes cannot wholly explain, some intervention of God over and above the strict terms of the guarantee.

Consider now, not the whole vast section of humanity that constitutes the Church upon earth, but the men chosen out of it to be popes. I have said that you will find anything and everything in the popes—pretty well every sin, pretty well every virtue—that is to be found among men in general. But in what proportion? To me it seems that the mass of sheer sanctity and sheer human greatness is immeasurably beyond any human average; the number of "unworthy" popes (even by the most hostile judgment) is tiny in proportion to the whole number. This, of course, is only a personal impression. Another man might feel quite differently. But in either event it is not of the essence. Our faith is rooted in Christ, not in the human instruments He uses. In a given age, a Catholic might revere the reigning pope and rejoice in his policies, and this would be an extra stimulation. On the other hand, he might find the pope's life disedifying or his policies unpleasing: and that would be depressing. But whether the pope's personality and policy stimulate him or depress him, the substance of our Catholicity is something distinct from them: what primarily matters is what we find in the Church of which the pope is the earthly ruler—the grace of the sacraments, the offering of the Sacrifice, the certitude of the truth, the unity of the Fellowship, and Christ, in whom all these are.

Much of what I have said about the popes could be said, I think, about the mass of Catholics. Every sin that is found outside the Church will be found inside; but the proportion of virtue to sin—if there were any way of measuring such things for statistical purposes—would, I think, be found to be very different. An individual Catholic might very well be less pleasing to God than an individual non-Catholic. But the over-all picture would not be the same. All that stream of truth and grace, flowing through every channel that Christ made to carry the flow to men's souls, does not go for nothing. But if we want to form to ourselves some notion of the richness of the stream, we must look not at Catholics who make no use of it, nor even at good average Catholics, but at the saints. If you want to know how wet the rain is, do not judge by someone who went out into it with an umbrella. Most of us are like that in relation to the shower of truth and life. We do not give ourselves to it wholly but set up all sorts of pathetic protections against the terrifying downrush of it. But the saints have gone out into it stripped. There, but for resistance to the grace of God, goes every one of us.

22. The Mystical Body of Christ

What we have now seen is the Church at the first level of our understanding—the Kingdom, a society of human beings to which we come to receive God's gifts of truth and life through the Holy Spirit, a society in which we are in the company of Christ since He is with it. If the Church were no more than that, it would still be glorious; but it is in fact much more than that, and we should come to a deeper level of understanding, for it would be a shame for a Catholic to live out his life in the Church without the fullest realization of the magnificence that is his.

(i) Cells of a living Body

This deeper level is bound up with the meaning of Our Lord's words "I am with you." Go back to the words He used of Himself in answer to St. Thomas' question at the Last Supper: "I am the Way and the Truth and the Life." We have already used these words as headings under which to examine what Our Lord came to do. But Our Lord used them to describe not His work but Himself. They apply to His work only because they already apply to Him. Once we examine the phrase exactly as Our Lord said it, we are struck with its extreme strangeness. What makes it strange is the word "am", particularly as followed by the words "truth" and "life". We might have expected Him to say: "I have the truth", and "I have the life"; but what He says is "I am the Truth" and "I am the Life". The difference between what He said and what we might have expected makes an enormous difference to us. Had He said, "I have the truth", we could have asked Him to fill our minds with it, since truth is the mind's first need. But He said, "I am the Truth", so that we must ask Him to fill our minds with Himself, we must ask Him, not to enlighten our minds, but to be the light of our minds. Likewise if He had said, "I have the life", we could have asked Him to give it to us. But He said, "I am the Life", so that we can only ask Him to live in us. The gifts are not distinct from the giver. We take possession of the gifts only by taking possession of the giver. The gifts and the giver are the one same Christ. The Church in which we are to receive His gifts is now seen to be the Church in which we are to receive Him. The union with Him which is ours as members of the Church is now seen as intimate as that of truth with the mind and love with the will.

As the key to an understanding of this new concept of the Church, take the statement just made that since Christ *is* the life, we cannot have life unless He lives in us. This precise thing He has Himself said. In particular it is the recurrent theme of His long discourse at the Last Supper.

We have already noticed the phrase of Our Lord in His prayer to the Father for the unity of His Church, "that while Thou art in Me, *I* may be *in them,* and so they may be perfectly made one." *I in them.* This is the truth which St. Paul puts so grandly: "I am alive; or rather, not I; it is Christ that lives in me" (Gal 2:20). But parallel with this, there is another idea which at first sight seems to introduce a complication. Christ is

to live in us; but also we are to live in Him. Thus we find Our
Lord saying at the Last Supper: "It is only a little while now,
before the world is to see me no more; but you can see me,
because I live on, and you too will have life. When that day
comes, you will learn for yourselves that I am in my Father, and
you are in me, and I am in you" (Jn 14:19–20). He makes this
double in-living even more explicit in the parable of the Vine
and the Branches. "You have only to live in me, and I will live
on in you. The branch that does not live on in the Vine can
yield no fruit of itself; no more can you, if you do not live on
in Me. I am the vine, you are its branches; if a man lives on in
me, and I in him, then he will yield abundant fruit" (Jn 15:3–5).

This double necessity that He should live in us and we
should live in Him brings us to the very heart of the truth
about His Church. It is only in a living body that the verb "to
live in" can be used both ways. So Our Lord had shown by
speaking of the living body of a vine. St. Paul has worked out
the idea still more fully by the comparison to the living body
of a man. I can say of the cells of my body that I live in them,
because it is by my life that they live; but equally I can say that
they live in me, because though it is from me that their life
comes, it actually does make *them* alive. If we are to live in
Christ and He is to live in us, then there must be some such
relationship between us and Him as that between a person and
the cells of his body. It is in this sense that the Church is the
Body of Christ. It is not merely an organization, something to
which we resort for the gifts our souls need; it is an organism, a
living body with its own life-secret and its own life-stream.
But He whose Body it is, is Christ, so that He is the life-secret;
and the life-stream flows from Him to every cell in the Body,
so that, insofar as we are alive, it is with His life. We are living
in Him because He is living in us.

This, then, is the reality of the Church, men bound together into one by the one life-stream flowing from the Head, which is Christ. So St. Paul can say to the Romans, "We, though many in number, form one body in Christ" (12:5); and to the Ephesians, "God has put everything under His dominion, and made Him the head to which the whole Church is joined, so that the Church is His body, the completion of Him Who everywhere and in all things is complete" (1:22–23); and to the Galatians, "All you who have been baptized in Christ's name have put on the person of Christ; no more Jew or Gentile, no more slave and freeman, no more male and female; you are all one person in Jesus Christ" (3:27–28).

(ii) The fullness of redemption

St. Paul's Epistles indeed are alive with the doctrine. And not unnaturally. For the first word Our Lord said to him—in the vision on the road to Damascus, which converted him—announced it: "Saul, Saul, why dost thou persecute me?" Persecuting Christ's Church, persecuting Christ, it is all one, for Church and Christ are one.

Everything that we have learnt about the Church must be re-translated into this new language of organic union with Christ. Baptism, as we have just seen, no longer means merely entry into the Church, or even merely rebirth into the supernatural life. It means rebirth into Christ. By our rebirth in baptism we are incorporated with Christ, as by our natural birth we are incorporated with mankind. By our incorporation with Christ, we share alike in the satisfaction that He offered for sin, and the supernatural union with God that He merited.

Redemption was won for all on Calvary; it is made actual in each person at baptism. By baptism we die, as He did, and rise again, as He did. "You, by baptism, have been united with His burial, united, too, with His resurrection; . . . in giving life to Him, God gave life to you too, when you lay dead in your sins" (Col 2:12–13). St. Paul gives the same teaching to the Romans (6:3–7): "We who were taken up into Christ by baptism have been taken up, all of us, into His death. In our baptism, we have been buried with Him, died like Him, so that, just as Christ was raised up by His Father's power from the dead, we too might live and move in a new kind of existence. We have to be closely fitted into the pattern of His resurrection, as we have been into the pattern of His death; we have to be sure of this, that our former nature has been crucified with Him, and the living power of our guilt annihilated, so that we are slaves of guilt no longer."

Our incorporation with Christ is so real that, in the phrase of St. Thomas, "His sufferings avail for us as if we had suffered them ourselves" (S.T. III, q. 69): the words are the natural development of St. Paul's phrase (Gal 2:19) "with Christ I hang upon the cross". Thus, the satisfaction He made is ours because we are in Him. The supernatural union with God, which is the purpose and crown of redemption, is likewise ours because we are in Him. We have seen why Our Lord said I *am* the Life. We can also see why He said I *am* the Way. He not only opens the way for us and points the way to us: He *is* the Way. What we must do is enter into Him and abide in Him. That is salvation. United thus organically with His sacred humanity, we are united with His Person, that is to say, with the Second Person of the Blessed Trinity, and so with the Triune God. In our life in Him, the breach between man and God is healed and the relation of oneness restored. It is the formula of restoration He had uttered at the Last Supper: "I am in my Father, and you in Me, and I in you."

Redemption, then, finds a new statement in terms of the Mystical Body; so does the work of the Holy Spirit. We have already seen how the Holy Spirit was sent to the Church to do for the Church as a whole and for all its members the work of supernatural sanctification and illumination which He did for the human nature of Christ. Now we are in a position to see deeper into this sending. The Holy Spirit comes to us *because* we are inbuilt into Christ, in whom He is. The life which is Christ's—and ours because His—is the operation of the Holy Spirit in His human nature. Therefore we may speak of life in the Body as Christ living in us: or the Holy Spirit living in us. Our Lord speaks of both in-living, and so does St. Paul. In one passage (Rom 8:9-11) Paul has them both—"Christ lives in you", "the Spirit dwells in you", "a man *cannot* belong to Christ unless he has the Spirit of Christ." Just as both live in us, both operate in us: "All this is the work of one and the same Spirit" (1 Cor 12:11): "So effectually does His [Christ's] power manifest itself in me."

It is because of the indwelling and operation of the Holy Spirit in Christ our Lord that we cannot be incorporated in Christ without sharing the same indwelling and operation. "Your bodies belong to the body of Christ", says St. Paul (1 Cor 6:15); and a few verses later, "Your bodies are the shrines of the Holy Spirit."

For this twofold presence, the Church has found various phrases: Christ is the source, the Holy Spirit the operative principle: Christ is the Head of the Body, the Holy Spirit the Soul. There is one lovely variant of this last phrase used by St. Thomas and again by Pope Leo XIII (*Divinum illud Munus*): the Holy Spirit is the Heart.

(iii) Relation to Christ and to one another

By birth in Adam we are Jew or Gentile, slave or free, man or woman; by our rebirth in Christ we have put on the person of Christ. The second incorporation is immeasurably more living and intimate than the first. By birth we are members of a family; by rebirth, of a body. At its very best, the unity of the members of a family is only a shadow of the organic unity of the members of a body—to be brothers of one another is as nothing compared to being members of one another. And the human family into which we enter by birth is by no means the family at its very best, but a widely scattered family, which has largely forgotten that it *is* a family: for its head, Adam, died in a dim and dateless past, and most of his children have never heard of him. Adam communicated life to his son, and he to his son, and at last in its long winding it reached us, so that we owe our life to him; and in that sense he lives in us, but only in that sense. By countless intermediaries he gave us our life, but he can do no more about it: if our life weakens and dwindles, we cannot turn to him for renewal. But in the Body, we are in immediate and continuing contact with our Head, Christ, and the flow of His life through us His members never ceases but is always there for our growth and renewal.

Thus our relation to Christ is closer than the natural relation of brothers to a brother or even of children to a parent. It is that of cells in a body to the person whose body it is. It is therefore closer than *any* relationship that one human being can have with another. By membership in the Mystical Body we are more closely related to Christ our Lord than Our Lady is, simply as His mother in the natural order. Motherhood, even her motherhood, is not so close as membership of Christ's Body, which involves living from instant to instant by the selfsame life that He is living by. Needless to say, Our Lady is also a member of the Mystical Body, living more totally and intensely by His life than we shall ever live. But it remains that her relation to Him as mother is less not only than her relation to Him as a member of His Mystical Body but also than the relation of every one of us to Him as members of His Mystical Body.

There is a lesser consequence, which can startle us a great deal more: our relationship to one another as members of Christ's Body is closer than any possible natural relationship. Each one of us is more closely related to every other member of the Church by this life of grace than to his own mother by the life of nature. "And you are Christ's body, organs of it depending upon each other" (1 Cor 12:27). This is easy enough to say. But if we were ever to let ourselves look squarely at it and really try to live by it, its immediate effect would be a remaking of ourselves so thorough that nature shrinks from it; and the ultimate effect would be to renew the face of the earth.

(iv) The Church re-lives His life

Guided by the same Holy Spirit, through the same world, under pressure from the same Devil, one would expect the Mystical Body to relive the life of Christ, produce actions like His, stir the reactions that He stirred. And so it is. To take some of the reactions first, we see that there is not an accusation hurled at Him that has not been hurled at His Church. And notice that she is most bitterly hated not for what is most human in her, the faults—sometimes the appalling faults—of her members, but for what is most clearly the operation of Christ. Her insistence on the primacy of the spiritual is twisted into the same accusation that was brought against Him, that she is setting up a kingdom to dominate the kingdoms of men; she is hated as He was for both of her teachings on the body—that it is subordinate to the spirit, and that it is capable of sanctification; for her assertion that divine truth and divine law are absolute, not to be modified by human circumstances; for her assertion of infallibility; for her claim to judge the world. She is hated for her claim to be unique; she is hated for *being* in fact unique.

But the similarity of the world's reaction is a small thing compared with the similarity of the actions she produces to the actions of Christ upon earth. She lives the very details of His life: His public ministry is continued in the active work of the hierarchy and the missionary; His hidden life at Nazareth, in the lives of the contemplative orders of men and women. The Church has the same alteration of fasting and feasting, the same sudden intervention of God by miracles, the same glorification of virginity, the same fruits of virginity. It is hardly too much to say that if we had no Gospels we could reconstruct the whole picture of Christ from studying the daily life of the Church — the whole picture, not excluding His redemptive suffering.

(v) Our Lady and the com-passion

There is light for the understanding both of the Church and of our own lives in the truth, that the Church as a whole and we its members have some kind of share in the redemptive suffering of Christ. This truth, like almost everything else relevant to membership in the Mystical Body, may best be studied in relation to Christ's mother, because she is the one perfect member of the Body. Every element in the life of the Body will be seen at its most intense in her.

The Church has always had a sense of the enormous love of Christ for His mother. But if we confine ourselves to the Gospel record, it is very difficult to find any concrete evidence of it. The Gospels do not record a single word of tenderness. It is possible that at the very moment of His death, when He gives her St. John to take His own place as her Son, there is profound tenderness, yet the actual words of it could hardly be briefer or more objective: "Woman, behold thy son." The word "woman" is a term of honor, with none of that offensive implication which the progress of the English language has fixed upon it; but it is a term of honor, hardly a term of affection. There is no record in the Gospel that He ever addressed her as mother.

All this, of course, may have no significance. The Gospels are the briefest possible record of a life fuller than the life any other man ever lived. Following upon the description of Our Lord's infancy, there is complete silence upon the next twelve years; then a single incident; then silence upon eighteen years. The main concern of the evangelists is with the three years of the public ministry, and even here everything is so compressed that nothing can be argued from the absence of anything from the record. And it would take a great deal more than the mere silence of the Gospels to persuade anyone that the perfect Son did not love His mother with perfect love.

But we have not only silence to puzzle us: there is a certain note of remoteness in what is actually recorded. And the Church, in her doctrine of the com-passion of Our Lady, explains in marvelous combination both the apparent remoteness and the immeasurable love. Let us begin with that episode of Our Lord's twelfth year, told in St. Luke's second chapter, when His parents, returning from Jerusalem, find that He is not with them, search for Him for three days, and find Him at last in the Temple asking the doctors questions and proposing solutions at which the doctors marvel. Our Lady said to him, "My Son, why hast thou treated us so? Think what anguish of mind thy father and I have endured, searching for thee." He answered, "What reason had you to search for me? Could you not tell that I must needs be in the place which belongs to my Father?" The answer, coming from a boy of twelve to a mother who has had three days of anguish through His action, is startling. Here is remoteness to the point of bleakness. No word of regret or sympathy. We need not be surprised that we are puzzled, for so were Mary and Joseph. These words which He spoke to them were beyond their understanding. In any event, the strange episode came to its close. He went back with them to Nazareth. But "His mother kept in her heart the memory of all this." Remember how Simeon had said that a sword should pierce her heart; these words of her Son, kept in her heart and pondered, may have been part of the turning of the sword.

Examine them closely. Her question to Christ is, "My Son, why hast thou treated us so?" What exactly had He done to them? Gone away from them. It seems possible that this cry of Our Lady is an echo long in advance of a more famous cry yet to be uttered: "My God, my God, why hast Thou forsaken Me?" What she cries to her Son in her anguish is so very close to what He cries to His Father in His anguish. So theologians have seen it, and seen it not as a mere chance, but as part of the very design of our redemption.

In the natural order, one imagines that Christ must have been like His mother—this was one infant, at least, about whom no question could arise as to which parent He resembled; and she found it, probably, as much of a delight as most mothers find it, that her Son was like her. But that remains in the natural order. In the supernatural order her supreme glory is that she was like her Son. That she was like Him is for any Catholic a commonplace, yet we may miss certain important elements in the likeness. He was sinless and the Man of Sorrows. She was sinless, and we think of her most naturally as the Mother of Sorrows. From the moment of her Son's birth, almost all that we know of her is shot through with grief—the flight into Egypt to save her Child from murder, the knowledge of the other mothers' children massacred by Herod, the three days' loss of Christ when He was twelve, His death while she stood by the cross. He suffered; she suffered; but the analysis we have just made of that strange episode in the Temple points to a relation between her suffering and His that we might otherwise have failed to see. Her suffering was related to His; but it was not merely her reaction to His, it was hers. She suffered not simply *with* Him, as any mother must suffer in the suffering of her child, but in her own right. Before He experienced His desolation, she experienced her desolation. He had His Passion, but she had her passion too. And while His accomplished everything, hers was not for nothing. It was part of the design of the Redemption that while the Divine Person suffered the Passion that redeemed us, a human person should suffer a passion parallel with His.

There is almost impenetrable darkness here, but St. Paul helps us to penetrate it a little: "I am glad of my sufferings on your behalf, as, in this mortal frame of mine, I help to pay off the debt which the afflictions of Christ leave still to be paid, for the sake of His body, the Church." The Douay Version has: "I fill up those things that are wanting of the suffering of Christ, in my flesh, for his body which is the Church" (Col 1:24). In either translation the words are startling and at first almost stunning. St. Paul says that something is wanting, something left still to be paid, something apparently not accomplished by the sufferings of Christ; and to make the shock of this more formidable, he says that by his own sufferings he will help to supply what the sufferings of Christ did not accomplish. St. Paul, of course, is writing not to stun but to teach.

There is something, needed by Christ's Body, the Church, which Christ's suffering has not accomplished and which St. Paul—and presumably other members of the Church—must help to supply. Obviously nothing could be lacking in what the Divine Person did for the Church. Whatever could be done by God for men has been done. The lack could be only something which in the nature of the case *could not* be done by

God for men, something which in the nature of the case men must do for themselves. In other words, there is a part in mankind's redemption—a subsidiary part having no effect at all save in relation to the total effectiveness of Christ's action—that mankind must play for itself. The thing is very subtle, difficult to say as clearly as one sees it.

Remember that in the redemptive act itself there were two elements, the human nature *in which* the act was done, and the divine Person by *whom* the act was done. Because it was an act in human nature, it could rightly be offered for the sin of the human race. Because it was the act of the Divine Person, it had an infinite value which no merely human act could have had. That being so, we considered the question why some lesser act in the human nature could not have sufficed and we saw how it accorded with the demand of all that is best in man that in expiating the sin of man human nature should give of its very uttermost, and in the human nature of Christ it did.

In the human nature of Christ it did: but if only there, then human nature has not given of its uttermost, for in the event the rest of men would be merely spectators, the human nature that is in them contributing nothing. The infinite Person of Christ did not need so total a giving in His human nature, yet it was fitting that He should redeem us by that total giving. Similarly our redemption thus effected did not require that humanity as a whole should give what it has to give. But it was in the glorious design of God that human love should not be denied all place in the expiation of human sin, and men be condemned to be no more than spectators of their own redemption. Redeemed humanity should suffer in union with Christ, and in union with Christ these sufferings should be co-redemptive. When St. Paul says that in a body the head cannot say to the foot, "I have no need of you", he may be speaking in all strictness of the *Body* and the *Head.*

There is then a co-redemptive action of Christ; and in this co-redemptive activity every member of the Mystical Body plays some part insofar as he unites his sufferings with Christ's: human nature is privileged to repeat in the persons of men what it has completed in the person of Christ. But what all of us may do according to our imperfection, Our Lady did perfectly. Even St. Paul could not make all his sufferings available for the Church, since some at least must be set against his own sins. Our Lady had no sins, and whatever she suffered could be wholly for the sins of mankind. But how could she suffer? She could suffer like any other mother to see her child suffer, and more than any other mother because she was better than any other and had a Child more worthy of love. But for the completion of suffering, she must have sufferings of her own, and at their highest these must be in the soul. Her son chose for her and she chose for herself the suffering that would lead to the uttermost increase of her sanctification, and give her the most to contribute to the spiritual needs of all of us. Her Son loved her supernaturally, as God loves all who have His sanctifying grace in their souls, and more than all others because no spirit of man or angel has ever received and responded to so vast a measure of His grace. Her Son loved her naturally, as a human son loves a human mother, and again more than any other because of His perfection and hers. It was a wonderful thing for her, this second sort of love, but it was still second. So vast a thing is supernatural relationship, that every one of us in the state of grace is more closely related to her Son supernaturally than she merely by her natural relationship as His mother. And if our relation by grace is closer than hers by nature, how immeasurably closer still was *her* relation by grace.

It does seem at least possible that for the increase of supernatural love, she denied herself not, of course, any tiniest degree of His natural love, but some of the intimacies and consolations that normally flow from the natural relation of mother and son. At first approach, we find the idea almost unbearable: and so must she have found it in its actuality. But seeing as clearly as she saw, immeasurably more clearly than we can see, she would have realized the thing we half glimpse, that all the external accompaniments of natural love are not in themselves of the essence of it; and that self-denial in their regard would lead not only to a growth of that which matters most, supernatural love, but thereby to a growth of natural love too. She could see that this is so, and could act by it; but that would not diminish the suffering that flowed from the denial. Like us all, she had to deny herself in order to follow Christ. What else had she that she could deny herself?

We may carry the doctrine of Our Lady's suffering one stage further. We all have a share in the co-redemptive suffering of the Mystical Body by uniting our sufferings with the sufferings of our Head. But when Our Lady did perfectly what we must do in our own fashion, she was suffering not simply as one of us, even as the best one, the one closest to Christ, but as our representative. We shall not see her clearly if we do not grasp this representative function of hers. And not only here. When in answer to the angel's message that she was to bear the world's Redeemer she said, "Be it done unto me according to thy word", she was uttering the consent of the whole human race. When she died, she was taken up into heaven, body and soul, and there till the Day of Judgment she will be the one human person complete with soul and body standing before the throne of God. So here God allowed that the suffering of the Divine Person should be accompanied by a wholly human suffering, as earnest of the suffering of redeemed humanity that was to be spread throughout the ages. As Christ represents humanity in the Redemptive Act, she represents humanity in the co-redemptive act. His suffering was the essential thing, and hers valuable only by derivation. His was the Passion, hers the com-passion. He was the Redeemer, but the Church loves to call her Co-Redemptrix.

As we look back over what we have so far seen of the Mystical Body of Christ, we recognize that it is a difficult doctrine, but that the difficulty is of a special kind. It is not difficult to grasp what the Church is saying, as it is, for example, with the Blessed Trinity. In that sense it is a comparatively simple doctrine. The difficulty is to grasp that the Church really means it, that a thing at once so simple, and so glorious, and so glorifying to us, is actually so. It is the hardest thing in the world to comprehend that we are what this doctrine says we are. We feel that we are not upon the scale for such magnificence. But we must become reconciled to our own magnificence as Christians, not deluded by our meagerness as men. "Agnosce Christiane dignitatem tuam"—Learn, O Christian, thy dignity. This is what St. Leo meant.

23. Life in the Body

So far we have been considering the Mystical Body insofar as it means Christ living in the Church. We may now consider it insofar as it means the Christian living in Christ. All that we have so far learnt about the life of the soul must be re-seen in this new context.

(i) Life-processes of the Body

The supernatural life—of faith, hope, and charity, the moral
virtues, the gifts of the Holy Spirit—is the vital operation of
Christ our Lord in us His members. As St. Thomas says (S.T.
III, q. 48), grace was given to Christ not simply for Himself
but as Head of the Church, that it might flow from Him to His
members. The life of God flows through the Head to the
Body. It really *is* the life of God, up to the level of our capacity
to receive it. It does not make the finite infinite, but it is
hard to find any limit short of that to what it can do: if we will
let it.

For this life is ours only if, and insofar as, we will take it. In
the Mystical Body we are still men, and men have free will.
Even in the Body our will remains free. It is solicited by grace,
but not stormed by grace. The problem of our development
lies not in the destruction of our human will, but in its free
union with the will of God; and the free union is not normally
a simple matter, attainable in one swift stride, but a goal to be
striven for with great effort. By our re-birth in Baptism, we are
cells in Christ's Body and so we are in His life stream. But to
what degree that stream flows into us and makes us supernaturally alive depends upon our will. If we will to open our
being wholly, then the life flows into it and vivifies it wholly.
If we will to open our being, yet not wholly but reserving this
or that small element ungiven to God, then the life will still
flow to us: but whatever element in ourselves we have kept as
our own will remain as our own, unvivified. We shall be alive
but not wholly alive. There is one further possibility. We may
set our will firmly against God's by the free choice of serious
sin, to the destruction of the love which is the life secret. So
doing we close our being to the life flow. We are still in the
Body, but as dead cells, living with our natural life, but

supernaturally not alive. While we remain in this life upon earth, it is always possible for the dead cell that we have become to be reopened and made alive by true sorrow for sin and the sacrament of Penance; just as it is always possible for the cell that is alive to grow in life.

That we should grow is the essential thing. And growth means growing in likeness to Christ; or rather it means growing first *into* likeness, by growing away from all that is unlike; then growing *in* likeness, growing in being and in power. The cell must become the image of the Head. So St. Paul tells the Galatians: "My little children, I am in travail over you afresh, until I can see Christ's image formed in you" (4:19). We sometimes feel that the saints are overdoing their anguish at their own imperfections. We are so much more imperfect, so much less agonized. Somewhat similarly, we feel that a pianist's misery over a performance that we should be proud of cannot be sincere. But it is. The pianist is comparing himself not with us but with Rachmaninoff. The saint is comparing himself not with us but with Christ, for he is consumed—as we all should be—with desire to be remade in His perfect image. For this end above all, Christ works upon us, giving us His gifts of truth and life through the men whom He has appointed to special functions in the Body. "Some he has appointed to be apostles, others to be prophets, others to be evangelists, or pastors, or teachers. They are to order the lives of the faithful, minister to their needs, build up the frame of Christ's body, until we all realize our common unity through faith in the Son of God, and fuller knowledge of him. So we shall reach perfect manhood, that maturity which is proportioned to the completed growth of Christ; we are no longer to be children, no longer to be like storm-tossed sailors, driven before the wind of each new doctrine that human subtlety, human skill in fabricating lies, may propound. We are to follow the truth, in a spirit of charity, and so grow up, in everything, into a due proportion with Christ, who is our head. On him all the body depends; it is organized and unified by each contact with the source which supplies it; and thus, each limb receiving the active power it needs, it achieves its natural growth, building itself up through charity" (Eph 4:11–16).

Thus the Body is not simply composed of a Head and an undifferentiated mass of human cells, all alike and all functioning alike. It is, like any other body, an organism, a structure, with different parts functioning differently for the perfection of the whole. Pope and bishops and priests and laymen must each become the image of Christ: so far there is no difference: there is not some greater likeness of Christ reserved to popes, some lesser likeness kept for the laity. But in the life processes of the Body, different members have different functions—which merely means that Christ uses them in different ways. This Body, like any other body, has an order and a proportion and a complexity of elements working together. We see this again in considering the sacraments, the principal means by which the energizing of the Holy Spirit flows to us from Christ. Just as in our own bodies the blood does not surge upon us in a tidal wave but flows silently to every part of the body through arteries and veins; so sanctifying grace does not come upon the Mystical Body like a cloudburst, more likely to drown than to vivify, but flows through a multiplicity of channels made by God for its flow. As in the individual soul, so in the Mystical Body, the Kingdom of God is like a leaven working secretly. Holiness is not best served by chaos.

In our first consideration of the sacraments, we saw that the Blessed Eucharist differs vitally from the others. We now see the same difference in the new context. By Baptism we enter into the life of the Body: or, to put it another way, the life of the Body enters into us. Either way, we become alive supernaturally. A living thing needs food, and without food will almost certainly perish. But all life must be fed by bodies, of animal or vegetable. Our mental life is fed by minds, the minds of those who instruct us. But this new life of sanctifying grace is Christ Himself living in us: the only food that could feed a life which *is* Christ must itself *be* Christ. And what we receive in the Eucharist *is* Christ. Thus Our Lord can say: "He who eats my flesh, and drinks my blood, lives continually in me, and I in him. As I live because of the Father, the living Father who has sent me, so he who eats me will live, in his turn, because of me" (Jn 6:57–58).

Receiving Christ our Lord thus, we are in the profoundest sense one with Him, and this is the great thing; but also we are one with all, in all ages, who by receiving Him have become likewise one with Him. And this is no small thing. The Blessed Eucharist serves the growth of each member of the Body in holiness; but it serves also the unity of the Body as a whole, drawing the whole more profoundly into oneness with Christ. "The one bread makes us one body though we are many in number" (1 Cor 10:17). There is a sense in which the Eucharist is the life-principle of the Church even more than of the individual soul.

(ii) The Mass

From God's end, the channels of grace are the means of union between Him and us; from man's end, the means of union is prayer. In its broadest sense, prayer is the direction of life to God. In its special sense, it is the converse of the soul with God, the intellect concentrated upon God, uttering itself to Him and silently receptive to His utterance, and the will given wholly to him in love. So much prayer should be in any event, given that God exists and man exists. We know from the experience of the mystics how far this converse can go. With the aid of special graces from God, the prayer of contemplation can bring the soul into an awareness of God as immediately present— not seen face to face by the intellect as the souls in heaven see Him, but felt, touched, savored (the words for this experience-beyond-utterance vary) in a direct contact of love. Some of the saints have told us that in this contact they have had an awareness of the Triplicity of Persons in the Godhead.

But even at the highest intensity, this movement of the individual soul to God is not the whole of prayer. Because man is not an isolated unit, each person related only to God and no one to any other, but all related to God and therefore to one another, there must be a social element in prayer, as well as an individual. Men may go apart to pray, for each has his own incommunicable self, which is only his; but they must come together to pray too. This again would be true in any event, given that every human being exists in the solidarity of the human race. But it reaches a new depth in the unity of the Mystical Body. There is a prayer of the whole Body, a prayer that Christ as the Head of the Body makes His own and offers as His own; and it would be an appalling impoverishment of our life in the Body to take no conscious, willed part in it. The Christian's private prayer, the conversation of himself as *himself* with God, is essential, though even in this the Christian remains *in* the Body and prays from his place in the Body; but liturgical prayer, the prayer of the Body itself, is essential too. God loves both, and the Christian grows by both.

The highest point of the prayer of the Body is the offering of the Sacrifice of the Mass. We have already seen that there were to be priests in Christ's Kingdom and a Sacrifice. We can now see more closely what that means. If we consider what Our Lord did for men while He was upon earth, we shall find that He is still doing all the same things for men through the Church. Upon earth He taught, forgave sins, vivified, gave men the Holy Spirit; and he does all these things still, through His Mystical Body. But, underlying all these actions of His upon earth was the thing He came to do—to offer Himself as a sacrifice for the redemption of men; and this too He continues to do: that is the precise meaning of the Mass.

Consider what the action of the Mass is. The priest, we have seen, consecrates bread and wine so that they are changed into the body and blood of Christ: Christ Himself, slain once upon Calvary but now forever living, is upon the altar. "Panem vinum in salutis consecramus hostiam"—the bread and wine are changed into the Victim of our salvation. And Him who was slain for us the priest offers to the Father for the application to men's souls of what His Passion and Death made available for us. The key to all this is that the priest gives himself to be used by Christ, so that Christ is the real offerer, the priest taking the role of Christ, acting in the person of Christ. Thus the Mass is seen aright only when Christ is seen as not only the Victim offered, but as the Priest who offers. In the Mass as upon Calvary, Christ is offering Himself to God for the sins of the world: the Mass is a re-presentation of Calvary. There is no new slaying of Christ in the Mass: for in the first place, death has no more dominion over Him, and in the second, if the priest in any sense slew Him, this would be to introduce into the Mass an element that was not in Calvary, for Christ did not slay Himself but was slain by His enemies. Yet that it is the Christ who was slain upon Calvary is shown sacramentally by the separate consecration of bread to become His body and wine to become His blood. The essence of the Mass is that Christ is making an offering to the Father of Himself, who was slain for us upon Calvary. The Mass is Calvary, *as Christ now offers it to His Father.*

Thus Our Lord is continuing upon earth what we have already seen He is doing in Heaven. "Jesus continues for ever, and his priestly office is unchanging; . . . he lives on still to make intercession in our behalf" (Heb 7:24–25). That intercession is the continuing presentation before the face of God of Himself, who was slain for us: "He has entered heaven itself, where He now appears in God's sight on our behalf" (Heb 9:24). So the Book of Revelation (Apocalypse) shows Him in heaven, "a Lamb standing upright, yet slain (as I thought) in sacrifice". In some way the marks of His victim-state are still upon Him, not diminishing His glory but adding to it.

The Mass is the breaking through to earth of the offering of Himself that Christ makes continuously in heaven simply by His presence there. We can now go one level deeper. Christ makes His offering in heaven in His own sacred humanity; Christ makes His offering on earth through His Mystical Body. The priest is the organ of His Mystical Body that He uses to consecrate and offer Himself. But we are united with Christ in the act of offering as really as the priest is. So in the Mass, the priest speaks to the congregation of the sacrifice he is offering as "our offering". After the Consecration we — "Christ's holy people" — are named as offering "the pure, the consecrated, the spotless Victim".

But because we are cells in the Body of Christ, we are associated with Him not only as offerer but as Victim offered. So St. Peter reminds us (1 Pet 3:18): Christ died once for our sins, "so as to present us in God's sight" (or, in the Douay Version, "that He might offer us to God"). So St. Gregory the Great urges us "who celebrate the mysteries of the Passion" to "offer ourselves as victims". And this is simply a most marvelous elevation to a new power of the plain truth that if we do not offer our own selves, God will not be moved by any other offering we may make.

(iii) The human element

The Church, then, is the body of Christ, His Mystical Body we call it, using the adjective both to emphasize the extreme mysteriousness of this unique body-to-person relationship, and to distinguish this Body from His natural body. The distinction is worth stating explicitly. His natural body is that which He received from His mother, in which He lived His human life in Palestine and died upon the cross. In that same natural body, but now glorified, He rose from the dead, ascended into heaven, and is forever at the right hand of the Father. It is that same body which we receive sacramentally in the Blessed Eucharist. The Mystical Body, His Church, we may think of as the successor to His natural body, or, perhaps better, to His human nature as a whole, because in it He continues to operate among men as formerly in His human nature. Think of the two as successive instruments by which He works among men.

Thus the Church is in its deepest reality Christ Himself still living and operating on earth. The trouble is that the Church does not always look like it. The Church is in the world, but a great deal of the world is in the Church. There is a sense in which the Real Presence of Christ in the Church is as difficult to believe as the Real Presence of Christ in the Eucharist. In the one case we say, "It looks like bread", in the other we say, "It doesn't look like Christ." Both statements are correct; but neither settles the reality. What looks like bread is in fact the body of Christ; what looks like a very much too human society is in fact the Body of Christ. Upon this second clash of appearance and reality we may get some light from a further comparison between Our Lord's two lives upon earth, the first in His natural body, the second in His Mystical. In each case God chose to take to Himself and operate in a human body. In each case He is faithful to the logic of His choice. His human nature was a real human nature, and in accepting it, He accepted the limitations proper to it. It goes with being a natural body to have limitations, and when it presses against these limitations it is bound to appear deficient. It does not begin mature, but in the helplessness of babyhood. The body God took began so. Anyone looking at Christ in His mother's arms could only have said, "It doesn't look like God." So it was when, still following the strict logic of His choice, He bled when He was scourged, fell under the weight of a cross too heavy for His natural powers, and died and was buried. He chose to have a body like ours, and these are the deficiencies that go with a body like ours. At those points especially He did not look like God, but He *was* God.

Just as there are limitations, deficiencies, and weaknesses that go with a material body, so also with that other kind of body, a society of human beings each with his own free will; and among these limitations we find a new element, the possibility of sin. But here again Christ is faithful to the logic of His choice. He did not force His natural body; He does not force His Mystical Body. Each follows the laws of the kind of being it is, so that its appearance often serves rather to mask Christ than to reveal Him. Assuredly He did not allow to His natural body a perfection that would have robbed His sacrifice of its meaning; nor does He confer upon the members of His Mystical Body an automatic perfection that would rob their life upon earth of its meaning. But just as His natural body was glorified and its defects ceased, so His Mystical Body too will one day be glorified and in all its members sinless.

The upshot of all this is that, just as in thinking about Our Lord we distinguish between the human nature and the divine, so we must distinguish between the human and the divine element in the Church—the divine being all that sphere where Christ guarantees that what is done shall be without defect because in actual fact He is doing it: the human being that sphere in which he leaves it to men and women to respond to what He offers them, that is, to let Him operate wholly in them, or partially, or not at all.

24. Life after Death

Thus we live our life in the Mystical Body, well or less well or altogether ill. We have seen the three possible states—we may unite our wills wholly to Christ's; or we may unite our wills partially to His, reserving something of self unyielded; or we may separate our wills wholly from His, choosing self as apart from God, closing our soul to the flow of His life. In one or other of these states we are, at any given moment of our life upon earth; in one or other of them we die. Pause for a moment to consider this matter of natural death, the separation of soul and body, which ends our life upon this earth, our time of testing and of growth.

A point comes—suddenly if there is violence, or by slow wearing—when the body can no longer respond to the lifegiving energy of the soul. That, precisely, is death. The body, unvivified, falls away into its elements, not to be re-united with the soul, and once more whole and entire, till the end of the world. But the soul does not die with the body. Why should it? As a spirit, it does not depend for its life upon the body: matter cannot give life to spirit. In the absence of the body, the soul cannot exercise its powers as the animator of a body, so that these must remain wrapt within it till the body rises again at the last day. But in its own nature as a spirit with intellect and will it lives on. In what state? According to the state in which death finds it.

(i) Death's formidable finality

If we die wholly separated, then we are cut out from the Body forever. Our lot is forever with the angel who created the precedent, so to speak, who was the first to opt for self as against God. If we die united, even if not wholly—that is, if any flicker of the supernatural life is in us—then we shall be saved. If we are wholly united, wholly penetrated by Christ's life, then, with no break or interval, the soul enters heaven and, in the Beatific Vision of the unveiled face of God, comes at last to its goal. If there still are elements of self unsurrendered, then there is first cleansing by the suffering of purgatory, so that life may take possession of every tiniest element in our being, so that we may be made perfect as our heavenly Father is perfect, and so with no defilement left in us, can enter heaven.

All this suggests a formidable finality about death, and finality is precisely what marks it. Death is an end, an end not of life but of wavering. At any given moment of our life upon earth, we are in one of the three possible states. But we are not fixed in them: we pass from one to another and back again. Time in its flow brings into the foreground one, or another, or another, of all the myriad objects that can attract the will, so that the will finds itself played upon almost intolerably by competing fascinations. And to an ordeal so continuously exacting, the will brings different energies of acceptance and resistance.

The objects themselves are inconceivably various, and so are their ways of drawing the will to them. But for all their variousness, they are reducible to two categories—they are, according to God's will, for us or against; and for all the ways in which the will reacts to them, it is always doing one of two things—choosing God, or choosing self as against God; that is to say, choosing either increase of being or diminution of being, reality undiluted or reality mingled with illusion. This choice is the determining element in our life. And, as we have seen, most of us do not steadily and without variation choose either the one way or the other. Consider the person in a state of grace, but not perfect. Some object attracts him, which he knows to be against God's will for him. If he chooses it, he sins. If it is some small thing, not involving a deliberate assertion of self as against God, a thing inconsiderable in itself so that he gives no particular thought to it at all, we have venial sin. It does not break the relation of love, and so of life, between himself and God. Yet it means that there is this small element of self not wholly given to God. If it is a great thing, chosen with deliberation, then we have mortal sin. It is a definite choice of self as against God; it breaks the bond of love, and so empties the soul of life.

It is not easy to draw a line in any given case between venial and mortal sin; but the distinction is wholly in keeping with our strangeness. A man can love his country passionately, yet break its law by driving his automobile too fast or doing a little mild cheating on his income tax; there is all the difference between things like that and going over to the enemy in time of war. So a man can love God, yet fall into small sins: and though they are breaches of the law of God, there is a world between them and the deliberate enthronement of self in God's place.

Anyhow, venial sins or mortal sins, we can fall into them;

but we do not necessarily stay in them. By contrition, true sorrow for the love of God, we can repair our venial sins. By contrition for mortal sins and the sacrament of Penance, we can restore the relation of love and the flow of life to the soul. And then some other temptation comes our way, and perhaps we resist or perhaps we yield to it: and if we yield, we can be restored as before, either soon or after many years. Any flashback of the mind over our past shows a series of falls and rises and falls again and more rises: not much to be proud of, plenty of cause to be disheartened. But actually, though the will is always liable to swing violently, there is a certain defining of its choice. As life proceeds, we tend either toward God, or toward self and away from God. There will be flickering still, but the range will be narrower, and the general movement unmistakable. The will is setting in a direction. By the end of this life upon earth, its direction is generally fixed. It loves God; or it loves self as against God. There is life in it, or it is empty of life.

(ii) Eternal separation from God

Take the second possibility. The soul has chosen self. In this life it may hardly be aware of it. Life is full of all sorts of interests; the soul occupied with them may not have adverted to the choice it was making, the direction in which it was setting. But the reality is there: the soul has come to love self exclusively. Even in this life, that state may have its natural consequence of realized hatred of God, for the majesty of God is an intolerable affront to self-love grown so monstrous. Yet again the mere multiplicity of life may have prevented the soul from seeing clearly either its own state or God's majesty. But once death comes, there is nothing to stand between the soul and its awareness both of itself and of God: and loving self so totally, it can only hate God.

Understand that the will is now fixed: it will not change; of its own choice it loves self to the hatred of God. Therefore it cannot go to God. Heaven is closed to it both by its lack of the supernatural life, which makes living in heaven possible, and by its own continuing hatred of God. Nor can it cease to exist, for it is by nature immortal. God could, of course, annihilate it, but will not. Our Lord has told us (Mt 25:41) what is its lot: to be separated from Him (whom it hates): to go into the everlasting fire that was prepared for the Devil and his angels. Enough has already been said of hell in Chapter 13. The soul will be there forever: kept there by its unchanging will to love self and hate God. There will be vast suffering in the nature of the case: for man was made for God, needs God therefore, and, in the absence of the God he needs with every fiber of his being, must suffer as one always suffers from needs unsatisfied. One has heard of preachers licking their lips over what the demons will do to the lost. There is none of that in Scripture. It tells only of sufferings from within the self—weeping and wailing. These vary, one imagines, from person to person, as self-torment varies here on earth. But for all alike there is the pain that flows from the loss of God—which is hell's meaning. Of this pain we can form some faint notion from our experience in this life. The body needs food and drink and suffers agonies in their absence; the whole of man's being needs God: the need can be blunted in this life by every sort of thing less than God: but in hell the soul is naked to its own insufficiency, with nothing to lull it or distract it. It is one aching need, turned resolutely and finally from the only Reality that could satisfy it.

If we face the truth of this squarely, there is real nightmare in it—a sense of horror that man's will can pervert itself so utterly. If we see it only superficially, there is illusion of nightmare—a sense of horror that God can treat man so cruelly. We should know that this is illusion, if only because the fact of hell is taught us by Our Lord, who showed His love for mankind as no one else has ever shown it. If Christ teaches hell, then hell is no contradiction of love. So much we should be certain of simply from our knowledge of Him. But we should also be able to glimpse why. It is the will of man that makes the choice. Given that man *can,* freely, choose love of self and hatred of God, the rest follows. In all reverence we can say that God, respecting the will's freedom, can do nothing about it. He does not thrust devils or men into hell: they go there, because that is their place. Accordingly, Scripture tells us in so many words of Judas: he died "and went to his own place". It is a spiritual nature finding its place, somewhat as a material thing finds its place by the law of gravity: so Our Lord could say, "I saw Satan, like lightning, falling from heaven."

(iii) Purgatory

St. Thomas, among others, has developed this notion of a spiritual law of gravity: "Hence, as a body, unless prevented, is borne to its place by its weight or lightness, so souls, when the bond of flesh by which they were held in the condition of this life, is dissolved, immediately attain their reward or punishment, unless something intervenes" (In IV *Sent.,* dist. XLV, q. 1). Long before, St. Augustine had used the same idea: weight, he says, takes a material thing where it is to go, if it is heavy, downward, if it is light, upward. But for himself (as for all men) "Amor meus pondus meum"—love is my weight. If a man loves God, then he is, by a sort of natural movement, drawn Godward; if a man loves self in preference to God, then as naturally he is drawn away from God. And we make our own weight: God gives us the wherewithal, but it is we who make it.

So far we have been considering the person who dies with his love set away from God. He finds his place. But so too does the person who dies loving God. This love, as we have seen, may be total, a uniting of his will with the will of God so complete that there is no element of self unyielded. But there is the other possibility: a real love of God, and a union of the will with the will of God, yet with some small element of self left unsurrendered. This may be by way of sins committed—venial sins not taken seriously enough for serious repentance, or mortal sins repented with genuine sorrow yet with something lacking to the intensity of the sorrow. Or it may be sins of omission, which consist fundamentally in the absence of a total yielding of the self at this or that small point. Either way it comes to the same thing. The real love really there would bear man directly to God, but these lightless, lifeless elements hinder the movement. It is for them that purgatory exists.

Not a great deal has been revealed to us of the nature of purgatory. It is a place of waiting where, by suffering lovingly accepted, the soul is cleansed of all these smaller defilements. Purity means the giving of oneself to the will of God without any admixture of other influence: to hold back any element in oneself, however slight, is an adulteration, and so a defilement: and nothing defiled can enter heaven. What the suffering is by which the soul is brought to perfection in purgatory, we do not know. But that it should be suffering is natural enough. The defilement consists precisely in the assertion of self. By nothing is self-assertion so radically healed as by the acceptance of what the self shrinks from as it shrinks from suffering.

(iv) Heaven

For the soul totally united with God, whether at death or after the purifying of purgatory, there is immediately the direct vision of the Blessed Trinity. Man has attained the thing God made him for. Union with God now takes on a closeness for which we have no words or concepts adequate. God has revealed the essential of it, and we can repeat the words, but the mind can hardly make more than a step or two in their realization. So St. Paul reminds us (1 Cor 13): "Our knowledge, our prophecy, are only glimpses of the truth; and these glimpses will be swept away when the time of fulfillment comes. . . . At present, we are looking at a confused reflection in a mirror; then, we shall see face to face." St. John says the same thing: "We are sons of God even now, and what we shall be hereafter, has not been made known as yet. But we know that when He comes we shall be like Him; we shall see Him, then, as He is" (1 Jn 3:2).

Observe how St. John and St. Paul emphasize seeing: we shall see Him as He is, we shall see Him face to face. This is the doctrine of the Beatific Vision—the seeing that brings bliss. The mind knows God, not by an idea of God however rich or full, but directly. We have no experience of direct knowledge here below, since we know everything by means of ideas. We can try to figure it to ourselves as so close a contact between the soul and God, that God takes the place of the idea of God. So we stammer and stumble in our effort at comprehension. What we must hold on to is the certainty of a union with God of inconceivable closeness. The intellect will see Him, with nothing between. The will will love Him at the level of this new vision. Intellect and will and every power of the soul will be utterly fulfilled in the contact. The whole of the soul's energy will be working at its highest upon the highest: there will be no frustration from unused or misused energy: there will be total happiness.

This happiness, though total for each, will not be equal in all. Will and intellect will be working *at their highest,* with no element in them unused or unfed. But how high will my highest or yours be? As high as our co-operation with grace in this life has made it. It is in this life that the soul grows; every piece of truth, every channel of grace, can be used by us, if we will, for growth. Whatever capacity the soul has grown to at death, that capacity will be filled in the glory and the joy of heaven. A man who does not accept the Catholic Church may be saved; that is, he may enter heaven. But not having all the truths or all the means of grace, he will not have grown to the soul-capacity that the totality of Christ's gifts would have meant for him. A given non-Catholic may indeed have made better use of his smaller share of gifts than a given Catholic has made of the totality. Yet his capacity, though it may be greater than this or that Catholic actually has, is not as great as he himself as a Catholic would have had. And the difference matters far beyond our power to conceive.

But great soul or small, we shall all be filled. In our total contact with God, we shall be wholly happy, and imperishably happy. There are two possibilities of misunderstanding here. One may feel that some more substantial sort of happiness than knowledge and love of God would suit us better; one may feel that eternity is too long for us anyhow.

The first feeling is commoner: as we think upon the things we have enjoyed in this life, the joys of heaven seem noble, of course, but definitely thin: with a slight sinking in the pit of the heart, we find ourselves hoping that it may turn out better than it sounds. This is an amiable weakness, much as if a small child, learning that adults like poetry or science or mathematics, should feel how ill such things compare with the tin soldiers and the rocking horse and the plum tarts of his own ecstacy.

We must not let imagination fool us. All the things we have enjoyed are made by God of nothing. Whatever reality is in them God gave them. But God does not give what He has not got. Any reality He has put into things, He must already have in Himself. It will be in Him according to His infinity, but it will not be less for that but greater. The things we have enjoyed with their mingling of nothingness, we shall possess in God unmingled. A man who had lived all his life by a muddy stream and never had anything to slake his thirst but muddy water might recoil from his first sight of a spring of clear water. It would look so thin and bodiless. But let him drink it. For the first time he knows the lovely taste of water, and in that act knows the mud for what it is. Reality mirrored in nothingness has given man exquisite moments—reality mirrored in nothingness, reality muddied by nothingness. What reality unmirrored, unmuddied, has to give will not be less.

The second feeling was expressed by Engels in his jibe at "the tedium of personal immortality". The error arises from a profound sense of the emptiness of life upon earth, combined with a notion of eternity as time that does not end—Macbeth's tomorrow and tomorrow and tomorrow creeping on their petty pace from day to day. But the "pace" of heaven is not petty. And there is no succession of tomorrows. In heaven we shall not be in eternity, the changeless Now of God; but we shall be out of the ceaseless flow of change that time measures.

Aeviternity, we have seen in Chapter 2, is the proper duration of spirit; in heaven, the spirit abides with no distracting awareness of moments flowing away, nor any weariness from needs or powers unsatisfied to make it restless for change, in the bliss of a total experience. Even when the body is restored to it at the Last Day, its awareness of the body's less perfect hold upon an abiding present will not be a distraction, for the body will no longer draw the spirit downward to its own lesser level of being. The detail of this new relation of soul and body is beyond us; but the reality of it is certain. We have seen how here below, the body imposes its subjection to time so forcefully upon the soul that we have almost forgotten that the soul has a proper duration of its own. In heaven it will not be so. The soul's changeless contemplation of God will be the dominating reality; its relations with the body, though not of the same order, will not diminish it but somehow fall within it; so, mysteriously, will our relations with angels and other souls in heaven.

For observe that the soul in its lifegiving contact with the Absolute is not merged in the Absolute. It remains itself, a value willed by God. And just as total love of God in this life does not exclude but flows naturally into love of neighbor because God loves him too, so the total vision of God does not exclude but flows naturally into an awareness of all those other beings who are in the same loving contact. So Benedict XII, in the Encyclical *Benedictus Deus,* wrote of the souls of the just who "see the divine essence with an intuitive and face to face vision", that they are in heaven with Christ, linked together with the company of the angels. It is not only the angels in whose companionship we shall be in heaven. We shall be with one another. Thus in the Mass for the Dead, the Church has special prayers for one's parents who have died: "Give them eternal joy in the land of the living, and let us join them one day in the happiness of the saints."

What our companionship with one another in heaven will mean is another of the things we cannot know in detail; and there is no great point, though quite a lot of pleasure, in speculating.

What is more practical is to grasp that we upon earth have a true companionship with them *here and now*. The souls in heaven and in purgatory are still members of the Mystical Body, confirmed forever in their membership as we upon earth are not, but members of one Body with us for all that. The doctrine of the Communion of Saints takes on a new dimension. We can help the souls in purgatory by our prayers, and there are many theologians who hold that they can help us similarly; the souls in heaven certainly can. Before the face of God, they can join their prayers to ours. They are not less with us for being in heaven, but more, because they are more profoundly in Christ, in whom we also are. This is the sense in which we say that sin separates but death does not. The cares of this life still stand between us and them, but not between them and us. They are more closely united to us now than in any closeness known upon earth. It was noted earlier that we do not join the Church for the company, but for the gifts Christ gives through it. But if we do not join the Church for the company, we do find ourselves in pretty remarkable company all the same: "The scene of your approach now is mount Sion, is the heavenly Jerusalem, city of the living God; here are gathered thousands upon thousands of angels, here is the assembly of those first-born sons whose names are written in heaven, here is God sitting in judgment on all men, here are the spirits of just men, now made perfect; here is Jesus, the spokesman of the new covenant, and the sprinkling of His blood, which has better things to say than Abel's had" (Heb 12:22–24).

25. The End of the World

So men die and go to bliss or woe. Meanwhile the world goes on. Christ died at the hands of sinners and rose again in victory over sin and death. But sin and death go on. The victory, complete in Christ, is progressive in men: its completion lies somewhere in the future. Satan is dethroned, but not driven from the field. He has lost the human race, but may still win individuals, and go close to winning many more, and trouble many whom he does not even go close to winning. It was after Our Lord's Resurrection and Ascension that St. Paul wrote to the Ephesians (6:11): "You must wear all the weapons in God's armoury, if you would find strength to resist the cunning of the devil. It is not against flesh and blood that we enter the lists; we have to do with princedoms and powers, with those who have mastery of the world in these dark days, with malign influences in an order higher than ours."

The world is filled with the turbulence of men. The writer of the Book of Wisdom would not have to soften a line in his harsh picture: the proportions may be different, the world makes certain advances, but all these things are still here—"They neither keep life nor marriage undefiled: but one kills another by envy or grieves him by adultery. And all things are mingled together,

blood; murder, theft and dissimulation, corruption and unfaith-
fulness, tumults and perjury, disquieting of the good; forgetfulness of God, defiling of souls, changing of nature, disorder
in marriage, and the irregularity of adultery and uncleanness."

(i) The Body growing to maturity

But all this is only the colorful front face of things. This is humanity tormented by its own evil and by powers of evil greater
than its own. Behind it and within it Christ is forming the new
humanity, re-born and re-made in Him. The Mystical Body continues to grow. There are the millions who have died in Christ
and are inbuilt into the Body forever, and there are the millions still on earth in whom His life principle is working, evidently or secretly. Behind all the turbulence, the building of the
Mystical Body of Christ goes on ceaselessly, and it is humanity's
real work, little as so many humans suspect it, perversely as so
many work against it, tepidly as so many cooperate.

The building goes on ceaselessly, but not by mere addition of
more and more. It is growing toward something. So St. Paul
tells the Ephesians: "Far off or near, united in the same Spirit,
we have access through him to the Father. You are no longer
exiles, then, or aliens; the saints are your fellow-citizens, you
belong to God's household. Apostles and prophets are the foundation on which you were built, and the chief corner-stone of
it is Jesus Christ himself. In him the whole fabric is bound
together, as *it grows into a temple,* dedicated to the Lord" (2:18–21).

Here the Church is seen as a building growing into a temple.
Two chapters later we see it as a Body growing to maturity.
We have already seen the application of the verses that follow
to the individual soul, but they apply equally to the Body as a
whole: "So we shall reach perfect manhood, that maturity which

is proportioned to the completed growth of Christ. . . . We are to follow the truth, in a spirit of charity, and so grow up, in everything, into a due proportion with Christ, who is our head."

Both figures convey the same truth. The building of a temple is more than an endless heaping together of stones. It is an adding and an arrangement, and it has a term: a moment comes when the temple is built. Only God knows the shape and proportion of the temple He is building; only God knows how close the temple is to completion. So with a body: it is not merely an endless growing of new cells: it has a shape and proportion, and grows toward a maturity. How close Christ's Mystical Body is to its maturity, He knows and we do not. But it is not fanciful to think that with the completion of the temple, the maturity of the Body, the human race will cease to generate. To what purpose would new generations be born, when the Mystical Body of Christ is complete?

(ii) Anti-Christ

Soon or late our world will end, and the Day of the Lord will be here. We do not know when the end will come: all that we have upon that is Our Lord's word: "This gospel of the kingdom must first be preached all over the world, so that all nations may hear the truth; only after that will the end come" (Mt 24). But if we do not know the time, we know what the signs will be. Our Lord has told us especially in the twenty-fourth chapter of St. Matthew. We have it in the Prophet Daniel (especially chapters 7, 11, and 12), and again in the second epistle of St. Paul to the Thessalonians. Of these signs, two are stated with immense clarity, namely, a general apostasy and the coming of Anti-Christ: "Do not be terrified out of your senses . . . by any spiritual utterance . . . purporting to come from us, which suggests that the day of the Lord is close at hand. ... The apostasy must come first; the champion of wickedness must appear first, destined to inherit perdition. This is the rebel who is to lift up his head above every divine name, above all that men hold in reverence, till at last he enthrones himself in God's temple, and proclaims himself as God. ... At present there is a power (you know what I mean) which holds him in check, so that he may not show himself before the time appointed to him; meanwhile, the conspiracy of revolt is already at work; only, he who checks it now will be able to check it, until he is removed from the enemy's path. Then it is that the rebel will show himself; and the Lord Jesus will destroy him with the breath of His mouth. ... He will come, when he comes, with all Satan's influence to aid him; there will be no lack of power, of counterfeit signs and wonders; and his wickedness will deceive the souls that are doomed, to punish them for refusing that fellowship in the truth which would have saved them" (2 Th 2:2–10).

A third sign seems to be suggested by St. Paul. It is the conversion of the Jews: "Blindness has fallen upon a part of Israel, but only until the tale of the Gentile nations is complete; then the whole of Israel will find salvation" (Rom 11:25). St. Paul is alone in telling us of this. It is upon the Apostasy and the coming of Anti-Christ that Scripture insists continually. Iniquity will abound, love will grow cold, and Anti-Christ will come; and then very soon after, Christ will come.

Both St. Paul and St. Peter give us some account of the evil state of men at the Apostasy. St. Paul writes (2 Tim 3–5): "Know also this, that in the last days, shall come dangerous times. Men shall be lovers of themselves, covetous, haughty, proud, blasphemers, disobedient to parents, ungrateful, wicked, without affection, without peace, slanderers, incontinent, unmerciful, without kindness, traitors, stubborn, puffed up, and lovers of pleasures more than of God: Having an appearance indeed of godliness, but denying the power thereof." St. Peter gives a description which seems to apply with special aptness to our own moment, as he speaks of "those especially, who follow the defiling appetites of their corrupt nature, and make light of authority. . . . Their eyes feast on adultery, insatiable of sin; and they know how to win wavering souls to their purpose, so skilled is all their accursed brood at gaining its own ends. . . . Using fine phrases that have no meaning, they bait their hook with the wanton appetites of sense, to catch those who have had but a short respite from false teaching. What do they offer them? Liberty. And all the time they themselves are enslaved to worldly corruption" (2 Pet 2:10, 19).

Anti-Christ's success is to be spectacular while it lasts. St. John, recounting his vision of it (Rev 13), writes: "All the dwellers on earth fell down in adoration of him, except those whose names the Lamb had written down in his book of life, the Lamb slain in sacrifice ever since the world was made."

Part of this universal success is the work of another mysterious figure, the "false prophet", Anti-Christ's chief minister—"Such wonders could it accomplish that it brought down fire, before men's eyes, from heaven to earth; and by these wonders, which it was able to do in its master's presence, it deluded the inhabitants of the world."

We have just seen who were saved—those whose names were written in the book of life; and a moment ago we have seen St. Paul indicating *how* they escaped the error of the rest: there is *a fellowship in the truth,* which in that day will save those who trust in it. However overwhelming the miracles of Anti-Christ, the Teaching Church will be there for those who will hold fast to it. And the trial, though fierce, will not be long. Christ will come: the false Christ and his false prophet will be overthrown: mankind will be judged.

What of Anti-Christ himself? In Scripture, it is very difficult to see him as anything but an individual. We have seen
that St. Paul described him as "the rebel who is to lift up his
head above every divine name, above all that men hold in
reverence, till at last he enthrones himself in God's temple and
proclaims himself as God". Daniel says of him (11:36): "He shall
be lifted up and shall magnify himself against every god: and
he shall speak great things against the God of gods: and shall
prosper, till the wrath be accomplished. For the determination
is made. And he shall make no account of the God of his
fathers: and he shall follow the lust of women, and he shall not
regard any gods: for he shall rise up against all things."

But if Anti-Christ is to be a real person and the Apostasy a
real Apostasy coming at the end of the world, both Anti-Christ
and Apostasy have their forerunners in every age of the world.
For the truth is that just as every death is the end of the world in
miniature, so every age is the last age in miniature. In that sense
we are all in the last age. Anti-Christ is to come; but we have
heard St. Paul say that "the conspiracy of revolt is *already at
work*". In his First Epistle (4:3), St. John tells us the same thing:
"Every spirit which acknowledges Jesus Christ as having come
to us in human flesh has God for its author; and no spirit which
would disunite Jesus comes from God. This is the power of
Anti-Christ, whose coming you have been told to expect; now
you must know that he is here in the world already."

(iii) The Judgment: a new heaven and a new earth

Of the coming of Jesus in power to judge the world, Scripture
also tells us something. St. Paul writes: "That is for the day
when the Lord Jesus appears from Heaven, with Angels to
proclaim His power; with fire flaming about Him"—an echo

of Our Lord's own phrase: "When the Son of Man comes, it will be like the lightning that springs up from the East and flashes across to the West." There will be the sound of a trumpet, and the dead will arise in their bodies. Thus Our Lord tells us: "Immediately after the distress of those days, the sun will be darkened, and the moon will refuse her light, and the stars will fall from heaven, and the powers of heaven will rock; and then the sign of the Son of Man will be seen in heaven; then it is that all the tribes of the land will mourn, and they will see the Son of Man coming upon the clouds of heaven, with great power and glory; and he will send out his angels with a loud blast of the trumpet, to gather his elect from the four winds, from one end of heaven to the other" (Mt 24:29–32).

St. Paul gives a further detail concerning those who are still alive upon earth when that day comes: "It will happen in a moment, in the twinkling of an eye, when the last trumpet sounds; the trumpet will sound, and the dead will rise again, free from corruption, and we shall find ourselves changed; this corruptible nature of ours must be clothed with incorruptible life, this mortal nature with immortality" (1 Cor 14:52–54).

It is not only the just who will be there: "When the Son of Man comes in His glory, and all the angels with Him, He will sit down upon the throne of His glory, and all nations will be gathered in His presence, where He will divide men one from the other, as the shepherd divides the sheep from the goats; He will set the sheep on His right, and the goats on His left. Then the King will say to those who are on His right hand, Come, you that have received a blessing from my Father, take possession of the kingdom which has been prepared for you since the foundation of the world. . . . Then He will say to those who are on His left hand, in their turn, Go far from me, you that are accursed, into that eternal fire which has been prepared for the

devil and his angels.... And these shall pass on to eternal
punishment, and the just to eternal life" (Mt 25:31–46).

Of the detail of the judging we are told little. In the passage
just quoted, Our Lord makes the sentence depend upon works
of charity done or refused by us to men, and therefore done or
refused to Himself. It is the common teaching that these works
of charity are used here as representative of the virtues in
general. The Judgment will be a complete judgment, in which
men will see their own actions in their true value, and in the
whole of their context — that is to say, in relation to the actions
of all other men, and these in relation to the overruling providence of God: so that in a sense there will be spread before the
mind of man a picture of the whole created order and of
the marvelous pattern of God's work in it and upon it. At last
we shall see the shape and bearing of all things.

The Kingdom of God will then be established in its fullness.
What will be the place of matter in it? Souls will once more be
united with bodies, so that we shall be constituted in the
completeness of our personality. Will these bodies have any
connection with the bodies we now have? The answer is yes,
but the detail is not clear. After all, while I have the same body
now that I had twenty years ago, no single cell in it is the same:
every cell I had then is gone, and a new one has taken its place.
Yet it is not mere verbalism to say that I still have the same
body. Clearly apart from the cells there is an element which
somehow persists, and by persisting preserves the identity of
my body. It would be beyond the scope of this book to set out
the philosophic and scientific theories as to the nature of the
persisting element. But it may be this element, whatever it is,
that will be re-united with the soul in the resurrection of the
body and constitute the identity of the new body with the old.
Anyhow, our resurrection bodies will be, in the theological

phrase, glorified bodies: corruption will be clothed with incorruptible life, mortal nature with immortality. At last we shall know what it is to be a man, for the union of soul and body will exist with no rebellion or inertia on the body's part to diminish the union. As Christopher Dawson said, "Matter will be once more the extension of spirit, not its limit; the instrument of spirit, not the enemy."

What matter will be there apart from the human body, or in what condition, we do not know very well. Scripture, both Old Testament and New, is filled with the promise of new heavens and a new earth. Here is St. Peter: "The day of the Lord is coming, and when it comes, it will be upon you like a thief. The heavens will vanish in a whirlwind, the elements will be scorched up and dissolve, earth, and all earth's achievements, will burn away. . . . And meanwhile, we have new heavens and a new earth to look forward to, the dwelling place of holiness" (2 Pet 3:10, 13). The whole twenty-first chapter of the last book of the New Testament should be read. I quote here the opening verses:

"Then I saw a new heaven, and a new earth. The old heaven, the old earth had vanished, and there was no more sea. And I, John, saw in my vision that holy city which is the new Jerusalem, being sent down by God from heaven, all clothed in readiness, like a bride who has adorned herself to meet her husband. I heard, too, a voice which cried aloud from the throne, Here is God's tabernacle pitched among men; he will dwell with them, and they will be his own people, and he will be among them, their own God. He will wipe away every tear from their eyes, and there will be no more death, or mourning, or cries of distress, no more sorrow; those old things have passed away. And he who sat on the throne said, Behold, I make all things new."

That inanimate nature will in some way be involved in the Kingdom that shall never end seems certain, however mysterious may be the detail. St. Paul writes much upon this aspect. Thus to the Romans (8:19–22): "If creation is full of expectancy, that is because it is waiting for the sons of God to be made known. Created nature has been condemned to frustration; not for some deliberate fault of its own, but for the sake of him who so condemned it, with a hope to look forward to; namely, that nature in its turn will be set free from the tyranny of corruption, to share in the glorious freedom of God's sons."

This destiny of the material creation is bound up with the role of the Second Person of the Blessed Trinity, in and through whom all things were created and who became man for the remaking of the design that man had spoiled. Consider two of the things St. Paul said. The first is to the Colossians (1:15–20): "He is the true likeness of the God we cannot see; His is that first birth which precedes every act of creation. Yes, in Him all created things took their being, heavenly and earthly, visible and invisible.... He takes precedency of all, and in Him all subsist.... It was God's good pleasure to let all completeness dwell in Him, and through Him to win back all things, whether on earth or in heaven, into union with Himself, making peace with them through His blood, shed on the cross." And to the Ephesians (1:8–10): "So rich is God's grace, that has overflowed upon us in a full stream of wisdom and discernment, to make known to us the hidden purpose of His Will. It was His loving design, centered in Christ, to give history its fulfillment by resuming everything in Him, all that is in heaven, all that is on earth"; or in the Douay version, "In the dispensation of the fulness of times to re-establish all things in Christ."

The essential of life in the Kingdom will be in this, that

in union with Christ we shall gaze upon the face of God, our whole being uttering itself in knowledge and love of Him. But just as God's infinite knowledge and love of Himself do not exclude creatures but flow over into knowing and loving them, so our total knowledge and love of God likewise will not exclude creatures but will flow over into knowledge and love of them. And God will be all in all.

PART IV

ONESELF

26. Habituation to Reality

The first part of this book was about God. The second part was about the story of God's action upon the human race. Note the word "story". Christianity is a historical religion: time has always been its fourth dimension. In studying man's relation with God, time is vital. His relation to God has a history, a shape, an unfolding; in fact, a plot. It matters enormously when a man was born. It is not a case of a static higher world with which man has had, and could only have, a fixed relation. That world and we have had a great many changes of relation. Things that have happened are part of our religion, as well as things that are. Not to know the story is not to know the religion; and not to know the religion is not to know reality. For the facts of religion are not simply facts of religion, but facts, and the most important facts. What we have been studying is that context of reality in which we are, and from which we can in no way escape. Given that the context is what it is, it remains for us to study our own being and our own life in it; and this will be the theme of the third and last section of this book.

(i) Knowing the context

In summary, we see the context as statable in terms of three actors and four events. The actors are God, Adam, Christ: all of them are in us in various ways, and we cannot know ourselves without understanding them. The events are the Creation, the Fall, the Redemption, and the Judgment. Knowing this context, we know where we are, what we are, and what we exist for; knowing the totality, we can know our place in it and establish our relation to everything else in it. We can do nothing to alter the context, for it is reality. As I have said, we cannot escape from it, there is nowhere to escape *to*, for apart from it is only nothingness. The only thing left to our choice is the mental attitude we shall adopt to it. No subordinate choice that we can make can ever be as important as this fundamental choice.

What choices are open to us? Roughly, three. We can do our best to understand reality, the context in which we are, and harmonize ourselves with it. Or we can understand the context and rebel against it; that is, rebel against reality, and what could be bleaker? Or we can ignore the context, and either invent one of our own by selecting such elements in the context as we happen, mentally or temperamentally, to find appealing, or else act in no context at all. Maturity lies with the first choice.

Maturity is preparedness to accept reality, cooperate with reality, not kick against reality: remembering that the reality we accept does not mean any situation that merely happens to be, and is in fact within our power to change, but only the vast framework of reality which by God's will is what it is.

We are existent in a universe: we and it alike are created by God, held in existence from moment to moment by God; we enter life born in Adam and enfolded in the results of his fall:

we are meant for a supernatural destiny and can reach it only by entering a supernatural life through rebirth in Christ our Redeemer: we are fully ourselves, that is, in a condition to be all that we are meant to be and do all that we are meant to do, only as members of the Mystical Body of Christ. These are the inescapable facts about ourselves. To be unaware of any element in them is to falsify everything. Whatever one proposes to *do* about the facts, there is only ignorance and error, darkness and double darkness, in not seeing them.

(ii) The theologian and the novelist

In that darkness we cannot get our relation to anything right. The sociologist, for instance, is not *directly* concerned with men's relation to God, but with their relation to one another; and the same is true of the novelist, too, for the most part. But men are in fact related to God, fallen in Adam, redeemed by Christ, on their way to heaven or hell; and if the novelist or sociologist does not know this, he does not know men; that is, he does not know his business. Even what he does see, he does not see right. Our own age is very fastidious about novels, and particularly about their reality. We say a novel is artificial, and so saying damn it out of hand, when the characters are unreal. Yet no one seems to mind that the world he inhabits is unreal. The novelist is continually in the absurd position of making laws for his characters in a universe he did not make, and he is forced to this absurdity simply because he does not know the laws of the real universe. Lacking this knowledge, no matter how profound his insight into human character and passion and motive and motivelessness, he is doomed to unreality. A work of art is not composed in order to illustrate the moral law, any more than a cathedral is built to illustrate mechanical laws. But if the builder ignores the laws of mechanics, his cathedral will show its unreality by falling down; and if the artist ignores the moral law, his work will in the long run show its unreality just as certainly.

This, fundamentally, is why the theologian finds the modern novel chaotic. To one who has grasped the shape of reality, the most solemn, somber, closely observed modern novel seems as grotesque and fantastic as *Alice in Wonderland*. What makes that masterpiece obviously fantastic is that the law of cause and effect does not operate; but this lack of connection between cause and effect is at the level of the most superficial of secondary causes. Consider what derangement must follow if the First Cause is utterly unknown. The grotesqueness is not less because the cause ignored is more fundamental; it is only less obvious because the mind has lost contact with its own depths.

But if the theologian dismisses the novelist's world as lacking shape, the novelist dismisses the theologian's world as lacking flesh and blood. This counter-charge is worth examination, because it draws attention to a real danger that lies in wait for the student of ultimate reality. There *is* a danger that in handling elements so far beyond the reach of daily experience one might come to treat them as abstractions; and in that event our philosophizing would come to be an exercise in getting these abstractions rightly related to one another, in getting the shape of reality right. But the universe is not simply something that has a shape. It is something. The trouble is that the student, in his student days at least, must to a large extent be conditioned by his examinations; and examinations are almost invariably about shape; it is difficult to devise examinations that can test how real reality is to a man. It is possible to have a less detailed knowledge of all the relations that exist between all the various elements of reality, yet know reality better; a man who has never heard of some of the subtler truths may have a far better hold upon reality, because of the intensity of his apprehension of it. To know all the ins and outs of the diagram of reality is very valuable, but not if reality is in the mind simply as a diagram. We must never mistake intricacy for depth.

Therefore it is necessary to balance our study of the relations of things by a growing intimacy with the very being of things. Thus we must study creation, not simply the process, the transition from nothingness to something by the exercise of God's omnipotence, but the result of the process, the created universe. Studying it, we will come not only to a better knowledge of it but to a better knowledge of God, who created it; and this again not only in the sense already discussed, that we learn something of any maker from the thing he has made, but in the less obvious sense, that from the study of created being we come to an awareness of *being,* which we can bring to our study of the Uncreated Being. The theologian studying only God might come to a pretty thin notion of God. The primary truth about God is that He is. The more *is* means to us, the richer our knowledge of God. For a beginning of our study of *is,* finite being lies ready to our hand, accessible, apt to our habits. It is only a shadow of infinite Being, but even a shadow is still something immense if infinite Being has cast it. Just as finite language is inadequate to express our knowledge, yet is the best we have and not to be spurned without loss, so finite being is an inadequate expression of infinite Being, yet is the best we have as a starting point and can yield immense fruit of knowledge.

(iii) Study the created universe

We must study being, not simply as a philosophical concept, but as a reality expressed in everything that exists. We shall do better if we arrive at our own mental relation with being from our own experience of the things that are, and not simply from books in which other men abstract for us the fruit of theirs. Certainly it would be folly to think that we are likely to get a better notion of infinite Being by ignoring finite being. For in the first place, as we have seen, it bears at its lowest the imprint, and at its highest the likeness, of its Maker. It would be a singular aberration to think one could learn nothing about God from the things He has made — from the heavens, for example, which show forth God's glory. The mind really aware of the splendor of creation cannot but feel how superb must be the infinite Being, if He can make this admirable stuff out of nothing. It is no compliment to God's omnipotence to treat what He has made of nothing as if it were little better than nothing. It is no compliment to a poet to be always seeking him and resolutely refusing to read his poetry. God *is* communicating with us, telling us something, by way of his universe. There is something verging on the monstrous about knowing God and not being interested in the things He has made, the things in which His infinite power is energizing. The logical development of so strange an attitude would be to love God so exclusively that we could not love men — an exclusiveness which He has forbidden. We have to love our neighbor because God loves him, and love demands knowledge. We cannot at once love our neighbor and ignore him; and we have to love the world, because God loves the world; and coming to know the world, we find that we are knowing God better. Provided that we keep the proportion right, our relation to God is better and richer because of our use, with mind and will and body, of what He has made.

But note again: in its way the created universe *is,* and from it we can get a real if quite unsayable notion of what *is* means. But as our knowledge grows, we are conscious of a kind of two-way effect—a growing sense of the wonder of it, and a growing awareness of the element of nothingness in it. As against not-being, nothing, it is so measurelessly great. As against Infinity, it barely is at all.

Given that the created universe has to be studied, how shall we study it? There is no one set way. Once one has the shape of reality, there is almost no way of *not* studying it, if one's mind is not abnormally lethargic. Once one has the main elements of reality clear in the mind, everything can add to the richness. Indeed a great deal of the enriching process will be spontaneous and unmeditated. We have not to be forever setting our teeth and working conscientiously at the enrichment of our mind. Direct study of the universe there must be, but it will not be the whole of the mind's action or the best part of it. Any living activity will serve. There is, for example, an immense amount to be learned about being, and therefore about God if one knows how to apply it, merely by having a cold plunge on a winter morning.

(iv) Learn from poet and scientist

On the same principle of learning from our own experience in living, there is much to be learned by sharing the fruit of the experience of others by reading—not simply reading philosophy, but the words of those especially gifted to react to reality. The theologian may well have something to gain from the novelist. For if the novelist has only a vague notion, or no notion at all, of the total meaning of life, he has usually a highly developed awareness of the flesh and blood of it. But far more than novels, the theologian might gain by reading the poets—and not only because they might improve his style, though that is more important than he always understands. In that *awareness* of reality which is so vital, the poet really has something to give the theologian.

Wordsworth's

> *The moon doth with delight*
> *Look round her when the heavens are bare*

and Virgil's "Sunt lachrymae rerum" witness across eighteen hundred years to the same truth: the poets cannot be happy with the idea that nature is dead. They feel the life in it, though they do not always know what the life is that they feel. The Christian is exactly the reverse: he knows what the mystery is, but for the most part does not feel it. He knows as a fact of Christian doctrine that God is at the very center of all things whatsoever, sustaining them by His own continuing life above the surface of that nothingness from which He drew them: but he does not experience things that way. What the Christian knows as a truth, the poet responds to as a living fact: he sees things so. That is the one half of his gift. By the other half, he can communicate his experience, so that we see them so, too. Thus the poet can help many people who know a great deal more about creation than he does. He can help them by making creation come alive to them.

But as we have said, there is need of direct study of the created universe. Consider matter first. The natural sciences serve the lesser purpose of helping to make the world more habitable and the greater purpose of increasing our knowledge of it. This order of values is not simply a fad of my own. The scientist himself holds it. *Science* is from the Latin verb *scire,* "to know". Science does not mean doing; it means knowing. We have the electric light, not because scientists wanted to give us a handier illuminant than gas, but because they wanted to know more about the nature of light and the nature of electricity. The handy-men may hang around the scientist, seeing how they can put to use what he discovers; but it is he that discovers, not they. And he is driven on to his discoveries by a passionate desire to know. But for him, and that quality in him, the handy-men would be helpless.

It would be incredible, we have shown, for a theologian to think he could learn nothing about God from the things God made—any of them, therefore the material things too. The scientist has information to give the theologian, which the theologian can turn to gold. The scientist is not, as such, a theologian. He is dealing with causes and arrangements and relations less fundamental than the First Cause and the First Principle of Order. Further, he keeps within the field of material things. Therefore *as a scientist* he does not and cannot know what it is all about. He can know an incredible amount about the things upon which he specializes, but from his science he cannot learn the totality of being, and therefore he cannot know the full meaning, or any large part of the meaning, even of what he does know. He knows it out of its context. To repeat an illustration used very early in this book: the scientist who is only a scientist is in the position of a man who attempts to make a most detailed study of a human eye, never having seen a human face. The scientist is dealing with the relations of material things to one another; and his is valid and valuable knowledge, requiring its own sort of asceticism and devotion. But it is very bad for him if he confines himself exclusively to it, for a scientist is also a man with a man's need to know and a man's capacity to know the meaning of his own life.

Nothing is valueless that God has made, but the things the

scientist studies are the lowest in value; and apart from their relation to God and to the higher things of that creation which in their lowliness they complete, they would be of no value at all: this is how he tends to study them. For him to be engaged so closely in their study that larger realities remain unseen is to neglect the better part of his own humanity. No amount of excellence as a scientist can compensate for stuntedness and crippledness as a man. Yet these brilliant workers upon the lowest things may well be compensated by the good God for the blindness so many of them have inflicted upon themselves.

The scientist loses more by not learning from the theologian than the theologian loses by not learning from the scientist: in any event the theologian has never ignored the stuff of the universe as the scientist has ignored the mind behind the universe. The theologian can hardly help knowing that bread nourishes, that poison kills, that sex perturbs. But if one loses less than the other, both lose. The scientist's loss is not here our concern, but the theologian's is, since we are taking our first steps along his road. He and we can learn from all the things that bear God's imprint, but still more from those higher things that He made in His likeness—angels and the souls of men. There is more to be learned from studying angels, but not by us. Man lies more immediately to our hand. We can study him more conveniently than we can study the angels. We can study him not only in psychology classrooms or history classrooms but in the workshop, the bus, the shaving mirror. The stupidest couplet that Alexander Pope ever wrote is

> *Presume not the illimitable to scan,*
> *The proper study of mankind is man.*

In divorcing the study of the illimitable from the study of man he was wrong both ways; for man is a most excellent starting point for our study of the illimitable, while man cannot be understood apart from his relation to the illimitable—that is, out of his context. The remainder of this book will be concerned with the study of man, for we have already paid the beginning of attention to the illimitable.

27. Habituation to Man

One is at first startled to be told that only in the Mystical Body can man be fully and satisfactorily himself. The real difficulty about the doctrine of the Mystical Body, as we have seen, is not to grasp it but to believe that the Church really means it. It is not hard to believe in the Catholic Church as an organization established by Christ to which its members go for Christ's gifts of life and truth; but, about the idea of the Church as an organism into which we are built that we may live in the full stream of Christ's life as members of Christ, there is an extraordinariness which dazzles or baffles by seeming so utterly out of scale with us. The ordinary Catholic's first reaction on being told that this is his condition in the Church is an incredulous "What, me!" He feels not only that the thing is beyond his powers, but that it is rather beyond his desires. Our meagerness would have been satisfied—even, as we feel in this first reaction, better satisfied—by something less. Some less ardent context, we feel, would suit our ordinariness better.

(i) Man's extraordinariness

We have already considered this difficulty in the mind. Here we may look at it again from a rather different angle. Man must grasp that man is extraordinary. He is extraordinary like all creatures—there is nothing prosaic about being held in existence out of one's native nothingness by the continuing will of Omnipotence; but he is more extraordinary than other creatures, both by what God made him and by what he has made of himself.

Let us consider ourselves a little. We are made from nothing, but we are not made for nothing and will never return into nothing. Without God we would be nothing, but we are not without Him and will never be without Him. He made us not only into something, but into something that is like Him; and again not only into something that is like Him but into something that He could Himself become, something that He thought enough of to die for. Spiritual and immortal, made in the likeness of God, redeemed by Christ, we are clustered with splendors. Consider man's glory as we know it against the dreariness of man as the atheist thinks him. We have nothing as our origin, but eternity as our destiny; the atheist has a cloud about his origin but nothing as his destiny. We come from nothing, he is going to nothing. Fortunately his thinking so does not make it so. Eternity will have surprises for him too.

In any event never think that the way of man is prosaic. We are a mixture of matter and spirit, and thus we resemble no other creature (at least in the universe known to us: of possible inhabitants of other planets I know as little as the rest of men). We are the only beings who die and do not stay dead: it seems an odd way to our goal that as the last stage on the way to it all of us, saint and sinner, should fall apart. We are the only beings with an everlasting destiny who have not reached their final state. By comparison there is something cozy and settled about angels, good and bad. Men are the only beings whose destiny is uncertain.

There is an effect of this in our consciousness, if we choose to analyze it. There is a two-way drag in all of us, and nothing could be more actual and less academic than this curious fact. How actual it is we can see if we compare our knowledge that the planet we live on is not anchored in space. This ought to be, one would think, the first thing we should be aware of, yet it was only a few centuries ago that scientists arrived at it; and most of us still have to take the word of scientists for it. No one of us has ever felt the whizz of the world through space and the counter-drag of whatever power it is that keeps us upon the earth's surface. But we *do* feel the almost continuous drag in ourselves downward toward nothingness and the all too occasional upward thrust. Man is the cockpit of a battle. We are the only creatures who can choose their side and change their side in this battle. We are the only beings left who can either choose or refuse God. All the excitement of our universe is centered in man.

For observe that we started extraordinary, and from extraordinary have grown monstrous—body rebelling against soul, imagination playing the devil with intellect, passion storming will. The mediaeval travelers' stories of men with their heads under their shoulders were not unjustly felt to be pretty startling. But men with their intellects under their imaginations and their wills under their passions are more startling still. The only reason we are not startled is that we are more sensitive to the shape, and therefore to any misshapenness, of body than of soul. Whatever other reasons we might have or think we have for rejecting the doctrine of the Mystical Body, let us not think of ourselves as too ordinary for so marvelous a context. No context could be too extraordinary for creatures like men.

(ii) The Church alone sees man as (a) spirit and matter, (b) individual
 and social

But the extraordinariness of both is not the only link between
man and the Church. At every point in the nature of man, the
Church fits it. We may summarize the truth about all men in
two pairs of facts: first, man is at once spirit and matter;
second, he is at once an individual person and a social being. In
each pair, the Church sees both elements.

As to the first pair, she makes such provision for the needs
and powers of the soul as are undreamed of elsewhere; but the
body is fully realized too, by way of asceticism fitting it for full
partnership with the soul, by way of sacrament and sacramental fitting it for companionship to the very furthest point the
soul can go. Within the Church there is a consecration of soul
and body, an awareness of sacredness in soul and body.

As to the second pair, the Church has turned the social
element in man's nature to the uses of religion beyond any
other church, seeing man united with his fellows in relation
to God, uniting with his fellows in the worship of God,
receiving God's gifts of truth and life through the fellowship.
Yet the person remains himself, not merged in the human
society here or in the divine nature hereafter, under God an
end in himself, not a pawn in a game. Nowhere can a person
more fully feel at once his kinship with all human beings and
the worth of his own personality.

In relation to both our key facts, notice the two tides that
have beaten on the Church in these last centuries, Protestantism
and Secularism. Just as in each the Church preserved both
components, so in each her assailants chose one component
and let the other go. Protestantism stressed the soul and the
individual. Secularism stressed the body and society. Consider
these a little more closely.

Protestantism, we say, opted for the soul and largely ignored the body, or at least made no provision for it. It ruled out asceticism, most of the sacraments, and all the sacramentals. It produced a religion for the soul only, which would have been well enough had man been a soul only, but was no religion for man. With the onrush of Secularism, the ignored element had its revenge. Secularism concentrated on the body, ignoring the spirit as completely as Protestantism ignored the body. Its aims are primarily the body's good, comfort and security, on the general assumption that, if man does happen to have a soul, it too will be satisfied by improved material conditions. The result is the starvation of the spirit.

Again, the emphasis of Protestantism was on the relation of the individual soul to God, any cooperation of man being regarded as an intrusion. There is a truth in this, but it is not the whole truth. There is an element in man beyond the reach of his fellows, something incommunicable which must have its own unshared relation with God, but that element is not the whole of man; and the effort to build the whole of religion upon it as if it were, means ultimately that even it does not reach its fullest achievement. It is within the Catholic Church that mysticism has reached its most marvelous point, as indeed the spiritual non-Catholic shows by reading the works of our mystics in preference to his own. There is the same revenge of the ignored element here as earlier. Secularism came, betting everything upon the social order as against the human person. We see this at its logical extreme in Communism and Nazism, where the collective is everything and the individual has literally no meaning and certainly no destiny apart from it. But though in these two the tendency has gone furthest, the same tendency runs through all modern sociology. The only home left for personality is the Church. Only for the Church is everyone someone.

Thus both Protestantism and Secularism maim man by treating him as half of himself. The Church alone treats man as the whole of himself in the whole of his context.

(iii) Man as union of spirit and matter

But if the Church gives us the whole truth in perfect balance, there is a danger that we, receiving it thus whole and balanced, may not use our own minds sufficiently upon it. It is a great thing to preserve truth inviolate, but less so if one keeps it unexamined. And within this danger there is the subtler danger of thinking one's mind active upon the truth when one is in fact merely exercising it upon words. In this matter of what man is, the Catholic is in real danger of stopping at the words of the definition as though knowing them were equivalent to knowing man.

Man, says the Catholic philosopher, is a rational animal. He is indeed. As a definition, the phrase is perfect; but as a description it would be totally inadequate. The object of a definition is to define, that is, to make a statement about a thing which will apply to that thing exclusively. It is a pointer which points to one single thing, the thing it defines. The phrase "rational animal" manages to point at *man* and at nothing else within our experience: the word "animal" cuts out every being that is not animal; the word "rational" cuts out every animal that is not man. The phrase distinguishes man from the octopus, say, and from the angel (just as the derisive phrase "unfeathered biped" distinguishes him from bird and beast, since no beast is biped and no bird unfeathered). Once one has put enough into the definition to exclude every other thing, to add anything further would be superfluous. But this means that there is far more in anything than its definition tells. Too many treat the phrase "rational animal" or the alternative phrase "union of spirit and matter" as a sort of blackboard diagram upon which they proceed to base their thinking on the affairs of man. But in fact either phrase is too meager a foundation. It leaves out too much — the fact, for instance, that man is fallen.

The truth is that no book and no statement by someone else can tell us what man is. Only life can do that. Every person one meets can add to our knowledge of what man is, provided that we know how to learn. If we want really to understand man, it is not enough to study animality and rationality, on the principle of the man in *Pickwick Papers* who, having to write an article on Chinese Metaphysics, looked up China in the encyclopedia, then Metaphysics, and combined the information. If you want to find out what a rational animal is, study man; neither animality nor rationality will be the same when the two are wed: the marriage does strange things to both of them. Rationality functioning in union with a body is not just rationality, animality is so ennobled by its marriage with spirit that no mere animal would know what to do with it. The way to find all this is to meet man and think hard about the experience.

As an example of the mass of actuality that can be wrapped up in a phrase, consider some of the first things that experience shows, and the phrase does not in itself tell us, about man as a union of spirit and matter. The word "union" is a word with a vast variety of meanings. If one is content with the word without getting at the one special meaning which applies to man, then one will never know what man is at all, and this would be a pity since it means a profound ignorance about oneself. Not to know what an angel is is a misfortune; not to know what a man is threatens sanity.

Let us glance at our phrase, beginning with the word "union", The union is of two beings, one of them spatial, one of them spaceless. Two unlikelier beings for a union it would be hard to conceive. If we had not the fact of it under our noses, we should be inclined to think that if any union were possible between two such, it could be only a very sketchy and casual union. But the fact is that these two beings are united so closely that they constitute one being, one person, one subsistent operative thing. We have already considered the union in a rather abstract way, but it may be worth repeating something of what has been said and adding some further points.

You may remember the illustration, used in Chapter 12, of a pot of water boiling on a flame. We have here a union of flame and water, the flame enflaming every part of the water, so that the water is immeasurably different from water unflamed both in what it is and in what it can do; so in the human compound, the body acted on by a spiritual soul is immeasurably different from a merely animal body. If ever there were a water and a flame, so related that that flame could heat only that water and that water be heated by no flame but that, we should have a figure closer still. For the soul of man and the body of man can in the one case give and in the other case receive the lifegiving energy only in relation to each other. My soul could not animate your body. In the most literal sense a man's soul and body are made for one another.

A union so close—and here the figure of the flame and the water becomes totally inadequate—might be expected to affect the soul in its own proper activities. And so we find it. There is not only that border region of emotion and passion where it is hard to tell which is more in operation, but, in the activity of intellectual knowledge, which is the soul's own special affair and for which the body as such has no competence at all, the body does in fact play a part. The soul receives all that information about the outside world—upon which it does its own thinking and from which it draws knowledge amounting ultimately to the knowledge of God himself—through the door-ways of the body's senses. While soul and body maintain their union here upon earth, the body must play this organic part in the soul's knowing, or the soul not know.

The interrelation of soul and body in the concrete living of life is the commonest fact of experience. States of the soul produce effects upon the body. What happens to the body produces states of the soul. And all this, Protestantism chooses to ignore. At any rate it will not be ignorable in heaven. We have observed that the flame can go on flaming even after the water is taken away. And the soul can continue in its own spiritual activities even after the body has reached a point where it can no longer respond to the animating energies of the soul and we have the separation called death. But the separation is not to be permanent. For this immeasurably close union constitutes the fullness of man. And man's ultimate destiny is to live the life of heaven not as part of himself, even the noblest part, but as his whole self.

(iv) Man as rational animal

We have glanced a little at the union of spirit and matter; we may now look at its other face, the union of rationality and animality. At first sight, these two look, if anything, less apt for life together than "spaceless" and "spatial". In terms of marriage it looks like the most impossible *mésalliance*. Friendly angels may well have shaken their heads and malicious devils rubbed their hands to see a marriage that looked so certain to go on the rocks, and which very soon looked as if it had in fact gone on the rocks. Rationality and animality are so oddly assorted in themselves that they seemed to need ideal circum-stances to give them any chance, and ideal circumstances are just what they did not get, at least for long. In our own experience we know how bothersome a union it is. An archangel or a cat would be driven mad in twenty-four hours by the problem of living in two such various worlds at once. Indeed madness sometimes looks like a pretty good summarization of what man has made of the problem himself, a madness we have got used to.

The trouble is that animality is so much easier than rationality. For one thing it is quite effortless, whereas rationality demands effort. We are good at animality and very much attached to it: we find rationality difficult and not so immediately rewarding. What makes it worse is that the soul can enjoy the body's pleasures as the body cannot enjoy the soul's. The dice seem heavily loaded in favor of animality, especially in a generation as fatigued as ours. Yet we *have* spiritual and not only animal needs. The body is on the quest, but the spirit is on the quest too. The body quests more clamorously, but the spirit is never wholly silent, and its hungers can be as real and even as torturing as the body's. We shall see more of these hungers of the soul, but pause here long enough to grant their reality. The soul can enjoy the body's satisfactions, but it cannot be satisfied with them. There is a trouble in it, and an unawareness of what is troubling it. H. G. Wells half hit it in his description of one of his heroes—"a street arab in love with unimaginable goddesses".

There is a conflict in man between these two so different sets of needs, and the result is a kind of near-chaos. Rationality and animality either complete each other (and that, if the relation is exactly right), or perturb each other, neither knowing what is the matter. They tend to fissure, making two beings of us instead of one: but two incomplete beings. The needs of the body inflame the soul; and the needs of the soul torment the whole man, in such a way as to mar the perfection of the body's pleasure in its pleasure; and the animality is spurred further to provide what it cannot provide, namely, satisfaction for the whole person; and so we get every sort of perversion and that sort of depravity which in our exasperation we call animal but which is not animal at all and would shock an animal to the root of his being if he could comprehend it; and mixed with the perversion and the depravity, strange streaks of magnificence. Chaos is the only word, and if we are not aware of the chaos, then we do not know man. The chaos roars or mutters or only whimpers, according to the energy of the man and what he has made of the conflict. It may be only a kind of uneasy shifting or sense of insecurity. But it must always be taken into account.

The fact of this conflict within man is one reason why we should not judge other men. Our Lord tells us not to judge, "lest we be judged". That is one reason, but it is not the only reason. We should refrain from judgment not only because we expose ourselves to judgment, but because we have not the knowledge that judgment needs. The quick slick confident judgments we are forever making are merely silly. Who can read the chaos in another's soul from which his actions proceed? Who can read the chaos in his own soul?

What we have just seen is simply a sample of what beginners in the study of man can find out for themselves on their way to deeper knowledge. Such a study once entered upon must not be allowed to cease. We must keep on studying man. We may not be able to say, that is, to cast into words, the new knowledge we gain; but there is an intimacy, a new feel and instinct for man such as a good sculptor gets for stone, which will make the most enormous difference to our handling of all men, and especially of the man who is ourself. Each must make the study for himself.

But we may summarize here two of the things that will

become always clearer. The first is that man is incalculable. Man is a rational animal. But that does not mean that he is a reasonable animal. It means only that he has reason, and therefore can misuse it. If he had not reason, he could not be unreasonable. But he has, and is. That is what I mean by his incalculability. But once you have said that man is incalculable, you have said that the definition is not enough, that no definition could be enough, and indeed no description. We must never take our eye off him: he is always liable to surprise us, and himself too.

The second truth that will emerge is that man is insufficient for himself. His insufficiency is so essential to an understanding of the religion God made for him that it must have its own chapter.

28. The Insufficiency of Man

Man is insufficient for himself, not only by the ill use he has made of himself, but in any event. There must be clarity here. So many of our troubles flow from a defective use of the intelligence or will or energy we have, that we are in danger of thinking that all our troubles could be cured by a better use of our own powers—in other words, that man has the secret of sufficiency within himself if he will but use it. But apart from failings that we can do something about, there is a radical insufficiency in us flowing altogether from our being.

(i) Action, mind, will: doomed to frustration apart from God

Man is insufficient without God because without God he would not even be. It is easy for man to think himself autonomous, if he does not think very much: for God does not jerk his elbow, so to speak, but only solicits his mind. But that a being who does not bring himself into existence and who cannot put himself out of existence should think that it is by any power of his own that he is maintained in existence is a sign that his mind must be engaged upon other matters. For fullness of being, man must have a knowledge of and a cooperation with that which maintains him in existence, that which is the very condition of his be-ing at all. To be wrong about that, is to be wrong about oneself—to see oneself as one is not, to act as one is not, to aim at what is not (which means loving things for what they are not). There is an abyss of nothingness at the very heart of our being, and we had better counter it by the fullest possible use of our kinship with the Infinite, who is also at the very heart of our being. To be ignorant of that is to live in unreality, and there can be no satisfaction for ourselves or any adequate coping with anything.

Apart from the will of God, man's action is doomed to frustration, since the ground-rule of all things—of man himself who acts, of that upon which he acts, of the universe within which he acts—is the will of God. We cannot thwart God's will. We can disobey His laws, but the disobedience does not frustrate them, it frustrates us. We can glorify God's will in two ways—by obeying it, in which event we glorify ourselves too; or by disobeying it, in which event we degrade ourselves. God's glory is not in question: only ours. That is why the end does not justify the means: morally, of course, it is not *permissible* to use evil means to obtain a good result; more profoundly still, it is not *possible* to achieve a good result by evil means. It may succeed for the moment, as opium may give pleasure for the moment: but in a universe directed by supreme intelligence and supreme goodness, evil means of themselves must produce an evil result. "Nisi Dominus frustra." Without God there is only frustration. So reason shows. So history shows.

But there is not only frustration of man's action when it is not in harmony with God's will. There is a profounder frustration in our very being itself, showing most obviously in our highest faculties, mind and will.

The *mind* is doomed to unsatisfaction unless it sees things in God. It sees everything wrong: there are so many things it cannot see at all, that it cannot get the meaning of the things it can see. It is living in a world of bits and pieces; and that hunger for order, which the mind has because it is a mind, cannot be satisfied by an order of bits and pieces. Nor is that other hunger of the mind, the hunger for purpose, in any better case. The mind, if it be sufficiently active, can propose to itself all sorts of immediate purposes, short-range sectionalized purposes; but it can have no over-all sense of what reality is all about, and is ultimately brought to a stand-still by a sense of futility.

Similarly the *will* is doomed to unsatisfaction insofar as it aims at things separate from God. By the will, we move toward things, love them, desire to make them our own. As a matter of plain experience we can fix our heart's desire anywhere between nothing and the Infinite. But without God, all things are nothing. To love things without loving God means loving shadows and expecting from shadows what only reality can give. One most tragic result is the disappointment of men and women in each other, each expecting what the other cannot give. That is the reason for the horrible disproportion between the ravenous not-to-be-denied hunger and the enjoyment. The shadowiness of things apart from God, which we see at its most piercing in the relation of men and women, is in fact generalized over all life. It is hard to tell whether the poets mourn more for the pleasure that vanished too soon or the pleasure that lasted too long. Let a sunset or a piece of music be as beautiful as we can conceive, we find it hard to go on contemplating the beauty of a sunset even for the short while that the sun takes in setting, and we should be driven quite mad by the music half a dozen times repeated without interval. The mind shudders and the will fails at the thought of seeing any play one half as often as we hear Mass. But there is no weariness for mind or will in the Mass itself.

So far we have been considering the total absence of God from man's conscious relation with reality. Total absence is hardly the phrase for what we may take as the general state of the world we live in. For the most part it does not actually deny that God is. But, if it has not forgotten *that* He is, it has so largely forgotten *what* He is, that it can see no function for Him and therefore in the actual conduct of life tends more and more to omit Him. There is only a step from this to actual atheism, and a sufficient number of people have already taken that step. Let us at least take account of what must follow. Omitting God leaves man on top, but of a diminished universe; and to live in a diminished universe diminishes oneself. To take a rough analogy: if we choose to ignore music and poetry, then we are not humbled by the comparison of our own more mediocre equipment with the greater power of the musician and the poet: our ego is spared that wound. But we are not fed by their music and their poetry.

Cutting off the head leaves the neck on top, but of what a body. Ignoring the head, leaving it unused, is almost as bad: there are so many things the head can do that the neck cannot.

(ii) The danger of devitalization

The frustrations, the hungers, the despairs are facts that we can see by observing men, even if they do not know the reason for them. Let us look a little at that sense of futility which can bring all action close to a stop. We are wholly caused by God. So is everything else. Therefore without God everything is literally inexplicable, not only in the sense that man cannot find the explanation, but also in the sense that there is none. Therefore, again, apart from the knowledge of God, man really is doomed to live in a meaningless universe, and he can but grow weary of the effort to live a meaningful life in a context that has no meaning. Not knowing God, he does not know what he is; equally he does not know what he is here for, where he is supposed to be going, how to go there. He is on a journey, but does not know his destination, has neither a map of the road nor the rules of the road. Lacking this indispensable knowledge, men occupy themselves with other matters, beer or women or rare stamps or science. One man, for instance, is a great authority on butterflies. Upon his subject he will talk endlessly and with an admirable enthusiasm. But interrupt his discourse on butterflies to ask him what he knows about himself and where he is supposed to be going and how: he will answer that those are religious questions, and that he has no time for them, being so deeply engaged with his butterflies. The thing is farcical but terrifying. One can make no sense of a man who gives so much attention to butterflies that he has none left for his own meaning. The little creatures should be flattered. But the man is hardly sane. And he is the perfect type of our world.

One calamitous result of this unawareness that the road of life leads anywhere in particular is that hope dies. "The mass of men", says Thoreau, "lead lives of quiet desperation". I do not know how true that was of his generation but it is fiercely true of ours. Note that it is quiet desperation: not so much active despair as the absence of hope. Men live from one day to the next, hoping that tomorrow may be a little better than today, or if not better then not much worse, occasionally stimulated a little by some extra surge of hope that this or that venture, intellectual or financial or athletic or amatory or what you will, may turn out well. But for most men, even these hopes are impermanent; and just as there is no over-all purpose in life, so there is no over-all hope. They are not living *toward* anything. There is no great thing in the future drawing them on: no goal.

Occasionally a whole society will have some such surge of hope as we have noted in the individual. It may be a new social or political creed that makes life seem purposeful; or new techniques that give men a sense of mastery that is wholly intoxicating. For a long moment the air is electric with new hope. But new creeds become old creeds and the fire dies out of them; man's limitations lie sickeningly in wait for him, and the illusion of mastery is seen for mockery. The golden moment passes and hope with it. But hope and vitality are bound up together; where hope grows pallid, vitality weakens; where hope dies, vitality dies. Nor do men have to be aware of their own lack of hope to be devitalized by it. Many have died of malnutrition who never heard of vitamin B. Men are dying from lack of hope who do not even know that they are hopeless. The hold upon life is pretty precarious when men are living only for lack of any specific reason for dying.

This devitalization is contributed to by something else, resultant, like hopelessness, from ignorance of life's meaning. The hopelessness results from not knowing the goal of life's road; this second weakness results from not knowing the rules of the road. Where God is not sufficiently acknowledged, men find themselves without any standards by which to decide the rightness or wrongness of conduct. What of conscience? That there is an inner voice telling us that we should or should not do thus or thus, is a pretty universal experience; but the experience may be misinterpreted. Conscience is not the voice of God but of our own intellect. Yet God is not for nothing in it. Our intellect is judging by a standard, and primarily the standard is the law of God written in our nature. God did not first make us and then impose laws: He made us according to laws, so that the laws find their expression in the way we are made; and actions contrary to them tend to provoke a revolt in our nature, and the intellect expresses the revolt in the judgments we call conscience. The trouble is that we are no longer as God made us: the generations have introduced distortions, so that no one of us has in his nature a clear clean copy of God's law. The intellect, if it judges only by the smudged copy we have within us, can judge wrong. For certainty, we need also the objective statement that God has given us of His law for us—the ten commandments, the teaching of the Church. Conscience must always guide us, but, if the intellect has not this surer knowledge of God's law, conscience may guide us wrong. But either way—known in its totality or only in part—God's law is the foundation of the intellect's moral judgments.

Whether this point is grasped or not, a moral code must be founded on something. A society can accept a moral code without any conscious awareness of its foundation, provided the code is of long standing and not questioned. But in a generation like ours where everything is questioned, the foundation must be clearly seen; and apart from God the foundation cannot be clearly seen. The practical result for the average man of our generation is that when he is faced with what his grandparents would have called a temptation, he has nothing to judge it by. His first reaction is "Why shouldn't I?" Conscience may put up a brief resistance; but conscience, as we have seen, is the judgment of our intellect, and it is precisely our intellect that is confused; and in any event our modern man will have heard half a dozen theories to explain conscience away. All this is too weak a barrier against any really strong rush of temptation. From the initial "Why shouldn't I?" he passes with an uneasiness too slight to affect his decision to "I don't see why I shouldn't." As we have already seen, this last statement is precise almost to the point of pedantry. He does not see why he shouldn't: he does not *see* anything, because he has turned out the lights, or had them turned out for him: he is simply conscious of a lot of urges and appetites in the dark, and there is no mistaking their direction.

There is no mistaking their direction. It is the line of least resistance. It is the following of one's inclination: it is the avoidance of suffering, the avoidance of effort. For our special consideration here, it is the avoidance of effort that matters. Even if the moral law had no foundation at all, it still remains true that the will whose only rule is to avoid effort must grow flabby and unmuscular.

This simple principle—"I don't see why I shouldn't"—so sane, so reasonable, begins by justifying divorce and promiscuity; it has already gone on to justify every kind of sexual perversion. Yet in the absence of a moral law explicitly forbidding them, why should the will fight against the things which promise pleasure? The few might be willing to impose a discipline upon their own desires, not in the interests of morality but in the interests of spiritual fitness, of well-toned spiritual muscles. But not the mass of men. For them, unless there is the clearest and most compelling reason against, there can be only the following of inclination, the avoidance of effort, flabbiness and unmuscularity of soul. But those qualities in the soul, as in the body, lead to a general sense of unfitness, in plain words reduced vitality. Men thus devitalized by their own softness, by the lack of a goal for their hope, by a sense of futility, can still respond to a major stimulation like war; but under the quieter stimulations of peace, they are in danger of complete collapse.

(iii) An unhappy generation

Naturally a generation living a devitalized life, half wasted in looking for happiness where it is not and avoiding suffering that cannot be avoided, is not happy. It may be only a minority that is definitely unhappy; but the mass of men and women are quite definitely not happy. Unhappiness is always unused or ill-used spiritual energy; and man has within himself so many energies made for God that, lacking God, these energies cannot be satisfied and can only turn in upon the man and rend him. There are moments when one feels that if one wanted to fill out the definition of man into a description, one might say first that man is a rational animal who can despair.

Yet there is a worse state than despair. The moral theologians tell us that there are two sins against hope, despair and presumption; we might as truly say that there are two alternatives to despair, hope and apathy. By hope we rise above it; by apathy we fall below it. Despair is one particular form of unhappiness resulting from spiritual energy unused; but where there is no spiritual energy, there is no unhappiness. There is nothing. There are people whose minds and wills have so few hungers and so unacute that they are not actively unhappy. They would probably regard themselves as happy if asked, because their spiritual energies are so reduced that they are not conscious of, still less tormented by, their unsatisfaction. But no one would mistake that for happiness who knows what happiness is. Happiness is not to be defined as the absence of unhappiness. It is a splendor resultant from spiritual energies functioning at their maximum. The man has sunk low who has neither God *nor* despair. Therefore one service we can render men is to make them see the face of their own hopelessness. A man who does not even know that he is hungry will not make the effort for food.

An unhappy generation has of necessity to distract itself from its own emptiness. Since the beginning of the world, man has sought distraction in sin; our own world has found a further distraction, special to itself, in science. Take science first. It is incredible how long science has succeeded in keeping men's minds off their fundamental unhappiness and its own very limited power to remedy their fundamental unhappiness. One marvel follows another—electric light, phonograph, motor car, telephone, radio, airplane, television. It is a curious list, and very pathetic. The soul of man is crying for hope or purpose or meaning; and the scientist says, "Here is a telephone", or "Look, television!"—exactly as one tries to distract a baby crying for its mother by offering it sugar-sticks and making funny faces at it. The leaping stream of invention has served extraordinarily well to keep man occupied, to keep him from remembering that which is troubling him. He is only troubled. His sense of futility he has never got round to analyzing. But he is half strangled by it.

How long science will continue to distract man from his own misery one does not know. It may pass. But it is a reasonable bet that sin will not pass, especially that sort which makes for the quieting of the mind's appetites by the indulgence of the body. We are concerned here not with sinning through passion but with sinning through sheer futility. That is the gaping wound everywhere. Men are either tormented by it, or without torment have their vitality quietly sapped by it. That is why some people seek to overturn the order of the world by revolution, and these tend to be the most energetic; it is the livest nerve that needs the anesthetic most. But the majority are not as energetic as all that. Yet they too must have their outlet, and there is something about the indulgence of the body, especially sexual indulgence, which makes it the almost inevitable resource of futility. The act itself is so easy, so effortless. And it gives a kind of reassurance to the battered and discouraged ego. For many a person it seems to mark the only time when he is acting as himself, doing what he chooses, expressing his personality, being someone, being at once himself and lifted above himself. It is only a seeming, of course. In fact, it means a further dispersal of man's powers, leaving him less and less master of himself. It rewards him little, but gets a terrible grip on blood and bone.

How all this affects social life is obvious enough. Men and women are rational animals who need one another and do not possess themselves. We are fallible in judgment and muddied in will, not clear sighted, not disinterested. Our judgments differ, and passions madden differences. Yet social life has to be carried on. It is bad enough for the individual not to know what man is and where man is supposed to be going and how he is to get there; but it is more chaotic still for society. The individual can choose for himself a goal which, even if the wrong one, does satisfy something in him and unifies his effort; society is a mass of individuals, pursuing a variety of goals. Only if men are rightly related to God can men be rightly related to one another. Only to the extent that this fundamental unity exists among men can secondary unities—marriage for instance, social order, international society—be healthy. But there can be no coercion here. Men must freely accept. While men refuse the fundamental unity of the right relation to each other in God, we still have to strive for such success as we can get in the secondary unities. We have, bleak but inescapable, the job of working for a second best. But the real job of the moment is to re-Christianize the world—beginning with ourselves, of course, but not postponing the rest of the world till our own Christianization is completed.

We must work for the good of the secondary social reality; we must work for the primary reality. Either way it is a race against time. There is devitalization and fatigue in the very air of our world, and spreading fast. Death is staring us in the face. There is no guarantee of immortality to any human order. Civilizations have died before, and time has eaten them. Our own civilization might die. No one looking honestly at it can fail to see the danger signs, the possibility that men may grow weary, beyond the safety point, of the efforts and resistances life demands. Aside from the obvious and nameable dangers that threaten, there is the greatest danger of all, the danger of nothing in particular, of mere drift, seeing nothing, shaping nothing, living for nothing.

29. Sufficiency in the Church

Without God, man is insufficient for his own life, because life cannot be lived intelligently or vitally without a knowledge of its meaning and purpose, the stimulation of hope, the clear grasp of the laws which will bring life to its goal. None of these can man provide of himself if he omits God.

(i) Meaning, hope, law unattainable without God

Men cannot produce a secular meaning and purpose: they cannot *discover* one as something already there and only awaiting discovery, because it is hard for men to persuade themselves or anyone else that a story that has no author can have a plot; nor can they arbitrarily *invent* a meaning and purpose and impose them upon life, because too much has happened already to condition mankind, including the would-be author of the new design, and because no one ever knows what is going to happen next. A secular hope is equally impossible. If the individual man has no future, but must ultimately merge again into that general mass of reality from which for no known reason he has temporarily emerged, it is idle to talk of offering him hope; one may invent the brightest conceivable future for the race of man, but for each individual in it there is only transience and extinction of personality.

On the whole, men have not been much concerned to provide a secular meaning for life and a secular hope, not appreciating their urgency. But willy-nilly they have been forced to provide some sort of ethics, since without general agreement upon what conduct is right or wrong, society would fall to pieces at once. But even here the effort has not been very energetic. In our own world, we still tend to live by what remains of the Christian ethic, though there is no longer any clear grasp of its foundation; and concessions to human weakness have left it pretty tattered. Of actual efforts to frame a strictly secular ethic, there is little to be said. In the nature of the case they must fail because the man who would frame a secular ethic cannot prove to himself that there is no God and no next life. He may feel sure of both negations, but if he knows what knowing means, he cannot think that he knows either.

Observe that the most convinced atheist not only does not succeed in proving that there is no God, but does not even try to prove it. He does one or all of three things: one, he tries to find a theory which would account for the universe without bringing God into it—in other words, he tries to show how the universe *might* exist without God; two, he attacks the various arguments that have led men to believe in the existence of God and tries to show that these arguments are not conclusive; three, he stresses elements in the universe (suffering, for example) which ought not to be there if God exists—which, to put it brutally, is equivalent to saying that if he had been God he would have acted differently. He may state his arguments well or ill under these heads. But let him state them as well as can be conceived, they still do not disprove the existence of God. We might analyze his arguments against a future life in roughly the same way, and with the same result.

But God and the next life are vast things to be unsure about. If either exists, it must wreck any system of human conduct that ignores it. Take the next life, the effect of ignoring which might be less obvious. If one is to invent a secular ethic, a system of laws of conduct for men and women, it must be aimed at something. Almost certainly it will be aimed at the production of the maximum happiness for mankind, however differently happiness might be conceived by different lawmakers. But how can people know whether such and such conduct would produce happiness for mankind if they do not know whether the whole span of human life is available for inspection? If there be a next life, then it must be part of the evidence too; and there is no way of bringing it into evidence. Any secular ethic must fail through its inability to discover the effect of our actions upon the next life, and in its inability to prove that there *is* no next life. In any event, the question is academic. So far no one has been able to persuade any large section of men to adopt any system of secular ethics. The secular philosopher's contempt for the moral law is as nothing to the world's ignoring of his secular ethic. The ignoring is total. There is not even the compliment of contempt. Secular ethics are only in books.

(ii) The Church provides meaning, hope, and law

Meaning and hope and law remain as needs, and man cannot supply them for himself. Religion is the only answer. Every religion, to the extent of the truth in it and its power to help men to a living awareness of God, can give some part of the answer. But for the whole answer we must come to the Church that God founded. We have already considered this necessity from the point of view of God's will, and that is decisive. But consider it now from the point of view of man's need. A non-infallible, non-dogmatic answer would leave man's needs very much where they were. Consider for one instant the nonsense of a non-dogmatic hope—*to the best of our knowledge* there is the possibility of fullness of life with God in heaven: to the best of our knowledge: what could be less stimulating? Let us have the sure and certain hope of a glorious resurrection; *or* let us talk about something else. Anything short of complete certainty is uncertainty. Consider again for as short a moment the morality of a non-dogmatic ethic—*it seems to us* that God does not like remarriage after divorce or sexual experience outside marriage. That is too frail a barrier to set against passion: there is a kind of cruelty in it, throwing in a probability to worry the mind instead of a certain truth to sustain it.

Observe how, in the Church, man's need for happiness is met at every point. Where there is spiritual energy unused, man cannot be happy, as we have seen. There is so much energy in man that was meant to be used upon God and cannot be adequately used upon any lesser object, so that if it is not used upon God it must turn in upon man and torment him. That is what St. Augustine meant by saying that our hearts are restless until they rest in God. We have a need for contact with God at every point of our being, more still in the higher part of our being, the soul, and above all in the soul's highest faculties of intellect and will. In the Church, the intellect may know God to the limit of every man's capacity to know, and the will may love God with a love as high as the love of the saints, and the whole being of man may be in contact with God, with the reality of God and no half-reality, to the limit of every man's capacity for union. Yet in that total contact, men do not lose themselves but find themselves. There is no merging and absorption of human personality in the Absolute, but a total union between man and God in which man remains himself as truly as God remains Himself.

As against the devitalization of life, there is the life of grace; as against the diseases of human society, there is in the Mystical Body a relation of every man with every other man, which, if even half comprehended, could remake the natural relationship upon which all the secondary unities of men depend for their health. Catholicism meets the complexity of man; in its simplicity it is as complex as man. In the Church, every need of man's nature is met; and not simply every need of *man's* nature, but of this person's nature and that person's nature. Neither the Church nor God will let man lose his personality. The Church is the paradise of unstandardized men. Thus this Church, more rigid than any in dogma and law, is, as no other Church ever has been, the home of every type of human being, of every nation and of every sort of person within every nation. Because only in the Church is man fully himself.

(iii) Why men do not see it

Why do not all men see it? Because they have lost the very notion of the gifts, the gifts of life and truth, given by Christ, given through the Church. Having lost the notion of the gifts which are the Church's reason for existence, they naturally do not see the Church's reason for existence. Therefore they test the Church by such notions as they *have* got. Generally they test her and dismiss her by two lines of inquiry which they would see as irrelevant if they had any awareness of the things which constitute her purpose.

The commonest criticism is of the character of Catholics — of popes, bishops, priests, and lay people. People observe that this or that pope was immoral, this or that bishop is worldly, this or that priest is a bully or a snob or lazy, this or that layman is a corrupt politician or an unjust employer or a defaulting bookmaker or a scandalmonger. Catholics can be found in all these categories. But even if the proportion of unpleasing Catholics at every level were as great as the Church's severest critic thinks, the criterion would still be the wrong one. We have already discussed this at some length, but it is worth repeating the main point here. And the main point is that it is through this strange assortment of human beings that Christ our Lord gives the gifts of truth and life. No one who knows his own desperate need of those gifts would be kept at a distance by the character of the human means through which Christ has chosen that they shall have them, any more than a man hungry for bread will be kept from it by doubts about the moral excellence of the baker. But if a man does not know about the gifts, he is bound to have strong views about the character of the purveyors, for the Catholic Church is a spectacular body and the vices of Catholics are not likely to be overlooked.

The second criticism is that the Church is failing to take her part in the improvement of the social order, is not producing or working in support of plans for the organization of the nations, or social reforms within the nation. Man, so says the critic, is striving for a better life upon earth, and the Church stands aside from the strife. Upon the detail of this, books could be written and libraries filled with them. One might say with truth that the Church has done more for the betterment of life upon this earth than all other institutions put together. One might say with equal truth that the popes have thought and written most profoundly and constructively upon the earthly life of man. One might say, not unjustifiably, that the civil order is the affair of the citizen: that when things go well the citizen clamors that this is his sphere and the Church must keep out of it: and that only when he has got himself into a complete mess does he suddenly whine that the Church is neglectful. All this is true and massive. Yet there are areas where the Church seems to have acquiesced in, if not actually encouraged, great social evils. Here again there are all sorts of considerations, but we cannot rule out the part that sloth has played in the lives of churchmen—the sloth of the intellect, accepting the customary because it is customary without even seeing how evil it is, the sloth of the will which finds it easier to take things as they are than to raise the devil by trying to put them right.

Yet when the Church in any given place is doing the least for the social betterment of men's lives, it still remains that by comparison with the truth and the life which God *is* giving through her, to treat these other things as though their absence were a reduction to nothing of the Church's function is a kind of frivolity. Certainly there is no sanity in foregoing the vaster thing which the Church is giving because of such lesser things as she is not giving. What the world wants of her and what the Church is actually offering the world are plainly incommensurable—provided one recognizes what the gifts of God are.

Indeed, however just a complaint might be made against the Church in this or that place, the complaints actually made about what the Church is not doing in the social order are almost invariably made with no appreciation whatever of the things that she exists to do. This failure of appreciation varies. At one end is the Catholic who accepts the gifts as a matter of habit, is indeed attached to them and would miss them if they were withdrawn, yet has no profound awareness of them or response to them. At the other end is the non-Catholic who regards the Church's own work as a lot of nonsense, but would be willing to overlook it as an unaccountable but harmless eccentricity if only the Church would concentrate on what seems to him the vital business of mankind. The soul's needs are the Church's business. If you are not interested in souls, then she will seem to have no business at all.

These two things—preoccupation with the defects of Catholics, impatience that the Church holds secondary what others hold primary—stand between men and the recognition that the Church is their true home. Therefore we must try to help men to see what are those gifts of God through the Church which make human defects and earthly reforms of secondary importance. We must show men the gifts. But here comes the third, and in the long run the greatest, difficulty. Even when men do know something of what the gifts are, they are not necessarily attracted but may even shrink from them. More often than not, their first reaction is that they have not the muscles to take hold of them, nor any taste for them or likelihood of happiness from them. Merely to grasp the vision of reality calls for mental muscles they have never used. The moral law, which is the law of reality, threatens the loss of pleasures which, if they leave our deeper hungers unfed, have their own exquisiteness all the same. The world of spirit seems so thin and remote, the world we are used to so solid and close, that in finding reality we feel as if we were losing reality. Our poor hearts cling to the things of this world in a desperate fear that if they lose them they will lose all. We must have something to cling to, for we cannot stand our own solitariness: so we cling to things as empty as ourselves—shadows certainly, but "what lovely things these shadows be." People are not likely to give up shadows so lovely save for the seen loveliness of reality—seen, and seen to be greater. Our Lord's cry "Ah! if thou couldst understand the ways that can bring thee peace" utters the deepest trouble of men upon earth. To know the things that are for our peace involves knowing so much: about ourselves, and about things, and especially about these things, especially about the life of grace and about the landscape of reality that Truth opens to our gaze. Life and landscape each need a chapter.

30. The Life of Grace

By grace we are indwelt by God. At first sight there seems to be a problem here. Since God is present in us, maintaining us in existence, what further indwelling can there be? What is the difference between God's presence in us by nature and His indwelling of us by grace? The primary difference is that, as to the first, we have no choice. We were not consulted before God brought us into existence; we are not consulted at any subsequent time as to our remaining in existence. We cannot escape this existence-giving presence of God. The demons in hell cannot escape it, nor the lost souls. For them is the awful fate of having nothing of God but His presence, awful because it sustains in existence beings who for their own fulfillment need all sorts of other gifts from Him and must suffer in their absence.

In order to *be,* we need do nothing. But in order to *be supernaturally,* we must do something. God's presence, we have seen, is by no invitation of ours: but His indwelling *is* by invitation. There is a sense in which we may say of an earthly visitor, that no one can enter our home unless we invite him. He can enter our house without our invitation, but not our home. God's indwelling means God's making Himself at home in us, and depends upon our invitation. When we are infants, the sponsor extends the invitation to Him on our behalf; when we reach the use of reason, we confirm the invitation. We can withdraw it at any time, and so lose God's indwelling and be left with only His presence.

(i) *Meaning and indwelling: grace and the virtues*

Thus we may see the indwelling of the Blessed Trinity by grace not simply as God's action upon our souls but as the result of the soul's reaction to God's action. God is present, says St. Thomas, much as something known is present in the knower, something loved in the lover. Our invitation to God to make Himself at home in us produces a vast energizing of God in our soul, or, if you will, a vast development of the soul as a result of its willing response to God's energizing.

It is important to grasp that sanctifying grace is a real transformation of the soul. Where Luther taught that the soul in grace is wearing the garment of Christ's merits, the Church teaches that the very substance of the soul is renewed; the soul is affected in its very being so that it can well be called a new creation: it has a new life in it, a life with its own vital "organs" and operations, so that it can now perform actions at the level of its new being, actions which because they are supernatural can merit a supernatural reward. Thus it is that St. Paul speaks of us as "in Christ a new creature" (2 Cor 5:17), "the new man, who according to God is created in justice and holiness of truth".

Yet it remains the same soul, with the same faculties: soul and faculties are not destroyed so that some new thing may take their place, but elevated to a new level of life and the operations that go with it. Grace does not destroy nature, but is built into it, and from within elevates it. The intellect has the new power of faith; the will, the new powers of hope and charity. The point is so important that one must take the risk of laboring it. A rough analogy may help: the wire in an electric light bulb, when connected with the battery, is luminous; so much so that, looking at it, we seemed to see only light, and no wire, and might be tempted to think that the wire was gone and that the light had taken its place. But it is the same wire, only luminous. And if the connection with the source of power be broken, we see that it is the same wire. The soul in grace is luminous, but it does not cease to be the soul.

With what is the soul luminous? With sanctifying grace: with the theological virtues, Faith, Hope, and Charity; with the moral virtues, Prudence, Justice, Temperance, and Fortitude; with the gifts of the Holy Spirit, Knowledge, Understanding, Wisdom, Counsel, Fortitude, Piety, and Fear of the Lord. We shall discuss all this in the course of the chapter.

Meanwhile, let us note the distinction between the theological virtues and the moral virtues (sometimes called the cardinal virtues). To understand the distinction, we must distinguish in our minds between the end of an action and its object. The end of every virtue is God. It is for God that we do it. But the object of a virtue may not be God, but some created thing. If a boy is serving on the altar at Benediction, the end of his action is the glory of God; but the object of his action is the censer. If he concentrates so exclusively upon the end of his action that he neglects the object, he will probably spill the censer. The reason why Faith, Hope, and Charity are called theological virtues is that God, or some attribute of God, is not only their end, but their object too. By Faith we believe God; by Hope we desire to come to God; by Charity we love God. Thus, as St. Thomas says (S.T. I–II, q. 64, a. 4), "God Himself is the measure and rule of a theological virtue: our faith is regulated according to God's truth, charity according to His goodness, hope according to the greatness of His omnipotence and His love for us." The moral virtues, on the other hand, have God for their end, but their object is the created universe. By Prudence, Justice, Temperance, and Fortitude, we are given the power so to handle created things, ourselves, and other things, that we may attain God.

Observe that while there are two ways of receiving the supernatural Life — the easy way of the baptized infant and the harder way of the one who comes to it in adult life — either way one can receive it only as the whole of it, theological virtues, moral virtues, and gifts of the Holy Spirit. This life in us can grow, as we have seen. But just as it is received only as a whole, so it can grow only as a whole.

We may be brought to a clearer understanding of this supernatural Life and its reception, if we consider for a moment those who receive it in adult life. They cannot receive supernatural Life unless God gives it. By their own strength, they could not merit that God should give it, because no natural action could merit a supernatural reward. Prior to the reception of sanctifying grace, they must receive that special help from God which is called *"actual grace"*.

The use of the word "grace" for two things so different may easily confuse us. It may simplify our understanding if we think of sanctifying grace as supernatural life, and actual grace as supernatural impulsion. By actual grace, God assists us, thereby making us capable of an action which without that special assistance would be beyond our powers. Actual grace is a sort of thrust or impetus, in the power of which we can act above our powers. But if we cooperate with this impulsion from God, let ourselves go with it, then we shall receive supernatural Life, either a beginning of it if we lack it, or an increase of it if we already have it. What is to be noted here is that there could be no beginning of supernatural Life without supernatural impulsion. There is no seed of supernatural Life in our nature, no faintest beginning of it; it is wholly a gift.

(ii) Faith

The root of the supernatural Life, when God gives it to us, is Faith. So St. Paul writes: "Once justified, then, on the ground of our faith, let us enjoy peace with God through Our Lord Jesus Christ, as it was through Him that we have obtained access, by faith, to that grace in which we stand" (Rom 5:1-2). The first Vatican Council gives us the definition:

> Faith is a supernatural virtue
> by which, under the inspiration and with the aid of God's
> grace (*gratia Dei inspirante et adjuvante*),
> we hold for true what God has revealed
> not because we have perceived its intrinsic truth by the
> natural light of reason
> but on the authority of God Himself as its revealer, who
> can neither deceive nor be deceived.

The last three sections are so clear that they hardly need comment even for the newcomer to theology. But so much is wrapped up in the first two that some expansion is needed.

Faith is defined by St. Thomas (S.T. II–II, q. 4, a. 2) as an act of the intellect assenting to a divine truth owing to the movement of the will, the will in its turn being moved by the grace of God: the act of the intellect is the intellect's assent to whatever God has said because He has said it. Taking this statement to pieces, we see what happens. God gives actual grace, that is, a supernatural impulsion, to the will; the will thus moved moves the intellect to make its act of assent. Observe that this says nothing of evidence, of argument, of what we sometimes call "grounds of belief"; nor of prayer, humility, and such like. The whole process is attributed to God. This does not leave prayer and intellectual inquiry no function at all; but their function is solely preparatory: in the production of the virtue of faith itself they have no direct role.

God, we say, moves the will, which moves the intellect. But God does not do violence to nature. He does not force either will or intellect to act against the nature He has given them. The function of prayer and humility is so to prepare the will that when the impulsion comes from God it is ready to go with that impulsion, with no violence done to its own nature as a will. The function of evidence and argument is so to prepare the intellect that when it feels the impulsion of the God-moved will, it too will be prepared to co-operate with that impulsion, with no violence to its own nature as an intellect. It would be outside God's normal mode of working upon man to move his intellect to an assent for which nothing had prepared it, against which much of its own experience as an intellect might well have predisposed it.

Thus, provided that intellectual inquiry by way of argument upon the evidence has prepared the intellect to go along with the impulsion from God, it has served its purpose. The virtue of faith in no way depends upon it, but solely upon God's moving the soul to it and sustaining the soul in it. Reason can produce a flawless chain of arguments, showing that there is a God, that God became man and revealed certain truths; and a man might, one imagines (though I have never met such a man), by the sole power of reason, unmoved by God's grace, follow the arguments and assent to the truths. But this assent would not be the supernatural virtue of faith, for it would be produced in him and sustained in him by arguments, whereas the assent of faith is produced in us and sustained in us by God. Again though the arguments for revelation are flawless in themselves, they are not necessarily so as seen by every believer. One may see them vaguely, or superficially; one may be quite unable to sustain them against an objector. But just as the most perfect grasp of the arguments is no substitute for the grace of faith, so defect in them as they have worked upon a given man does not weaken or invalidate his faith, because faith is in fact not produced by arguments, or founded on them, or kept in being by them. They do not produce faith in our souls, but only make us willing to let God produce it. They make us willing to open the shutter to let the light pour in. The opening of the shutter is necessary if there is to be light in the room, but it does not produce the light. However slight the reason for which one has opened the shutter, there is the light.

It is pleasant, given our human stumblingness, to know that we can stumble toward the light. Given the rarity of powerful intellects, it is fortunate that sure faith can be had by imperfect intellects. The light is the fact. The believer cannot always prove, that is, state a flawless logical case for his faith, very much as a man in a lighted room might have no clear notion how electricity works. But he is in no doubt about the light. He is living in it. That is why faith carries with it a kind of certainty which no chain of argument can produce. By logic we see that a thing must be so: by faith we see it so—at any rate, when, as we shall see, faith is perfected by the gift of Understanding. I do not mean that we see it as if we were gazing at the object itself, for faith "is that which gives substance to our hopes, which convinces us of things we cannot see". But it is more than seeing the conclusion of an argument. It is a living awareness that reality is so. That is why one who has faith cannot convey what it is to one who has not got it. You cannot tell a blind man what seeing is. Indeed you cannot prove to him that color exists at all. If one puts this analogy to an unbeliever, it will very naturally irritate him to madness. But it is exact.

Although faith is in the intellect, it will be noted that the intellect is moved to it by the will; and this might at first sight seem puzzling, savoring somewhat of wishful thinking. The intellect, one feels, is the faculty whose job is to know, and any interference by the will seems like a usurpation. There is some color of truth in this in relation to natural knowing, where the assent of the intellect is based upon the evidence presented to it. But this color of truth is not the whole truth as to the relation of will and intellect even in the natural activity of knowing, and in any event the assent of faith, with which we are here concerned, does not depend upon the evidence presented to the intellect, but upon the grace of God. Once we grasp this, we can see what part God's prior action upon the will plays.

God does not do violence to nature, and a direct impulsion

producing the utter certitude of faith in the intellect might do very great violence to nature indeed. The will is deeply concerned in the intellect's decision, for an obvious reason, and for a reason less obvious. The obvious reason is that the will is so profoundly affected by all the things that may follow upon the assent of faith—the interference with pride, for instance, and the necessity of union with the will of God—that left to itself it would be quite capable of preventing the intellect from giving the assent. The less obvious reason is that all men find certitude, complete and utter certitude, difficult; and some men find it impossibly difficult. There is something about the absoluteness of certitude, the inescapable yes or no of it, from which all in some measure and some in vast measure shrink. It is a shrinking from finalities, comparable to that of a man who cannot decide to get married: he would like to marry, and he would like to marry that particular person, but he cannot be sure and hesitates: and someone else marries her, and the marriage works out well or ill, but anyhow the human race is carried on, while the man who cannot be sure lives in the fine balance of conflicting possibilities and dies without issue. This fear of certitude is a disease of the will. The intellect is not really in doubt. It is the will that persuades it that it is.

That may be one reason why God gives the impulsion of grace to the will. But even apart from this, the truths to which we assent by faith are remote from our daily habits, not presented directly to the intellect with their own evidence but only with the evidence that God has revealed them, and not stated as they are in their own reality but only so far as human language can utter them—so that even with such illumination as God gives to the intellect, it still needs the support of the God-moved will. If we find this first action of the will in the assent of faith mysterious, observe that it has one superb consequence: the root of the supernatural Life is faith, and the first movement of faith is in the will, the faculty by which we love: so that as love is the fruit, it is also the root of Life.

We have now considered all the elements of the definition save one. When we gain the virtue of faith and make the act of faith, what is it that we believe? We believe God; that is to say, we believe that what God has said is true because He has said it. Faith puts our mind in the attitude of unquestioning acceptance of what God has said. But it does not mean that we know all that God has said; it does not exclude the possibility of ignorance or actual error as to what God has said. We believe all that God has said, and thus implicitly possess it. But that we may actually know it, we must use our intellect to find it, that is, to find the teacher who can tell us with certainty what things God has said. When we have found that teacher and learned what he has to teach us, then we possess certain truths, but the possession of these truths is not precisely the same thing as the virtue of faith. Here we must distinguish three elements: one, the preliminary preparation of will and intellect to cooperate with God's grace; two, the virtue of faith; three, the truths we possess by faith.

Observe that defects in the first or third of these elements do not mean defects in our faith. We may have fallen into erroneous arguments on the way to it; we may have misunderstood some of the teachings of God and not even heard of others. Neither sort of defect is a defect in our faith, the virtue by which the intellect adheres to God as the source of truth. If the preliminary inquiry as to where the truths God has revealed are to be found is *totally* successful, then we discover that the Church is their repository and their custodian and their teacher. But even one who has not come so far may still have found truths revealed by God, and by God's grace accepted them, and so have the virtue of faith. The teaching of the Church is the rule of faith: one who has not found it will not have access to *all* the truths God has revealed, so that his faith will not be doing all for him that faith can do. But it is still the supernatural virtue of faith, the root of the supernatural life.

(iii) Hope and charity

With faith there enters the soul the whole of our supernatural equipment, the theological virtues, the moral virtues, the gifts of the Holy Spirit. We are supernaturally alive. The soul is made new in its essence and its operations. It *is,* has its be-ing, *does* its be-ing, at a higher level; and it not only has its be-ing at a higher level, it has the power to act at a higher level. Grace and the virtues are not something external of which the soul is given the use, as an eye might be enabled to see by a microscope things otherwise too small for it. Grace and the virtues are in the soul itself, very much as seeing is in the very eye itself. The theologians call them "habits", and the word is worth dwelling on. It is not a mere piece of terminology, but will later help us to solve some of the practical problems affecting the running of our own lives. Here let us grasp what they mean by it. Habit is a modification of a nature whereby it is made more apt to act in one way or another. Thus the habit of piano playing is a real modification—in this instance a development—of mind and body whereby we can produce music from a piano. It is something real and objective. One either has it or lacks it. The whole point of it is that it enables us to do something which without it we could not do, or not do so well.

The virtues we are discussing have in themselves all three elements of habit: they are a modification of our nature, something actually in our nature, not merely an external aid; they are real and objective, not a matter of feeling thus and thus;

and they enable us to do specific things which without them we should not be able to do at all—to believe supernaturally, hope supernaturally, love supernaturally and so on. They differ from natural habits in the way we acquire them. The supernatural habits we receive in one act from God. A natural habit is acquired by the continual repetition of certain acts: we do not acquire the habit of playing the piano in one lesson, nor the habit of craving alcohol by one glass. But though the mode of acquisition is different, the supernatural virtues are habits as truly as those we acquire for ourselves.

Let us look at them now in some little detail. Faith we have already discussed. It is simply the acceptance of God as our teacher. Hope cannot be stated so simply. It is a complex of three things: we desire God, that is, our final union with God; we see this as difficult; we see it as possible. With all three in full operation, we hope. We long for union with God in Heaven, and we rely upon His promise that we shall attain it. We know that our own powers are totally insufficient, so that without His help it is impossible. In that sense our salvation is wholly a work of God. But we know also that God will not save us without our cooperation. We must obey His laws and use the means He has set for us. To err upon either of these would be a sin of presumption: for it is presumptuous to think that God will save us if we make no effort at all; more presumptuous still to think that we can save ourselves by our own unaided effort.

At the opposite end from presumption is despair, an absence of the virtue of hope, which again may be one of two failures: we may cease to hope by no longer particularly wanting to achieve union with God and therefore setting our aim upon created things, or by feeling that we ourselves have reached so low a point that even the grace of God can no longer save us. The first is a cheaper thing. By comparison there is almost nobility in the second—at least we may feel that a certain fineness of spirit is necessary before a man could be so aware, so over-aware as it happens, of his own baseness. But it is a lack of trust in God all the same, and an exaggeration of the part that the self is meant to play in salvation. St. Paul has told us of the magnificence of hope: "Who will separate us from the love of Christ? Will affliction, or distress, or persecution, or hunger, or nakedness, or peril, or the sword? For thy sake, says the Scripture, we face death at every moment, reckoned no better than sheep marked down for slaughter. Yet in all this we are conquerors, through him who has granted us his love. Of this I am fully persuaded; neither death nor life, no angels or principalities or powers, neither what is present nor what is to come, no force whatever, neither the height above us nor the depth beneath us, nor any other creature, will be able to separate us from the love of God, which comes to us in Christ Jesus Our Lord" (Rom 8:35-39).

Charity, like faith, is simple. By charity we love. We love God, and we love our neighbor because God loves him. Charity has suffered both from those who do not know that it means love and from many of those who do. For the modern world, charity has become associated with help to the poor, given without heart and poisoned by condescension. It is the coldest word in the language. But charity *means* love. And the trouble is that this meaning has led to almost as great a debasement of the notion.

It is a great thing to know that charity means love, provided one knows what *love* means. Unfortunately, if the word *charity* has become a cold word in the modern mouth, the word *love* has become a sentimental word, with all sorts of emotional overtones. We must carefully separate love from its emotional accompaniment. Love will emerge the stronger for the distinction. Love is the highest and strongest act of the will. In relation to God, it means that the will has deliberately chosen God as the supreme value, by which all others must be measured. In relation to our neighbor, it means willing his good; and how much good must we will to him? As much as we will to ourselves. In the natural order, love will inevitably have some accompaniment in the emotions. There is no space here to go into the psychology of the emotions, but we may say generally that the emotions belong neither wholly to the soul, nor wholly to the body; they are a certain excitement in our organism made possible because our soul is united to our body, in such a way that the states of the soul have bodily effects. An angel, having no body, has no emotions. Thus love is not an emotion but can produce an emotion; that is to say, it can set up certain vibrations in the bodily organism, which in turn have their effect upon the state of the soul.

But we must grasp that our supernatural life has no direct access to the emotions. Insofar as our supernatural love of God brings our natural power of loving into play, that in turn will tend to produce a feeling of love. But neither the feeling of love, nor the operation of our natural power of loving, is the thing that matters essentially, but that supernatural gift by which, feeling or no feeling, we steadily choose God as our supreme good. The emotional accompaniment will depend very much upon the temperament of the individual. Its absence is no matter for concern. Certainly we should not harry our souls in the effort to make them "feel" that they love God. For most of us the prayer of the psalmist will suffice on the side of feeling: "Concupivit anima mea desiderare te"—My soul has longed to yearn for You.

How little any sort of external action matters in comparison with charity, St. Paul has told us (1 Cor 8:1–3): "I may speak with every tongue that men and angels use; yet, if I lack charity, I am no better than echoing bronze, or the clash of cymbals. I may have powers of prophecy, no secret hidden from me, no knowledge too deep for me; I may have utter faith, so that I can move mountains; yet if I lack charity, I count for nothing. I may give away all that I have, to feed the poor; I may give myself up to be burnt at the stake; if I lack charity, it goes for nothing."

So the thirteenth chapter opens, and the opening prepares us for the closing verse: "Meanwhile faith, hope and charity persist, all three; but the greatest of them all is charity." Charity is the lifegiving virtue, and makes the other virtues to be alive. It is possible, as we shall see, to lose charity by mortal sin, yet retain faith and hope. But in the absence of charity, they are dead. The reason for this lifegiving function of charity may be stated in two ways, which in the end are one way. Charity is the union of man's will with God's will; lose charity, and the union is broken, the invitation to God to dwell in us withdrawn; so that the life which flows from His indwelling ceases in us. Again, charity is love; and throughout all that is, the uncreated being of God and the universe at all levels, love and life go together. Love is life-giving. The denial of love is the destruction of life.

(iv) The Moral Virtues

The theological virtues are concerned directly with God. The moral virtues deal with the conduct by which we are to come to God. A brief reflection upon the ways in which we may deviate from the road that leads to our goal will show the relation of the moral virtues to man's necessity. We may deviate either by a failure of the intellect to grasp the bearing of our actions, or by a failure of the will to act, either in the control of ourselves or in relation to other men, according to the true light that the intellect has.

That our *intellect* may rightly see what things help toward our eternal salvation and what things hinder, there is the virtue of Prudence. Its direct work is upon the intellect, but thereby it provides a rule according to which the activities of the will may be regulated too. The will operates properly when it keeps to the right path, which the intellect, operating properly, sees. Like Charity, Prudence has suffered from a degradation of its name in common speech. Prudence is not a timid virtue. It is not that virtue by which we avoid all occasion for the use of the virtue of Fortitude. Prudence is a bold virtue. It sees the bearing of conduct, not upon our immediate convenience, but upon our ultimate salvation. It is by the virtue of Prudence that the martyr clearly sees his way to martyrdom. There are occasions when the avoidance of martyrdom would be highly imprudent. The word *prudence* itself is simply another form of the word *providence,* and providence is from the Latin word "to see": it is the virtue that sees in advance and provides.

The other three virtues furnish the *will* with what it requires to act prudently—in the meaning of Prudence just given. Justice has to do with our relations with others. It means that the will is set toward their having whatever is due to them. Observe, again, that Justice is not simply a willingness to restrict our own desires to what is strictly our due, but a firm will that all men should have their due. Our Lord urges that we hunger and thirst after justice, and this hunger and thirst are very different from that sort of diffused niceness which, provided that we have what is due to us, finds a sort of agreeableness in the thought that others should be as fortunate.

Temperance and Fortitude are for the perfecting of our conduct in relation to ourselves. Between them they cover the two principal deviations that come from within the will. By Temperance we control our natural impulse toward the things we should shun; by Fortitude we control our natural impulse to avoid the things we should face. Temperance strengthens us against certain pleasures that solicit us; Fortitude, against certain dangers and difficulties that frighten us. Temperance moderates; Fortitude stimulates.

(v) The Gifts of the Holy Spirit

It might seem that man's supernatural equipment as described so far is so complete that no more would be required. With grace perfecting his soul in its very being, the theological virtues relating his faculties at this new level to God, the moral virtues regulating his activity in relation to created things, it would hardly seem that more could be required. There are theologians who hold that more is not required. But the majority, among them St. Thomas, teach that, though with this equipment and no more a man could obtain beatitude, it would be but haltingly. By the virtue of faith, for instance, he believes without doubt whatever God has revealed; but the virtue of faith does not of itself tell him all that God has revealed, nor give him any profound understanding of those truths that he does know about. It gives him the utter certainty that what God has revealed is true, but does not tell him what it is nor what it means. For each of these, short of some new supernatural aid from God, he would have to use his own powers of inquiry and judgment as best he might—that is, with an alarming admixture of ignorance and error. He might or might not find the Church, through which God gives the fullness of His revelation; having found the Church, he might or might not understand the truths she gave him. In any event, there arise all sorts of special situations to which no teaching of the Church seems specifically to apply, and he might or might not succeed in making the right application of some more general principle.

What has been said of Faith, applies in principle to Prudence also. By it our intellects are so formed that they will judge concrete situations in the light of God's revelation as to the reality of things, but only insofar as they know God's revelation; that is, insofar as they have been able by the best use of their intellect to discover it.

It seems clear that even with sanctifying grace and the theological and moral virtues, the intellect would not be equipped for action with speed or certainty. Insofar as the will depends upon the intellect for light, the operation of the will would be affected by this dimness in the intellect; and in any event the will finds such appalling difficulty that even if strictly speaking it needs no further aid from God than the virtues which perfect it, one could hardly be other than glad if in fact God gave such further aid. It is for this double function of more and more certain light for the intellect, and special aid for the will when special difficulties call for it, that God gives us, along with the virtues, the Gifts of the Holy Spirit. To illumine our mind and to strengthen our will, God is continually giving us actual graces, impulses of the divine energy which, if the soul responds to them, will move intellect and will in the way they should go. The Gifts of the Holy Spirit are habits residing in the soul in a state of grace, by which the soul is capable of responding readily and fruitfully to these actual graces when God gives them.

To use the illustration which is by now traditional, the Gifts are like sails catching the wind of the Spirit. The wind will move a boat, even when the boat has no sails; but incomparably less swiftly and surely. The soul, even without the Gifts, could receive some motion from actual grace, but incomparably less swift and certain motion. The action of the Spirit, says Our

Lord (Jn 3:8), is like a wind that breathes where it will, and we can hear the sound of it but know nothing of the way it came or the way it goes: but by the Gifts of the Spirit we can go with it.

Isaiah lists the Gifts for us: "The Spirit of the Lord shall rest upon him: the spirit of wisdom, and of understanding, the spirit of counsel and of fortitude, the spirit of knowledge and of godliness (piety). And he shall be filled with the spirit of the fear of the Lord. He shall not judge according to the sight of the eyes, nor approve according to the hearing of the ears" (Is 11:2–3). Thus the Vulgate, following the Septuagint, gives us seven gifts. The Hebrew has only six, for one Hebrew word stands for both Piety and Fear of the Lord.

Four of these gifts—Understanding, Wisdom, Knowledge, Counsel—are for the perfection of the *intellect*. By Understanding the intellect is equipped to respond to the power of God bringing a comprehension of the truths of revelation and a power to explore them more deeply. Roughly we may think of the gift of Understanding as giving new eyes to the virtue of faith. Wisdom and Knowledge make the soul responsive to the true, the spiritual, value of things, Wisdom in relation to God Himself, Knowledge in relation to created things. Understanding is of special value in enabling us to see the difficulties of Faith and not be troubled by them. Counsel makes the mind responsive to God's guidance in relation to the individual here-and-now problems that face us. It has the same sort of relation to the moral virtue of Prudence that Understanding has to the theological virtue of Faith.

The three Gifts by which the *will* responds to the wind of the Spirit of God are Fortitude, Piety, and Fear of the Lord. Fortitude corresponds to the moral virtue of Fortitude; the Fear of the Lord to the moral virtue of Temperance, especially in controlling the turbulence of the flesh—"Pierce thou my flesh with thy spear, for I am afraid of thy judgment." Piety is primarily the love of the instructed heart for God. Piety is in itself the love between two who are already bound by the bond of authority. The gift of Piety leads us to a love of God precisely because of the reverence we owe Him: and gives a keener sensitiveness than Justice alone implies in dealing with our fellow men, because God loves them too.

The limits of this book will not allow of a fuller treatment of the Gifts, nor of what theologians call the Fruits and the Beatitudes. They are immensely worth following up. But enough is here to show what the Life is which Christ came that we might have, and have more abundantly.

31. The Landscape of Reality

At the start, the object of this book was stated. It was the health of the intellect, which is sanity. Sanity involves seeing what is; in relation to ourself it means seeing what we are, where we are, what life is about. Our object was to come mentally to citizenship of the real world, that we might be at home in it, familiar with it—knowing its realities and its laws, knowing how to conduct ourselves in it. And all this not merely as something known, so that if questioned about it we could answer correctly, but as something seen, as a kind of landscape in which the mind habitually lives: not something that we have to recall when some special occasion arises, but something that we see as a matter of course when we see anything at all.

(i) What we see

From all that has gone before, it is evident that the fullest possession of this whole vision of reality—without which no individual section of reality is intelligible—is made possible only when we receive the supernatural virtue of Faith and the gift of Understanding. We are now in position to make some rather summary survey of the reality that now lies before the mind's gaze.

Notice in the first place how vast an enlargement of the universe it is. Man has built walls around and about him, through which no light of infinity can break, rather like an eccentric millionaire who, having inherited a mansion, chooses to live in the coal cellar. It is a kind of insanity within an insanity to have built the walls of our own prison. Even without Faith, the powers of the mind were sufficient to blow those self-invented walls away and see something of infinity and eternity and its own kinship with both. But the awareness the mind could get for itself is only a pallid shadow of what the revelation of God lays wide open to Faith. There is an increase beyond measure in the range of things we are aware of and in the vividness of our awareness.

We are aware of God, Infinite and Eternal, and we are in vitalizing contact with Him, loved by Him, utterly certain, in Dame Julian of Norwich's phrase, that "love is His meaning". If our only deficiency were to be less than He, this awareness would still be a marvelous thing. But in the actual fact of us, with an abyss of nothingness at the core of our being, always tormenting us and drawing us toward it, it is vital that we should grasp and use every existent fact of kinship, and possibility of contact, with the Infinite.

We are aware of the spiritual world, not simply of the reality that is under our noses but of all that is. We live in a universe where angels good and evil and souls of living and dead are greater realities than the bodies which throng upon our awareness so powerfully by way of senses and imagination. We are saved from the intellectual destitution that comes of being aware of a teeming material world beneath us, and above us only emptiness.

We are aware of the human race, and our membership of it, of its movement through time and of our place in the movement. As part of that awareness, we are aware of our membership of Christ and so of one another.

We are aware of ourselves and of the war within ourselves. Above all, we know what by no supreme effort of the mind we could have ever so dimly suspected—the grandeur of our own nature, which God could take and make His own. We see our life as a road with a beginning and a goal, for we know the realities from which, through which, and to which it proceeds. In the only true sense of an abused phrase, we know the facts of life.

We know not only that spirit is real and valuable, but that matter is real and valuable, and we know how real and how valuable: no one who knows the dignity of matter will underrate the dignity of labor.

We know totality, so that we do not mistake parts for wholes, giving them a sufficiency which they have not and expecting from them a satisfaction which only the whole can give.

(ii) Complexity and simplicity

The plain blunt man finds all this rather complicated. He has a plain blunt feeling that religion should be simple: why? Because it would be simpler that way. In plain truth he does not want to have to use his mind on religion, but only his emotions—his mind being needed for more pressing matters: and indeed even emotion is too strong a word for what has become only an uncertain sentiment turning to vapor.

This attitude is at once so curious and so widespread that it is worth a second look. Observe that it is only in regard to religion that men demand this sort of barbaric simplification. In science, for instance, they take mystery and complexity for granted. Imagine how the plain blunt man would snort if it was the Church and not science which taught that the sun does not go round the earth. Incomprehensible nonsense, he would call it: a lot of mystification: why, hang it, he has *seen* the sun moving across the sky. But since science teaches it, he not only does not snort, he actually purrs. He is pleased with the mysteriousness of the universe, feeling, reasonably enough, that it confers a certain mysteriousness upon him. "Wonderful fellow, Einstein," he chuckles delightedly; "only six men in the world understand him."

However superficially silly the expression of this attitude may be, or however profoundly silly the man may be who expresses it, yet there is great truth in it. Reality *is* mysterious and highly complex; science is right to see it so and to say it so, and the layman is right to find a certain joy in it and a sense that he is the gainer by it. But if science is rightly complex in its explanation of part of reality, why must religion be simple in its explanation of the whole of reality? Religion is not something distinct from reality and unrelated to it. It is (among other things) a light by which we see reality. It is hard that the explanation of the lowest section should be praised for complexity, and indeed incomprehensibility, while for the whole some rule-of-thumb explanation must be found which calls for no effort of mind at all.

What we see of science, applies to the natural life of man as a whole: it would be horribly impoverished by the kind of simplification proposed for religion. But there is another point. Like most vital functions, religion is complex to analyze, but simple in operation. Complexity in structure actually simplifies things for us. Breathing, for instance, is a simple and satisfying operation resulting from a highly complicated mechanism. Eliminate some of the elements of the mechanism by which we breathe, and breathing would cease to be simple, and might even cease to be breathing. Simplicity, indeed, is one of those qualities which has suffered from being praised without much thought. One leg is simpler than (that is, half as complicated as) two; but to have only one leg would complicate walking. Similarly to explain life by one principle, either spirit or matter, would be simpler than to explain it by two. But it would leave life quite inexplicable.

In fact, the mind, enabled by faith and its own cooperative activity to see reality as it is, does not find itself impeded by overcomplication, but for the first time can move freely about reality. In the realization of the Infinite, there is a sense of enlargement and confidence, not lessened but added to by the resultant awareness of our own finiteness; for finiteness is no constraint to a being that is simply trying to be itself. The mind is not forever baffled by the multiplicity of things, once it sees them related to God, whose meaning is love, and so to each other. A heap of human features tossed pell-mell onto a table, or even arranged in some arbitrary order—in order of size, for instance, or in alphabetical order—would be very baffling indeed; but in their proper order in the human face they are not baffling.

Just as the mind finds freedom and not confusion in the seen complexity of things, so life and action find freedom and not frustration. For there is a miraculous principle of simplification in seeing that the significant movement of life, to which all other movements are secondary, is according to whether we are going toward God, the logical end being sanctity, or toward self as distinct from God, with the logical end of damnation. There is nothing in human life that cannot be related to this single simple principle. It is with this that the Church is concerned, to the great puzzlement of those who do not possess this key to simplicity. To take one obvious illustration: whereas, in the light of natural justice, we tend to see men primarily as exploiters and exploited, with the result that we see as a first duty the overthrow of the exploiters and the relief of their victims, the Church sees them primarily as saints and sinners, her job being to turn the sinners into saints and the saints into greater saints. The practical consequences of this way of seeing are enormous and frequently disturbing. Where the world sees a strong man triumphant in tyranny, who must be put down, the Church sees a poor stunted soul in peril of damnation, who must somehow be saved from that mortal peril. To the world, arrogance is a provocation and we rage against it; to the Church, arrogance is a disease in the soul, arousing compassion and a loving desire to heal. Other considerations may intervene—the good of souls endangered by the sinner—leading the Church to resist. But even then her action is still guided by the principle that what matters is the movement of souls toward God or away from God. It is good, since this *is* the principal question, that someone should specialize on it, so that it is not left merely to take its chance among the myriad motives for which people act.

(iii) The laws of reality

The vision of reality involves seeing not only what is, but how we should conduct ourselves in this now-seen universe. Reality has laws, and we can know them.

God did not make a chaos, in which any cause might have any effect. That would make intelligent living impossible. We must see laws primarily as statements of cause and effect. In other words, laws may be seen from one of two angles. Primarily they are statements, secondarily they are commands. As statements they tell us what the relations are between one reality and another: reality *is so*. As commands they order us to act in accordance with reality thus shown to us: reality being *so, do so*.

Apply this to the moral law. It is a law of reality that fidelity in marriage is right for the kind of being man is; from this law it follows that if we commit adultery, we must suffer damage to our soul. So far we are dealing with a truth about man, seizable by the intellect. But God has made a command of it, "Thou shalt not commit adultery." This is addressed to the will, so that to disobey it is sin; but it is still seen by the intellect as an instruction from our maker as to how we should best run ourselves, so that to ignore it is folly. Obviously our obedience to the command is aided enormously by our awareness of the reality about ourselves upon which it is based.

Return for a moment to consider law as statement rather than command. It says that a particular course of conduct is best for man, because he is what he is. To act otherwise always damages man, either by some positive damage, a real wound in his nature, or by stunting his development so that, though there is no actual wound, he does not grow as he might have grown. All this is obvious enough to us in regard to material bodies, because in the disordered state of our nature, bodies are so especially seeable. But there are elements in man more difficult to see than his body, and the laws that govern these elements are more difficult to see than, say, the law of gravity. But they *are* laws, for there is no chaos in this nobler part of reality either; and they are more vital, precisely because this part of us is nobler. We need to know them in order to be ourselves. Knowledge of law is a condition of freedom, material or moral. Such knowledge limits our freedom to guess, but increases our freedom to act and to think. Observe that there is no such thing as freedom from law, but only freedom within the law. As we have seen, we cannot frustrate God's law at any point. There is no such thing as breaking the law of gravity. We can ignore it, but we literally cannot break it. It can break us. Similarly there is no such thing as breaking the law of purity. We can disobey the command, but the law is not broken, *we* are. There is a common fear that religion, with its insistence upon acceptance, shackles the mind; in fact it shackles the mind no more than knowledge of the law of gravity shackles the body.

But if the moral law is always a condition of our freedom, it is not always an immediate convenience. It is often highly inconvenient. So indeed is the material law. Thus the law of gravity may mean that if from the top of a high cliff you see a man drowning, you may have to go miles around to reach the sea-level—in other words you have to let him drown—instead of jumping. Jumping represents a short-cut, but it would destroy you and not help the drowning man. Immorality similarly represents a short-cut, but it always damages and may destroy us. The trouble is that man finds a short-cut almost irresistible. It may help us to see how a clear view of reality helps us to observe the moral law, if we consider a couple of cases; and it will help most if we choose instances where the sin is all the more tempting because it does not appear to damage some other persons. It is still something to our credit that we shrink—even if not uncontrollably—from sins that will hurt others.

There is a small but already growing—and likely to grow larger—movement for euthanasia, the painless killing of patients suffering agonies from an incurable disease. The case for it is put very persuasively, and there is something in us to which it makes a very powerful appeal. As Catholics, we know that there is a plain command of God by which it is murder. That settles the matter, but leaves us with an unsatisfied feeling. Yet, quite apart from the command of God according to which it is murder, there are certain plain facts of reality by which it is madness. The argument for it is usually clinched by the reminder that we would not let a dog suffer so, but would put him out of his misery. But the cases are not parallel. We put the dog out of his misery, and there the matter ends. We put the man out of his misery, and there the matter does not end. The further question arises, what do we put him into? If he happens to be in a state of unrepented rebellion against God, then we have put him into hell. It is true that we cannot know, but precisely because we cannot know, we should not take an action which might involve a catastrophe so vast and so final. Only in this life can repentance be made, grace gained or regained. Even if (what we cannot know) the sufferer be in a state of grace, it is also true that only in this life can grace be added to and the soul's capacity grow. It may well be that in the agony of that unrelievable suffering, the soul might thus grow, so that when death finally came the soul would enter heaven with a far greater capacity to live the life and receive the joy of heaven. Again we cannot know; but to risk sending a man either to hell or to a "lower circle" of heaven to save him from bodily pain however great would (like so much well-meant meddling) do credit to our heart perhaps, but none at all to our head.

So far we have considered only the effects in the next world of this particular disobedience to the law of God. Obviously there can be no effects upon the sufferer in this world, since we are putting him out of it. But there *are* effects in this world all the same, not upon the man but upon the whole structure of society. A society lives or dies by the values it holds. This truth is almost always omitted from modern discussion of problems that used to be called moral. Our tendency is simply to count the number of people immediately benefited by a proposed line of conduct and the number of people harmed by it, and if there be a clear preponderance of people benefited, to assume that no further argument is required: that line of conduct is justified. But this statistical simplification of morality will not do. Only a society which values life so that it will not sacrifice it save for values indubitably higher is a healthy society. Escape from bodily suffering is not a higher value. To allow that a man's life may be taken, even with his own consent, in order to save him from bodily suffering is to reduce the value of life; and the whole of society lives in the shadow of that diminished value.

We may take one further instance of a sin which seems to hurt no one. A man marries a woman whose husband has already left her. Who is damaged, and how? We are assuming that neither party is Catholic. Now obviously this is not one of the worst breaches of the law of God. The parties concerned do not know of God's positive law against their act, and the modern conscience is no longer very lively on the point, so that there is no question of a deliberate setting of their own will against God's will, which is the really destructive element in sin. But the law of monogamy is as real a law as the law of gravity, and whether we know it or not, to break a law of reality is to suffer damage. But in this event what damage? To the persons concerned, probably, there is not much positive damage, of the kind we have compared to a wound in the body; but they have missed the development that living by the law of morality, which is the law of reality, would have brought them. Because the law is God's law, God sees to it that those who live by it will grow by it. The absence of knowledge may very well mean that there is no guilt, in fact no sin. But there is a law by which they might have gained something, and they have not gained it.

Further we have the same consideration as to the effect upon the social order that we have already seen in the matter of euthanasia. The sacredness of life is one value by which society lives healthfully. The unity of marriage is another. To allow that a particular marriage may be dissolved is to assume that marriage as such is dissoluble; and everyone's marriage is thereby weakened.

Summarizing the various considerations upon law, we observe that the will of God is a reality. The sensible, indeed the only rational, thing to do is to learn it and live by it. There is only childishness in letting oneself be broken by reality because one would like reality to be different. There is no great harm in wishing reality different, provided we do not proceed to act as if it were different: for that is to act in unreality. There is no more point in objecting that the moral law has no right to constrain you and that you will act as you please in regard to it than in objecting that cold air has no right to freeze you, that you will go where you like and wear what you like—that you will, for example, stroll through a blizzard in a bathing suit. That would be madness in relation to physical law. The other would be no less madness in relation to the moral law.

The first point of maturity is to accept law. The highest point of maturity is to be in love with law: for law is the will of God, and God is love. In between this first and last step lies the acceptance of law not because we fear the consequences but because we love the Lawgiver: "If you love Me, keep My commandments." We have already seen the frenzied effort to read personality out of the universe: and with personality gone, will goes, and law is only mechanism. But the universe we are in *is* an expression of will, and the will it expresses is love.

(iv) The problem of suffering

The vision of life and law is splendid, but there is mystery in it. The higher sort of mystery we have already discussed—mystery about the great realities: mysteries like all that we cannot see about the Blessed Trinity, mysteries about that lesser but still great thing the soul of man—his free will, for example. To be too much bothered by the questions we cannot answer is to be irked at not being God. Above all we must not be so bothered by the darkness ringing our circle of light that we cannot enjoy the light. Nor is there any reason why we should be bothered. The mind may well be tormented by truths seemingly irreconcilable, by its own inability to see their reconciliation, if it cannot see *why* it cannot see. But we, knowing the great things with which we are dealing, see why we cannot see further. So that in fact (as we saw early in this exploration) our very darkness is a kind of light.

But in our vision there is a mystery of a more practical sort, and we have not yet discussed it. It is the mystery of suffering. Observe first that while it is right to call suffering a mystery, or a problem, the mystery or problem is commonly misconceived. We talk as if we had to explain suffering away, to defend God in relation to it; whereas our real task is to see the meaning of it and to use it. The chief problem of suffering is how not to waste it. Certainly no one who has followed the thought of this book thus far will come to the question as if we were putting God on trial. We come to it in full knowledge of His omnipotence and His love. We seek to understand it, for ourselves, and to help others to understand it if we can. If we are aiming to justify the ways of God to men, it is not for the sake of clearing God's character, but of preventing men from being kept from Him.

The question *Why does God allow suffering?* is all but meaningless. It could only mean: why does God allow us? He could prevent suffering by preventing us, a cure more drastic than we should desire. This is not mere flippancy, but the most obvious truth. Given that we are what we are, we can get into a wrong relation to reality. To be in a wrong relation to reality *must* have an effect on us. The name for the effect is suffering. The suffering will be related to the kind of being we are, to the elements in us which have got into the wrong relation to reality. Thus we may inherit or acquire bodily defects: our lungs, for example, may be wrongly related to reality because they cannot handle air properly for the good of the body; or there may be a famine, so that we cannot get food, and our body's right relation to reality depends upon food. Again the want of harmony with reality may be in the mind: a man may want something that he cannot have—a woman, for example. He may be unable to have her because she is dead, or because she is married. In the one case his desire has collided with a physical law, in the other with a moral law.

The wrong relation with reality may be one that we can easily put right. The defect in the body may be healed, the energy of the mind may be directed to something attainable. We may very well seek relief from suffering, if relief is to be had. But we must be careful not to deceive ourselves and act as if relief were to be had when it is not. In the instance of the man and the woman above noted, he will know that he cannot have her if she is dead: the physical law does not allow of question. But in face of the moral law he may have an illusion of freedom: although she is married, he can in fact have her, if she is willing. But the law remains a law. He has merely turned from one wrong relation to reality—wanting what he should not have—to another wrong relation to reality—taking what he should not have. His felt suffering may be relieved; but the damage to him is greater and not less.

Anyhow the principle remains: we can get into the wrong relation with reality in one way or another: we suffer as a result. This is the sense in which I have said that God could prevent suffering by preventing us. But a second question remains, and it is in the practical order the heart of the problem. Given that finite creatures with fallible intellects and free will are pretty certain to bring suffering upon themselves, the question still remains to torment us—why did God make us so that we can suffer so much? Some part of the answer may emerge as we continue our examination of the working of our first principle.

Let us apply it to bodily suffering first. The reality to which we belong and from which we cannot subtract ourselves has laws, expressive of real and knowable sequences of cause and effect. We can collide with these laws, through our own fault or someone else's or, as it sometimes seems to us, through nobody's. To suggest that God should intervene every time we come into collision with reality and prevent the causes taking their effects would mean that we should not be living in a universe of law at all. If the universe were not run by laws, but by myriads of special interventions by God, we could hardly handle our lives intelligently: we could simply passively let ourselves be handled. God does intervene, of course. We call His intervention miracle. In the nature of the case, miracle is exceptional. It means that the cause we see does not produce its usual effect, or that the effect we see has no relation to a natural cause. This is invariably a surprise, pleasant if we benefit by a miracle, disconcerting if it is against us. But if ever miracles ceased to be exceptional and became common, considered action would have to cease. We could not master our environment, grow in our environment, exercise our will by choice, or take the consequences of our choice. We should never be sure what the consequences of our choice were. It is hard to see how we could reach maturity.

The laws of reality represent real sequences of cause and effect. Some of these laws we know, some we do not know yet: even these last we can sense; we live in the effect of them, and may someday get to learn them. But we could never learn them if they were never allowed to operate to our disadvantage but were always interfered with by special acts of God. None of this means that the laws of reality are merely mechanical, acting automatically like a machine long ago wound up and capable of running only as it is wound. There is a continuous personal will in operation. It operates even in the laws that seem most mechanical; it operates to make them what they are and to enable them to function as they function. But beyond that there is the continuous possibility of intervention by God, not only by miracle, nor because someone has asked Him and He has heard the prayer, but rather by way of a higher law. As part of this higher law God lavishes gifts upon men as a reward, lavishes punishment upon men either simply as punishment demanded by justice or as healing because He is merciful. What I have called the mechanical laws function in the framework of the universal law of God's love. One of mankind's tasks is to find the principle of this higher action of God in the universe. There are unquestionably spiritual laws which set material laws in motion. So much we might suspect, even without revelation. But if we live by the revelation of God, we shall come to see more and more clearly what these laws are. What is true of law in the material order, where its operation is most obvious to us, is true also in the order of rational action, the order of our psychological life and our social life. Man's right relation to God is needed if the world is to go right for man. It is surprising how little this truth is grasped, even by people who have some general notion of God. Men who have only the faintest beginning of faith or hope or charity expect God to act as if they had them in full measure. This sort of strain we are always putting upon the reality of things. We make ourselves un-men and expect God to treat us as men. We are to ignore God's laws, and God is to treat us as if we had observed them; men are to be selfish, and God is to prevent wars; men are to be sinful, and God is to prevent evil. All this as though men were to be forever jumping off cliffs and God forever catching them in mid-air.

In this connection, notice that we are still, by nature, members of the human race, as we are of the material universe. Each man must live in an environment created by all men. We cannot subtract ourselves from the human context and expect God to treat us thus in total isolation. We do not know what problems the race is setting God. Therefore we do not understand how God's treatment of those problems must incidentally affect us. Even naturally we are members one of another, and the disease of one will bring suffering to another. We must see the conflict of giants in which we are. The perspective of individual suffering is all wrong if we do not. Just as in the physical order, a tidal wave cannot be expected to drown everybody else but choose out me for survival; so in the social order the evils which the human race brings upon itself by its massive ignoring of God's law, which is the law of reality, cannot be expected to single out me for exemption from suffering.

But though it would be unreasonable to expect as of right, or even as of rule, that God would prevent our suffering along with the race to which we belong, we know for our consolation that God can see to it that we do not thereby lose. We cannot be saved from suffering pain, but we can be saved from suffering loss. This does not mean only that God can compensate us by happiness in the next life. Even if it did, this would still be something vast. St. Paul tells us that he counts the sufferings of this world as unworthy to be compared with the glory to come. Nor was this a mere mouthing of platitudes. When St. Paul said that, he knew very well what the sufferings of this world could be: "Five times the Jews scourged me, and spared me but one lash in the forty; three times I was beaten with rods, once I was stoned; I have been shipwrecked three times; I have spent a night and a day as a castaway on the sea. What journeys I have undertaken, in danger from rivers, in danger from robbers, in danger from my own people, in danger from the Gentiles; danger in cities, danger in the wilderness, danger in the sea, danger from false brethren! I have met with toil and weariness, so often been sleepless, hungry and thirsty; so often denied myself food, gone cold and naked" (2 Cor 11:24–27).

But in saying that God sees to it that we do not lose by that suffering which comes to us not for any fault of our own but simply because we are not excepted from the calamities that flow from our place in the material universe and the human race, I had not in mind merely the possibility of eternal compensation for suffering that ends. What the phrase meant was that our suffering itself should not be wasted. It is not merely an unfortunate by-product of broken laws, a by-product in whose power we unfortunately find ourselves so that we cannot but be involved in it: something, therefore, from which we cannot be exempted but for which we can be compensated.

Suffering is more than that. It is constructive, it is building-stuff, God uses it. Our suffering can be used directly for ourselves; in the solidarity of the human race, our suffering can be used for the building of others, and theirs for ours.

There is a tendency to dismiss impatiently any answer to the problem of suffering which brings in God's action. The unbeliever mocks at it, and even the Christian feels that it is something of an anti-climax: he would like some explanation which did not call upon God for so much. What we are looking for, to comfort ourselves and to quieten the derider, is some self-contained theory which would be equally valid if there were no God. But we can hardly expect God to leave what He Himself would do out of account when planning the universe. If we continue to study the problem with an awareness of God as the most important element in it, we shall find not that the darkness vanishes, but that there is a pretty solid increase of light all the same.

Our problem is, as we have said, to see how suffering may be used and not wasted. Ordinary human experience shows that suffering can be maturing; indeed, that anyone who is spared from suffering too rigorously will never reach maturity at all. But suffering, as the same experience shows, can be destructive too. Whether it shall develop a man or shatter him is not simply a matter of the quantity of suffering. Of two men suffering greatly but so far as we can judge unevenly, the one who suffers less may be shattered and the one who suffers more may be immensely developed by it. Which way it shall go does not depend upon the suffering, but upon the will. The beginning of a positive answer to suffering, at any level of intensity conceivable, lies in the will's acceptance of it as a part of reality, whether reality seen impersonally as the order of things, or personally as the will of God. Of itself and necessarily, this acceptance cuts at the central point of man's profoundest disease.

That central point is the over-assertion of self. Suffering can come to us in a thousand guises: the element common to them all, the element therefore which constitutes suffering as such, is that something is happening to us which we intensely dislike. Given that our deepest-lying disease is the over-assertion of self, then to accept what we intensely dislike, and not merely disintegrate in impotent rebellion against it, is of itself and directly a healing and strengthening of the will, fitting it for, helping it toward, restoring it to, its proper domination of the whole man. Self-control is the first condition of any control. No matter how vast an empire a man may have, if he does not control himself then he does not control the empire either: whatever controls him controls it.

This healing and strengthening effect of suffering operates even if it is merely the acceptance of reality, a determination to cope with what is; still more if it is the acceptance of reality as a moral law, even if this is only dimly apprehended in conscience and not seen in relation to a personal lawgiver; but above all if it is a conscious union of the will with God. Acceptance at the first level is difficult. To suffer in a universe directed by no mind is to be tortured by blind forces which know nothing of man and care nothing for man. This could easily lead to despair, even in a mind of great vitality. Where the mind is already devitalized, it can hardly do otherwise: life is futile anyway, without having torture thrown in. But if we see the universe directed by a mind, then the suffering might be directed too, might be for our gain. Thus, if we accept the impact upon us of the laws of reality by uniting our own will to God's will, suffering has the chance to do a vast constructive work in us; and this constructiveness reaches its peak when, as we saw in Chapter 22, we reach the point where we can unite our sufferings to the redemptive sufferings of Christ. "For as the sufferings of Christ abound in us: so also by Christ doth our comfort abound" (2 Cor 1:5).

Let us pause a moment to consider one almost universal reaction to any such attempt as I am making to see suffering as constructive, to see how there can be comfort in it. It is the answer contained in Kipling's rhyme—

> The toad beneath the harrow knows
> Exactly where each toothpoint goes;
> The butterfly upon the road
> Preaches contentment to that toad.

A man suffering intensely will always feel something of this as he listens to what must seem to him a cold-blooded rationalization of suffering by one who sounds as if he has never suffered. That is why I quote St. Paul: I could as easily quote a hundred other saints: and beyond these there is the massive testimony of millions who have fallen short of sainthood but would have fallen shorter still but for suffering.

Because we are living in a universe and not a chaos—because, that is, the laws of reality are made by a God of infinite knowledge and infinite love—we can be sure that no one gets more suffering than he can, with God's help, bear. It would not be possible to prove this empirically, or disprove it either, for that matter. It is simply a case for trusting God. If we cannot trust God, we cannot trust: for no one else has given us God's reasons for trust.

So much for suffering that can develop the sufferer—and this whether he be innocent or guilty. But the mind is more profoundly troubled by suffering that seems as if it could in no way bring growth to the sufferer; for example, suffering which kills while the suffering itself is of such intensity that the sufferer's reaction to it seems little more than an animal reaction to torture in which the spirit is for the moment drowned;

or again, the death in agony of tiny children. Here we see less clearly or perhaps not at all. But we have one firm principle for our support. If a thing seems wildly cruel and unfair to us, it still remains that God loves men more than we do, for He has done two great things for them that we have never done— created all of them, and died for all of them. If it really were cruel and unfair, He would know it.

But that is not all: it is the greatest thing we can say, but it is not the only thing we can say. Here again we can remind ourselves of the rewards that God has laid up for us in heaven, the glory to come, which St. Paul saw as an incomparably greater thing than any suffering here. The child who died in agony yesterday is saying that today. But there is another consideration too, arising from the solidarity of the human race. We have seen how suffering does of itself balance sin. The acceptance of what we intensely dislike is a direct healing for the over-assertion of self, which is the key to sin. Suffering can be an energy filling up the energy spilled away in sin. But as reality is constituted, God can use the suffering of one for the healing of another, or the suffering of all for the strengthening of all. This is one of those laws of the universe which are not merely mechanical. The infant has no sin of his own to be made up for by suffering. But his suffering can be used by God. Thus the infant is given the enormous privilege of doing something for others. Under God, there is no higher privilege.

Many readers will find the theory of suffering just stated fairly satisfactory. Every so often some type of suffering will occur to them which this does not explicitly cover—for example, the deliberate and seemingly permanent moral corruption of the innocent young by older people. Nonetheless, for the vast mass of the world's suffering there is some light in it. But we shoud assure ourselves that the line of answer here suggested is not for us simply something academic, satisfactory enough while we are considering suffering in the abstract but liable to collapse in the face of real suffering really apprehended. When we discuss the problem of suffering, it is not the problem of a word or a notion. The reader should test how firmly the principles here suggested hold his mind, by reading some of the classic accounts of various sorts of human suffering. If we are honest with ourselves, we may have to admit that these accounts of suffering in the concrete do give our princples a pretty thorough testing. The chances are that they leave us with our theories still standing if shaken, but with no tendency whatever to think that there is any slick glib answer. It may help us to clarify our own mind if we see certain intellectual defects in ourselves which make the seen fact of suffering such a temptation not only against trusting God, but against those principles which in tranquillity our mind had seen and balanced.

The first difficulty lies in the simple fact that we do see the suffering, but we do not see the application God makes of it to the soul here and now; still less do we see the glory that is to come. Suffering causes so vast a shuddering in the soul, God so tiny a vibration; often enough when we think we are seeing the suffering in relation to God, we are only feeling how much greater the shuddering is than the vibration. Things seen are mightier than things heard; things that can seize the imagination loom larger than those that must appeal directly to the intellect. Not only in relation to suffering, but in relation to all things whatsoever, we must be aware of this defect in ourselves and able to make allowances for it. It is worse still when unbelievers challenge us upon suffering. We give an answer to people to whom suffering is real but God is not. They are aware of God only as a word, and the word carries none of the living implications that it has for us.

The second difficulty lies in our almost incurable habit of seeing this life as the whole and judging accordingly; seeing its tragedies as final, whereas the one tragedy is to make the fundamental choice of self in preference to God; for that means to leave life unfit for what lies before us. Since this life is a preparation, the only ultimate tragedy is to leave it unprepared. Our heart may tell us otherwise, but the heart is not the teller. Nor can our heart tell us, either by its hopes or its fears, what souls have in fact left this life unprepared. Sanctifying grace, which is the principle of eternal life, may be in men as no more than a grain of mustard seed. We cannot tell. They cannot tell. Grace is like the little leaven that leavens the whole lump. Until it *has* leavened the whole lump, we can see only lump and no leaven. But the tiniest fragment of leaven is sufficient for salvation. In all our consideration of this life, we must try to make it utterly matter of course to see it as a preparation. We waste so much apologetic effort trying to "justify" God's action on us in this life as if this life were not preparatory but complete in itself; whereas frequently the only justification is that it does prepare, even if we do not see how. There is a rough comparison in the way in which pre-marital purity is a preparation for marriage. At the time it may seem pointless and dreary and even painful: its perfection as preparation is seen only when marriage comes. So with this life as a whole in relation to the next. In a sense we may think of it as the tuning of the instruments, so that it gives only a hint of the glory of the symphony when all the instruments are tuned and all are obeying the conductor.

One final point. If we reject this answer to the problem of suffering, we are left with no answer. At best we can have an indignant sympathy with the sufferer which does not help him, least of all if the sufferer happens to be ourselves. The true answer is hard but vitalizing. The alternative is despair.

It may seem that in our survey of the vision of reality, we have given a disproportionate space to one of the elements which may cloud the vision. The disproportion is only apparent. The whole book has been about the vision, whereas suffering is treated in detail here only. The vision is the thing. Suffering is an appalling problem to one who sees it, but does not see the whole context of reality. The believer may find it as unanswerable as the unbeliever; but he is not troubled by it in the same way, for he sees so much, has experienced so much, has quite simply lived so much. His real life is lived consciously in the company of God and of the Mother of God and of the gifts of God. A given patch of experience may be one hundred per cent dark, but it is not ten per cent of the whole landscape. That is the sense in which we have spoken earlier in this book of the necessity of seeing reality as a whole, as a preparation for living wholly in it. Seeing it is not the same thing as living wholly in it, but it is an excellent preparation. Our wrestling is still, as St. Paul saw it, "not against flesh and blood, but against Principalities and Powers, against the rulers of the world of this darkness" (Eph 6:12). But our foot is upon firm ground.

32. Idyll and Fact

From the Catholic life and the Catholic vision, it is something of a shock to come to the Catholic. We are so appallingly commonplace. Illumined by such truths, fed by such food, we yet look so horribly like everyone else. Living within one split second of the judgment seat of God, we are so intent upon other matters. At Mass we are taking part in an action of inconceivable wonder, and our problem is to keep our minds upon it at all. These things, and a score of other manifestations of the same trouble, puzzle the unbeliever.

(i) Our mediocrity

There is no doubt at all that the principal argument against the Church is the Catholic. Not the bad Catholic: any man of intelligence can see that members of the Church who do not listen to her teaching or receive her sacraments or obey her laws constitute no case at all against the Church. It is the Catholics who do in a general way listen to the teachings and receive the sacraments, who stand more than any other single factor between the unbeliever and belief. He hears of the immensities that we believe, and he feels that if he believed such things his life would be utterly revolutionized; he would be made new. But we do not look new, or anything else in particular. He meets us, for instance, after we have received Communion, and he finds the Real Presence of Christ in the communicant rather harder to believe than the Real Presence of Christ in the Host. Before Communion, the bread does not look as if Christ were present in it; after Communion, the Catholic does not look as if Christ were really present in him. The unbeliever feels certain that he could not believe such things and be to all appearance so little affected outwardly or inwardly. He can account for it only by assuming that we do not really believe the things we say we do, and this comforts him in his own aimlessness, or at least helps to keep him in it.

As I say, the unbeliever is troubled, and that is tragic. But it is not his puzzlement that I am concerned with now, but our own. We puzzle ourselves, when we stop to contemplate ourselves, and unless we see the key to our own puzzle we may easily get a mistaken view of the vital realities which seem to vitalize us so little.

The truth about us is, of course, that grace is working in a nature that fell in Adam. Grace is in itself as glorious a treasure as we have described it. But in St. Paul's phrase, we carry that treasure in earthen vessels; and the vessels are not something distinct from ourselves: they are ourselves. *Gratia supponit naturam,* say the theologians. They mean that grace does not supply us with a new nature but works in the nature it finds. Grace is a supernature, but it does not supersede nature. It sets a new principle of life in the very core of the nature we have, which gives it new and greater powers. But it does not directly improve it as a nature. It is rather like electricity, which gives a wire the power to light up a whole room. But the electricity does not correct any defects there may be in the wire. The analogy must not be pressed further, because grace does, as we shall see, bring aid to nature. It brings aid not by direct action upon nature's defects, nor, usually, at all quickly or spectacularly. Grace is necessary for the healing of our nature. But it will not itself heal our nature. Our cooperation with grace will do that, and in the measure of our cooperation. We are the trouble.

If you want to see the effects of the Fall upon human nature, there is no need to find an unbaptized man: stop the first Christian you meet and study him. We all of us inherit natures tainted and vulnerable from Adam and every ancestor since, and it is only too probable that we have contributed our own share to their worsening.

Grace, then, has to work in a damaged nature. Consider first the clouded intellect in which the theological virtue of Faith, the moral virtue of Prudence, and the Gifts of Understanding, Knowledge, Wisdom, and Counsel have to operate. Vast and luminous realities are spread out before our gaze: why are we not dazzled? Our intellect is defective at three levels. There are

truths it simply does not know;
truths it knows but does not advert to;
truths it knows and adverts to but does not comprehend.

Take the first. For a variety of reasons, one finds that a great number of Catholics have made almost no study of their religion. They believe it, would probably die rather than deny it, but are not interested enough to find out very much about its meaning. They have grasped that knowledge is not the most important part of religion, and have proceeded from that to a sort of working theory that it is not important for themselves at all. They know that they can be saved with a very minimum of knowledge, and have not grasped that more knowledge might help. Consider, for instance, one piece of truth not grasped even by all practicing Catholics. They know that sanctifying grace is necessary to salvation; they have been accustomed all their lives to being urged so to live that they will increase in sanctifying grace. But for the most part they have only the vaguest notion of what sanctifying grace is. From this lack, two practical consequences follow; first, that they think of their destiny after death as rather a matter of whether they are in sin than as a matter of whether they are in the state of sanctifying grace; second, that they think of salvation simply as a matter of getting into heaven and thus avoiding all the unpleasantness of hell. They have not grasped that there are degrees of glory in heaven, dependent upon the intensity of the life of grace in the soul at death. The result of this hodge-podge of light and darkness in the mind is that one adopts as a practical rule of life the question: How much can I have of this world without losing heaven? It is very much like the small child speculating how much he can eat without getting sick. The extremely practical question How little of heaven am I likely to get by this system? does not arise at all.

There is no awareness, as I have said, of degrees of glory in heaven; nor very much awareness of glory in heaven at all. The motive of such a life is not desire for heaven, but desire to avoid hell.

In this category of truths not known is a widespread failure to grasp the whole truth about sin. At any level of instruction or uninstruction, a Catholic can hardly fail to know that the moral law is a command of God; but he may easily fail to see the other half of the truth, that it is a statement about reality, that it is comparable with the maker's instructions as to the running of an automobile. In the light of that truth, sin is folly. But one may easily not know that truth— much less a truth deeper still, in the light of which, sin is totally ridiculous.

Given that God made us all of nothing and continues to hold us in existence, it follows that we depend for our existence entirely upon the will of God. Sin is an effort to gain some happiness for ourselves against the will of God, against the one thing that is holding us in existence at all. What could be more ridiculous? We are being kept from God by our attachment to things that are wholly of God. Which is a reminder of that defect in the intellect which underlies all others, our tendency to take the part for the whole, to treat the part as if it were the whole, to try to get from it that total satisfaction which can only be got from the whole. The trouble is that our minds have not the muscles for totality. But they can grow them.

The second defect in the mind concerns the truths it knows, but does not advert to. Our intellects are always harassed and often dominated by our imagination; the thing seen close has greater power than the greater thing on the horizon. We are obsessed with the immediate. We have already considered this in the matter of our reaction to suffering. Under the impact of some pain especially terrible, we tend to ask impatiently, Why does not God intervene? If the question meant what it says, it would mean, "I would act thus and thus if I were God: why doesn't God?" So stated, it is ridiculous. But it would be unfair so to state it. It is the almost automatic reaction of a mind which sees the part and not the whole, is all aquiver with realization of what it does see and naturally not affected by what it does not advert to. One can think of a dozen such instances: there is, for example, the tendency to be unduly affected by the appearance of unworthy conduct in a priest. It means that his personal conduct, which is immediately under our gaze, is "more real" to us than his office as the channel of God's gifts.

The third effect concerns things known and adverted to but not comprehended. The unbeliever is wrong when he thinks that we do not really believe the immensities we profess. We do quite really believe them, with no admixture of doubt; but we do not always comprehend them. It is of the plainest historical evidence that Catholics will die for the Mass: they would not die for something they did not really believe. Yet the vast majority of those same Catholics were almost certainly distracted at every Mass they ever attended, and may very well have spent more time thinking of other things. The test of belief is willingness to die for a truth; the test of comprehension is ability to live by it. It takes time for the mind, and an effort of habituation, if we are to live at the level of our new knowledge. Comprehension requires muscles which the ordinary conduct of life has never called upon us to use. They will not instantly come to full power and functioning. We are not dazzled by the immensitites we believe, simply because the mind can hardly cope with them at all—much as a man does not stagger under a weight that he has not the muscles to lift.

More serious than the damaged intellect is the damaged

will. For in the will lies the issue of salvation or damnation. It is the will that loves, and as we have seen it can fix its love anywhere between nothingness and God. Ultimately we are saved or damned by what we love; here and now we are made or unmade by what we love. We are not consulted about our creation, about that act of God which brought us into existence—what we may call the initiation of our creation. But creation will not be fully accomplished in us without our consent. It is by no act of our will that we are men: but as to what sort of men, our will is decisive.

We have already seen that just as the continuing action of God is necessary if we are to exist, so the continuing action of God is necessary if we are to act. It is not thinkable that beings whose very existence results from God's action upon nothingness should themselves be able to act without God's concurrence in their action. The same God who lends us the energy to exist with, lends us the energy to act with. Apart from God, there is nothing in ourselves for action to proceed from. But if it is part of the consequence of the freedom God willed us to have, that same God will concur in the actions our will chooses, even if these actions are not the best for us. If the will insists, God will give it the energy which will allow it to damage itself. In other words, God treats us as grown-up. He will lend our will the energy to act against His will if that is what our will chooses. This choice is sin.

Observe the list that the Church gives of the seven capital sins, the sins from which all other sins flow. They are Pride, Envy, Avarice, Anger, Sloth, Gluttony, and Lust. Note that all are in the will; for sin is always a defect of the will. Its act may be in the intellect, or in the body; but the sin itself is in the will. No action whatsoever, merely as action, can damn us; but the will can damn us without any action at all save merely willing. For it is by the will that our relation of harmony or disharmony with reality (that is to say, with God) is established.

Observe that sin is always assertion of self as against reality. Pride is the worst sin, for it is positive assertion of self, positive choice of self in place of God as the supreme object of our love and our actions. Being the worst sin, it is also the most ridiculous. In order to set oneself up in place of God, one must borrow from God the energy to do it: if we insist upon defying God, God lends us the energy to defy Him with. No sin is its own contradiction more instantly and obviously; no sin, therefore, means a more total break with reality. The other six sins avoid the crowning folly of Pride. Whereas Pride is a positive assertion of self as against God, these others choose creatures in place of God, without necessarily making any explicit assertion at all about the nature of God or themselves. But there is always an assertion of one's desires as against the reality of things. And it is always an assertion that negates. It always involves choosing less than we might have, less than we need. And it never pays full dividends.

Why then do we sin? For the sins of the mind, there is the plain uncomplicated pleasure of egoism. There is an appearance of autonomy in asserting self with the appearance of impunity. Indeed there is a disease in the will which can find some sort of pleasure in the assertion of self, even where the appearance of impunity has vanished away and the wretched inadequacy of self in the face of reality is altogether obvious.

But for sins of the body, the position is different. They are the lesser sins (not that they cannot damn us all the same) because they affect the lesser part of us; because they are rather a yielding of weakness than an assertion of strength; because the temptation is fiercer. Our bodies are so made that there is a clean joy to be got through their senses, and this joy is a splendid thing, meant by God. It turns to total evil in the extreme case when we are able to get joy from nothing else. But short of that extreme, the body can urge its desires upon the will with altogether disproportionate effect. There is an intensity and exquisiteness and immediacy and vibrancy in bodily pleasure which for most of us is not in the pleasure of the mind. Serving God does not give us the same kind of here-and-now pleasure that sin gives. To eyes as little trained to reality as ours, there is a color and energy in sin, by comparison with which virtues look pallid and half alive. It is in this sense that Swinburne speaks of

> The lilies and languors of virtue
> And the roses and raptures of vice.

There is something in us all that stirs into life in response to that. But it is illusion all the same. Chesterton has the truth of it when he makes Swinburne's mistress reply,

> The notion impels me to anger
> That vice is all rapture for me,
> And if you think virtue is languor
> Just try it and see.

Sin is always a following of the line of least resistance, toward the deficiency of life. It is a going-with-the-stream-of-one's-inclinations. But it takes no vitality to go with the stream: a dead dog can do it.

In any event there is quite enough in ourselves to account for our sinning. And we are not left to ourselves. There are other men to urge us on. And there is the Devil. What the Devil gets out of it, it is hard to see. There is a futility in all that he does. His own sins and the sins he leads others to commit serve only to illustrate the unbreakableness of God's law. The Devil is the supreme example of the assertion of self at all costs and with no gain, of the pure rejoicing of self in self, the world well lost for love, self-love. That God allows the Devil to tempt man, we have already seen. But how does the Devil go about it? He has no direct power over our souls: he has not even a power to read our souls. He can form extraordinarily good guesses as to what is in our mind, but they remain guesses. His power relates to the matter of our bodies. All angels have, as a mere consequence of their own superiority in being, a power over matter. They cannot create it or annihilate it, but they can move material things in space, and redistribute the elements within material things themselves. They cannot exercise this power without the permission of God; but God does give permission to the fallen angels to make a certain use of their power as part of the testing of man. The Devil can stir the flesh of man at its most sensitive points; he can move the eye of man to see what otherwise he might not have seen; he can produce certain images in the bodily organism, the brain for example, which man will find at once distracting and soliciting.

One way or another, under the impulse of his own desires and other men's urgings and the Devil's tempting, man is in constant peril of sin; and no one of us can feel that our own performance is particularly impressive. Baptized or unbaptized, we all sin, though some less than others, certain of the saints probably only venially, and only Our Lady not at all. But leaving out the saints, the rest of us are a pretty unimpressive lot. And the Church knows it, as indeed she well might after hearing our confessions for the best part of two thousand years. If you want realism about the weakness of Christians, read the Missal carefully. The worst things our enemies charge us with, the Church has already mentioned on her own account in her official prayer book. In one of the forms of the Penitential Rite at the beginning of Mass, for instance, the priest, the minister of God, joins the people in saying, "I have sinned through my own fault in my thoughts and in my words, in

what I have done and in what I have failed to do." What is
there left for anyone else to say against him? One might
embroider that, as the Church's enemies often do, but one
cannot add to it. It says everything. This same realism is to be
found on almost every page, so that we are tempted sometimes
to wonder if we are as bad as that. But we are.

(ii) Imperfect response to grace

All this is plain fact. But how is it to be reconciled with the
presence in our souls of sanctifying grace? To bring the problem to a point: how is it that a person with the virtue of
Charity acts cruelly, or a person with the virtue of Temperance
gets drunk?

To answer the question, we must return to what was said in
an earlier chapter about sanctifying grace and the theological
and moral virtues as habits. A natural habit is acquired by a
constant repetition of certain acts, and results in a facility in the
performance of these acts. The good habit of speaking English,
the bad habit of drinking too much alcohol, the dubious habit
of playing the piano, are all illustrations. The supernatural
habits are not acquired by the continuous repetition of acts,
but are given to us in one act by God. Nor do they give the
same facility in action that the natural habit gives. But they are
habits all the same, as truly as our natural habits. For they are a
real modification of our nature, giving us the power to act
in a special way.

Along with the gift of sanctifying grace we get supernatural
habits, but we do not lose our natural habits. We are in the
curious position of having two sets of habits in one person.
With sanctifying grace, a naturally cold man gets the virtue of
Charity, and remains cold; a naturally lustful man gets the

virtue of Temperance and remains lustful; a naturally timid man gets the virtue of Fortitude and remains timid.

I have called this curious, and so it is; but there is no contradiction. Grace gives us a power (which without it we should not have) to act supernaturally—for example, to be temperate for the love of God or courageous for the love of God. But though it gives us the power to act supernaturally, it does not remove our natural power to act sinfully. It does not even remove our natural desire to act sinfully. What it does is to insert a new desire to act for the love of God, so that there is a new war in our powers.

The result is that a man with the virtue of Temperance may find it appallingly hard to act temperately and may often collapse into intemperance. Yet the virtue of Temperance is a real power all the same. It is rather like a great pianist with a bad piano. His power to produce music is truly real and objective; but because of the state of the piano he finds it all but impossible to produce music at all.

This same illustration may help to throw light upon another problem. The Church teaches that when we are in a state of grace, we have all the supernatural virtues at the same level of intensity. There is no such thing as a man having more Prudence than Fortitude. Yet is seems to be a matter of every-day experience that a given Christian has more of one virtue than another. We can now see why we fall into this error. Suppose a man who could play all the instruments in an orchestra equally well: yet if the piano is good, and the violin less good, and the oboe hopeless, the listeners might conclude that he had a greater gift of playing the piano than of playing the violin and that he had no gift at all for the oboe. The illustration will serve, provided we remember that the instru-ments upon which grace must make its music are our natural faculties of soul and body, not something distinct from ourselves, but part of ourselves: and that grace does aid in their repairing.

Not all our powers are equally apt to manifest our supernatural virtues. But our supernatural virtues are equally powerful. For they all go with the Life: it is to that, not to any single effect of it, that God gives increase. God does not give us an increase of Faith, for instance, as distinct from Hope and Charity. He gives us an increase of Life, which means an increase of all the virtues and gifts that flow from Life. When we pray, as against a particular temptation, for an increase of Faith, our prayer is not for more of the supernatural virtue of Faith as distinct from the other virtues, but for an increase of sanctifying grace and a strengthening of our nature, so that it may not be prevented, by its own natural scepticism, for instance, from acting in harmony with the supernatural virtue of Faith.

Thus our problem is to bring our natural habits into harmony with our supernatural habits. Grace has to operate through our faculties; we have to work for the destruction of habits that make our faculties bad instruments for grace and for the development of habits that make them good instruments—to the point where the supernature has become a sort of second nature, and the supernatural habits give the same facility as natural habits. And there is only one way in which that can be done—by the steady repetition of actions, actions against the bad habit, actions tending to form a good habit. That is the law of our nature for the formation of natural habits, and the supernatural life does not supersede it.

But then, you may wonder how grace and the virtues fulfill the second part of the definition of habit. A habit is a modification of a being, disposing it to act in a particular way. How can grace and the virtues be said to dispose our nature to act according to them? First there is the truth we have already seen: that by grace we have real powers, even if our nature is too damaged to act in harmony with them. But there is something else. Grace helps us in the effort to acquire good natural habits by setting this new energizing of divine life in the very center of our being, and by showing us God closer and clearer, as a stimulus to action that will please Him and bring us to Him. It gives us not only a supernatural power to act in relation to God thus seen close and clear, but a stimulus that our nature itself can respond to. It brings not only God all-knowing and all-loving thus close to us, but the rest of reality as well, and especially the truth about ourselves: It analyzes sin for us, telling us what the war within ourselves is about; telling us why man is unsatisfied and must go on being unsatisfied with things less than God, because the central fact about man is that he is *capax Dei,* capable of being filled with God.

In these and a dozen other ways, grace helps nature to do nature's own job of remaking itself. But it is, as it cannot help being, a long job. At first, all we can say is that there are now two sets of habits at conflict within us, and that now one is victorious, now the other—which is at least an improvement on our earlier stage, when the natural habit invariably won because there was no contest. But from that first effect—disturbing our peace, ruining our previous simple joy in our sins, by initiating a conflict which was not there before—to the successful issue of the struggle when we find peace at a new level, there is a long way to go. It is vital that we should understand just what the struggle involves. As we have seen, the precise problem is the healing of our nature *as nature,* which cannot be effected without grace or by grace alone, but by the development of natural habits in harmony with grace. As between different people, one will find less resistance in his nature than another—his passions are less stormy perhaps, or his sins bring less delight. But in all people there is some resistance, some sort of warfare, and the general principles on which the war must be fought are the same for all. First, we must use every means of increasing the supernatural life in us. Second, we must work upon our natures with toil and pain that may amount to agony, fighting against bad habits and forming good.

At the risk of wearying, it must be repeated that grace alone is not the answer. We often deceive ourselves by trying to make the supernatural do the work of the natural, and falling into despair because it does not. We multiply Communions against a particular temptation, and often enough the only result is to increase the strife within us without producing the virtuous act or preventing the sin. The charity of God troubles us, but does not seem to aid us. Once we have grasped the real nature of the struggle, we shall be in no danger of being led by it to despair, least of all to despair of the supernatural, because the supernatural was never promised for that purpose. God could, of course, root out the bad habit or tendency by one act of His power, but He has not promised to do so, and it would be something in the nature of miracle if He did. By all means, pray for a miracle, but do not be discouraged if you do not get it.

The direct work upon our nature has to be done, as we have seen, with labor and pain. In our damaged state, in the wrongness of our relation to reality, we are not healable or rightly treatable without pain caused. *Dulce et decorum est pro patria mori* — It is sweet and right to die for our country. So says Horace, and the first word surprises. That it is "right", one does not doubt. But "sweet"? There is a sweetness in it, but for most of us it would hardly be the specifying element. It is true that all right action *can* be sweet, but only if we are in complete harmony with reality. To get ourselves to the state where virtue is sweet, the road is by no means sweet. Immediate enjoyment is almost invariably incompatible with healing, and without healing there is no permanent enjoyment.

Part of healing is the bringing back of our powers into their proper relation to one another. The body must be made subject to the mind. This subjection will mean that where the body wants something which the instructed mind knows it should not have, the body's claims must be denied. The mere keeping of the commandments will tend to bring upon the body a great deal of very unpleasant pressure, which may amount to real pain. Over and above that, all who have had any success in bringing their body into proper subjection to the mind testify that there must be definite unpleasantness caused to the body or pleasure refused to the body, not simply in the avoidance of sin but as a direct training of the body for its proper part in the human compound, not only for the soul's good, but ultimately for the body's too.

But if the body must be brought into right relation with the mind, the mind must be brought into right relation with God. And the obvious method is prayer. Prayer does of itself, even more directly than suffering, tend to correct the disharmony between ourselves and reality. For of itself it asserts every element in the relation that ought to exist between the creature and God, and it brings the soul into that sort of contact with God in which He is closest and clearest. And if that be true of prayer in general, it is most true of prayer at its highest point, the Mass.

The harmonizing of the two wills, man's will and God's will, must be brought about by shared life: that is, not simply by *effort* on the will's part, but by a loving cooperation with God's action. In the Mass, there is precisely this co-action of man with God, with no sense of effort or strain; and the richness of that experience falls back upon those other areas of life where the cooperation is most difficult.

But even here, the cooperation is not simply a matter of our acting as God wills, but of God acting *with* us. When St. Paul said, "I live, yet now not I, but Christ lives in me", he was speaking a precise truth, not simply giving us a stimulating figure of speech. In his epistle to the Colossians (1:29), he tells us the same thing even more clearly: "In Christ Jesus I labor, striving *according to His working which He worketh in me in power.*" The same truth that our struggle to live the life of grace is not ours only but God's too, he tells the Romans: "Only, as before, the Spirit comes to the aid of our weakness; when we do not know what prayer to offer, to pray as we ought, the Spirit himself intercedes for us, with groans beyond all utterance" (8:26). St. Paul sees our prayer and the Holy Spirit's part in our prayer as so interwoven that he hardly bothers to distinguish them. We are praying, but it is really the Spirit praying in us and with us; and St. Paul attributes to the Spirit the unspeakable groanings which are ours, because He has given us the power to utter them.

(iii) Sanity points toward sanctity

In the ordinary Christian life, the struggle is lifelong. The victories go sometimes one way and sometimes the other; but the oscillation grows definitely less. With all sorts of defects, the Christian's nature does come into something like harmony with grace, his natural habits into some sort of correspondence with his supernatural. Temptations may remain, but his power over them grows. If he falls into sin, his repentance comes more quickly and certainly. Again not always, though this tends to be the story for the Christian who makes a real effort to grasp the Church's teaching, use the Church's sacraments, obey the Church's laws. If the oscillation does not cease, it does, as I have said, grow less violent. In the saint, it ceases. His nature has been brought fully into harmony with his supernature. If temptation remains, it can only solicit him and not conquer him.

Because the saint is a person who had made a total success of man's prime job of being a man, we may look at him for a moment a little more closely. What makes him a saint is the union of vast supernatural love of God, and a nature through which the supernatural love can manifest itself without flaw or discord. This correspondence of nature with grace—which he has attained and we are still toiling toward—may or may not have been for him a matter of hard striving. There is a romantic notion abroad that the greatest sinners make the greatest saints. It is an error, but it hints at certain truths. Persons who begin life with an equipment of strong passions may actually be aided on their way to sanctity by that very fact. Those of strong passions, in the first place, are more likely to be driven to actions which will shock themselves into the recognition of their own sinfulness and their need of aid from God. There is a certain danger in weak passions: a danger that one may mistake the absence of any very spectacular sin for virtue; the danger that one may seem to oneself to be a good enough sort of person, because one happens to be temperamentally incapable of doing anything bad enough to force one to see one's own badness.

And there is a second way in which this original natural equipment may help. Sanctity does not mean the absence of sins, though it will result in that, but the right direction of energy. There is no particular virtue in not committing sins for which one has not the taste or the temperament. It is in this sense that St. Teresa of Avila said that chastity is no bad preparation for purity. Chastity as such is merely a fact of one's autobiography. It means that one has not had a particular bodily experience. If this abstinence is for the love of God, it is a virtue; but not if it is only because one is afraid of women, or has no natural inclination toward persons of the opposite sex, or prefers one's stamp collection. But purity means the direction of energy to God with no admixture of self. Given that sanctity is the right direction of energy, then great natural energy, which if it take the wrong direction runs into sins of passion, will if it turn tc the right direction produce the heroic virtue of the saint.

The saint, we may say, is the successful man. He is so, even by natural standards. For he has found peace, and peace is what all human beings are seeking at all times. They would say that they are seeking for happiness, but peace *is* happiness and nothing else is. Peace, of course, is not the absence of activity, but the absence of discordancy. It is not the beginning of our life in the Church. Anyone who joins the Church, as the common misunderstanding has it, to find tranquillity will soon begin to wonder what he has found: not tranquillity certainly, but struggle. Peace is not given along with faith. We shall find peace at the end, if we persevere to the end. The danger is that in seeking peace we may be led away from the road to peace: the struggle to harmonize our will with God's, and our body with our will, seems to bring so much discord into our very being, and we want happiness so urgently. "If thou couldst understand the ways that can bring thee to peace": so cries Our Lord, and it is the heart of our tragedy. But the saint's tragedy is resolved. This book is not about sanctity, only about sanity. But sanity points stright toward sanctity.

INDEX